Teams:
Their Training and Performance

edited by

Robert W. Swezey
Eduardo Salas

ABLEX PUBLISHING CORPORATION
NORWOOD, NEW JERSEY

Library of Congress Cataloging-in-Publication Data

Teams : their training and performance / edited by Robert W. Swezey,
  Eduardo Salas.
      p.   cm.
   Includes bibliographical references and index.
   ISBN 0-89391-852-0; 0-89391-942-X (ppb)
   1. Work groups.   2. Organizational behavior.   3. Industrial
organization.   I. Swezey, Robert W.   II. Salas, Eduardo.
HD66.T437   1992
658.3′128—dc20   91-44960
                                                            CIP

Ablex Publishing Corporation
355 Chestnut Street
Norwood, New Jersey 07648

To Susan E. Swezey — who was a team player

Table of Contents

The Authors

Robert W. Swezey is the Senior Vice President of ISA Associates, Sterling, Virginia, and President of its subsidiary InterScience America. He also serves as a Professorial Lecturer in the Department of Psychology at The George Washington University. He holds a Ph.D. in industrial psychology from the University of Maryland.

Eduardo Salas is a Senior Research Psychologist in the Human Factors Division of the U.S. Naval Training Systems Center, Orlando, Florida, where he heads the research thrust in team training and performance. He holds a Ph.D. in industrial/organizational psychology from Old Dominion University.

Earl A. Alluisi is a member of the research staff of the Science and Technology Division at the Institute for Defense Analysis. He holds a Ph.D. in psychology from the Ohio State University.

Dee H. Andrews is Technical Director of the Aircrew Training Research Division of the U.S. Air Force Human Resources Laboratory at Williams AFB, Arizona. He holds a Ph.D. in instructional systems from Florida State University.

Eva L. Baker is a Professor of Educational Psychology at UCLA, where she heads the Center for the Study of Evaluation. She holds an Ed.D. in educational psychology from UCLA.

Herbert H. Bell is a Research Psychologist with the U.S. Air Force Human Resources Laboratory at Williams AFB, Arizona. He holds a Ph.D. in experimental psychology from Vanderbilt University.

Clint Bowers is an Assistant Research Scientist in the Team Performance Laboratory at the University of Central Florida. He holds a Ph.D. in clinical/counseling psychology from the University of South Florida.

Janis A. Cannon-Bowers is a Research Psychologist in the Human Factors Division of the Naval Training Systems Center, Orlando, Florida. She holds a Ph.D. in industrial/organizational psychology from the University of South Florida.

Thomas R. Chidester is a Research Psychologist with American Airlines. He holds a Ph.D. from the University of Texas at Austin.

Sharolyn A. Converse is Assistant Professor of Psychology at North Carolina State University, Raleigh, North Carolina. She holds a Ph.D. from Old Dominion University.

Michael D. Coovert is an Associate Professor at the University of South Florida. He holds a Ph.D. from the Ohio State University in industrial/organizational psychology.

J. Philip Craiger is a doctoral student in the industrial/organizational psychology department at the University of South Florida. He holds an M.A. from the University of South Florida.

Terry L. Dickinson is Professor of Psychology and Director of the Personnel Research Laboratory at Old Dominion University. He holds a Ph.D. in industrial/organizational psychology from Ohio State University.

James E. Driskell is President of Florida Maxima Corporation in Orlando, Florida. He holds a Ph.D. in counseling psychology from the University of South Carolina.

Deborah L. Flanagan is a Graduate Research Assistant at the Naval Training Systems Center. She holds a B.A. from the University of North Carolina.

Edwin A. Fleishman is a Distinguished University Professor in the Department of Psychology at George Mason University, Fairfax, Virginia. He holds a Ph.D. from Ohio State University.

Catherine D. Gaddy is Principal Scientist at the General Physics Corporation in Columbia, Maryland. She holds a Ph.D. in psychology from the Catholic University of America.

Edward J. Kazlauskas is an Associate Professor of Instructional Technology at the University of Southern California. He holds a Ph.D. in instructional technology from USC.

David L. Kleinman is Professor of Electrical and Systems Engineering at the University of Connecticut. He holds a Ph.D. in electrical engineering, control systems, from the Massachusetts Institute of Technology.

Donald L. Lassiter is Assistant Professor of Psychology at Tarkio College, Tarkio, Missouri. He holds a Ph.D. in engineering psychology from the Georgia Institute of Technology.

Peter B. Luh is an Associate Professor in the Department of Electrical and Systems Engineering at the University of Connecticut. He holds a Ph.D. in applied mathematics from Harvard University.

Kathleen McNelis is a Testing Research Psychologist with the Florida Power Company in St. Petersburg, Florida. She holds a Ph.D. in industrial/organizational psychology from Ohio State University.

Ben B. Morgan, Jr. is a Professor of Psychology at the University of Central Florida, where he heads the Team Performance Laboratory. He holds a Ph.D. in psychology from the University of Louisville.

Glenda Nogami is Director of Curriculum Research at the U.S. Army War

College, Carlisle Barracks, Pennsylvania. She holds a Ph.D. in social psychology from Purdue University.

Harold F. O'Neil, Jr. is a Professor in the Department of Educational Psychology and Technology at the University of Southern California. He holds a Ph.D. in psychology from Florida State University.

Randall Oser is a Research Psychologist at the Naval Training Systems Center in Orlando, Florida. He holds an M.S. in industrial/organizational psychology from the University of South Florida.

Krishna R. Pattipati is an Associate Professor in the Department of Electrical and Systems Engineering at the University of Connecticut. He holds a Ph.D. in electrical engineering, control and communication from the University of Connecticut.

Louis A. Penner is Professor and Chair of the Psychology Department at the University of South Florida. He holds a Ph.D. in social psychology from Michigan State University.

Carolyn Prince is a Research Psychologist at the Naval Training Systems Center in Orlando, Florida. She holds a Ph.D. in industrial/organizational psychology from the University of South Florida.

Daniel Serfaty is Group Leader, Decision Systems at ALPHATECH, Inc. He holds an M.S. in aeronautical engineering from Technion, Haifa, Israel; and an M.B.A. in international management from the University of Connecticut.

Siegfried Streufert is a Professor of Behavioral Science at the Pennsylvania State University School of Medicine, Hershey, Pennsylvania. He holds a Ph.D. in social psychology from Princeton University.

Scott I. Tannenbaum is an Assistant Professor of Management at the State University of New York at Albany. He holds a Ph.D. in industrial/organizational psychology from Old Dominion University.

Jerry A. Wachtel is a Senior Engineering Psychologist with the Nuclear Regulatory Commission. He holds an M.B.A. from the City University of New York.

Wayne L. Waag is a Senior Scientist with the Aircrew Training Research Division, at the Air Force Human Resources Laboratory, Williams AFB, Arizona. He holds a Ph.D. from Texas Tech University.

Stephen J. Zaccaro is an Associate Professor of Psychology at George Mason University, Fairfax, Virginia. He holds a Ph.D. from the University of Connecticut.

Foreword

Earl A. Alluisi

Picture a two-by-two matrix in which one dimension represents the *type of training*, individual vs. collective (or not individual), and the other, the *site of training*, in schools vs. in on-the-job sites (or not in schools). Since most meaningful human work occurs in the context of team or group performance, logic suggests that a great deal of training research should deal with *collective training in on-the-job sites*. Yet in the past, most training research has been concentrated in the cell associated with *individual training in schools*.

Team training, arguably one of the most important topics in psychological science and training technology today, has been one of the least emphasized topics in past psychological research. With a few notable exceptions (e.g., a recent text that has several relevant sections on training strategies in different corporations; Casner-Lotto, 1988), there is little or nothing in the psychological literature on team training in civilian academic education or industrial training.

For example, there have been four chapters on training in the 41-year publication history of the *Annual Review of Psychology*. The three later chapters devote essentially no space to the topic of team training (cf. Goldstein, 1980; Latham, 1988; Wexley, 1984), and the earliest (Campbell, 1971) has only a brief one-page section on the topic, which it summarizes as follows:

> team training has value for transfer to tasks requiring interaction, but the additional increment is quite fragile and can be largely obviated by such things as lack of stimulus fidelity in the task or lack of individual reinforcement. However, the tasks used to study the benefits of team training have been quite limited and we have no good definitions of such concepts as team, coordination, or fidelity. (p. 592)

If this was the situation in 1971, it had improved but little, if at all, by the mid-1970s, when the Director of Defense Research and Engineering sponsored a Defense Science Board (DSB) study of training technology research and development in the Department of Defense. The *DSB Task Force on Training Technology* concluded that insufficient attention was being given in Defense technology-based efforts to the training of military units—such as to collective training.

The Task Force suggested that increases in team training research and development could lead to substantial improvements in the efficiency and effectiveness of both the training and the performance of military crews or units (Defense Science Board, 1976, pp. xi, 36–37). Now, nearly 15 years later, the situation has begun to change, with the Department of Defense developing technology for military team training—for example, a prototype battle-engagement simulation network for the collective training of military elements in the conduct of air–land battles (Rhea, 1989).

But what of civilian academic education and industrial training? Education and training differ. They have different goals. The goal of education is the *dissipation of ignorance* and the fear that ignorance breeds. It is obvious that a great deal of the educational process can be (and is) adequately, efficiently, and effectively conducted individually in schools.

On the other hand, the goal of training is the *acquisition of skill*. Where those skills involve performances of the members of a collective interacting with other members of the same or different collectives, it is reasonable to expect that the skills could be quite well acquired in the course of normal work performances—that is, in on-the-job collective training. Indeed, experiences in many different work settings verify that groups acquire team-performance skills as the team members work together collectively on the job, where the group tasks are performed relatively frequently and the working team is relatively stable. Special efforts to provide team training are called for where these conditions do not hold—for example, where there is moderate-to-great personnel turnover or turbulence, or where important collective tasks are only infrequently performed.

Experience with special cases, such as the training of team sports or musical groups, attests to the need and potential impact of collective training on the skills and performances of working groups and teams. Individual skills alone, however great, may be relatively useless or ineffective without the cooperative, coordinated, and supporting efforts of others where group or team performances are required. It is in such cases that collective or team training is likely to be both necessary and of benefit to group performances.

This is not to negate the value of individual training in schools or on the job. An athlete can (and perhaps can best) practice or train on some functions individually (running, tossing, catching, maneuvering, etc.), but must also practice collectively with other members of the team to train for game (or team) play.

Likewise, a musician must certainly train individually to master his or her instrument, but must also train collectively with the accompanist, ensemble, or orchestra to prepare for a performance. Similar observations hold for other group performances that depend, not only on the individuals' skills with their "instruments," but also on their skills in interacting with the other members of the team.

Team training research and development is aimed at discovering and exploiting those phenomena which, if better understood and applied, could increase the efficiency and effectiveness, not only of the training, but also of the collective performances that are affected by it. The present text reports recent advances in team training research, as well as progress being made in the measurement of team performances.

There is not yet a generally accepted answer to the question, "What are the collective performance skills that team training is to improve?" Rather, the skills are hypothesized at this point to include in some measure the "seven Cs" of good military team performances: command, control, and communication; cooperation, coordination, and cohesion; and cybernation—all appropriately adapted to fit the broader range of collectives that includes nonmilitary teams and groups as well.

Command, control, and communication relate primarily to between-team interactions—to interactions of one collective with another, either horizontally at the same or a similar level, or vertically up or down the hierarchical organization. On the other hand, *cooperation, coordination, and cohesion* relate primarily to within-team interactions—to interactions among the members of the collective with one another.

Cybernation occurs both within and between teams. It represents that high degree of skill that all leaders strive to have their teams or groups exhibit, be they sport team captains or coaches, orchestra conductors, or military commanders. It is that high degree of "readiness" attained when teams perform their collective tasks, not only correctly, but also with the rapid and smooth automaticity that is the hallmark of real expertise—of a championship team in any sport, a world-class orchestra with any music, or a battle-wise, veteran warfighting unit of any army, navy, or air force.

The key to this kind of success is training—*team training*—whatever its form, and whether it be called "training," "practice," or "exercising." It is the kind of training that is based on the collective (team or group) performances of relevant tasks in contexts that support the acquisition of team performance skills—and those are the skills that differentiate winning from losing teams.

The present text is focused on this kind of training—*team training*. Thus, its publication marks a milestone in the psychological literature. It is doubtless the most comprehensive psychological document published on team training and performance to date. Let us hope that it is only the first of many volumes aimed toward advancing the science and technology of team training.

REFERENCES

Campbell, J. P. (1971). Personnel training and development. In P. H. Mussen & M. R. Rosenzweig (Eds.), *Annual review of psychology: Vol. 22* (pp. 565–602). Palo Alto, CA: Annual Reviews.

Casner-Lotto, J. (Ed.). (1988). *Successful training strategies: Twenty-six innovative corporate models. The Jossey-Bass Management series.* San Francisco: Jossey-Bass.

Defense Science Board. (1976, February). *Summary Report of the Task Force on Training Technology.* Washington, DC: Office of the Director of Defense Research and Engineering.

Goldstein, I. L. (1980). Training in work organizations. In M. R. Rosenzweig & L. W. Porter (Eds.), *Annual review of psychology: Vol. 31* (pp. 229–272). Palo Alto, CA: Annual Reviews.

Latham, G. P. (1988). Human resource training and development. In M. R. Rosenzweig & L. W. Porter (Eds.), *Annual review of psychology: Vol. 39* (pp. 545–582). Palo Alto, CA: Annual Reviews.

Rhea, J. (1989, August). Planet SIMNET. *Air Force Magazine,* pp. 60–64.

Wexley, K. N. (1984). Personnel training. In M. R. Rosenzweig & L. W. Porter (Eds.), *Annual review of psychology: Vol. 35* (pp. 519–551). Palo Alto, CA: Annual Reviews.

Preface

This book is the first of its kind. Although it deals with a widely recognized topic—teamwork—it does so from a research-based perspective. Herein, readers will find both new ideas on this topic, and old ideas explored via new methodologies.

In our view, the contents of this book deal only with a subset of the team literature. Its orientation is toward actual team *behavior,* as well as toward the research and training bases which underlie team operations and performance. The book does not deal with management and human resources aspects of teamwork. Nor does it deal with such topics as team building, sales, and organizational development. The emphasis here is on performance orientation as it applies to teamwork. It is our hope that this book can be used by researchers to develop hypotheses for additional investigation, and by practitioners to expand applications of teamwork practical situations. In these respects, we think, it is unique.

ORGANIZATION OF THE BOOK

We have organized the 14 chapters of this book into three major sections. The first of these deals with *Team Organization and Functioning.* In this section are chapters which address basic models of teamwork and team performance (by Salas, Dickinson, Converse, and Tannenbaum), the development of a taxonomy of team performance functions (by Fleishman and Zaccaro), the performance of individual team members (by Penner and Craiger), and the staffing and composition of teams (by Morgan and Lassiter).

The second section of the book concerns the *Research Base* and its application in teamwork. This section includes chapters on small group research (by Driskell and Salas), cognitive complexity and team decision making (by Streufert and Nogami), the assessment of team performance (by O'Neil, Baker, and Kazlauskas), mathematical models of team decision making (by Kleinman, Luh,

Pattipati, and Serfaty), guidelines for use in developing team training programs (by Swezey and Salas), and a review of team decision-making research, and application of Petri Net technology to teamwork (by Coovert and McNelis).

The final section of the book deals with *Applications of Teamwork Skills*. This section includes chapters on military team training (by Andrews, Waag, and Bell), aircrew coordination training (by Prince, Chidester, Cannon-Bowers, and Bowers), industrial work teams (by Cannon-Bowers, Oser, and Flanagan), and teamwork in the nuclear power industry (by Gaddy and Wachtel).

Robert W. Swezey
Eduardo Salas
Leesburg, Virginia
Orlando, Florida
December, 1990

Part I
TEAM ORGANIZATION AND FUNCTIONING

1

Toward an Understanding of Team Performance and Training*

Eduardo Salas
Terry L. Dickinson
Sharolyn A. Converse
Scott I. Tannenbaum

INTRODUCTION

The ability of individuals to work together productively as a team is vitally important to the success of many organizations and work groups. Recent technological developments, global competition, and world events have made teamwork increasingly important, because modern tasks often impose mental and physical demands that are too large for one individual to perform in isolation. If such demanding and dynamic tasks are to be completed successfully, individuals must work together as a team (Modrick, 1986). This trend has stimulated the development of a body of research that is directed toward the identification of

*The views expressed herein are those of the authors and do not reflect the official position of the organizations with which they are affiliated. The authors are grateful to Ben B. Morgan, Jr., Janis A. Cannon-Bowers, Joan Hall, Catherine Baker, and Robert W. Swezey for their useful comments in earlier drafts of this chapter.

factors that determine the quality of team performance and the training strategies needed to ensure team effectiveness.

This chapter will address two issues. First, selected conceptual frameworks and theories are described for guiding the understanding of team performance and training research. Second, a brief overview of factors that influence team performance and training is provided, as well as a discussion of what we still need to know about team performance and training.

✳ WHAT IS A TEAM?

A fundamental question that must be addressed in team performance and training research concerns the nature of teams. That is, what is a team? To some this may be a trivial question. However, we believe that the failure of the research literature to address this question adequately has created confusion and prevented the systematic accumulation of knowledge. Today, after more than 50 years of team research, few principles and guidelines are available for guiding the composition or management of teams (Swezey & Salas, 1989) or for distinguishing good and poor teams (Driskell, Hogan, & Salas, 1987).

Several researchers have advanced definitions or taxonomies of team type (e.g., Dyer, 1984; Hall & Rizzo, 1975; Modrick, 1986), but they lack consensus about the different kinds of teams that exist. We do not advocate a discrete taxonomy. On the contrary, we argue that types of teams can be conceived to fall on a continuum. At one extreme of the continuum fall highly structured, interdependent teams, and at the other extreme fall teams whose members interact minimally and perform individual tasks in a group context. The placement of a team on this continuum is probably moderated by the task demands imposed on the team. This chapter will focus on the more highly structured interdependent teams.

For our purposes, a *team* is defined as a distinguishable set of two or more people who interact, dynamically, interdependently, and adaptively toward a common and valued goal/objective/mission, who have each been assigned specific roles or functions to perform, and who have a limited life-span of membership. This definition of a team has been shaped by the input from many authors (e.g., Dyer, 1984; Hall & Rizzo, 1975; Nieva, Fleishman, & Reick, 1978; Morgan, Glickman, Woodard, Blaiwes, & Salas, 1986; Modrick, 1986).

The central point of the definition is that task completion requires: (a) a dynamic exchange of information and resources among team members, (b) coordination of task activities (e.g., active communication, back-up behaviors), (c) constant adjustments to task demands, and (d) some organizational structuring of members. Clearly, some form of task dependency must exist among members in order for them to interact and accomplish their objective. Member interdependency is one key element in distinguishing teams from groups. All teams share some form of member interdependency, either explicit (e.g., verbal communication) or implicit (e.g., members anticipating the actions of other members). In addition to task structure, several other factors impact team performance. For example, teams perform under various decision structures (e.g., centralized or distributed) that require different levels of interaction and communication.

The element of time is also critical for understanding teams. Most teams perform for a limited life-span that can last for a few hours (e.g., the duration of a flight for an air crew) to several days or months (e.g., a military tactical team). During the period of performance, depending on the task demands, team members may go through countless behavioral or cognitive events to achieve their goal.

NOTHING MORE PRACTICAL THAN A GOOD THEORY

In order to design research that provides a comprehensive understanding of the practical issues that teams face, Lewin's argument for good theory is as important today as it was several decades ago (see Marrow, 1969). In recent years, many conceptual frameworks or theories have been developed, ranging from applications of sociopsychological constructs (Mullen & Goethals, 1987) to those that are more complex, naturalistic, and developmental in nature (e.g., Morgan et al., 1986; Gersick, 1988; Gladstein, 1984). The conceptual frameworks presented below were selected to illustrate underlying concepts and issues that characterize various perspectives, as well as to help develop an understanding of team performance and training.

Normative Model

In general, Hackman's (1983) normative model represents a comprehensive conceptualization of group processes in an organizational environment. Although this model does not strictly deal with highly structured teams, it does identify the broad range of variables that can influence team performance and training.

The basic assumption of the normative model (see Figure 1.1) is that organizational context and group design (i.e., input variables) affect the member interaction process, and that that, in turn, affects the quality of team performance (i.e., the output variables). Hackman (1983) postulates that team effectiveness is facilitated by the capability of team members to work together over time, the satisfaction of member needs, and the acceptability of task outcomes by those individuals who demand or receive them. Moreover, team effectiveness is dependent upon the level of effort exerted by the team members, the amount of knowledge and skill they can apply to the task, and the appropriateness of task

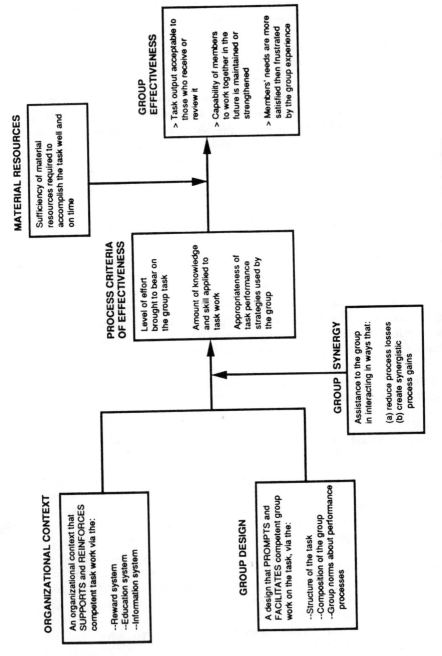

MATERIAL RESOURCES

Sufficiency of material resources required to accomplish the task well and on time

GROUP EFFECTIVENESS

> Task output acceptable to those who receive or review it

> Capability of members to work together in the future is maintained or strengthened

> Members' needs are more satisfied then frustrated by the group experience

PROCESS CRITERIA OF EFFECTIVENESS

Level of effort brought to bear on the group task

Amount of knowledge and skill applied to task work

Appropriateness of task performance strategies used by the group

GROUP SYNERGY

Assistance to the group in interacting in ways that:

(a) reduce process losses
(b) create synergistic process gains

ORGANIZATIONAL CONTEXT

An organizational context that SUPPORTS and REINFORCES competent task work via the:

--Reward system
--Education system
--Information system

GROUP DESIGN

A design that PROMPTS and FACILITATES competent group work on the task, via the:

--Structure of the task
--Composition of the group
--Group norms about performance processes

Figure 1.1. Normative Model (adapted from Hackman, 1983)

6

performance strategies. Effectiveness is also influenced by the resources allocated to the team. Appropriate tools, equipment, space, raw materials, and human resources are factors that enhance a team's performance. The normative model is Hackman's alternative and extension to the descriptive research approach for understanding team performance (e.g., McGrath, 1964). The descriptive approach seeks to develop new knowledge about what happens in groups/teams and to generalize about the relationships among the variables investigated and its context. Hackman (1983) argues that descriptive research is limited by its piecemeal focus on a few variables and by its failure to consider the impact of contextual variables. Further, he maintains that researchers employing the descriptive approach place too much emphasis on the theoretically idealized level of team performance, as well as understanding the "process loss" that prevents a team from achieving optimum performance. Furthermore, the descriptive approach fails to investigate possible interactions among variables that impact on team performance, and, consequently, it fails to suggest interventions that consistently improve team functioning. In sum, it appears that the strength of the descriptive research approach (i.e., helping to describe team performance) is also its weakness. That is, the descriptive models tell us very little about what should be done to improve team functioning.

Hackman's normative model offers several conceptual elements for understanding team performance and training. First, it argues that the organizational context or environment surrounding a team cannot be ignored. Much of what goes on in the environment may facilitate or hinder the team process and performance. This implies that teams need to be studied and trained in settings representative of the actual performance environment. Second, a thorough understanding is required of the effort, knowledge, skill, and performance strategies that enhance team performance. That is, these factors allows us to understand what motivates team members to work together and whether members have the skill and knowledge of the procedures that must be used to accomplish the team task. The manipulation of these factors would allow us to compose or manage teams more effectively. Finally, Hackman's normative model begins to articulate, not only the conditions that are necessary for effective team functioning, but also how to create them. Although not directly related to team training, Hackman (1983) outlines how to diagnose the task demands, the boundaries, and the development of norms in teams. A better understanding of these three issues can help with designing and developing appropriate team training interventions.

Time and Transition Model

Gersick (1985, 1988) describes a time and transition model for work teams. Gersick's model is based on a study of eight teams ranging from a team composed within a graduate management course to a team organized as a bank task

|1ST MEETING   PHASE I   TRANSITION   PHASE II   COMPLETION|
- -/ / / / / / / / / /- -
|start   halfway   deadline|
time ➔

Figure 1.2.   Time and Transition Model (adapted from Gersick, 1985)

force. Gersick collected handwritten records of various types of behavior, the number of incidents, and (subjective) measures of the quality of work or "energy" that team members displayed during the meetings. The transcripts were used to discern patterns of behavior the teams displayed (for a more detailed summary, see Gersick, 1988). The data revealed only one clear pattern of behavior across the teams. In each case, the team established a method of performing its given task in the first meeting. Each team consistently maintained the agreed-upon method of task performance until midway through the predetermined time given to complete the task. At this halfway point, without exception, the teams decided to pursue a different strategy to complete their task. This amended approach to task completion was maintained by the teams until the task was completed (see Figure 1.2). Apparently, team members adhered to an "alarm clock" at midpoint that heightened their awareness of time. This heightened awareness initiated the transition of the team towards a new method of performing the task.

Gersick's contribution to understanding team performance and training is twofold. First, the dynamic nature of team performance is emphasized. Gersick's model and data (see also Gersick, 1989) show that team performance results from a dynamic exchange of information and resources among team members. Second, the transition concept emphasizes that teams adapt their performance strategies during certain periods of their lifecycle (in this case the midpoint).

Task Group Effectiveness Model

Gladstein's (1984) model focuses on groups in organizational environments. Although the model does not focus per se on highly structured teams, it is one of the few models tested with a large sample from the work environment (Goodman & Assoc., 1986). As indicated in Figure 1.3, group process and group effectiveness are central to this type of model, with group task demands serving as a moderating factor. Group process is defined as the intra- and intergroup events and behaviors that transform group and organizational resources into group effectiveness.

According to the model, the degree of group effectiveness (i.e., a group's terminal performance and its satisfaction with the job done) is a function of the elements of group process (e.g., open communications, discussion of strategy, weighing individual inputs) moderated by the group task demands. Task complexity, environmental uncertainty, and the level of team interdependence neces-

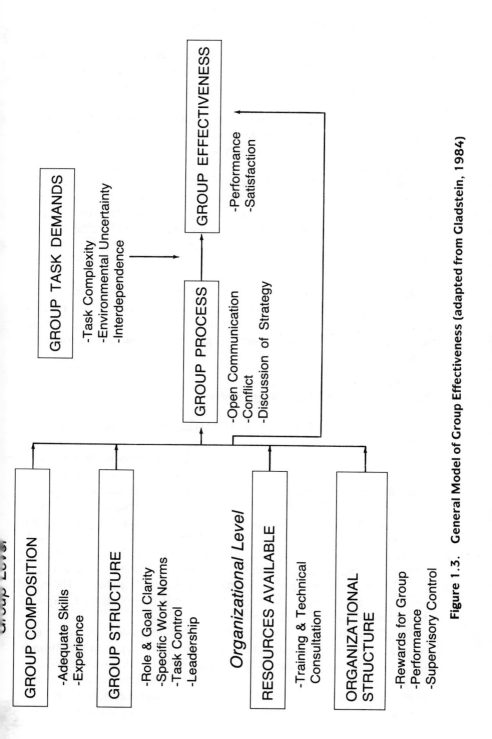

Figure 1.3. General Model of Group Effectiveness (adapted from Gladstein, 1984)

GROUP TASK DEMANDS

-Task Complexity
-Environmental Uncertainty
-Interdependence

GROUP EFFECTIVENESS

-Performance
-Satisfaction

GROUP PROCESS

-Open Communication
-Conflict
-Discussion of Strategy

GROUP COMPOSITION

-Adequate Skills
-Experience

GROUP STRUCTURE

-Role & Goal Clarity
-Specific Work Norms
-Task Control
-Leadership

Organizational Level

RESOURCES AVAILABLE

-Training & Technical
Consultation

ORGANIZATIONAL STRUCTURE

-Rewards for Group
-Performance
-Supervisory Control

9

sary to complete the task are the relevant determinants of group task demands. Group composition, group structure, resources available, and the organizational structure are the external factors preceding and impacting group process and group effectiveness.

Gladstein's (1984) research on sales teams in the communications industry indicated that theories of effectiveness need to account for the impact of the organizational context and the process by which teams manage their interactions. More specifically, Gladstein (1984) found that open communication, supportiveness, active leadership, experience, and training were positively related to ratings of group satisfaction and performance. The relationship between group structure and group process was also established, suggesting that group processes may not be effective without a group structure characterized by clear roles and goals, and specific work norms. Gladstein's model underscores the complexity of team performance and suggests that training alone does not enhance team effectiveness.

Recurring themes in this model that are important for understanding team performance are: (a) the conceptualization and importance of processes for determining team performance, (b) the fact that the task moderates the process–performance link, and (c) the impact of organizational context and environment on team performance.

Team Evolution and Maturation Model

The Team Evolution and Maturation (TEAM) model (see Figure 1.4) developed by Morgan et al. (1986) combines two concepts of team performance. The constructs developed by Tuckman (1965), and the findings of Gersick (1988, 1989), are combined to create a model of team performance that predicts the stages that teams go through before, during, and after performance of a task.

Essentially, the TEAM model suggests that task-oriented teams evolve through a series of developmental phases. It also indicates that teams begin at different stages of development and spend different amounts of time in the various phases. The beginning stage depends upon the members' experience as a team, their individual expertise, task characteristics, and the environmental context. Not all teams are expected to progress through all the phases. The model serves as a framework to document the potential development of teamwork during task performance and training.

The TEAM model also hypothesizes that teams have two tracks which must be successfully resolved before they can reach satisfactory team performance. The track of "operational team skills training" represents the task-oriented skills that the members must understand and acquire for task performance. Here, team members spend their time understanding the task requirements, discovering the operating procedures, and acquiring task information and other task-oriented

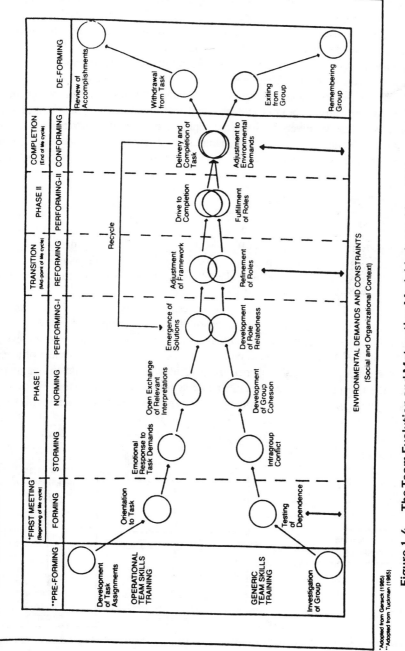

Figure 1.4. The Team Evolution and Maturation Model (adapted from Morgan et al., 1986)

issues. The track of "generic team skills training" reflects the behavioral interactions and attitudinal responses that team members must develop before they can function effectively as a team. Specific behaviors included in the "teamwork" track are coordination, adaptation to varying situational demands, effective communication, compensatory behavior, mutual performance monitoring, and giving and receiving feedback. The convergence of the activity tracks symbolizes the belief that, at some time after the point of "intragroup conflict," the teams must experience a merging of tasks and teamwork skills, before, or at the point of task performance. The divergent lines are representative of the fact that all teams disperse eventually, as a result of change in team composition or the advent of some disrupting outside influence.

Team Performance Model

The Nieva, Fleishman, and Reick (1978) conceptual model of team performance derives from conclusions draws from their review of team performance research. The review focused on the relationship between team performance and what they considered to be the major variables affecting group performance. Figure 1.5 depicts the conceptual model of team performance.

Team performance is viewed as a set of responses separate from the task itself. The task is considered an outside set of stimuli. Team performance has two major components: task behaviors by individuals, and task functions at the team level. The authors maintain that these components determine the effectiveness of team performance. Individual task performance may be a primary determinator of team performance, or team member interactions may predominate. For many tasks, team performance is probably determined by both components.

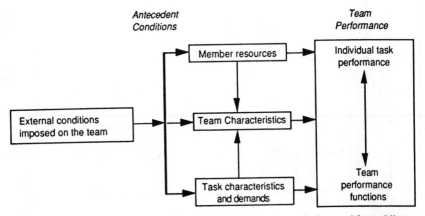

Figure 1.5.   Conceptual Model of Team Performance (adapted from Nieva, Fleishman, and Reick, 1978)

External conditions imposed on the team is the first of four types of antecedents of team performance. For example, operational teams usually work within a larger organizational/social context. This predominating context sets the task and the standard operating procedure to be used by the team, and to a large extent determines the membership of the group. These external conditions (outside influences) can serve to aid or hinder task completion.

Other antecedents include the resources of individual skills, abilities, and personality characteristics that each member brings to the team. These resources can combine to form relationships that enhance team performance (e.g., complementary abilities of the members). In contrast, personality conflicts (relating to dimensions such as adjustment, dominance, and extroversion), and varying levels of individual proficiencies, can degrade team performance.

Team characteristics define the team as an entity. They are size, group cohesiveness, intra- and interteam cooperation, communication, standard communication networks, homogeneity/heterogeneity across a variety of dimensions, power distribution within the team, and team training. Team characteristics are influenced by member resources and task characteristics and demands. The team characteristics are also influenced by external conditions imposed on the team (e.g., authority structure, team composition, and task assignment).

Task characteristics and demands determine the critical requirements for successful performance and affect the interactions that team members have with each other. Task characteristics dictate individual task functions and team-level operations. Research has demonstrated relationships between task type and such team-related processes as originality and quality (Hackman & Morris, 1975), and structuring, generating, and elaborating (Sorenson, 1971).

Task-Oriented Model

Several models have been proposed that emphasize a task-oriented analysis of team performance (cf. Dickinson, 1969; Dieterly, 1988; Naylor & Dickinson, 1969; Shiflett, Eisner, Price, & Schemmer, 1982). These models emphasize that team performance is a function of the subtasks that members must perform effectively for the accomplishment of team goals. Further, they suggest an analysis of the performance requirements of these subtasks to indicate the relative emphasis that should be given to individual and team skills training.

According to the task-oriented model developed by Dickinson and his colleagues, an analysis of performance requirements involves the examination of interrelated aspects of task structure, work structure, and communication structure. *Task structure* is described by the complexity and organization of the subtasks to be accomplished. *Task complexity* refers to the demand characteristics of the subtasks. Relatively simple tasks are defined as tasks of low complexity, while relatively difficult tasks are of high complexity. Complexity can be assessed by many metrics, including subjective and objective measures of information processing demands, time demands, and workload. No single metric applies to all team tasks, and the use of several metrics is advocated for the analysis of a team task.

Task organization refers to the interdependencies that exist between various subtasks of a team task. When few such interdependencies exist, task organization is low. However, when many subtasks are interrelated, task organization is high. The nature of task organization varies with the team task and must be determined through task analysis. Types of interdependencies include information that must be shared between subtasks, the degree to which the products of one subtask serve as the input for other subtasks, and the degree to which the completion of one dictates the need to perform subsequent subtasks (cf. Cooper, Shiflett, Korotkin, & Fleishman, 1984).

The *work structure* of a team refers to the manner in which subtasks are assigned to and shared by various team members. For example, subtasks may be assigned so that individual team members perform the same (i.e., redundant) subtasks in order to promote reliability of performance, or subtasks may be assigned in a manner that requires individual team members to complete several subtasks independently. According to Naylor and Dickinson (1969), the identification of the appropriate work structure requires consideration of the subtasks that must be performed, analysis of the task organization, determination of the sequence in which subtasks must be accomplished, and evaluation of task complexity.

Within the task-oriented model, the communication structure of a team consists of patterns of interaction between team members that develop as a function of task organization, task complexity, and work structure. For example, team tasks that are characterized by low task organization, low task complexity, and an hierarchical work structure require very little communication among team members. Thus, the communication structure of a team performing under such conditions is not likely to be a rich network for communication. However, when team tasks are highly organized, quite complex, and employ a decentralized work structure, team members must communicate frequently and effectively in order to perform together successfully. Thus, the communication structure for such teams is likely to be quite elaborate. In sum, the communication structure of a team develops as a function of task organization, task complexity, and work structure (cf. Shiflett, 1972). As such, communication structure is viewed as a dependent, rather than as an independent, variable.

The task-oriented model of team performance implies that task organization and task complexity not only determine the optimal work and communication structures, but also interact to moderate requirements for individual and team skills training for enhancing team performance. For tasks in which few interdependencies exist among subtasks (i.e., low task organization), team members are able to focus almost exclusively on performance of their assigned subtasks.

Further, a team task of low task complexity allows each team member to perform a relatively large number of subtasks. Thus, communication and coordination requirements are not likely to be key determinants of successful team performance for a simple task (i.e., characterized by low task complexity and organization). Under such task conditions, training of individual skills is likely to be an efficient training strategy.

When the subtasks of a team task are highly interrelated (i.e., high task organization), team members must coordinate the flow of individual work inputs and outputs, and they must communicate frequently and effectively with one another. High task complexity may also require that team members coordinate their work flow, especially when several members must be assigned to perform the same subtask. Thus, when the team task is characterized by high task organization, and perhaps by high task complexity, team training should focus on team skills for effective coordination and communication (Denson, 1981; Dyer, 1984; Hackman & Morris, 1975; McRae, 1966; Naylor & Dickinson, 1969; Nieva et al., 1978).

The predictions of the task-oriented model of team performance have received impressive support in the literature. For team tasks characterized by high task organization, the training of coordination and communication skills becomes more effective as the complexity of the team task increases (Bass & Barrett, 1981; Briggs & Johnston, 1967; Meister, 1976; Naylor & Dickinson, 1969; Wagner, Hibbitts, Rosenblatt, & Schulz, 1977). This finding explains the results of earlier research on the effects of various communication structures on team performance. The earlier research failed to assess the moderating effects of task structure on the relationship between communication structure and the level of team performance (Jones, 1984).

Models of Team Performance and Training: Summary

All of the models described previously aid in the understanding of team performance and training. For example, Hackman's (1983) model contributes by emphasizing organizational context as well as the effort, skills, and strategies of team members in performing the tasks. The Gersick (1988) model highlights the dynamic and evolving nature of team performance. Similarly, the TEAM model translates the dynamic nature of teams into developmental phases in which the interaction of task and teamwork skills are merged. This model also may suggest how team training might proceed and how teamwork evolves. Nieva et al. (1978) emphasize that individual characteristics cannot be ignored in team functioning. Finally, the task-oriented model conveys the criticality of task and work structures in understanding team performance and designing team training.

Figure 1.6 represents a framework that integrates the models described here. In general, team performance is the outcome of dynamic processes reflected in

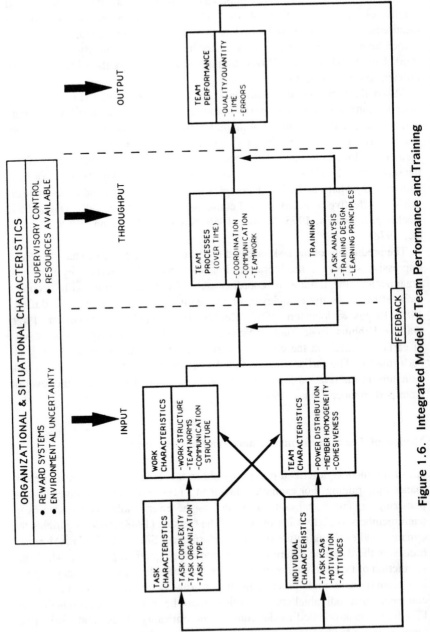

Figure 1.6. Integrated Model of Team Performance and Training

16

the coordination and communication patterns that teams develop over time. The processes are influenced by organizational and situational characteristics, and task and work characteristics, as well as individual and team characteristics. As implied by several of the models, training could and should be used to impact these processes and their relation to team performance. We turn now to a discussion of the nature of team training that includes a consideration of design and learning principles.

THE NATURE OF TEAM TRAINING

Individual Skills

Historically, the expected performance of a team has been considered to be a function of the average skill level of the individuals who comprised the team. Early research supported this view with the repeated findings that the accuracy and speed of team performance were positively related to the average skill level of individual team members, and that the teams comprised of members with high individual skills reached criterion performance with less training than did teams composed of members with average or poor individual skills (e.g., Bouchard, 1969; George, Hoak, & Boutwell, 1963; Hall & Rizzo, 1975; Kabanoff & O'Brien, 1979; Klaus & Glaser, 1965; Terborg, Castore, & DeNinno, 1976; Tziner & Eden, 1985).

Individual skills undoubtedly are important to team success. However, individual skills appear to be necessary but not sufficient for good team performance. The magnitude of the positive relationship between the average skill level of team members and the quality of team performance typically is small (Bass & Barrett, 1981). For example, Terborg et al. (1976) reported that individual skills only accounted for 3% of the variance in performance of a land survey task. The implication of this finding is that enhancing team performance is often a more complex undertaking than simply training team members to master individual skills (Denson, 1981; Nieva et al., 1978).

Several researchers hypothesized that the ability of team members to work together productively depends upon the interpersonal skill levels of team members. Tuckman (1965) reported that studies of team development indicated that good interpersonal relationships between team members must be established before team members are able to focus effectively on the performance of the team task. Bass and Barrett (1981) hypothesized that the ability of team members to interact effectively modifies the development of their individual task skills, because team members provide cues and reinforcements of behavior that are important for learning the team task.

Unfortunately, training of interpersonal skills has received mixed support in the literature. For example, Johnston and Briggs (1968) provided support for the hypothesis with evidence that performance errors are less frequent when team members are allowed to correct and provide feedback to one another. However, in other research, Briggs and Johnston (1967) reported that interpersonal skills training did not enhance team performance as much as did individual skills training. Further, Parsons (1981) compared the effects of group dynamics and individual skills training, and found that teams receiving only individual skills training performed better than teams receiving group dynamics training and better than teams receiving both types of training.

Teamwork

Steiner (1972) suggested that the relatively small relationship between the average skill level of team members and overall team performance is due to "process loss." According to Steiner, team performance is not only a function of the potential of team members to perform their assigned subtasks, but also a function of the necessity for team members to coordinate their work flow and communicate effectively with one another. Process loss occurs whenever team member efforts are wasted or duplicated in the course of meeting the coordination and communication requirements for team performance.

An implication of the concept of process loss is that training team members to coordinate their activities and to communicate effectively should enhance team performance, regardless of the average skill level of team members (Hackman & Morris, 1975). Indeed, the training of coordination and communication skills has received support in the literature. For example, McRae (1966) and Parsons (1981) reported that team skills training resulted in better team performance overall than did exposure only to individual skills training.

Unfortunately, team skills training has not always proven to be the most effective method of training team members to work together productively. For example, Horrocks, Krug, and Heermann (1960) reported no difference in the quality of team performance when team members were exposed either to individual or to team skills training. Further, Briggs and Naylor (1964) reported that team performance was superior following individual skills training than following training that required team members to interact and communicate.

The determination of factors that moderate the success of individual and team skills training is an important research question. Yet nearly 30 years after conflicting results were reported, there is little understanding as to why both individual and team skills training improve team performance in some investigations but fail to do so in others. This situation is unfortunate, because the determination of training appropriate to enhancing team performance is essential for many organizations.

ᵒ Coordination and Communication

While effective communication and coordination among team members appear to be vitally important when team tasks are characterized by high task organization and high task complexity, team training most often has emphasized only the learning of individual skills within a team setting, regardless of the nature of the team task (Briggs & Johnston, 1967; Converse, Dickinson, Tannenbaum, & Salas, 1988; Mesiter, 1976). In sum, team training has tended to ignore the development of teamwork skills and behaviors that are demanded by the interaction requirements of the team task.

The tendency of researchers and trainers to focus team training on the communal learning of individual skills may be because effective methods have not been clearly identified for the training of communication and coordination demands (Jones, 1984). However, research suggests that informing team members of the nature of other members' subtasks emphasizes the requirements for coordination and communication and enhances the quality of team performance (Krumm, 1958). Furthermore, training for coordination should help team members to recognize and identify their task interdependencies and should emphasize the undesirable consequences of failure to coordinate team members efforts correctly (George, 1967, 1979).

Chapman, Kennedy, Newall, and Biel (1959) suggested that teams should be allowed to develop flexible work structures, and recommended that team members experiment with different methods of coordinating their work flow under varying task conditions. Such experience would allow team members to use alternative methods of coordinating team member input under emergent or stressful task conditions. Chapman et al. tested this hypothesis by allowing teams of 40 operators of a simulated air defense system to use flexible work structures under varying levels of task difficulty. Their results indicated that a flexible coordination system allowed team members to handle task demands that were several times as large as those originally considered to be realistic for air defense teams to handle successfully.

Team Training Design and Learning Principles

Individual vs. team training. When individual and team skills training are combined with a training design, decisions must be made about the *optimum amount* of individual skills training relative to team training, including the *sequence* in which individual and team skills training should be presented, and the *time* that should be allowed to elapse between individual and team skills training. For example, Briggs and Johnston (1967) suggested that team training should be sequenced so that team members are allowed to master individual task skills before team skills training is begun. This training strategy is supported by numerous reports that team training proceeds most effectively and efficiently when team members develop individual task skills before receiving training on coordination and communication skills (e.g., Daniels, Alden, Kanarick, Gray, & Feuge, 1972; Denson, 1981; Johnston, 1966; Klaus & Glaser, 1970).

The amount of time delay between individual and team skills training does not appear to be an important determinant of the ultimate level of team performance. Nieva et al. (1978) surveyed the team-training literature and concluded that the ultimate quality of team performance is not different when team members are exposed to team skills training immediately after individual skills training compared to when they are exposed to team skills training as long as 1 month after individual skills training had been completed.

Training fidelity. Another factor to consider in team training design is the fidelity of the training environment to operational task conditions. It appears that the fidelity of the training environment is especially important when teams must coordinate individual subtask performance under stressful conditions. George (1967, 1979) and Driskell, Salas, and Hogan (1987) recommended that teams should be trained under stressful task conditions when the operational task setting itself is characterized by stress and pressure. George (1979) suggested that training under stressful conditions is useful, not only because it provides operational task fidelity to team members, but also because it allows researchers to identify the subtasks that tend to be degraded under stressful conditions. Such subtasks should be given additional emphasis in training design.

The fidelity of the training environment has been conceptualized in terms of stimulus fidelity, response fidelity, and equipment fidelity. Briggs and Naylor (1964) reported that high stimulus fidelity and high equipment fidelity resulted in superior transfer task performance. However, high response fidelity resulted in superior transfer task performance only when team members were allowed to communicate during training. When team members were not allowed to communicate during training, response fidelity did not moderate the level of operational task performance. No research has determined the generality of the effects of stimulus and response fidelity on communication for various combinations of task and work structures.

Performance feedback. Perhaps the most important factor to consider in team-training design is the performance feedback given to team members. Feedback enables team members to perform their subtasks competently and demonstrates the contribution of that performance to the performance of other members and the team as a whole. Researchers generally agree that feedback about the effectiveness of task performance should be provided to team members (Dyer, 1984; Nieva et al., 1978). In fact, Klaus and Glaser (1970) demonstrated that practice without feedback can degrade the proficiency attained by teams.

There is also general agreement that feedback should be provided in a timely manner (Dyer, 1984; Nieva et al., 1978). For example, Alexander and Cooperband (1965) reported that team performance was better when feedback was given immediately after each correct team response than when feedback was delayed. Briggs and Johnston (1967) replicated this finding and further suggested that, when feedback cannot be provided after each correct response, or at some point during task performance, debriefing sessions should be conducted immediately following task performance in order to provide feedback as rapidly as possible.

The focus of feedback also appears to be vitally important to the success of the team training. Feedback enhances performance on that aspect of performance about which feedback is provided; this finding has been replicated several times (Alexander & Cooperband, 1965; Chapman et al., 1959). In fact, Briggs and Johnston (1967) reported that teams maximize that aspect of performance about which feedback is given, even at the expense of other aspects of performance. Thus, team training should avoid emphasizing one characteristic of team performance at the expense of others.

Sequencing feedback (i.e., when feedback should be given) on various aspects of the team task is a useful method of training teams to enhance several aspects of performance. Feedback should be given only on one aspect of task performance during early training sessions, but feedback should refer to several aspects of task performance during later training sessions. When this sequencing procedure was employed, Briggs and Johnston (1967) found that teams attempted to enhance performance for all of the aspects of the team task on which they had received feedback, rather than to focus only on the aspect of performance for which they had originally received feedback.

Briggs and Johnston (1967) also addressed the issue of feedback specificity. They suggested that the specificity of feedback should be determined by the phase of training in which a team is participating. Briggs and Johnston (1967) suggested that feedback should be given about gross aspects of performance during early phases of team training, while feedback should be more specific during later phases of training in order to "fine tune" performance.

Another issue is the relative timing and amount of individual and team feedback. Klaus and Glaser (1970) suggested that individual and team feedback should be given according to the stage of training. Individual feedback should be given in initial training sessions, while feedback about overall performance should be provided in later phases of training. This strategy is designed to train individual skills to a criterion level of performance before team feedback is supplied. Team feedback provides little direct information about the quality of individual performance. Thus, when team feedback alone is supplied, team members may receive inappropriate reinforcement for their individual actions and misjudge the accuracy of their performance. Individual skills should be well developed before team feedback is supplied, because team feedback can disrupt the training of individual skills.

When individual and team feedback are combined and sequenced, transfer from individual to team feedback often produces a temporary decrement of individual skills performance. This is due to the fact that team feedback is less specific and generally is less frequent than is individual feedback. Klaus and Glaser (1970) suggested that the problem of performance decrement at the onset of team feedback can be alleviated by making individual feedback intermittent during later stages of individual skills training. This strategy trains team members to sustain performance with increasingly small amounts of feedback, and helps to develop resistance to performance decrement during early stages of team feedback.

The nature of the team task is also an important determinant of whether individual and team performance feedback should be supplied to team members during training. Feedback about individual performance should be provided during training only if individual feedback is a regular feature of the operational environment (Klaus & Glaser, 1970; Klaus, Grant, & Glaser, 1965). Furthermore, team feedback by itself can be a dangerous strategy when the good performance of one team member can compensate for the poor performance of a teammate. Without specific feedback on the relationship between poor and good performance, incorrect behaviors may be reinforced, and the performance of one or both team members may not improve. The nature of task organization would seem to moderate the timing and amounts of team and individual feedback. As suggested by Nadler (1979), the greater the number of interdependencies among team members, the greater the importance of team feedback. Unfortunately, no research has yet evaluated the relative effects of individual and team feedback.

Research Questions

While the task-oriented analysis of team performance, and recent literature (e.g., Morgan et al., 1986; Glickman et al., 1987; Prince, Chidester, Cannon-Bowers, & Bowers, this volume), identify important considerations in team training, research questions remain about the design of that training. First, what are teamwork skills? How are these different from individual skills? Second, what are the appropriate instructional strategies for teaching team skills? Third, as discussed earlier, we need to know about the sequencing of individual and team skills training. Further, we need to better understand the role of task structure on team training design. For example, when the team task is characterized by high task organization and low task complexity, what should be the nature of training? High task organization requires coordination and communication skills training, while low task complexity indicates that individual skills training will most effectively enhance overall team performance. Thus, a combination of individual skills and team skills training should be the superior design for training teams to perform such tasks.

Part vs. whole training. Within the context of individual skills or team skills training, "part" or "whole" training methods may be employed. "Part" training requires that specific components of the task be learned sequentially. When components of the task are learned, they are gradually integrated until the entire task is mastered. Conversely, "whole" training does not isolate task components but focuses on the entire task during all segments of the training procedure.

When the objective is to train team skills, the issue of "part" versus "whole" training becomes increasingly problematic. It may be most beneficial to train team members individually, or the superior strategy may be to train team members within the team context. As a result, four distinct training strategies can be identified. Individuals may be given individual skills training that includes a focus on the interactive requirements of the team task (individual–whole training) or they may be given individual skills training that ignores the team context (individual–part training). When members are trained within the team setting, each member may be trained on the specific subtask to which he or she is assigned (team–part training), or the training may focus on the development of coordination and communication skills that allows the teams to function successfully as a unit (team–whole training).

When the team task is characterized by a combination of high complexity and high organization, a combination of individual skills and team skills training (i.e., individual–whole and team–whole) may be the superior strategy. When both types of training are given, no standard exists for the sequencing of the two training types or for the appropriate ratio of each method. In addition, it is not clear how task characteristics affect these relationships. Thus, we need a determination of when individual/team and part/whole training paradigms are most beneficial.

Dual-task environment. The dual-task hypothesis suggests that team members must integrate (as the TEAM model also suggests) performance of taskwork behaviors with the performance of teamwork behaviors. Thus, team members work within a task environment where they must coordinate the performance of two separate types of behavior (B. B. Morgan, Jr., personal communication, March 18, 1990). However, it currently is not clear exactly how team members should coordinate the performance of task and teamwork behaviors, or how team members should be trained to develop this coordination strategy. As a result, the development of strategies for interweaving task and teamwork behaviors, and the creation of training programs to train these strategies, are important research issues.

Shared mental models. Recently, it has been suggested that the concept of mental models is useful for the understanding and training of teamwork skills (Cannon-Bowers & Salas, 1990). The concept is useful, because team members need to possess an accurate understanding of the various requirements of team performance if they are to perform effectively as a team member (Adelman, Zirk, Lehner, Moffett, & Hal, 1986). When team members possess accurate and equally detailed conceptualizations (i.e., mental models) of the requirements of team functioning, they can be said to have shared mental models (Klein, 1989; Noble, Grosz, & Boehm-Davis, 1987; Cannon-Bowers, Salas, & Converse, 1990). The greater the degree of accuracy and overlap among team member mental models, the greater the likelihood that the team members will predict, adapt, and coordinate with one another successfully, even under stressful or novel conditions.

Perhaps the most difficult problem for the shared mental models hypothesis is the identification of methods to measure the degree of overlap among mental models of team member. Measures of the degree of overlap are required to determine the covarying features of mental models and to determine the impact of the common features on the performance of task and teamwork behaviors and the quality of overall team performance.

With respect to training, empirical evidence suggests that fostering or changing mental models is not simply a matter of training people to understand general principles of system or task design. In fact, such training has been found to be of limited utility (Brigham & Laios, 1974; Morris & Rouse, 1985). Instead, it appears that effective training occurs when information is given about the various components that comprise a system, *and* about the relationships that exist among those components (Kieras & Bovair, 1984). In addition, strategies such as cross training team members may have utility in producing shared mental models of member task requirements (Cannon-Bowers & Salas, 1990). Cross training provides team members with experience and practice on the individual tasks of other team members. Thus, cross training should be an effective method of enriching a team member's interpositional knowledge regarding other members' task functions, information needs, and coordination requirements.

The notion of shared mental models appears to be a valuable means to understand, evaluate, and train for team performance. However, before the shared mental model construct can be applied to the training of teams, several kinds of research must be conducted. Valid and reliable methods of measuring mental models, and of measuring the degree of overlap among mental models, must be determined. The particular models of overall team function that should be shared by team members, and the specific team members who should share them also must be identified. Methods of training mental models will need to be explored and the utility of these training programs must be evaluated. Despite the methodological problems posed by the shared mental model hypothesis, the mental model construct appears to be unique in its utility for understanding how team members are able to perform the cognitive components of their jobs. The construct of shared mental models should be particularly useful for understanding how team members predict and adapt successfully. Further, the construct can serve as an organizing concept for understanding team processes, and for generating specific predictions about the quality of team performance.

FINAL THOUGHTS

In summary, some progress has been made in the last several years in understanding team performance and training; however, there is much to be done. Team training is not simple, because it depends on task and work characteristics, individual and team characteristics, and the environment in which the teams perform. Answers will not come easily or overnight, nor will they satisfy everybody. Team training research is expensive, difficult, and labor intensive. But there is hope.

REFERENCES

Adelman, L., Zirk, D. A., Lehner, P. E., Moffett, R. J., & Hal, R. (1986). Distributed tactical decision-making: Conceptual framework and empirical results. *IEEE Transactions on Systems, Man, and Cybernetics, SMC-16* (6), 794–805.

Alexander, L. T., & Cooperband, A. S. (1965). *System training and research in team behavior* (TM-2581). Santa Monica, CA: System Development Corp.

Bass, B. M., & Barrett, B. V. (1981). *People, work, and organizations.* Boston: Allyn and Bacon.

Bouchard, T. J. (1969). Personality, problem-solving procedure, and performance in small groups. *Journal of Applied Psychology Monographs, 53,* 1–29.

Briggs, G. E., & Johnston, W. A. (1967). *Team training* (NAVTRADEVCEN-1327-4, AD-660 019). Orlando, FL: Naval Training Device Center.

Briggs, G. E., & Naylor, J. C. (1964). *Experiments on team training in a CIC-type task environment* (NAVTRADEVCEN-1327-1, AD-608 309). Port Washington, NY: Naval Training Device Center.

Brigham, F., & Laios, L. (1974). Operator performance in the control of a Laboratory processing plant. *Ergonomics, 18,* 53–66.

Cannon-Bowers, J. A., Salas, E., & Converse, S. A. (1991). Cognitive psychology and team training: Shared mental models of complex systems. *Human Factors Society Bulletin,* pp. 1–4.

Cannon-Bowers, J. A., & Salas, E. (1990, April). Cognitive psychology and team training: Shared mental models in complex systems. In K. Kraiger (Chair), *Cognitive representations of work.* Symposium conducted at the annual meeting of the Society for Industrial/Organizational Psychology, Miami, FL.

Chapman, R. L., Kennedy, J. L., Newell, A., & Biel, W. C. (1959). The system research laboratory's air defense experiments. *Management Science, 5,* 250–269.

Converse, S. A., Dickinson, T. L., Tannenbaum, S. I., & Salas, E. (1988, April). *Team training and performance: A meta-analysis.* Paper presented at the annual meeting of the Southeastern Psychological Association, New Orleans, LA.

Cooper, M., Shiflett, S., Korotkin, A., & Fleishman, E. (1984). *Command and control teams: Technologies for assessing team performance* (AFHRL-TP-84-3). Wright-Patterson AFB, OH: Logistics and Human Factors Division, Air Force Human Resources Laboratory.

Daniels, R. W., Alder, D. G., Kanarick, A. F., Gray, T. H., & Feuge, R. L. (1972). *Automated operation instruction in team tactics* (NAVTRADEVCEN-70-c-0310-1, AD-736 970). Orlando, FL: Naval Training Device Center.

Denson, R. W. (1981). *Team training: Literature review and annotated bibliography* (AFHRL-TR-80-40, A9-A099994). Wright-Patterson AFB, OH: Logistics and Technical Training Division, Air Force Human Resources Laboratory.

Dickinson, T. L. (1969). The effects of work interaction and its interplay with task organization on team and member performance (Doctoral dissertation, The Ohio State University, 1968). *Dissertation Abstracts International, 30* (4-B), 1937–1938.

Dickinson, T. L., Salas, E., Converse, S. A., & Tannenbaum, S. I. (1987). Impact of task and work structure on team performance. In G. Lee (Ed.), *Proceedings of psychology in the Department of Defense symposium*. Colorado Springs, CO: U.S. Department of Commerce.

Dieterly, D. L. (1988). Team performance requirements. In S. Gael (Ed.), *The job analysis handbook for business, industry, and government* (Vol. 1, pp. 486–492). New York: John Wiley.

Driskell, J. E., Hogan, R., & Salas, E. (1987). Personality and group performance. *Review of Personality and Social Psychology, 9,* 91–112.

Driskell, J. E., Salas, E., & Hogan, R. (1987). *A taxonomy for composing effective naval teams* (NAVTRASYSCEN TR 87-002). Orlando, FL: Naval Training Systems Center.

Dyer, J. C. (1984). Team research and team training: State-of-the-art review. In F. A. Muckler (Ed.), *Human factors review* (pp. 285–323). Santa Monica, CA: Human Factors Society.

Friedlander, F. (1987). The ecology of work groups. In J. Lorsch (Ed.), *Handbook of organizational behavior* (pp. 301–314). Englewood Cliffs, NJ: Prentice-Hall.

George, C. E. (1967). Training for coordination with rifle squads. In T. O. Jacobs, J. S. Ward, T. R. Power, C. E. George, & H. H. McFann (Eds.), *Individual and small-unit training for combat operations*. Alexandria, VA: Human Resources Research Office.

George, C. E. (1979, March). *Team member coordination: Definition, measurement, and effect on performance*. Paper presented at the annual meeting of the Southeastern Psychological Association, New Orleans, LA.

George, C. E., Hoak, G., & Boutwell, J. (1963). *Pilot studies of team effectiveness* (Research Memorandum No. 28, AD-627, 217). Ft. Benning, GA: U.S. Army Infantry Human Research Unit, Human Resources Research Office.

Gersick, C. J. G. (1985). *Time and transition in work teams: Towards a new model of group development*. Unpublished manuscript, University of California, Los Angeles.

Gersick, C. J. G. (1988). Time and transition in work teams: Towards a new model of group development. *Academy of Management Review, 31,* 9–41.

Gersick, C. J. G. (1989). Marking time: Predictable transitions in task groups. *Academy of Management Journal, 32,* 274–309.

Gladstein, D. L. (1984). Groups in context: A model of task group effectiveness. *Administrative Science Quarterly, 29,* 499–517.

Glickman, A. S., Zimmer, S., Montero, R. C., Guerette, P. J., Campbell, W. S., Morgan, Jr., B. B., & Salas, E. (1987). *The evolution of teamwork skills: An empirical assessment with implications for training* (Tech. Rep. No. 87-016). Orlando, FL: Naval Training Systems Center.

Goodman, P. S., & Assoc., (1986). *Designing effective work groups*. San Francisco: Jossey-Bass.

Hackman, J. R. (1983). *A normative model of work team effectiveness* (Tech. Rep. No. 2). New Haven, CT: Yale University.

Hackman, J. R., & Morris, C. G. (1975). Group tasks, group interaction processes, and group performance effectiveness: A review and proposed integration. In L. Berkowitz (Ed.), *Advances in experimental social psychology* (Vol. 8, pp. 45–99). New York: Academic Press.

Hall, E. R., & Rizzo, W. A. (1975). *An assessment of U.S. tactical team training* (TAEG-18, AD-A011 452). Orlando, FL: Naval Training Equipment Center.

Horrocks, J. E., Krug, R., & Heermann, E. (1960). *Team training II: Individual learning and team performance* (NAVTRADEVCEN 198-2, AD-247 147). Port Washington, NY: Naval Training Device Center.

Johnston, W. A. (1966). Transfer of team skills as a function of type of training. *Journal of Applied Psychology, 52*, 89–94.

Johnston, W. A., & Briggs, G. (1968). Team performance as a function of team arrangement and work load. *Journal of Applied Psychology, 50*, 89–94.

Jones, J. E. (1984). *An analysis of constraints to coordinated tactical crew interaction in the P-3C aircraft* (AD-A147 220). Wright-Patterson AFB, OH: Air Force Institute of Technology.

Kabanoff, B., & O'Brien, G. E. (1979). The effects of task type and cooperation upon group products and performance. *Organizational Behavior and Human Performance, 23*, 163–181.

Kieras, D. E., & Bovair, S. (1984). The role of a mental model in learning to operate a device. *Cognitive Science, 8*, 255–273.

Klaus, D. J., & Glaser, R. (1965). *Increasing team proficiency through training. 5. Team learning as a function of member learning characteristics and practice conditions* (AIR-E1-4/65-TR, AD-215 621). Pittsburgh, PA: American Institutes for Research.

Klaus, D. J., & Glaser, R. (1970). Reinforcement determinants of team proficiency. *Organizational Behavior and Human Performance, 5*, 33–67.

Klaus, D. J., Grant, L. D., & Glaser, R. (1965). *Increasing team proficiency through training. 6. Supervisory furnished reinforcement in team training* (AIR-E1-5/65-TR, AD-471 470). Pittsburgh, PA: American Institute for Research.

Klein, G. A. (1989). Recognition-primed decisions. In W. B. Rouse (Ed.), *Advances in man-machine systems research* (Vol. 5, pp. 47–92). Greenwich, CT: JAI Press.

Krumm, R. L. (1958). *Crew member agreement on B-52 crew operating procedures as an index of crew proficiency* (AD-F630-317). Washington, DC: American Institute for Research.

Lawrence, P. R., & Lorsch, J. W. (1969). *Developing organizations: Diagnosis and action.* Reading, MA: Addison-Wesley.

Levinson, D. J. (1978). *The season's of a man's life.* New York: Alfred A. Knopf.

Marrow, A. J. (1969). *The practical theorist: The life and work of Kurt Lewin.* New York: Basic Books.

McGrath, J. E. (1964). *Social psychology: A brief introduction.* New York: Holt.

McRae, A. V. (1966). *Interaction content and team effectiveness* (HumRRO-TR-66-10, AD-637 311). Alexandria, VA: George Washington University, Human Resources Research Office.

Meister, D. (1976). Team functions. In D. Meister (Ed.), *Behavioral foundations of system development.* New York: Wiley & Sons.

Modrick, J. A. (1986). Team performance and training. In J. Zeidner (Ed.), *Human productivity enhancement: Training and human factors in systems design* (Vol. 1, pp. 130–166). New York: Praeger.

Morgan, B. B., Jr., Glickman, A. S., Woodard, E. A., Blaiwes, A. S., & Salas, E. (1986). *Measurement of team behaviors in a Navy environment* (Tech. Rep. No. NTSC TR-86-014). Orlando, FL: Naval Training Systems Center.

Morris, N. M., & Rouse, W. B. (1985). The effects of type of knowledge upon human problem solving in a process control task. *IEEE Transactions on Systems, Man and Cybernetics, SMC-15,* 698–707.

Mullen, B., & Goethals, G. R. (Eds.). (1987). *Theories of group behavior.* New York: Springer-Verlag.

Nadler, D. A. (1979). The effects of feedback on task group behavior: A review of the experimental research. *Organizational Behavior and Human Performance, 23,* 309–335.

Naylor, J. C., & Dickinson, T. L. (1969). Task structure, work structure, and team performance. *Journal of Applied Psychology, 53,* 167–177.

Nieva, V. F., Fleishman, E. A., & Reick, A. (1978). *Team dimensions: Their identity, their measurement and their relationships* (Contract No. DAHC 19-78-C-0001). Washington, DC: Advanced Research Resources Organization.

Nieva, V. F., Fleishman, E. A., & Reick, A. (1978). *Team dimensions: Their identity, their measurement and their relationships* (Contract No. DAHC19-78-C-0001). Washington, DC: Response Analysis Corporation.

Noble, D., Grosz, C., & Boehm-Davis, D. (1987). *Rules, schema, and decision making* (TR R-125-87). Vienna, VA: Engineering Research Association.

Parsons, K. L. (1981). The effects of load sharing system training upon team performance (Doctoral dissertation, Michigan State University, 1980). *Dissertation Abstracts International, 42* (6-A), 2876–2877.

Shiflett, S. C. (1972). Group performance as a function of task difficulty and organizational interdependence. *Organizational Behavior and Human Performance, 7,* 442–456.

Shiflett, S. C., Eisner, E. J., Price, S. J., & Schemmer, F. M. (1982). *The definition and measurement of team functions* (Final Report). Bethesda, MD: Advanced Research Resources Organization.

Siegel, A. I., & Federman, P. J. (1973). Communications content training as an ingredient in effective team performance. *Ergonomics, 16,* 403–416.

Sorenson, J. R. (1971). Task demands, group interaction and group performance. *Sociometry, 34,* 483–495.

Steiner, I. D. (1972). *Group processes and productivity.* New York: Academic Press.

Swezey, R. W., & Salas, E. (1989). Development of instructional design guidelines for individual and team training systems. *Proceedings of the 11th Interservice/Industry Training System Conference and Exhibition* (pp. 422–426). Fort Worth, TX: National Security Industrial Association.

Terborg, J. R., Castore, C. H., & DeNinno, J. A. (1976, May). *A longitudinal field investigation of the impact of group composition on group performance and cohesion.* Paper presented at the annual meeting of the Midwestern Psychological Association, Chicago.

Tuckman, B. W. (1965). Developmental sequences in small groups. *Psychological Bulletin, 63,* 384–399.

Tziner, A., & Eden, D. (1985). Effects of crew composition on crew performance: Does the whole equal the sum of its parts? *Journal of Applied Psychology, 70,* 85–93.

Wagner, H., Hibbits, N., Rosenblatt, R. D., & Salas, R. (1977). *Team training and evaluation strategies: State-of-the-art* (HumRRO-TR-77-1, AD-A039 505). Alexandria, VA: Human Resources Research Organization.

2

Toward a Taxonomy of Team Performance Functions *

Edwin A. Fleishman
Stephen J. Zaccaro

TOWARD A TAXONOMIC CLASSIFICATION
OF TEAM PERFORMANCE FUNCTIONS:
INITIAL CONSIDERATIONS, SUBSEQUENT
EVALUATIONS, AND CURRENT FORMULATIONS

Many human tasks are accomplished by groups of individuals. An essential characteristic of these tasks is that they often require synchronized actions rather than summed or aggregated responses. Performance on such tasks can be impaired, not because individuals within the group lack requisite abilities, but rather because the team as a whole fails to coordinate member capabilities and contributions (Hackman & Morris, 1975). Steiner (1972) defined such coordination deficiency in groups as process loss. Indeed, many group theorists have noted that groups fail to maximize their productivity because of process impairment (e.g., Hackman & Morris, 1975; Hill, 1982; Janis, 1982; Steiner, 1972; Watson & Michaelsen, 1988). Thus, understanding human performance often

*The authors acknowledge the contributions of Samuel Shiflett, Merri-Ann Cooper, Veronica Nieva, Angela Rieck, Ellen Eisner, Shelley Price, Mark Schemmer, and Arthur Korotkin at various stages of the research described in this chapter. The research described was supported in part by the Army Research Institute, and by the Air Force Human Resources Laboratory.

requires knowledge of how aggregations of individuals function to produce effective synchronized output.

Despite this requirement, relatively little formal knowledge exists regarding the description and analysis of team performance functions. This lack of sufficient information on those interdependent responses and member interactions that define group performance has been a long-standing complaint in the group performance literature (e.g., Glanzer & Glaser, 1955; Hackman & Morris, 1975). In a review of the small group performance literature, Davis and Stasson (1988) summarized a number of approaches to the assessment of team interaction dynamics. While they detailed advances in this area, they also noted the lack of a systematic framework linking measures of social processes to team performance.

Oser, McCallum, Salas, and Morgan (1989) have noted the problems of variable definition and measurement systems in current team performance research (see also McCallum, Oser, Morgan, & Salas, 1989; Salas, Blaiwes, Reynolds, Glickman, & Morgan, 1985). This imprecision in the specification and definition of performance measures has also been termed a formidable barrier to effective team-training efforts (e.g., Dyer, 1984; Hall & Rizzo, 1975; McCallum et al., 1989; Wagner, Hibbits, Rosenblatt, & Schultz, 1977). These observations indicate that there is still a need for an integrative classification of team performance functions.

In response to these issues, a number of researchers have developed classifications of group performance tasks (Davis, Laughlin, & Komorita, 1976; Hackman & Morris, 1975; McGrath, 1984; Steiner, 1972). These schemes, while extremely useful in understanding several domains of group performance, are typically too general to be of use in describing the specific coordinated activities engaged in by members completing group tasks. We cite as a good example the task taxonomy provided by McGrath (1984). This taxonomy effectively combined a number of prior taxonomies and classification schemes (Carter, Haythorn, & Howell, 1950; Shaw, 1973; Hackman, 1968; Steiner, 1972; Davis et al., 1976). It classified the specific tasks that may be presented to the group into such categories as planning, idea generation, problem solving, decision making, conflict resolution, and psychomotor performance. These tasks were subsumed under four broad performance processes—generate, choose, negotiate, and execute. This classification scheme provided an effective means of organizing a considerable body of knowledge about group performance (Goodman, 1986). However, the scheme did not specify the particular synchronized functions engaged in by team members as they perform different tasks. Also, it is not known how this classification scheme helps us generalize about the factors affecting synchronized functions across the task categories. What is necessary, then, is a taxonomic classification of team performance functions that includes coordinated member activities, is generalizable across diverse group task situations, and provides a foundation for a valid and reliable measurement system.

Taxonomic Classification: Basic Issues

Classification is defined as "the ordering or arrangement of entities into groups or sets on the basis of their relationship, based on observable or inferred properties" (Fleishman & Quaintance, 1984, p. 22). According to Fleishman and Quaintance (1984), the primary purpose of scientific classification is to describe the structure and relationships among similar objects in terms that afford general statements about classes of objects. Additional objectives include the definition of essential object properties, generation of hypotheses, and provision of a terminology that facilitates organization, understanding, and communication (Fleishman & Quaintance, 1984). The construction and evaluation of a taxonomic classification system involves the (a) operational definition of objects to be classified, (b) measurement of object properties and subsequently the degree of similarity among the objects to be classified, (c) application of decision rules regarding the appropriate degree of object similarity for inclusion in a particular category, and (d) evaluation of the system's validity. Three criteria used to evaluate classifications include internal validity, external validity, and degree of utility.

The conceptual issues, guidelines, and criteria for human performance taxonomies were elucidated by Fleishman and Quaintance (1984). They described an extensive and programmatic research effort that had as its goal the development and assessment of taxonomies of human performance (see also Fleishman, 1967, 1975a,b, 1982). Primary considerations were the adoption of task definitions that permitted reliable task description and discrimination, the specification of categories that were neither too specific nor too general to impede taxonomic utility, the development of measurement systems that correspond appropriately to taxonomic categories, and the establishment of criteria for the psychometric assessment of these approaches. Four primary conceptual bases of task classification, adapted from Hackman (1968), Altman (1966), and McGrath and Altman (1966), were examined in the research effort—the *behavioral description approach,* or task classification in terms of overt behaviors displayed while performing the task; the *behavior requirements approach,* or classification in terms of the inferred processes required to achieve performance criteria; *the ability requirements approach,* or classification according to the abilities required of the task performer; and the *task characteristics approach,* or classification according to the task conditions or task properties eliciting performance.

This research program, summarized in Fleishman and Quaintance (1984), established in the behavioral sciences the role of a taxonomic analysis of individual performance. Fleishman and Quaintance also noted a number of uses for a performance taxonomy, several of which are pertinent to the aforementioned gaps in the team performance literature. These include such scientific/theoretical benefits as generalizing results to new tasks, exposing knowledge gaps, and assisting theory development. The applied/practical benefits include a basis for task definition and job analysis, training specifications, and performance measurement and enhancement.

The research to be described in this chapter represents an extension and application of this work on individual performance taxonomies to an analysis of team performance. Specifically, we summarize and update efforts by Fleishman and his associates (e.g., Nieva, Fleishman, & Rieck, 1978; Shiflett, Eisner, Price, & Schemmer, 1982; Cooper, Shiflett, Korotkin, & Fleishman, 1984) directed toward the development and evaluation of a team performance taxonomy that met the criteria for a successful classification system. We begin with a model of group performance and an initial taxonomy of team performance functions. We then present several subsequent evaluations of this provisional taxonomy and provide some suggested modifications.

A MODEL OF TEAM PERFORMANCE

A lack of clarity regarding the concept of *team* has hindered research on team performance. Nieva et al. (1978) defined *team* as "two or more interdependent individuals performing coordinated tasks toward the achievement of specific task goals" (p. 51). This definition assumes a shared task orientation and task interdependence among group members. *Team performance* is defined as "the goal-directed behaviors/activities/functions accomplished by the team in performing the task" (Nieva et al., 1978, p. 52). Performance is viewed then as a set of responses, independent and synchronized, that is separated from the task itself. A model of team performance, based both on these definitions and on an extensive review of the group performance literature, was provided by Nieva et al. (1978). This model is illustrated in Figure 2.1.

Team performance has two primary components (Guetzkow & Simon, 1955), individual task behaviors and coordinated task-related processes/functions/behaviors. Individual behaviors are those which are geared towards discrete task operations, requiring no coordination. Team functions are those that promote coordination among individual members and subtasks. In the research program to be discussed, Cooper et al. (1984) noted that team functions are strategies directed toward organizing personnel and material resources to match specific task requirements and goals. Such functions are based more on interactions among team members than on independent, individual acts. Both individual and team components determine the level and nature of group performance. For example, on intellective tasks where a single, compelling, and correct answer exists (Laughlin, 1980), group performance is based on the acts of the individual who knows the correct answer as well as on the coordinated activities of the group in eliciting and gaining acceptance of this answer (Hackman & Morris, 1975; Steiner, 1972). However, the weight of each component in terms of contri-

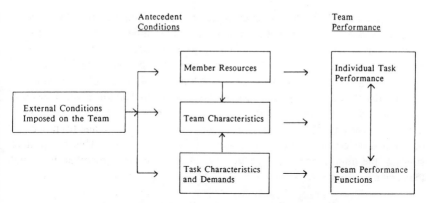

Figure 2.1. Conceptual Model of Team Performance
From Nieva, Fleishman, and Rieck (1978).

butions to overall team performance will vary according to the nature of the particular task characteristics. Individual acts may carry more weight on additive tasks, where team performance is defined as the sum of individual outputs (Steiner, 1972), than on decision tasks that require the group to plan and reach consensus on group actions (e.g., Hackman & Morris, 1975; McGrath, 1984).

Team performance is considered a result of four antecedent classes of variables—external conditions imposed on the team, member resources, task characteristics and demands, and team characteristics. The specification of these variable classes is based on an extensive review of the group performance literature (Nieva et al., 1978). What follows is a further explanation of each variable class.

External Conditions Imposed on the Team

Task groups are often embedded within larger organizational systems. These systems determine the boundaries of group process and performance. Member resources available for group action are generally a product of selection and choice processes within the embedding system. Furthermore, aspects of the group's physical environment may change the interaction dynamics of the group (Paulus & Nagar, 1987). Environmental uncertainty and threat can affect group processes by centralizing member communication (Argote, Turner, & Fichman, 1989) and restricting team information-processing functions (Gladstein & Reilly, 1985).

Organizations affect several other parameters of embedded task groups, including temporal boundaries of the group task, job operating procedures, intergroup communication patterns, and power and authority distribution. Ancona

(1987) noted that the embedded character of groups requires that "they must adapt to, model, or be influenced by changing environmental conditions. Therefore, a central activity of groups in context must be reaching out, directing activity outward" (p. 214). Ancona (1987) denoted five interactive linkages with respect to this outreach. These were (a) dealing with dependence through negotiation, (b) adapting to the environment through information acquisition and exchange, (c) strategic management through team representations to the embedding organization, (d) balancing internal and external demands, and (e) processes of population ecology (see also Ancona & Caldwell, 1988). This perspective suggests the importance of external conditions in influencing member, task, and team characteristics.

Member Resources

The knowledge, skills, abilities, and experiences that members bring to the task help define the maximum level of group performance (Steiner, 1972). For example, on an intellective task for which there exists a single correct answer, group performance is determined by the resources of the most capable member (Laughlin, 1980; Steiner, 1972). On other types of tasks, performance levels may be limited by the average member of the group or even by the least capable member (Hackman & Morris, 1975; Steiner, 1972). Furthermore, member resources contribute to the quality of group interaction (Hackman & Morris, 1975).

Members' motives, attitudes, personality characteristics, and traits are also included as performance-related resources. These variables can affect the level of individual effort devoted to group performance. Tziner and Eden (1985) found that member motivation and ability had additive effects on performance of three-person tank crews. However, they also demonstrated the importance of synchronized team functions. Teams having uniformly high-ability members performed better than expected form the sum of individual resources, while uniformly low-ability teams performed lower than expected from a summative model.

Task Characteristics

Task characteristics are those aspects of the task that determine process and performance requirements. They specify individual and synchronized activities that are necessary for effective team performance (Steiner, 1972). Several task classification and models exist that specify the distinctions among group tasks and the different requirements these tasks pose for successful performance (Hackman, 1968; Hackman & Morris, 1975; Laughlin, 1980; McGrath, 1984; Steiner, 1972).

Hackman and Oldham (1980) also point to the motivational aspects of group tasks. Extending their Job Characteristics Model of individual tasks to group tasks, they suggested that team members can be motivated through group tasks that (a) require a variety of member skills, (b) yield a whole and identifiable product, (c) yield significant outcomes that are meaningful for people and groups, (d) provide considerable autonomy to group members in completing the work, and (e) provide direct performance feedback.

Team Characteristics

Nieva et al. (1978) defined *team characteristics* as those that apply to the group as a whole rather than to specific individuals. This concept is similar to Cattell's (1948, p. 49) notion of syntality, which refers to dynamic, temperament, and ability aspects of the group as a totality. Examples of team characteristics include group cohesion, size, structure, and authority structure. The model of team performance specifies that team variables are affected both by member resources and task characteristics.

Nieva et al. (1978) provided an extensive review of the group performance literature, specifically focusing on how particular team characteristics relate to performance. A full summary of that review is beyond the scope of this chapter, and we refer the reader to Nieva et al. (1978) and to more recent reviews and models (Goodman, Ravlin, & Argote, 1986; Gist, Locke, & Taylor, 1987). However, to illustrate how team characteristics can affect team performance, we present abbreviated reviews of the performance literature on two team characteristics—size and cohesiveness.

Group size. In their review, Nieva et al. (1972) found that, on disjunctive tasks where group performance is determined by the most capable member of the group (Steiner, 1972), group size was positively related to performance (e.g., Cummings, Huber, & Arendt, 1974; Frank & Anderson, 1971; Goldman, 1971; Waag & Holcomb, 1972). More recently, Yetton and Bottger (1983) confirmed this relationship but reported decreasing performance increments with each additional group member. Nieva et al. also concluded from their review that size was negatively related to performance on conjunctive tasks, where maximum performance is defined by the least capable group member (e.g., Frank & Anderson, 1971; Marriott, 1949). Further, they argued that, on certain other tasks, group size may have a positive effect on performance up to an optimum size level, after which size has a negative impact on performance.

Recent work on the size–performance relationship has detailed more deleterious effects of group size. Based on a meta-analysis, Gooding and Wagner (1985) concluded that, although group size was not related to total unit output in organizational subunits, there was a negative effect on unit efficiency. Latane and his colleagues (Latane, Williams, & Harkins, 1979; Petty, Harkins, Williams, & Latane, 1977; Williams, Harkins, & Latane, 1981) illustrated the "social loafing" effect, whereby individual group members decrease their efforts as group size increases. This effect has been demonstrated on both physical (e.g., Latane et al., 1979; Kerr & Bruun, 1983; Zaccaro, 1984) and cognitive (e.g., Petty et al., 1977; Harkins & Petty, 1982; Weldon & Gargano, 1985) tasks. Social loafing effects, however, have been eliminated when member outputs are made identifiable (Williams et al., 1981), when the task was a difficult one (Harkins & Petty, 1982), when members have high personal involvement (Brickner, Harkins, & Ostrom, 1986), and when the task orientation of the group is enhanced (Zaccaro, 1984).

This brief review indicates that the effect of group size on performance varies according the type of task assigned the group. Further, when individual indices serve as the criteria, group size appears to reduce effort, even if overall group output is increasing. However, this particular effect is also modified by several tasks, group, and member characteristics.

Group cohesion. *Group cohesion,* defined as "the degree to which the members of a group desire to remain in the group" (Cartwright, 1968, p. 91), has also been demonstrated as having mixed effects on group productivity. Prior reviews indicate positive, negative, or zero associations. For example, Hare (1976) cited 14 studies showing a positive relationship between cohesion and performance. Lott and Lott (1965) cited 20 studies demonstrating a positive association, but also found 15 studies showing either a zero or a negative relationship. Similarly, Stogdill (1972) reported 12 studies supporting a positive relationship and 20 studies not supporting an association. Reflecting this ambivalence, Nieva et al. (1978) cited 8 studies of a positive relationship between cohesion and performance and 6 studies reporting a lack of or a negative effect.

Given this inconsistency, the primary emphasis has been on the identification of moderator variables that determine the direction of cohesion effects on performance. Early work in this area focused on the role of group performance norms. Schachter, Ellertson, McBride, and Gregory (1951) argued that group cohesion was related to performance only when groups established high performance standards. When groups establish low standards, cohesion is negatively related to performance. This is due to the ability of cohesive groups to command more effectively member adherence to group goals. Several studies have provided support for this argument (Berkowitz, 1954; Schachter et al., 1951; Seashore, 1954). Moreover, related arguments were offered by Stogdill (1972), who suggested that *group drive,* defined as "the intensity with which members invest expectation and energy on behalf of the group" (p. 27), moderates cohesion–performance relationships, such that cohesion has a positive effect only under conditions of high group drive. Support for Stogdill's view was offered by Greene (1989).

Some researchers have argued that leadership style affects the relationship between group cohesion and group performance. For example, Tziner and Vardi (1982) reported that performance effectiveness in Army tank crews was highest under two conditions: (a) high team cohesion with a leadership style reflecting both a task and people orientation, and (b) low team cohesion with a people-oriented leadership style.

Most prior research on these relationships has operationalized group cohesion as members' interpersonal liking for fellow group members. This stems from a unitary view of group cohesion (cf. Back, 1950; Schachter, 1952). Recently, theorists have begun to examine cohesion as a multidimensional construct, with different components of group cohesion having different consequences for group performance and process (cf. Carron, 1982; Carron, Widmeyer, & Brawley, 1985; Hackman, 1976; Tziner, 1982). In support of this view, Zaccaro and Lowe (1988) found that task-based cohesion was positively related to performance on an additive task (where performance is the sum of individual efforts—Steiner, 1972), while interpersonal cohesion had counterbalancing facilitative and deleterious effects. Zaccaro and McCoy (1988) found that groups having high levels of both task and interpersonal cohesion yielded highest performance scores on an arctic survival task (i.e., a disjunctive task). Groups high on one type of cohesion but low on the other performed no more effectively than groups low on both forms of cohesion. Zaccaro (1991) reported differential effects of task and interpersonal cohesion on individual performance and absenteeism in student cadet groups. These studies suggest that the association between cohesion and performance may also depend on the specific nature of the group's cohesiveness.

The four antecedents of team performance noted by Nieva et al. (1978)—external conditions, member resources, task characteristics, and team characteristics—determine the specific nature of individual and coordinated team responses. Their review suggested the ways these antecedents can alter the nature of team processes. However, to fully understand how the variables surveyed by Nieva et al. (1978) relate to team performance and its underlying processes, it is necessary to clearly specify particular team performance functions. This would allow a more precise and fine-grained analysis of the aforementioned associations. Accordingly, Nieva et al. (1978) proposed a taxonomy of team functions.

A PROVISIONAL TAXONOMY OF TEAM PERFORMANCE FUNCTIONS

As noted, team performance is composed of individual task-related activities and coordinated team functions. A considerable effort has been devoted to developing taxonomies of individual performance (Fleishman & Quaintance, 1984). The primary focus here is on the development and evaluation of a team performance taxonomy. The performance functions to be described refer to *synchronized* activities.

With this goal in mind, Nieva et al. (1978) developed a provisional taxonomy of team functions. Their assumption was that common team functions generalize across many diverse performance settings and may vary in frequency and intensity according to task and team characteristics. The taxonomy is shown in Table 2.1.

The taxonomy contains four major categories of team performance functions. They are orientation functions, organizational functions, adaptation functions,

Table 2.1.   Provisional Taxonomy of Team Performance

I. Team Orientation Functions
   A. Elicitation and distribution of information about team goals
   B. Elicitation and distribution of information about team tasks
   C. Elicitation and distribution of information about member resources and constraints
II. Team Organizational Functions
   A. Matching member resources to task requirements
   B. Response coordination and sequencing of activities
   C. Activity pacing
   D. Priority assignment among tasks
   E. Load balancing of tasks by members
III. Team Adaptation Functions
   A. Mutual critical evaluation and correction of error
   B. Mutual compensatory performance
   C. Mutual compensatory timing
IV. Team Motivational Functions
   A. Development of team performance norms
   B. Generating acceptance of team performance norms
   C. Establishing team-level performance–rewards linkages
   D. Reinforcement of task orientation
   E. Balancing team orientation with individual competition
   F. Resolution of performance–relevant conflicts

From Nieva, Fleishman, and Rieck (1978).

and motivational functions. Nieva et al. (1978, p. 62) defined three characteristics of these functions. First, each function reflects a focus on task accomplishment with a concern for member interconnectedness. Second, they are molar functions, cutting across specific member activities. Indeed, a specific act can correspond to multiple functions. Third, the functions reflect relative categories, meaning that they can be ordered with respect to each other.

Orientation functions refer to processes by team members to acquire and distribute information necessary for task accomplishment (cf. Lanzetta & Roby, 1960). Information acquisition can be directed toward internal aspects of the group as well as toward the organization and environment within which the group is embedded (cf. Alexander & Cooperbrand, 1965). An example of this function is a team facing environmental threat (e.g., uncertainty), which responds by seeking additional information regarding the nature of the threat and the range of potential solutions (Staw, Sandelands, & Dutton, 1981).

Nieva et al. (1978) offered the following behavior patterns as dimensions of orientation functions (cf. p. 63):

• Generation and distribution of relevant information about *team goals and missions,* including the relevant importance of these goals.

- Generation and distribution of information about team tasks and *situational resources and constraints.*
- Generation and distribution of information about member *resources* (e.g., abilities, information, training), and consequently about their possible requirements and constraints.

Organizational functions are those processes necessary for team members to perform their activities in coordination. These include team decisions regarding task allocation and the timing and nature of member contributions to team action. Nieva et al. (1978) defined the following as dimensions within this category (pp. 63–64):

- Matching member resources to task requirements, or what is typically referred to as "division of labor."
- Response coordination and sequencing of activities, such that team member activities flow smoothly and do not interfere with each other.
- Activity pacing, which is highly related to response coordination.
- Priority assignment amonb subtasks.
- Load balancing of tasks by members.

Adaptation functions refer to monitoring and compensatory processes that occur as members proceed according to normative performance strategies. Individual members evaluate their own activities and the coordinated actions of their peers. These functions include communications and mutual adjustments made in response to these evaluations.

Nieva et al. (1978) included the following in this category (p. 64).

- Mutual critical evaluation and correction of error, which imply opportunities for team members to view each other's performance, the presence of sufficient common ground to enable detection of error, and a sufficiently open climate to allow for the discussion and admission of error.
- Mutual compensatory performance, which includes processes by which team members perform tasks which are not typically defined as their responsibility. These compensatory performances tend to be called for in emergency situations (e.g., temporary overload on some members, equipment failure).
- Mutual compensatory timing, which includes processes by which team members informally adjust the time involved in carrying out specific subtasks, so that the overall task is accomplished effectively.

Motivational functions refer to processes of defining team objectives and motivating members to adhere to these objectives. They include the establishment and acceptance of performance norms and reward systems that prompt considerable effort from members on behalf of the group. These activities also include the maintenance of a task-based cohesiveness or shared task commitment among members (cf. Hackman, 1976; Zaccaro & Lowe, 1988; Zaccaro & McCoy, 1988). Hackman and Morris (1975) note the criticality of member effort for successful group interaction and performance.

Nieva et al. (1978) offered the following dimensions within this category (p. 65).

- Development of team norms regarding acceptable levels of performance.
- Generating acceptance of team performance norms.
- Establishing performance–reward linkages for the team as an entity.
- Reinforcement of task orientation, which includes informal rewards as well as sanctions for effective performance.
- Balancing overall team orientation with individual competitive orientations in the team.
- Resolution of informational, procedural, and interpersonal conflicts which interfere with task orientation.

EVALUATION AND REVISION
OF THE PROVISIONAL TAXONOMY

The taxonomy developed by Nieva et al. (1978) in the research program of Fleishman and his associates was considered a provisional classification requiring subsequent evaluation and adjustment. Within this research program, Shiflett et al. (1982) undertook the initial evaluation. They cited as their goals: (a) evaluating the adequacy of the taxonomy for describing team performance functions, (b) applying the taxonomy in military performance settings involving teams, (c) testing the comprehensiveness of the taxonomy in capturing the range of performance activities in military teams on routine military missions, and (d) developing reliable measures of the team performance functions in various military settings.

Shiflett et al. (1982) conducted initial validation efforts in several Army combat and combat support teams, including infantry rifle squads and platoons, combat engineer assault ribbon bridge platoons, and mortar squads. These performance teams were observed and videotaped during field-training exercise. These videotapes were then used to evaluate the team performance taxonomy and its associated measurement system. This research effort also involved the development of behaviorally anchored rating scales that corresponded to each of the performance functions. These scales are described later in this chapter.

Shiflett et al. (1982) first attempted operationally to define the team performance functions proposed by Nieva et al. (1978). However, they encountered a number of problems and issues. Some aspects of the provisional taxonomy appeared too general to provide an effective observational tool. The functions were defined such that many team actions could not be properly categorized. For example, information exchange about how to complete a particular task assignment could legitimately fit into dimensions describing team orientation (e.g., "Elicitation and distribution of information about team tasks") as well as dimensions describing team organization (e.g., "Priority assignment among subtasks"; "Response coordination and sequencing of activities"). Indeed, in their reexamination of the proposed taxonomy, Shiflett et al. (1982) concluded that "virtually all of the functions were found to serve a broader function of conveying either information or physical resources" (p. 15). Thus, a central issue was the need to define a particular team performance function so that it was neither too narrow to be indistinguishable from specific acts nor too broad to prevent its use as a discriminant category.

Accordingly, Shiflett et al. defined each function as a behavioral episode involving input and processing of information, action implementation, and monitoring and feedback. Thus, team performance functions were reflected, not in discrete actions, but rather in a sequence of related task-based activities. This view incorporates a systems perspective of team functions in that team members process information regarding external events and internal team structures, plan appropriate response patterns, act accordingly, monitor ongoing action, and adjust team responses according to performance feedback.

From this perspective, Shiflett revised the provisional taxonomy with the intent of improving the specification and operational clarity of the functional categories. To resolve the nondiscriminant character of the original classification, Shiflett et al. proposed five categories: (a) team orientation, (b) resource distribution, (c) timing and activity pacing, (d) response coordination, and (e) motivational functions. The major changes from the provisional taxonomy were to eliminate the adaptation functions category, to divide the organizational functions into three separate categories, and to include "priority assignment of tasks" as an orientation function rather than organizational function. Also, the taxonomy reflected the embedded nature of teams by including "informational exchange regarding environmental characteristics and constraints" as one of the team orientation functions.

The functions proposed by Shiflett et al. (1982) are viewed as occurring though all broad phases of a team performance mission. Two such phases can be identified, "action planning or preparation" and "action implementation or execution." Each performance function was defined as incorporating activities related to each of these phases. Thus, a particular function with its corresponding activity dimensions can occur in all stages of team performance, although a particular activity linked to a function may vary in nature and intensity during the different stages.

For example, *orientation functions* (see the aforementioned definition from Nieva et al., 1978) describe most of the activities in the planning stage of team performance, including "task and resource information exchange" and the "assignment of individual member task responsibilities." In the action implementation stage, orientation functions serve to provide information and feedback during ongoing action about team resources, goal path adherence, and environmental events. Shiflett et al. (1982) defined the following as activity dimensions reflecting team orientation (p. 25).

- Information exchange regarding member resources and constraints.
- Information exchange regarding team task and goals/mission.
- Information exchange regarding environmental characteristics and constraints.
- Priority assignment among tasks.

Resource distribution functions refer to decisions regarding the assignment of members and their resources to particular responsibilities linked to task accomplishment. They also refer to insuring the adequacy of resource assignment across subtasks. In the preparatory phase of task performance, these functions may be the assignment of members to tasks and the development of resource contingency plans. The execution phase may involve the shifting of team resources as required by changing external and internal conditions. Shiflett et al. listed two activity dimensions under this functional category (p. 25):

- Matching member resources to task requirements.
- Load balancing.

Timing functions are directed toward the organization of team resources and activities to ensure that performance tasks are completed within established temporal boundaries. Activity pacing refers to the regulation of the speed of task completion. The entire group, subsets of members, or specific individuals can be the focus of such functions. Timing functions in the preparatory phase of performance may take the form of planning the pace of team action and controlling for factors which may dictate or disrupt the intended pace. Activities directed toward regulating or altering the ongoing pace of team performance reflect timing functions in the execution phase of performance. Shiflett et al. (1982) suggested two dimensions for this category (p. 25).

- General activity pacing.
- Individually oriented activity pacing.

Response coordination functions are directed toward the smooth coordination and integration of independent and synchronized member activities. These functions involve response sequencing such that member responses are ordered according to perceived task requirements and in such a manner as to avoid conflict and interference. Also, establishing the timing of each team member's action in relation to the acts of other members when performing a synchronized task is also part of these functions.

In the preparatory stage of team performance, response coordination functions may involve planning the sequencing and timing of activities. Teams may also establish the cues that are used to initiate actions in the desired order and at the specified time. The execution phase involves the implementation of the sequencing plan as well as any changes in member response order instituted as an adaptation to changing environmental and team conditions.

Shiflett et al. (1982) included two dimensions under response coordination functions (p. 25):

- Response sequencing.
- Time and position coordination of responses.

The *motivational functions* as defined in the original taxonomy were left intact in the provisional classification scheme. However, Shiflett et al. (1982) noted the difficulty in observing the occurrence of these functions. Teams and members frequently establish the motivational context for performance long before actual task accomplishment. For example, the development and acceptance of group norms can occur during stages of group formation and development. Further, establishing performance–rewards linkages and reinforcing member task orientation, while critical aspects of the context for team performance, may actually be team maintenance activities that occur outside performance missions and episodes. Because of this noncontiguity of function and performance episode, motivational functions were difficult to operationalize and observe. Also, some motivation-directed activities can also be linked to other team functions. For example, the admonishment to "work harder" may represent team enforcement of performance norms; it can also reflect an individually oriented activity-pacing activity during the execution phase of team performance. In addition, observers of team action may not be able to distinguish team norm development from information exchange about team goals and missions.

Shiflett et al. (1982) noted the awkwardness of incorporating motivational functions into the revised taxonomy; however, because they do occur and are important for team performance, they were retained. Nevertheless, these functions remain an unexplored aspect of the team function taxonomy and require additional specification.

The revised taxonomy is shown in Table 2.2. This taxonomy was the basis for the development of assessment tools and for the laboratory validation study.

Development of Team Function Rating Scales

One objective of this research effort was to convert the revised taxonomy to a measurement system for describing team performance requirements. The general

Table 2.2.   Revised Taxonomy of Team Performance

I. Orientation Functions
   A. Information Exchange Regarding Member Resources and Constraints
   B. Information Exchange Regarding Team Task and Goals/Mission
   C. Information Exchange Regarding Environmental Characteristics and Constraints
   D. Priority Assignment Among Tasks
II. Resource Distribution Functions
   A. Matching Member Resources to Task Requirements
   B. Load Balancing
III. Timing Functions (Activity Pacing)
   A. General Activity Pacing
   B. Individually Oriented Activity Pacing
IV. Response Coordination Functions
   A. Response Sequencing
   B. Time and Position Coordination of Responses
V. Motivational Functions
   A. Development of Team Performance Norms
   B. Generating Acceptance of Team Performance Norms
   C. Establishing Team-Level Performance–Rewards Linkages
   D. Reinforcement of Task Orientation
   E. Balancing Team Orientation with Individual Competition
   F. Resolution of Performance–Relevant Conflicts

Adapted from Shiflett, Eisner, Price, and Schemmer (1982).

approach was patterned after the procedures developed by Fleishman and his associates for the description and measurement of abilities required to perform tasks in the cognitive, psychomotor, physical, and sensory-perceptual domains of human performance (Fleishman, 1975a,b, 1992; Fleishman & Mumford, 1988, 1991; Fleishman & Quaintance, 1984; Theologus & Fleishman, 1973; Theologus, Romashko, & Fleishman, 1973). In that previous work, a seven-point behaviorally anchored rating scale was developed for each of 50 different abilities identified across these domains. Each rating scale contained a carefully developed definition of the particular ability, statements of how each ability differed from other abilities, and empirically scaled task examples at high, medium, and low points on each scale. The ability requirements of new tasks and jobs could then be profiled in terms of best ability dimensions.

Shiflett et al. (1982) adapted this approach to the team performance situation. For each performance function in the taxonomy of team functions, a seven-point rating scale was developed. Each scale contained a definition of the particular team function and statements about how each function differed from other team functions. Each scale also included concrete examples of task conditions and team behavior anchors defining specific scale points. The anchors assisted raters by providing particular behavioral incidents that exemplified the high, middle, and low values of each team function. Scales were developed to provide an overall measure of the function as well as measures of specific dimensions describing each function. An example of the scale for Information Exchange about Member Resources and Constraints (IMR) is shown in Figure 2.2.

Shiflett et al. (1982) established a number of criteria for these scales in addition to acceptable psychometric properties. Primarily, the scales could not have values reflecting optimums in performance (i.e., higher values reflect "better" performance). For teams having one set of task requirements, lower scale ratings of particular functions may be more desirable than teams faced with an alternate set of task requirements. Along these lines, the scales also provide descriptions of task conditions, so that raters may be aware of and primed toward the context of team performance. A further consideration was that scale anchors be selected such that they can be applied across different teams and tasks.

Validation of the Revised Taxonomy and Measurement System

Shiflett et al. (1982) carried out a laboratory study to provide an initial validation attempt of the revised taxonomy and to test the feasibility of the developed measurement approach. The goal of the study was to determine if naive judges can detect and discriminate reliably among the proposed functions that were displayed in videotapes of performing military teams. Nineteen male college students received background information on the teams to be observed and their missions and activities. They then viewed tapes of 15 performance segments and rated the degree to which each of the team functions was evident. Tapes were constructed to portray either all, one, or none of the functions.

The results of the study indicated moderate reliabilities that were considered acceptable for the type of scales used in the study, for the naive and relatively unsophisticated character of the raters, and for the preliminary stages of scale and taxonomic development (Fleishman & Hogan, 1978; Fleishman & Mumford, 1988; Schemmer, 1982). The orientation functions consistently yielded the highest reliabilities. Problems were observed for specific dimensions within resource distribution and activity pacing. Nonetheless, this study offered empirical support for both the structure of the provisional taxonomy and the corresponding measurement system.

SECOND EVALUATION AND REVISION OF THE TEAM FUNCTIONS TAXONOMY: CURRENT FORMULATIONS

In this research program, another evaluation of the emerging team function taxonomy was conducted by Cooper et al. (1984). Their purpose was to study the

INFORMATION EXCHANGE ABOUT MEMBER RESOURCES AND CONSTRAINTS (IMR)

This is an information exchange function that serves to make team members aware of each others' resources and capabilities. It includes exchange of information about (a) team member/manpower status and (b) messages about physical/equipment resources. Information reflecting stable member skills as well as availability on a spontaneous basis is exchanged.

How IMR Is Different From Other Functions

Information regarding *internal* status of the unit	vs.	ISR-information about circumstances *external* to the unit; support, threat, environment
Ongoing exchange/*discovery* process with respect to member skills, resource availability	vs.	MMR-use of *known* information in role assignment/resources distribution to further task/mission completion

Task Conditions: Team Behavior Anchors:

Very complex task structure requiring high degree of information exchange about internal resources	Efficient exchange of available and critical information about team member and resource status

7 ┬

Breaking camp/10km march on cloudy night in dense terrain; no loss of equipment or personnel.	Total awareness of teammate whereabouts and status while under heavy shelling.

6 ┼

Conducting a large force assault.	With enemy in immediate vicinity, team quickly and without detection clarifies and disseminates information about ammunition availability and distribution.

5 ┼

4 ┼

3 ┼

2 ┼

Loading troops onto a truck.	Team unintentionally fires at own member(s).

1 ┴

Very simple **task** requiring little exchange of information about resources	Minimal information exchange about internal status of unit

Using the 7-point scale, please rate:
The demands of the task you observe in terms of *need* for IMR:

The level of IMR you observe during team team performance:

(Task: _____)

(Behaviors: _____)

Figure 2.2.   Example of a Prototype Scale.

From Fleishman and Quaintance (1984), adapted from Shiflett, Price, and Schemmer (1981).

performance of Air Force tactical Command and Control systems, examine existing performance assessment strategies, and to develop a prototype team assessment methodology. The revised taxonomy was proposed as a basis for this effort. Thus, this project provided a venue for evaluating the adequacy of the team functions taxonomy offered by Shiflett et al. (1982).

Command and Control (C^2) teams are used by the Air Force to manage combat missions and coordinate responses in crisis situations. Two C^2 teams were chosen for observation and study. The first was the Weapons Team in a Control and Reporting Center, which had as its missions intercepting unidentified aircraft and attacking identified hostile aircraft. The second team chosen was the Fighter Duty Officer Team in the Tactical Air Control Center. This team was responsible for monitoring theater action plans, implementing revisions in these plans when warranted, and maintaining information displays of the ongoing situation.

The methods of evaluation consisted of semistructured interviews with the teams' operations staffs, interviews with evaluation and assessment staffs (including reviews of existing evaluation reports and documents, observations of two war-simulation exercises, and interviews with exercise participants). The functions in the revised taxonomy provided a partial basis for interview items. The observational phase of this study was used in part to detect the presence of critical team characteristics and team functions.

From the results of their data collection Cooper et al. (1984) concluded that "the team functions taxonomy could be used to capture most team-related aspects of tactical C^2 teams" (p. 84). For example, observers of the Weapons Team noted (a) constant and updated displays of information about tasks, goals, and environmental conditions (i.e., orientation functions); (b) the allocation of team resources to specified targets (i.e., response distribution functions); (c) effort directed toward expediting the distribution of important information (i.e., timing and activity pacing functions); (d) sequencing of activities from surveillance teams to weapons controllers to interceptor pilots (i.e., response coordination functions); and (e) comments in response to undue socializing that was incompatible with the team's task orientation (i.e., motivational functions). A similar range of activities reflecting the five functional categories proposed by Shiflett et al. (1982) were also observed in the Fighter Duty Officer Team.

Cooper et al. (1984) also noted, however, that certain activities occurred repeatedly in the training exercises but were not readily classifiable within the existing taxonomic categories. These activities concerned detection and reporting of task errors, and monitoring team adherence to performance standards. Shiflett et al. (1982) included monitoring and feedback as elements of *each* team function. However, data from the interviews and observations in this study suggested that these activities were of such criticality that properly assessing team performance functions required their separation from the other functions.

Accordingly, Cooper et al. offered two additional categories for the team functions taxonomy—"systems monitoring" and "procedure maintenance."

Systems monitoring refers to actions directed toward the detection of errors in the nature and timing of ongoing activities. Both team (i.e., coordinated) and individual member responses are monitored. The discovery of any errors results in alterations of system functioning. Thus, we suggest as dimensions of this functional category:

- General Activity Monitoring.
- Individual Activity Monitoring.
- Adjustment of team and member activities in response to errors and omissions.

Procedure Maintenance refers to the monitoring of behavior to ensure compliance with established performance standards. The emphasis is not on error detection, but rather on conformity to specified performance protocols. Monitoring can be of both synchronized and individual actions. We offer two dimensions under this functional category:

- Monitoring of general procedural-based activities.
- Monitoring of individual procedural-based activities.
- Adjustments of nonstandard activities.

We present our revised (i.e., current) version of the Team Functions Taxonomy in Table 2.3. We expect that this is not a final version. Indeed, Cooper et al. (1984) indicated that their addition of systems monitoring and procedure maintenance represented finer specifications of the earlier functions. Accordingly, Fleishman (1982, p. 832) notes:

> Recent empirical work suggests that the most useful set of primary categories in contemporary taxonomy appears to involve a rather large and steadily increasing set of categories. . . . The increasing fractionation of categories, while perhaps complicating life, is consistent with empirical work on the interrelationships among human task performances.

Thus, we expect as additional research on the evaluation of team performance functions is carried out, finer distinctions among these functions will continue to emerge.

SUMMARY

In this chapter we described a research program directed toward the development of a taxonomy of team performance functions. Our emphasis has been primarily

Table 2.3.   Taxonomy of Team Functions: Current Version

I. Orientation Functions
    A. Information Exchange Regarding Member Resources and Constraints
    B. Information Exchange Regarding Team Task and Goals/ Mission
    C. Information Exchange Regarding Environmental Characteristics and Constraints
    D. Priority Assignment Among Tasks

II. Resource Distribution Functions
    A. Matching Member Resources to Task Requirements
    B. Load Balancing

III. Timing Functions (Activity Pacing)
    A. General Activity Pacing
    B. Individually Oriented Activity Pacing

IV. Response Coordination Functions
    A. Response Sequencing
    B. Time and Position Coordination of Responses

V. Motivational Functions
    A. Development of Team Performance Norms
    B. Generating Acceptance of Team Performance Norms
    C. Establishing Team-Level Performance–Rewards Linkages
    D. Reinforcement of Task Orientation
    E. Balancing Team Orientation with Individual Competition
    F. Resolution of Performance–Relevant Conflicts

VI. Systems Monitoring Functions
    A. General Activity Monitoring
    B. Individual Activity Monitoring
    C. Adjustment of Team and Member Activities in Response to Errors and Omissions

VII. Procedure Maintenance
    A. Monitoring of General Procedural-Based Activities
    B. Monitoring of Individual Procedural-Based Activities
    C. Adjustments of Nonstandard Activities

on coordinated actions of team members. We expect this taxonomy to provide a useful point of departure for group theorists and practitioners. Research on group performance can benefit from the more precise delineation of synchronized activities offered by this taxonomy compared with prior classification efforts. Researchers focusing on the training and improvement of team performance may find that the taxonomy offers a basis for developing training design and content and for providing criteria for training evaluation and team assessment. Our expectation is that, as the taxonomy is used in such endeavors, its categories will undergo further clarification and finer distinctions. The goal remains a better understanding of team performance.

REFERENCES

Alexander, L. T., & Cooperbrand, A. S. (1965). *System training and research in team behavior* (Tech. Memo TM-2581). Santa Monica, CA: System Development.

Altman, I. (1966). Aspects of the criterion problem in small group research: The analysis of group tasks (Vol. 2). *Acta Psychologica, 25,* 199–221.

Ancona, D. G. (1987). Groups in organizations: Extending laboratory models. In C. Hendrick (Ed.), *Group processes and intergroup relations.* Newbury Park, CA: Sage.

Ancona, D. G., & Caldwell, D. F. (1988). Beyond task and maintenance: Defining external functions in groups. *Group and Organization Studies, 13,* 468–494.

Argote, L., Turner, M. E., & Fichman, M. (1989). To centralize or not to centralize: The effects of uncertainty and threat on group structure and performance. *Organizational behavior and Human Decision Processes, 43,* 58–74.

Back, K. (1950). The exertion of influence through social communication. In L. Festinger, K. Back, S. Schachter, H. H. Kelley, & J. Thibaut (Eds.), *Theory and experiment in social communication* (pp. 21–36). Ann Arbor, MI: Edwards Bros.

Berkowitz, L. (1954). Group standards, cohesiveness, and productivity. *Human Relations, 7,* 509–519.

Brickner, M., Harkins, S., & Ostrom, T. (1986). Personal involvement: Thought provoking implications for social loafing. *Journal of Personality and Social Psychology, 51,* 763–769.

Carron, A. V. (1982). Cohesiveness in sport groups: Interpretations and considerations. *Journal of Sport Psychology, 4,* 123–138.

Carron, A. V., Widmeyer, W. N., & Brawley, L. R. (1985). The development of an instrument to assess cohesion in sport teams: The group environment questionnaire. *Journal of Sport Psychology, 7,* 244–266.

Carter, L. F., Haythorn, W. W., & Howell, M. A. (1950). A further investigation of the criteria of leadership. *Journal of Abnormal and Social Psychology, 45,* 350–358.

Cartwright, D. (1968). The nature of group cohesiveness. In D. Cartwright & A. Zander (Eds.), *Group dynamics: Research and theory* (3rd ed.). New York: Harper & Row, 1968.

Cattell, R. B. (1948). Concepts and methods in the measurement of group syntality. *Psychological Review, 55,* 48–65.

Cooper, M., Shiflett, S., Korotkin, A. L., & Fleishman, E. A. (1984). *Command and control teams: Techniques for assessing team performance* (ARRO Final Report). Washington, DC: ARRO.

Cummings, L. L., Huber, G. P., & Arendt, E. (1974). Effects of size and spatial arrangements on group decision making. *Academy of Management Journal, 17,* 460–475.

Davis, J. H., Laughlin, P. R., & Komorita, S. S. (1976). The social psychology of small groups: Cooperative and mixed-motive interaction. *Annual Review of Psychology, 27,* 501–541.

Davis, J. H., & Stasson, M. F. (1988). Small group performance: Past and present research trends. *Advances in Group Processes, 5,* 245–277.

Dyer, J. (1984). *State-of-the-art review on team training and performance.* Fort Benning, GA: ARI Field Unit.

Fleishman, E. A. (1967). Development of a behavior taxonomy for describing human tasks. A correlation-experimental approach. *Journal of Applied Psychology, 51,* 1–10.

Fleishman, E. A. (1975a). Taxonomic issues in human performance research. In W. T. Singleton & P. Spurgeon (Eds.), *Measurement of human resources.* New York: Halsted Press.

Fleishman, E. A. (1975b). Toward a taxonomy of human performance. *American Psychologist, 30,* 1127–1149.

Fleishman, E. A. (1978). Relating individual differences to the dimensions of human tasks. *Ergonomics, 21,* 1007–1019.

Fleishman, E. A. (1982). Systems for describing human tasks. *American Psychologist, 37,* 821–834.

Fleishman, E. A. (1992). *The Fleishman Job Analysis Survey (F-JAS).* Palo Alto: Consulting Psychologists Press.

Fleishman, E. A., & Hogan, J. C. (1978). *A taxonomic method for assessing the physical requirements of jobs: The physical abilities analysis approach* (Tech. Rep. R78-6). Washington, DC: Advanced Research Resources Organization.

Fleishman, E. A., & Mumford, M. (1988). The ability requirements scales. In S. Gael (Ed.), *Handbook of job analysis.* New York: Wiley.

Fleishman, E. A., & Mumford, M. D. (1991). Evaluating classifications of job behavior: A construct validation of the ability requirements scales. *Personnel Psychology, 44,* 523–578.

Fleishman, E. A., & Quaintance, M. (1984). *Taxonomies of human performance: The description of human tasks.* New York: Academic Press.

Frank, F., & Anderson, L. R. (1971). Effects of task and group size upon group productivity and member satisfaction. *Sociometry, 34,* 135–149.

Gist, M. E., Locke, E. A., & Taylor, M. S. (1987). Organizational behavior: Group structure, process, and effectiveness. *Journal of Management, 13,* 237–257.

Gladstein, D., & Reilly, N. (1985). Group decision making under threat: The tycoon game. *Academy of Management Journal, 28,* 613–627.

Glanzer, M., & Glaser, R. (1955). *A review of team training problems* (Tech. Rep.). Pittsburgh: American Institutes for Research.

Goldman, M. (1971). Group performance related to size and initial ability of group members. *Psychological Reports, 28,* 551–557.

Gooding, R. Z., & Wagner, J. A., III. (1985). A meta-analytic review of the relationship between size and performance: The productivity and efficiency of organizations and their subunits. *Administrative Science Quarterly, 30,* 462–481.

Goodman, P. S. (1986). Impact of task and technology on group performance. In P. S. Goodman & Associates (Eds.), *Designing effective work groups.* San Francisco: Jossey-Bass.

Goodman, P. S., Ravlin, E. C., & Argote, L. (1986). Current thinking about groups: Setting the stage for new ideas. In P. S. Goodman & Associates (Eds.), *Designing effective work groups.* San Francisco: Jossey-Bass.

Greene, C. N. (1989). Cohesion and productivity in work groups. *Small Group Behavior, 20,* 70–86.

Hackman, J. R. (1968). Effects of task characteristics on group products. *Journal of Experimental Social Psychology, 4,* 162–187.

Hackman, J. R. (1976). Group influences on individuals. In M. D. Dunnette (Ed.), *Handbook of industrial and organizational psychology*. Chicago: Rand-McNally.

Hackman, J. R., & Morris, C. G. (1975). Group tasks, group interaction process, and group performance effectiveness: A review and proposed integration. In L. Berkowitz (Ed.), *Advances in experimental social psychology* (Vol. 8). New York: Academic Press.

Hackman, J. R., & Oldman, G. R. (1980). *Work redesign*. Reading, MA: Addison-Wesley.

Hall, E. R., & Rizzo, W. A. (1975). *An assessment of U.S. Navy Tactical team training: Focus on the trained man* (TAEG Report No. 18). Orlando, FL: Training Analysis and Evaluation Group.

Hare, A. P. (1976). *Handbook of small group research*. New York: Free Press.

Harkins, S., & Petty, R. (1982). Effects of task difficulty and task uniqueness on social loafing. *Journal of Personality and Social Psychology, 43*, 1214–1229.

Hill, G. W. (1982). Group versus individual performance: Are N + 1 heads better than one? *Psychological Bulletin, 91*, 517–539.

Janis, I. L. (1982). *Groupthink: Psychological studies of policy decisions and fiascos*. Boston: Houghton-Mifflin.

Kerr, N., & Bruun, S. (1983). Dispensability of member effort and group motivation losses: Free rider effects. *Journal of Personality and Social Psychology, 44*, 78–94.

Lanzetta, J. T., & Roby, T. B. (1960). The relationship between certain group process variables and group problem-solving efficiency. *Journal of Social Psychology, 52*, 135–148.

Latane, B., Williams, K., & Harkins, S. (1979). Many hands make light the work: The causes and consequences of social loafing. *Journal of Personality and Social Psychology, 37*, 823–832.

Laughlin, P. R. (1980). Social combination processes of cooperative, problem-solving, groups as verbal intellective tasks. In M. Fishbein (Eds.), *Progress in social psychology* (Vol. 1). Hillsdale, NJ: Erlbaum.

Lott, A. J., & Lott, B. E. (1965). Group cohesiveness as interpersonal attraction: A review of relationships with antecedent and consequent variables. *Psychological Bulletin, 64*, 259–309.

Marriott, R. (1949). Size of working group and output. *Occupational Psychology, 23*, 47–57.

McCallum, A. G., Oser, R., Morgan, B. B., Jr., & Salas, E. (1989, August). *An investigation of the behavioral components of teamwork*. Paper presented at the annual meeting of the American Psychological Association, New Orleans, LA.

McGrath, J. E. (1984). *Groups: Interaction and performance*. Englewood Cliffs, NJ: Prentice-Hall.

McGrath, J. E., & Altman, I. (1966). *Small group research: A synthesis and critique of the field*. New York: Holt.

Nieva, V. F., Fleishman, E. A., & Rieck, A. M. (1978). *Team dimensions: Their identity, their measurement, and their relationships*. Washington, DC: ARRO.

Oser, R., McCallum, G. A., Salas, E., & Morgan, B. B., Jr. (1989). *Toward a definition of teamwork: An analysis of critical team behaviors* (NTSC Tech. Rep. 89-004). Orlando, FL: Naval Training Systems Center.

Paulus, P. B., & Nagar, D. (1987). Environmental influences on social interaction and group development. In C. Hendrick (Ed.), *Group processes and intergroup relations*. Newbury Park, CA: Sage Publications.

Petty, R., Harkins, S., Williams, K., & Latane, B. (1977). The effects of group size on cognitive effort and evaluation. *Personality and Social Psychology Bulletin, 3*, 579–582.

Salas, E., Blaiwes, A. R., Reynolds, R. E., Glickman, A. S., & Morgan, B. B., Jr. (1985). Teamwork from team training: New directions. *Proceedings of the 7th Interservice/Industry Training Equipment Conference and Exhibition*. Orlando, FL: American Defense Preparedness Association.

Schachter, S. (1952). Comment. *American Journal of Sociology, 57*, 554–562.

Schachter, S., Ellertson, N., McBride, D., & Gregory, D. (1951). An experimental study of cohesiveness and productivity. *Human Relations, 4*, 229–238.

Schemmer, F. M. (1982). *Development of rating scales for selected vision, auditory and speech abilities*. Washington, DC: Advanced Research Resources Organization.

Seashore, S. E. (1954). *Group cohesiveness in the industrial work group*. Ann Arbor, MI: Institute for Social Research.

Shaw, M. E. (1973). Scaling group tasks: A method for dimensional analysis. *JSAS Catalog of Selected Documents in Psychology, 3*, 8.

Shiflett, S. C., Eisner, E. J., Price, S. J., & Schemmer, F. M. (1982). *The definition and measurement of team functions* (Final Report). Bethesda, MD: ARRO.

Staw, B. M., Sandelands, L. E., & Dutton, J. E. (1981). Threat-rigidity effects in organizational behavior: A multi-level analysis. *Administrative Science Quarterly, 26*, 501–524.

Steiner, I. (1972). *Group process and productivity*. New York: Academic Press.

Stogdill, R. M. (1972). Group productivity, drive, and cohesiveness. *Organizational Behavior and Human Performance, 8*, 26–43.

Theologus, G. C., & Fleishman, E. A. (1973). Development of a taxonomy of human performance: Validation study of ability scales for classifying human tasks. *JSAS Catalog of Selected Documents in Psychology, 3*, 29.

Tziner, A. (1982). Differential effects of group cohesiveness types: A clarifying overview. *Social Behavior and Personality, 10*, 227–239.

Tziner, A., & Eden, D. (1985). Effects of crew composition on crew performance: Does the whole equal the sum of the parts? *Journal of Applied Psychology, 70*, 85–93.

Tziner, A., & Vardi, Y. (1982). Effects of command style and group cohesiveness on the performance effectiveness of self-selected tank crews. *Journal of Applied Psychology, 67*, 769–775.

Waag, W. L., & Halcomb, C. G. (1972). Team size and decision rule in the performance of simulated monitoring teams. *Human Factors, 14*, 309–314.

Wagner, H., Hibbits, N., Rosenblatt, R. D., & Schulz, R. (1977). *Team training and evaluation strategies: State of the art* (Tech. Rep. No. 77-1, HumRRO). Alexandria, VA.

Watson, W. E., & Michaelson, L. K. (1988). Group interaction behaviors that affect group performance on an intellective task. *Group and Organization Studies, 13*, 495–516.

Weldon, E., & Gargano, G. M. (1985). Cognitive effort in additive task groups. The

56   FLEISHMAN & ZACCARO

effects of shared responsibility on the quality of multiattribute judgements. *Organizational Behavior and Human Decision Processes, 36,* 348–361.

Williams, K., Harkins, S., & Latane, B. (1981). Identifiability as a deterrent to social loafing: Two cheering experiments. *Journal of Experimental Social Psychology, 40,* 303–311.

Yetton, P. W., & Bottger, P. C. (1983). The relationships among group size, member ability, social decision schemes, and performance. *Organizational Behavior and Human Performance, 32,* 145–159.

Zaccaro, S. J. (1984). Social loafing: The role of task attractiveness. *Personality and Social Psychology Bulletin, 10,* 99–106.

Zaccaro, S. J. (1991). Nonequivalent associations between forms of cohesion and group-related outcomes: Evidence for multidimensionality. *Journal of Social Psychology, 131,* 387–399.

Zaccaro, S. J., & Lowe, C. A. (1988). Cohesiveness and performance on an additive task: Evidence for multidimensionality. *Journal of Social Psychology, 128,* 547–558.

Zaccaro, S. J., & McCoy, M. C. (1988). The effects of task and interpersonal cohesiveness on performance of a disjunctive group task. *Journal of Applied Social Psychology, 18,* 837–851.

3

The Weakest Link: The Performance of Individual Team Members

Louis A. Penner
J. Philip Craiger

INTRODUCTION

This chapter is concerned with the performance of an individual team member. It will attempt to answer a rather simple question about the individual performance of members of a team. What variables affect the performance of an individual team member and why do these variables have these effects? In general, the answers to the first part of this question are rather well known. There is, for example, a substantial body of literature on how variables such as the presence of an audience, the number of people in a team, identifiability, or the ability to diffuse responsibility affect an individual's performance (see Forsyth, 1983; Penner, 1986). There is much less knowledge of, and consensus about, the reasons why such effects occur. Therefore, this chapter will focus on some of the mediational or underlying mechanisms which are believed to be responsible for improvements or declines in the performance of an individual team member.

Because of space limitations, this review will be restricted to the literature concerned with the psychological variables that affect the quantity and/or quality of the performance of an individual member of a team. For the purpose of this chapter, *psychological variables* will be defined as those that involve the direct or indirect influence of a person or persons on the cognitions and/or behavior of an individual. Thus, the effects of important variables such as team structure, team organization, task characteristics, and personal characteristics on individual performance will not be considered here (see Morgan, Lassiter, & Tressler, this volume). This omission should not be taken as a statement about the importance of these variables in the understanding of the factors that influence the performance of an individual team member.

To address the issues of interest in this chapter, we will draw from three separate but conceptually related research literatures. The first of these is the research on *coacting aggregates*: collections of two or more individuals who are present at the same time and place when one or more of them are engaging in some task or activity but there is no interaction among the people in the aggregate. The second is the group literature, which differs from the prior area primarily in the latter's emphasis on aggregates composed of individuals who influence one another through mutual interaction (Forsyth, 1983). And finally, there is the team literature, concerned with well-structured and organized aggregates, which work on tasks that can be successfully completed only if each member of the aggregate successfully performs a specific task which has been assigned to him or her (Dyer, 1984). Although these research areas have often been quite divergent, they all provide some information on the questions of interest in this chapter. (For a more extended discussion of the similarities and differences between coacting aggregates, groups and teams, see Salas and Swezey, this volume.)

The chapter begins with a very brief history of research on individual performance in the presence of others; then it presents the specific phenomena of interest and discusses the mechanisms that may be responsible for each of them. Finally, an integrated overview is presented of how these psychological variables affect individual performance in a team context.

In the Beginning . . . There was Facilitation

About 100 years ago, Norman Triplett, a bicycle-racing enthusiast and graduate student at Indiana University, made an interesting discovery. His examination of the records of over 2,000 bicycle racers indicted that racers who competed against the clock took over half a minute longer to complete a mile course than did racers who had another racer pace them or who competed against another racer. Intrigued by this finding, Triplett designed what may have been the first true social psychological experiment, in which he systematically investigated the effects of the presence of others on individual performance. He wanted to learn whether he could produce the facilitation effect found with the racers in a laboratory setting where variables such as wind resistance or experience as a racer could be controlled (Triplett, 1897). The "race" Triplett devised was to pull a small flag attached to a line across a "course" 20 yards in length, and he used children as his subjects. Sometimes the children competed against the clock and sometimes against one another. He found that the times were clearly faster when the children were competing against one another than when they were competing against the clock. A few years later, in 1904, Neumann reported that performance on a simple motor task was facilitated by the mere presence of a passive observer (cited by Cottrell, 1972). This phenomenon was called *social facilitation*—the tendency for the presence of others to cause an improvement in an individual's performance.

A Little Bit After the Beginning . . . There was Impairment

In 1913, about 15 years after Triplett published his article on social facilitation, a French agricultural engineer, Max Ringelmann published an article in which, among other things, he reported on the amount of force individuals exerted on a rope-pulling task when they were alone and when they were members of 7-person and 14-person teams (Kravitz & Martin, 1986). He found that the amount of force exerted by one person working alone was 1.31 times as great as that exerted by the same individual when he or she was a member of a 7-person team and 1.39 times as great as the force exerted when a member of a 14-person team. He also reported that, on other unspecified tasks, individuals exerted over twice as much effort when they were alone as when they were the member of an 8-person team. This phenomenon has been called *social impairment*—a decline in individual performance as the result of working with others on some task.

On first inspection, Ringelmann's findings would seem to contradict those of Triplett. Whereas Triplett had found that the presence of others facilitated performance, Ringelmann had found that they impaired performance. Researchers interested in these two phenomena did not, however, initially see any contradiction. It was suggested that the reason for these conflicting findings was the difference in the kinds of aggregates examined in each study. Whereas Triplett had studied individuals who were working by themselves while others watched, Ringelmann had studied interacting and interdependent individuals. In the latter circumstance, the presence of others made performance decline because of the difficulties in coordinating the activities of several people, all of whom were simultaneously engaging in the same task. This was called *process* or *coordination loss* (Forsyth, 1983). This explanation was widely accepted, and the literatures on facilitation in coacting aggregates and impairment in interacting aggregates developed somewhat independently. For example, in his 1966 textbook Robert Zajonc, one of the leading researches in this area, presented Triplett's social facilitation study in the chapter on coaction, and presented Ringelmann's social impairment study in the chapter on group performance (Harkins &

Szymanski, 1987). The conceptual independence of the two phenomena was seriously challenged, however, by the results of a study by Ingham, Levinger, Graves, and Peckham (1974). They devised a situation in which subjects were asked to pull a rope in the presence of others. On some trials, subjects believed they were pulling a rope along with others, but in fact they were pulling alone. Despite the fact that no process loss could have occurred on these trials, subjects put forth significantly less effort on them than on the trials when they believed they were pulling alone.

Facilitation and Impairment, Performance and Motivation

We would argue that Triplett and Ringelmann were, indeed, studying two separate phenomena. The critical difference between them, however, was not that one concerned facilitation and the other impairment, or that one occurred in a coacting aggregate and the other in an interacting one. As we shall discuss shortly, both effects can be found in either situation. Rather, it is our contention that the phenomenon identified by Triplett, and that identified by Ringelmann, differed in a much more basic way. Specifically, we believe that the former concerns how psychological variables can affect an individual's *performance* on a task, and the latter concerns how psychological variables can affect an individual's *motivation* to perform the task. That is, the effect that interested Triplett and many of his theoretical descendants (e.g., Baron, 1986; Cottrell, Wack, Sekerak, & Rittle, 1968; Geen & Gange, 1977; Zajonc, 1965) was why, despite the motivation to do as well as one can, people will often perform rather poorly on a task. On the other hand, the effect that interested Ringelmann and his theoretical descendants (e.g., Harkins & Szymanski, 1987; Latané, 1981; Mullen, 1983) was why, despite at least implicit inducements to perform well on a task, individuals are often poorly motivated to do their best on a task. The next two sections present different theoretical explanations of the mechanisms responsible for each of the phenomena. A comment about the order of presentation of these two topics is needed. Clearly, variables that affect performance on a task are largely irrelevant if the person is not motivated to perform the task. But we shall cover the performance-related variables first. We do this simply because, historically, interest in performance appears to have predated interest in motivation.

Factors which Influence Individual Performance

The traditional name for this research area, *social facilitation,* is a bit of a misnomer. Indeed, readers familiar with the social facilitation literature will know that our brief history of the origins of interest in this effect was rather incomplete and even inaccurate. The most glaring omission was the failure to note that, by the early 1920s, there were several studies that reported, in contrast to Triplett, that the mere presence of an observer served to impair performance (e.g., Moore, 1917). According to Geen (1989), the number of early studies that found impairment or inhibition of performance as the result of the presence of others was probably as great as that of those that found facilitation of performance. Further, Geen suggested that the absence of a coherent theoretical explanation of both effects led to a dearth of interest in social facilitation up until about the mid-1960s. Let us now consider the mechanisms which have been proposed to account for both improvements and declines in individual performance.

Arousal. The current interest in social facilitation is largely due to the 1965 article by Zajonc. As suggested above, up until the publication of Zajonc's article researchers were puzzled and frustrated by the fact that, sometimes, an individual's performance improved as the result of being observed by an audience, and sometimes an individual's performance declined as the result of being observed by an audience. Zajonc argued that the same underlying mechanism was responsible for both effects. He proposed that the primary effect of the presence of others was to increase a performer's general arousal level and drive when carrying out some task. The facilitating effects of this increased drive would be the greatest on easy or well-learned tasks, that is, tasks which did not require choosing between a number of competing responses in order to successfully complete them. If, however, the task was difficult or complex and required choosing between correct and incorrect responses, the presence of others might impair performance. Zajonc based this explanation on Hull's (1943) drive theory, which posits that generalized drive energizes both correct and incorrect responses. Thus, the presence of others interacts with task difficulty/complexity to affect an individual's performance. When the task is easy, it facilitates performance. When the task is difficult, it impairs performance.

Zajonc's brilliant attempt to explain both facilitation and impairment of individual performance rekindled interest in social facilitation effects. However, subsequent explanations of why the influence of observers on individual performance is moderated by task difficulty have differed from Zajonc's explanation in a number of substantial ways (Geen, 1989).

Evaluation. One of the first people to formally challenge Zajonc's ideas was Cottrell (Cottrell et al., 1968; Cottrell, 1972). Cottrell argued that it was not the mere presence of others that increased arousal in a performer; rather, it was the potential negative evaluation an audience might give the performer that created the drive or arousal. Once created, the arousal operated in the same manner as Zajonc proposed. Tests of the two explanations of the arousal audiences create in a performer have tended to support Zajonc's position over Cottrell's. Schmitt, Gilovich, Goore, and Joseph (1986), for example, found that even the presence of a person who was blindfolded and wore sound-attenuating earphones (and, thus, could not evaluate the person's performance) had the effect of facilitating performance on a simple task and impairing performance on a difficult task. But, as Geen (1989) pointed out, such findings only show that arousal can occur in the absence of evaluation. They do not exclude the possibility that, under certain circumstances, it is evaluation that is responsible for increased arousal and the resultant changes in performance.

More recently, some researchers have argued that evaluation may influence the quality of individual performance more directly than was suggested by either Zajonc or Cottrell (Harkins & Szymanski, 1987; Szymanski & Harkins, 1987; Jackson & Williams, 1985). Harkins and his associates proposed that, on simple tasks, the possibility that one's performance might be evaluated by others increases one's motivation to do well and thereby improves performance. On complex or difficult tasks, however, the evaluation carries with it the increased possibility that the performer will be criticized or ridiculed for his or her failure. This fear of negative evaluation interferes with performance. This view of the effects of evaluation leads to the prediction that evaluation itself will facilitate performance on simple tasks and impair performance on complex tasks. Jackson and Williams (1985) found exactly this effect. Subjects worked on either complex or simple mazes under conditions where either their performance was anonymous or could be identified by others. When the task was simple, subjects in the low-evaluation (anonymous performance) condition performed poorer than those in the high-evaluation (identified performance) condition. When the task was complex, the pattern was exactly the opposite. (The influence of evaluation specifically on the motivation to perform a task will be discussed below.)

Distraction/conflict. Another, related explanation of how the presence of others affects drive and thus individual performance was based on the premise that the presence of others distracts the individual from the task that confronts him or her (Baron, 1986; Baron, Moore, & Sanders, 1978; Sanders & Baron, 1975). According to Baron and his associates, the increased drive that is often observed when people perform in the presence of others is not due to the potential for evaluation but rather to the conflict between attending to other people and to the task at hand. If the task is simple, this distraction will serve to facilitate performance; if it is difficult, it will impair performance.

In more recent years, Baron has modified his ideas about how the presence of others affects individual performance. Baron (1986) argued that attending to both the audience and the task may produce a cognitive overload rather than increased drive or arousal. Because humans have difficulty attending to several stimuli at the same time, the presence of others may cause individual team members to defensively narrow their attention to a smaller range of task cues (Geen, 1989). The effect of this narrowing is moderated by task difficulty. In a task with only a few relevant cues for task completion (i.e., simple tasks), the narrowing may improve tasks performance. In tasks with many relevant cues (i.e., complex tasks), the narrowing may impair performance.

Social impact theory. Social impact theory attempts to describe the process by which the "feelings, motives, and emotions, cognitions . . . and behavior that occur in an individual [are changed by] the real, implied or imagined presence or actions of other individuals" (Latané, 1981). It proposes that the impact of the social forces that impinge on an individual is determined by three things: (a) the strength of other people—their status, power, influence, and so on; (b) the immediacy of the other people—their closeness in time and space; and (c) the number of other people. As each of these factors increases, so does its social impact; however, the rate of increase declines. For example, an increase in audience size from one to two people has more impact than does an increase from five to six people.

Social impact theory does not speak directly to how the presence of others affects the quality of individual performance. We believe, however, that the factors identified by the theory certainly add to one's understanding of failures in individual performances. Specifically, one consequence of increased social impact on the individual is a concomitant increase in anxiety. (Although, as suggested above, the "impact curve" is negatively accelerated and asymptopes rather quickly; Latané & Harkins, 1976.) Zajonc's work would suggest that the anxiety engendered by social impact will create facilitation on a simple task and impairment on a complex task. More generally, it seems reasonable to propose an interaction between the "social forces" described in this theory and task complexity. All other things being equal, these forces would help performance on simple tasks and hurt performance on complex tasks.

Self-attention. Mullen (1983, 1987; Mullen & Baumeister, 1987) has proposed that the influence of others on the individual is mediated through the mechanism of self-attention. The concept of self-attention concerns the extent to which people focus their attention on themselves and their own thoughts, ideas, feelings, and actions, as opposed to focusing it outward, onto the situation and the people around them. When self-attention (or self-awareness) is high, people become relatively more aware of their own performance and actions (Duval & Wicklund, 1972). Mullen (1987) proposed that the critical variable in how much self-attention a person displays is the person's perception of the number of people in his or her subgroup relative to the total group. As the size of one's subgroup becomes smaller in relation to the total group, self-attention increases (Mullen, 1983, 1987). Mullen used a formula he called the *other–total ratio* to describe this size relationship: "the number of people in the other subgroup divided by the total number of people in the group (Other Total Ratio = O/(O + S). As one's own subgroup (S) becomes proportionally smaller, the Other–Total Ratio becomes proportionally larger (and self-attention increases)" (Mullen & Baumeister, 1987, p. 191). Mullen argued that performing alone in front of others creates a very large other–total ratio and thus a situation where the performer directs most of his or her attention on himself or herself. When this occurs, the individual becomes quite concerned with how his or her performance compares with some standard of excellence on the task. Actual performance on the task will depend on how this self-attention is moderated by other variables. For example, if self-attention is high and the task is relatively simple, performance will improve. Under some circumstances, however, self-attention can have rather dramatic negative effects on performance. One such instance is called "choking" by Baumeister (1984; Baumeister & Showers, 1986). According to Baumeister, if a member of a team is required to engage in a well-learned task that requires considerable skill, the presence of observers who expect the person to do well may produce a performance decrement. For example, Baumeister and Steinhilber (1984) found that professional athletes performed poorly in crucial games that were played in front of their own fans. In a laboratory analogue study, Baumeister, Hamilton, and Tice (1985) found that, when subjects thought that others expected them to do well on a complex task, they performed more poorly than when they thought that others expected them to perform at an average level on the same task. Baumeister's explanation of this effect was that the other people's expectations caused the performers to focus too much attention on their performance, which, in turn, interfered with the smooth execution of compli-cated, well-learned, or highly skillful tasks (Baumeister & Showers, 1986).

Although changes in individual performance as the result of changes in the other–total ratio are rather well documented (see Mullen, 1987), there is much less direct empirical support for the mediational role of self-attention in this process. Mullen, Johnson, and Salas (in press) have reported on a series of laboratory and field studies designed to test the notion that changes in the other–total ratio are accompanied by changes in self-attention. They reported that as the size of one's own subgroup increased various indices of self-attentiveness de-creased. For example, the use of first-person pronouns and endorsements of statements which indicated self-focused attention declined as the size of one's own group increased. Thus, it does seem reasonable to suspect that the changes in performance are due to changes in self-attention.

Motivation to Perform

The phenomenon of interest in the section that follows occurs in a situation where it would seem that a person would want to do his or her best on a task, but for some reason his or her motivation to do well on the task is significantly reduced or nonexistent. This description is so broad that it could reasonably include a number of different motivational phenomena, such as self-handicap-ping (e.g., Berglas & Jones, 1978), overjustification effects (e.g., Deci & Ryan, 1980), and poor performance as part of an ingratiation strategy (see Jones & Wortman, 1973). We will not, however, consider these and other similar effects, because we do not believe they are particularly relevant to individual perfor-mance in a team context. There are a number, of course, a large number of variables that are likely to influence motivation in this context. The first of these is the performance norms that exist within the team.

Norms. Norms are standards or guides for people's behavior and beliefs

(Penner, 1986). According to Hackman (1976), groups can establish norms and use "discretionary stimuli," such as approval and disapproval by members of the group, to get members to conform to these norms. Sometimes these norms can involve a group's standards or expectations for how well or poorly an individual member should perform.

Mullen and Baumeister (1987) have used the term *diving* to describe a situation in which, because of norms or standards, an individual is motivated to perform at less than an optimum level. The norms established by the team can be based on expectations for the entire group that contains the individual as a member, or on expectations for just the individual group member. For example, one form of diving proposed by Mullen and Baumeister can result from a group norm that discourages excellence in performance by any group member. Group members socialize their co-workers as to this norm and are ready to punish anyone who violates it. This is essentially the rate-busting effect reported by Roethlisberger and Dickson (1939) in their classic studies at the Hawthorne Electric Plant. Other examples of this have been reported by Berkowitz and Levy (1956) among flight crews, and by Kett (1977) among college students. The other kind of diving occurs when the group determines that excellence in performance is inappropriate for a particular individual (Mullen & Baumeister, 1987). For example, high-status members of a team may communicate the message to other members of the team that excellence in performance by a low-status member of that team is not appropriate. As a result, the low-status member does not attempt to do his or her best on the task at hand.

Social loafing. The concept of *social loafing* comes from Latané's (1981) Social Impact Theory. Recall that this theory proposed a model of how social pressure is exerted on the individual. Social Impact Theory is also concerned with the manner in which this social pressure is reduced or diffused. Latané and his associates believe that, as the number of other people in a group increases, the social pressure on any individual to perform well is diffused. As a result, motivation to do well may also decline. This effect is called social loafing: in the absence of any explicit demands to decrease the effort one expends on some task, the tendency to expend less effort when one is in a group than when one is alone. The social loafing effect increases (up to a point) with increases in group size and/or decreases in the ability to identify an individual member of the group (Kerr & Bruun, 1981; Jackson & Williams, 1985; Latané, Williams, & Harkins, 1979). This is, of course, the effect that Ringelmann observed in his original study.

There is little question that, under most circumstances, as group size increases, individual performance declines, and this decline appears to be due to a decline in individual motivation. Social impact theory is not, however, terribly precise about why this decline in motivation occurs. That is, why does the increase in group size cause the individual to feel less of a need to perform at his or her maximum? One explanation appears to be that, in most situations, there is unstated but real social pressure on individual team members to perform well, and the increases in group size diffuse this performance pressure.

Another explanation of this well-documented phenomenon is the so-called *free-rider effect* (Kerr & Bruun, 1981). According to this explanation, social loafing is a "rationally" or "economically" based decision to decrease one's effort. The mechanism proposed to explain this behavior is the person's belief that, since he or she is one of several people working on a task, he or she can do relatively little but still reap the benefits of the group's performance. Closely related to this explanation of motivational declines under these conditions are those based on equity considerations (e.g., the "sucker effect," Orbell & Dawes, 1981; withdrawing, Mullen & Baumeister, 1987). These and other theorists proposed that, if, after comparing his or her own contributions to those of other team members, an individual comes to believe that the other members of the aggregate are taking advantage of his or her contributions to the task, the individual member may reduce his or her effort in an attempt to reestablish equity with regard to effort expended on the task (Tziner, 1986). Although these economic views of motivation in this context are intuitively appealing, they have been challenged by a number of other researchers.

It should be noted that this section, and the previous one, describe processes which appear to be rather conscious and planful. That is, in contrast to poor performances and some of the motivational mechanisms to be discussed shortly, the person who "takes a dive" because of team norms, or reduces his or her effort because of perceived inequity, is likely to be quite aware of what he or she is doing. In contrast, the sections which follow describe processes which seem to be much less consciously planned.

Evaluation. In the first portion of this chapter, the potential for evaluation was discussed as one factor that might directly and indirectly affect the performance of highly motivated individuals when performing in the presence of others. For example, the potential for evaluation may engender arousal, which will facilitate performance on simple tasks and impair performance on complex tasks (Cottrell, 1972). Harkins and Szymanski (1987) have proposed that the potential for evaluation of a person's performance may also influence how motivated he or she is to perform well. According to Harkins and Szymanski (1987), for a person's performance to be evaluated, two things must be known: how well the person performed on a task, and what the standard of performance is for this task. When the performer has reason to believe that evaluation may occur, he or she will be more motivated and, thus, perform better (unless, of course, the motivational level becomes so high that it interferes with performance). One factor which influences subjective estimates of the likelihood of such an evaluation occurring is group size. That is, as group size increases, individual members believe that the probability their individual performance can be identified and evaluated decreases. This reduces motivational levels and thus performance.

Szymanski and Harkins (1987) demonstrated that the potential for self-evaluation can affect a person's performance in the same manner as the potential for evaluation by others. That is, subjects who believed that an experimenter could evaluate their performance, and subjects who believed that they would be able to compare their performance to a standard, performed equally well, and both groups far outperformed subjects who believed that neither they or an experimenter could evaluate their performance. In a later study, Harkins and Szymanski (1989) found that even providing individual group members with a standard against to compare their *group's* performance produced an increase in the quantity and quality of individual performance.

Self-attention. Another explanation of the effects of group size on individual motivation is derived from self-attention theory, which was presented earlier as one explanation of changes in performances. Self-attention processes appear to affect motivational levels as well. According to self-attention theories (e.g., Carver & Scheier, 1981; Duval & Wicklund, 1972), when self-attention is low, the person is either unaware of and/or unconcerned with internal standards that define what actions are appropriate, acceptable, or expected in a given context. One possible consequence of low self-attention is a decrease in the motivation to do well on a task. According to Mullen and his associates, (Mullen, 1983, 1987, 1991; Mullen & Baumeister, 1987), the extent to which a member of an aggregate is self-attentive depends on the other–total ratio discussed earlier. As the relative size of one's own subgroup increases, self-attention decreases, and consequently both motivation and performance decline.

Deindividuation. According to Penner (1986), deindividuation is a psychological state in which a person has a decreased sense of personal identity and responsibility. Among the variables which can produce feelings of deindividuation are increases in group size, anonymity, and altered states of consciousness (Prentice-Dunn & Rogers, 1989). Although deindividuation involves many of the mechanisms that have already been discussed, it differs from the previously discussed concepts in both degree and kind. For example, whereas the effects of evaluation appear to be limited to changes in motivation, the effects of deindividuation can be much more dramatic. It can also produce aggression, vandalism, and other rather extreme forms of antisocial behavior (see, for example, Zimbardo, 1970; Prentice-Dunn & Rogers, 1983).

Most of the contemporary explanations of deindividuation are based on control theory (Carver & Scheier, 1981), a variant of self-attention theory. The basic premise of control theory is that humans are self-regulating systems that use negative feedback loops to achieve this self-regulation. When the person becomes aware of a discrepancy between his or her present behavior and some norm or standard relevant to that behavior, he or she is activated to bring the behavior into accord with the standard. This self-regulation goes on more or less continuously and ultimately is in the service of higher order standards, which Carver and Scheier (1981) called *principles*. Principles are much like values and would include things such as "I am an honest person." In deindividuation, the person becomes relatively inattentive to his or her principles, and the self-regulatory system breaks down. People's behavior is no longer controlled by their internal standards but rather by the standards created by the situation in which they presently find themselves. Situationally induced norms and standards may become the primary determinant of the individual's actions. But in contrast to "diving" because of team norms (discussed earlier), during deindividuation the person's actions are apparently not the result of any conscious decision to act in a certain way. The individual is essentially "swept away" by the situation he or she is in.

Among the factors that can produce deindividuation are excessive levels of physiological or psychological arousal and strong feelings of attraction to one's team or group (i.e., group cohesiveness). For example, Prentice-Dunn and Spivey (1986) found that prolonged exposure to loud rock music (arousal) while team members performed a task that required considerable cooperation among team members (cohesion) produced declines in private self-awareness and increases in antisocial actions.

Although deindividuation can clearly affect an individual's motivation level and thus his or her performance, it seems reasonable to ask whether deindividuation is likely to occur in the typical team situation. Given that teams are usually well-structured aggregates, where each member has a specific role or function to perform and the overriding purpose of the team is to complete some task (Dyer, 1984), it might seem unlikely that the conditions which give rise to true deindividuation would occur in a team. On the other hand, Zimbardo (1970) has demonstrated that, when subjects were given a specific role to perform (acting as a prison guard), the role appeared to override the subjects' internal standards regarding fair treatment of others. Specifically, normal subjects placed in this role engaged in cruel and sadistic behavior toward subjects assigned to play the role of prisoners. Also one might wish to consider the likelihood that deindividuation effects could occur among military teams. Under combat conditions, the prolonged arousal and increased group cohesion that is likely to develop could conceivably give rise to deindividuation. Indeed, Hersch's (1970) description of the My Lai massacre during the war in Vietnam would suggest that deindividuation generated by these variables may have been largely responsible for this tragedy. However, at this time, the question of the likelihood of deindividuation occurring in teams remains empirically unanswered.

Factors Affecting Motivation and Performance

Table 3.1 presents a matrix intended to summarize the material which has been presented in this chapter. The first major division in the matrix is motivation versus performance. The left side of the matrix concerns effects associated with the motivation to perform tasks; the right side concerns the performance of tasks.

Table 3.1.   The Effects of Selected Psychological Variables on an Individual Team Member's Motivation and Performance

	Motivation		Performance	
Variable	Simple Task	Complex Task	Simple Task	Complex Task
Arousal	NA/?	NA/?	+	−
Evaluation				
a. Indirect effect	NA	NA	+	−
b. Direct effect	+	+	+	−
Distraction/conflict	NA	NA	+	−
Stimulus overload	NA	NA	+	−
Self-Attention	+	+	+	−/+
Norms	−/+	−/+	NA	NA
Other/Total Ratio	−	−	+	−
Equity/social comparison	?	?	NA	NA
Deindividuation	−	−	NA/−	NA/−

Note 1. Legend: "+" indicates the variable will increase performance/motivation; "−" indicates the variable will decrease performance/motivation; "?" indicates that the variable's effects have been inconclusive, inconsistent, or depend on factors not in the matrix; "NA" indicates that the variable is irrelevant in this condition.

Note 2. A cell with two symbols separated by a slash indicates that the variable can produce both effects, depending upon circumstances.

Motivation is presented first in the matrix because, as noted earlier, it seems reasonable to give motivation precedence over performance. If the individual is not motivated to perform well, the information on the right side of the matrix becomes irrelevant. Each half of the matrix is further divided by the variable of task complexity. Along the left hand side of the matrix are the "independent variables" that have been considered in this chapter. Some of these variables reflect changes in the individual's environment that could be directly measured (e.g., number of people present, degree of arousal), while others are the more conceptual variables (e.g., self-attention, deindividuation). The cell entries are the best estimates, based on the previous literature review, of the effect of a variable in a specific condition. One or more of four symbols appear in each cell: "+", the variable will improve motivation/performance, or the association is positive; "−", the variable will impair motivation/performance, or the association is negative; "?", the effect of the variable on performance is unknown, inconsistent, or would depend on factors not included in the matrix; and "NA", the variable does not appear to be relevant to motivation/performance in this specific condition. Consider, for example, the third row. The direct effect of evaluation on motivation is positive irrespective of level of task complexity; the direct effect of evaluation on performance is positive on simple tasks, but negative on complex tasks. In some instances, a cell will contain more than one symbol. For example, general arousal (row one), in sufficient strength, may engender deindividuation and thus impair motivation to perform well ($-$), but usually general arousal is irrelevant (NA) to motivation to perform. Consider, as another example of this, the effect of self-attention on performance on complex tasks. Self-attention will improve performance on such tasks ($+$). But if the self-attention is excessive, and the task is an overlearned one that can be best performed if the performer does not focus too much on his or her actions, self-attention impairs performance ($-$). Even a cursory inspection of this division in the matrix makes something explicit that has been implicit throughout the chapter. Whereas task complexity/simplicity is an important moderator of performance, it is more or less irrelevant for motivation to perform.

Concluding Comments

In concluding this review of variables which affect individual performance and motivation, we must address the question of the importance of these variables to someone interested specifically in team performance. That is, how important are variables which affect individual performance in the typical team? For example, is social loafing even likely to occur in a well-organized aggregate, with well-defined roles and responsibilities for individual members, which are highly interdependent? And if social loafing occurs, how large an influence will it have on a team's final product? This question becomes more critical when one realizes that much of the literature on the variables discussed in this chapter has been dominated by laboratory studies of ad hoc groups rather than real-world teams.

In the absence of empirical studies on this question, the best that can be offered is informed speculation. First, it would seem that, in most team settings, concern about motivating individual members should be relatively low. As suggested above, in many teams the potential for evaluation of an individual member's performance would be quite high, because his or her assignment and responsibility are so clear-cut. Further, because of the extensive interdependence on most team tasks, individual failures to expend maximum effort would be easily identified and possibly punished by other team members. Thus, the literature on factors that affect the motivational levels of individuals performing a task may not be as important to an understanding of team performance as are the literatures on other team-related variables such as team structure, and on task structure.

The issue becomes considerably more complex when one adds performance to the picture. It would appear that, on complex tasks, the team characteristics that should increase motivational levels might also impair performance. The summary matrix in Table 3.1 provides an example of this. Consider the rows for the variables of evaluation and self-attention. It would seem that a leader concerned with the motivational levels of individual team members should build into the team's structure and organization characteristics that would increase both the individual members' belief that they would be evaluated and their levels of self-attention. But at the same time, the leader must be concerned about the characteristics of the task that is given to the individual team member. If it is complex or demanding, high levels of evaluation and self-attention may impair performance. This would suggest that one must carefully consider the nature of the tasks one assigns to the individual team members.

More generally, it would seem that, on team tasks, it is often true that each member has a very specific responsibility, which may not be duplicated by any other member, and this assignment is critical to successful completion of the task. To the extent that this situation obtains and there are not internal checks or feedback systems for the quality of individual performances, factors that might affect the quality of individual performance would appear to be of critical importance. A chain, after all, is only as strong as its weakest link.

REFERENCES

Baron, R. S. (1986). Distraction/conflict theory: Progress and problems. In L. Berkowitz (Ed.), *Advances in experimental and social psychology* (Vol. 19). New York: Academic Press.

Baron, R. S., Moore, D. L., & Sanders, G. S. (1978). Distraction as a source of drive in social facilitation research. *Journal of Personality and Social Psychology, 36,* 816–824.

Baumeister, R. F. (1984). Choking under pressure: Self-consciousness and paradoxical effects of incentives on skilled performance. *Journal of Personality and Social Psychology, 46,* 610–620.

Baumeister, R. F., & Showers, C. J. (1986). A review of paradoxical performance effects: Choking under pressure in sports and mental tests. *European Journal of Social Psychology, 16,* 361–383.

Baumeister, R. F., & Steinhilber, A. (1984). Paradoxical effects of supportive audiences on performance under pressure: The home killer choke effect in sports championships. *Journal of Personality and Social Psychology, 47,* 85–93.

Baumeister, R. F., Hamilton, J. C., & Tice, D. (1985). Public vs. private expectancy of success: Confidence booster or performance pressure? *Journal of Personality and Social Psychology, 47,* 85–93.

Berglas, S., & Jones, E. E. (1978). Drug choice as a self-handicapping strategy in response to noncontingent success. *Journal of Personality and Social Psychology, 36,* 405–417.

Berkowitz, L., & Levy, B. I. (1956). Pride in group performance and group-task motivation. *Journal of Abnormal and Social Psychology, 53,* 300–306.

Carver, C. S., & Scheier, M. F. (1981). *Attention and self-regulation: A control theory approach to human behavior engineering.* New York: Springer-Verlag.

Cottrell, N. B. (1972). Social facilitation. In C. G. McClintock (Ed.), *Experimental social psychology.* New York: Holt.

Cottrell, N. B., Wack, D. L., Sekerak, G. J., & Rittle, R. H. (1968). Social facilitation of dominant responses by the presence of an audience and the mere presence of others. *Journal of Personality and Social Psychology, 9,* 245–250.

Deci, E. L., & Ryan, R. M. (1980). The empirical exploration of intrinsic motivational processes. In L. Berkowitz (Ed.), *Advances in Experimental Social Psychology, 13,* 39–80.

Duval, S., & Wicklund, R. A. (1972). *A theory of objective self-awareness.* New York: Academic Press.

Dyer, J. L. (1984). Team research and team training. A state of the art review. *Human Factors Review,* pp. 285–323.

Forsyth, D. R. (1983). *An introduction to group dynamics.* Monterey, CA: Brooks/Cole.

Geen, R. G. (1989). Alternative conceptions of social facilitation. In P. B. Paulus (Ed.), *Psychology of group influence.* Hillsdale, NJ: Erlbaum.

Geen, R. G., & Gange, J. J. (1977). Drive theory of social facilitation: Twelve years of theory and research. *Psychological Bulletin, 84,* 1267–1288.

Hackman, J. R. (1976). Group influences on individuals. In M. D. Dunnette (Ed.), *Handbook of industrial and organizational psychology.* Chicago: Rand McNally.

Harkins, S. G., & Szymanski, K. (1987). Social loafing and social facilitation: New wine in old bottles. In C. Hendrick (Ed.), *Group processes and intergroup relations* (Vol. 9). Beverly Hills, CA: Sage.

Harkins, S. G., & Szymanski, K. (1989). Social loafing and group evaluation. *Journal of Personality and Social Psychology, 56,* 934–941.

Hersch, S. (1970). *My Lai 4: A report on the massacre and its aftermath.* New York: Vintage.

Hull, C. L. (1943). *Principles of behavior.* New York: Appleton-Century-Crofts.

Ingham, L. A., Levinger, G., Graves, J., & Peckham, V. (1974). The Ringelmann effect: Studies of group size and group performance. *Journal of Personality and Social Psychology, 10,* 371–384.

Jackson, J., & Williams, K. (1985). Social loafing on difficult tasks. Working collectively can improve performance. *Journal of Personality and Social Psychology, 49,* 937–942.

Jones, E. E., & Wortman, C. (1973). *Ingratiation: An attributional approach.* Morristown, NJ: General Learning Press.

Kerr, N., & Bruun, S. (1981). Ringelmann revisited: Alternative explanations for the social loafing effect. *Personality and Social Psychology Bulletin, 1,* 224–231.

Kett, J. F. (1977). *Rites of passage: Adolescence in America 1790 to the present.* New York: Basic Books.

Kravitz, D., & Martin, B. (1986). Ringelmann revisited: The original article. *Journal of Personality and Social Psychology, 50,* 936–941.

Latané, B. (1981). The psychology of social impact. *American Psychologist, 36,* 343–356.

Latané, B., & Harkins, S. (1976). Cross-modality matches suggest anticipated stage fright as a multiplicative power function of audience size and status. *Perceptions and Psychophysics, 20,* 482–488.

Latané, B., Williams, K., & Harkins, S. (1979). Many hands make light the work: The causes and consequences of social loafing. *Journal of Personality and Social Psychology, 37,* 823–832.

Moore, H. T. (1917). Laboratory tests of anger, fear, and sex interests. *American Journal of Psychology, 28,* 390–395.

Mullen, B. (1983). Operationalizing the effect of the group on the individual: A self-attention perspective. *Journal of Experimental Social Psychology, 19*, 295–322.

Mullen, B. (1987). Self-attention theory: The effects of group composition on the individual. In B. Mullen & G. R. Goethals (Eds.), *Theories of group behavior.* New York: Springer-Verlag.

Mullen, B. (1991). Group composition, salience, and cognitive representations: The phenomenology of being in a group. *Journal of Experimental Social Psychology, 27*, 1–27.

Mullen, B., & Baumeister, R. F. (1987). Group effects on self-attention and performance: Social loafing, social facilitation, and social impairment. In C. Hendrick (Ed.), *Review of personality and social psychology.* Beverly Hills, CA: Sage.

Mullen, B., Johnson, C., & Salas, E. (in press). Productivity loss in brainstorming groups: A meta-analytic integration. *Basic and Applied Social Psychology.*

Orbell, J., & Dawes, R. (1981). Social dilemmas. In G. Stephenson & J. H. Davis (Eds.), *Progress in applied social psychology.* New York: Wiley.

Penner, L. A. (1986). *Social psychology: Concepts and applications.* Minneapolis, MN: West.

Prentice-Dunn, S., & Rogers, R. W. (1983). Deindividuation in aggression. In R. Geen & E. Donnerstein (Eds.), *Aggression: Theoretical and empirical reviews* (Vol. 2). New York: Academic Press.

Prentice-Dunn, S., & Rogers, R. W. (1989). Deindividuation and the self-regulation of behavior. In P. B. Paulus (Ed.), *Psychology of group influence.* Hillsdale, NJ: Erlbaum.

Prentice-Dunn, S., & Spivey, C. B. (1986). Extreme deindividuation in the laboratory: Its magnitude and subjective components. *Personality and Social Psychology Bulletin, 12*, 206–215.

Ringelmann, M. (1913). Recherches sur les moteurs animes: Travail de l'humme. *Annales de l'Institut National Agronomique, 12*, 1–40.

Roethlisberger, F. J., & Dickson, W. J. (1939). *Management and the worker.* Cambridge, MA: Harvard University Press.

Sanders, G. S., & Baron, R. S. (1975). The motivating effects of distraction on task performance. *Journal of Personality and Social Psychology, 32*, 956–963.

Schmitt, B. H., Gilovich, T., Goore, N., & Joseph, L. (1986). Mere presence and social facilitation: One more time. *Journal of Experimental Social Psychology, 22*, 242–248.

Szymanski, K., & Harkins, S. G. (1987). Social loafing and self-evaluation with a social standard. *Journal of Personality and Social Psychology, 53*, 891–897.

Triplett, N. (1897). The dynamogenic factors in pacemaking and competition. *American Journal of Psychology, 9*, 507–533.

Tziner, A. E. (1986). Group composition effects on task performance: A theoretical approach. *Small Group Behavior, 17*, 343–354.

Zajonc, R. B. (1965). Social facilitation. *Science, 149*, 269–274.

Zajonc, R. B. (1966). *Social psychology: An experimental approach.* Belmont, CA: Wadsworth.

Zimbardo, P. G. (1970). The human choice: Individuation, reason, and order versus deindividuation, impulse, and chaos. In W. J. Arnold & D. Levine (Eds.), *Nebraska Symposium on Motivation.* Lincoln, NE: University of Nebraska Press.

4

Team Composition
and Staffing

Ben B. Morgan, Jr.
Donald L. Lassiter

OVERVIEW

A quick perusal of the chapters in this book suggests that current knowledge concerning team training and performance is based upon a very large and diverse body of research. In fact, the topics addressed here represent a rather limited coverage of the many topics that bear some relationship to the concerns of team training and performance. Many books, and literally thousands of studies, have been published in areas such as group development, team performance, unit cohesion and morale, cockpit resource management, organizational structure, crew coordination, communication networks, team decision making, team training, and so on. Much of this research has been designed to investigate factors that influence team behaviors and outcomes, thereby providing background information concerning how teams develop, interact, and perform. The collective results of these studies provide a great deal of information concerning the characteristics, dimensions, and properties of teams, and about the factors that influence team performance (see, for example, Denson, 1981; Dyer, 1984; Foushee & Helmreich, 1988; Hare, 1972; McGrath, 1984; McGrath & Altman, 1966; Modrick, 1986).

However, much has also been said about the problems that have limited the applicability of this past research to the situations encountered by operational teams in actual work situations (see Alluisi, 1977; Modrick, 1986; Salas, Blaiwes, Reynolds, Glickman, & Morgan, 1985; Swezey & Salas, 1987). One of

75

the major problems in this regard is the fact that relatively little research has been directly concerned with evaluating tools, techniques, or strategies for enhancing team processes or performance. For example, a recent metaanalysis of relevant literature (Salas, Dickinson, Tannenbaum, & Converse, in preparation) found that there have been very few empirical investigations of *team training* since the Ohio State studies of the 1960s (e.g., Briggs & Naylor, 1965; Johnston, 1966). Thus, in the face of a large collection of interrelated data, there have been relatively few direct evaluations of the applicability of these data to the enhancement of team performances and interaction processes. There is a clear need to identify, develop, and evaluate procedures that will optimize team interaction processes, team development, and team performance. The overall orientation of this book toward the identification of applicable research findings is an important step in this regard. The current chapter contributes to this objective by assessing the current state of knowledge concerning team composition and staffing, and by highlighting findings which can be applied to the enhancement of team training and performance.

Focus of Current Chapter

As noted by Chidester (1987), there are three primary approaches to the enhancement of team functioning. These are to (a) improve the design of tasks, equipment, or systems, or provide job aids, so as to enhance the team's performance; (b) train teams to perform their tasks more effectively; and (c) select team members so that all necessary skills will be represented within the team, interactions among team members will be optimized, and team performances will be enhanced. The first of these approaches is beyond the scope of this book. However, research related to aircraft accidents indicates that most accidents occur because of problems associated with crew interaction processes rather than equipment design problems (Foushee & Helmreich, 1988); therefore, it would seem that this book's emphasis on "training and performance" is justified. The second of Chidester's (1987) approaches is the primary focus of other chapters in this book (for example, Chapters 8 and 9). The final approach—the enhancement of team functioning through the selection of team members—is the topic of the current chapter.

It should be noted that team functioning will be considered here not only with respect to the enhancement of performance per se, but also with respect to the improvement of team interaction processes, coordination behaviors, and the processes of team development and maturation. Recent findings clearly indicate that teamwork and interaction skills are important contributors to overall team performance (cf. Foushee & Helmreich, 1988; Glickman, Zimmer, Montero, Guerette, Campbell, Morgan, & Salas, 1987; Oser, McCallum, Salas, & Morgan, 1989). For example, it has been reported that more effective teams can be distinguished from less effective teams on the basis of behavioral/process profiles (Glickman et al., 1987; Oser et al., 1989). Therefore, it is important to identify ways to enhance these interaction processes because of their potential impact on team performance.

A variety of models have been offered as frameworks for describing the variables that influence team behavior (Morgan, Salas, & Glickman, in preparation). Perhaps the most comprehensive and widely accepted of these models is McGrath's (1964) Input-Process-Output Model (see also Gladstein, 1984; Hackman, 1983, 1986; Hackman & Morris, 1975). This type of model categorizes the factors that influence team performance into three major classes: (a) input variables, which determine the "givens" associated with the composition and characteristics of the team as well as the task and situational requirements of the environment in which the team operates; (b) process variables, which include the behavioral processes through which team members interact, communicate, and coordinate activities in order to complete their mission; and (c) output variables, which include the measures of team performance, changes in team structure, cohesion, etc., and other organizational outcomes that result from the actions of the team. According to this model (McGrath, 1964), input variables are further subdivided into three groups: "environmental" factors, particularly the variables associated with task and situational design, which are largely beyond the scope of the current discussion but which have been discussed in detail by other authors (Hackman, 1968; Morris, 1966; McGrath, 1984); "individual-level" or individual-difference variables, which determine the characteristics and capabilities of the individual team members; and "group-level" or team-difference variables, which serve to define the nature and characteristics of the overall team.

Thus, with reference to the Input-Process-Output Model, the purpose of the current chapter is to review the growing literature (cf. McGrath, 1964, 1984) that suggests that team interaction processes and team performances are significantly impacted by input factors related to individual-difference variables (such as the team members' personalities, attitudes, and skill levels) and team-difference variables (such as the team's size, structure, and cohesion). Other factors from the model are discussed only as they relate to these two sets of variables. A specific effort is made to focus on findings that provide a basis for the selection of team members in ways that will optimize the composition of teams and enhance team functioning. While there have been relatively few investigations of the direct impact of selection strategies on the enhancement of team performance, the importance of such strategies is emphasized by recent research with airline pilots that indicates that selection and training effects interact to determine the behavior of teams (Chidester, 1987; Chidester, Helmreich, Gregorich, & Geis, 1991). Whereas the current chapter focuses on the selection of team members, issues related to the training of teams are discussed in other chapters of this book (e.g., Chapters 8 and 9). Given the findings of Chidester and his col leagues, it is suggested that these two topics should be considered together as a basis for developing optimal interventions for team improvement.

The major results of the current review are presented in two sections. The first section describes the results of studies that have focused on the effects of individual-difference variables, and the second presents findings from studies that have investigated the effects of team-difference variables. The final section of the chapter attempts to summarize the findings that have been reported and to draw conclusions for the staffing of teams. For broader coverages of related topics, the reader might also consult prior reviews by Bass (1982), Haythorn (1968), Kahan, Webb, Shavelson, and Stolzenberg (1985), and Shaw (1976).

INDIVIDUAL-DIFFERENCE VARIABLES

Teams are ultimately composed of individuals who "interact independently in order to accomplish mutual goals" (Morgan, Glickman, Woodard, Blaiwes, & Salas, 1986, p. 3). Each individual brings into the team environment certain characteristics that can influence the effectiveness of team-member interactions and the efficiency with which teams accomplish their goals. Therefore, an important strategy for enhancing team processes and performance is to select individuals who can contribute the performance resources and coordination capabilities necessary for the team to accomplish its mission effectively. This requires the identification of individual-difference characteristics which are predictive of the overall performance of teams or which are known to influence team interaction processes. For purposes of the current discussion, these differences which distinguish among team members at the individual level are classified into four broad areas: (a) biographical differences, (b) personality differences, (c) differences in general and task-relevant abilities, and (d) leadership differences. Each of these areas is discussed below in terms of its potential impact on team processes and performance.

Biographical Differences

There is evidence to suggest that biographical variables such as age, gender, race, sociocultural background, and so on, are important factors in the performance of teams (e.g., Shaw, 1976). In their survey of reported relationships between biographical characteristics and task performance in teams, McGrath and Altman (1966) found that 13 of 51 cases yielded significant positive relationships. They reported that factors such as age, gender, educational level, and so on, were predictive of team performances. As noted by Bass (1982), biographical differences might have produced performance effects in a larger number of these cases had it not been for the fact that these effects were probably attenuated in operational teams due to a restriction of range resulting from selection procedures. At any rate, these and other data indicate that biographical variables can have significant effects upon team performance.

For example, in a study of racial differences in groups, Fenelon and Megargee (1971) found that racially mixed groups were less efficient in their performance of very structured clerical tasks than racially uniform groups. The researchers attributed this finding to racial tension within the mixed groups, suggesting that team-member conflicts can reduce the effectiveness of teammember interactions and performances. On the other hand, in an unpublished doctoral dissertation (cited by Shaw, 1976), Rhue reported that racially mixed groups performed better than uniform groups on an unstructured task which required individual input to a group problem-solving exercise. This improvement in performance by the racially mixed groups probably resulted from the fact that these groups contained individuals with different backgrounds and different resources to allocate to the performance of the problem solving task. Other research indicates that this type of heterogeneity of composition can be beneficial to the performance of tasks that require problem solving and creativity; this topic will be discussed in more detail later.

Quite a few studies have investigated the effects of gender and gender mixes on team performance (see Shaw, 1976). While most of these studies have focused on the effects of gender mixes, relatively consistent differences have been reported between males and females in terms of the ways in which they interact, conform, and perform in teams. For example, as compared to females, males have been found to display more aggressive behavior, make less eye contact (Exline, Gray, & Schuette, 1965), and conform less to the group norm (Reitan & Shaw, 1964). Studies of the effects of gender mixes indicate that members of mixed-gender teams spend more time and effort on interpersonal issues than on task-relevant behaviors. Also, members of these teams tend to conform more than the members of nonmixed teams (Shaw, 1976). Members of nonmixed teams, on the other hand, are more task-oriented, individualistic (less social), and competitive than members of mixed teams (Kent & McGrath, 1969; Wyer & Malinowski, 1972). These results clearly indicate that selection on the basis of gender and gender mixing can significantly affect the nature of the social interactions of teams. They suggest that males and nonmixed groups should be selected for structured, production-oriented tasks, and that females and mixed groups might be best for less structured or creative tasks. It should be noted, however, that these conclusions are primarily based upon research which was conducted during the 1960s and 1970s. Because of the ever-changing sex roles in society, new studies are needed in order to evaluate the effects of gender mixes on team performance within the context of today's social milieu.

It has also been found that the chronological age of team members may have important implications for performance (McGrath & Altman, 1966), but findings in this regard have been inconsistent (Stogdill, 1948; Shaw, 1976). On the other hand, investigations of individual performances have documented the fact that aging causes significant decrements in sensory sensitivity, perceptual ability, cognitive functioning, reaction time, and motor performance, to name a few (see Birren & Schaie, 1977, for an extensive treatment of these findings). It has also been noted that aging affects performance such that, with increasing age, there is (a) a slowing of performance, (b) increased variability among individuals, and (c) proportionately greater changes in performance as the difficulty of the task increases (Coates & Kirby, 1982). Coates and Kirby (1982) report that worker productivity tends to remain relatively stable up to an age of about 55, after which there is some decline during the remainder of the work life. They also note, however, that, in job situations which involve time stress, there are likely to be greater declines in performance as age increases.

Generalizing to teams, these findings indicate that younger teams will generally perform better than older teams on tasks that require sensory/perceptual sensitivity, speed of responding, fine motor responding, or complex cognitive processing. It can also be expected that older team members will have proportionately greater difficulty interacting and performing under stress. In addition, it can also be predicted that teams which are homogeneous with respect to age are likely to interact and perform more efficiently than teams that are heterogeneous with respect to age. Finally, it should be noted that the effects of age are not always negative. Experience and competence are highly correlated with age, and these variables often contribute to improved performance (Shaw, 1976). For example, Bass and Wurster (1953) found that leadership performance was positively related to age and educational background. Thus, when possible, younger team members should be selected to perform more difficult and demanding tasks where speed of responding is important, and older team members should be chosen for jobs that require greater experience and stability of leadership. However, it is clear that a great deal of additional research is needed in this area. The increasing age of the American population and the trend toward greater reliance on work groups in industry make such research imperative.

Personality Differences

There has been considerable debate concerning whether or not the personality characteristics of team members affect the performance of the team as a whole. While some researchers claim that prior findings have been somewhat inconclusive, providing a weak case at best (Kahan et al., 1985), others report that the personality traits of individual team members can have a significant effect on team performance (Driskell, Salas, & Hogan, 1987; Haythorn, 1968; Helmreich, 1987; Hogan & Hogan, 1989). The negative position appears to be based on the notion that personality traits or dimensions represent constructs that are too broad to be of much use in predicting a specific team performance. For example,

Haythorn (1953) correlated group productivity with members' scores on Cattell's 16-PF and found that only two personality factors were related to productivity. In a study by Bouchard (1969), only 16 of 90 personality variables were found to be significantly correlated with performance. In a study involving military teams, Butler and Burr (1980) examined three locus-of-control personality types and reported that only one of them was even weakly related to team performance. Thus, it has been argued that most personality dimensions fail to predict team performance (Kahan et al., 1985).

On the other hand, supporters of the position that individual personality characteristics influence team performance point to results such as those of Haythorn, Couch, Haefner, Langham, and Carter (1956), who found that the behaviors demonstrated by teams of authoritarian members differed significantly from those of nonauthoritarian teams. Further support for this position is provided by Mann (1959), who identified seven personality factors (intelligence, adjustment, introversion–extroversion, dominance, masculinity–femininity, conservatism, and interpersonal sensitivity) that have been studied for their effects on group performance. He found that task activity level was positively related to each of the personality factors except interpersonal sensitivity; these relationships were not as strong, however, when total activity rate was factored out. In addition, three of the seven dimensions—intelligence, adjustment, and extroversion—were also positively related to the team's total activity rate.

Recent research by Helmreich and others (Chidester, 1987; Chidester et al., 1991; Gregorich, Helmreich, & Wilhelm, in press; Helmreich, 1984, 1987) has focused on the identification of personality correlates of aircrew attitudes and performances. This research indicates that aircrew attitudes and crew coordination behaviors may be predicted from personality measures of Instrumental and Expressive characteristics (Spence & Helmreich, 1978), achievement motives (Spence & Helmreich, 1978), and an Achievement Striving factor of the Type A behavior pattern (Spence, Helmreich, & Pred, 1987). While the relationship between these variables and crew performance needs further investigation, this research is among the most promising in this regard.

Another promising effort in this area has been reported by Driskell et al. (1987), who provide a structure for predicting the interaction between personality variables and team task characteristics. These authors argue that the debate concerning the effects of individual personality on team performance has been driven by three major factors; namely (a) studies of personality effects have focused on the psychopathological aspects rather than the desirable characteristics of personality, (b) there has been a lack of consensus concerning the operational definition of personality, and (c) personality studies have tended to ignore the interactive effects of different types of tasks. To address these problems, Driskell et al. (1987) present a taxonomy of six (social reputation) personality traits (i.e., intelligence, adjustment, ambition, prudence, sociability, and likability), which are hypothesized to impact team performance. In addition, they provide a scheme for sorting team tasks into one of six classes on the basis of the behaviors required for performance, and a framework for predicting the interactive effects of the personality traits on different types of tasks. For example, they suggest that, for tasks requiring supportive social skills (i.e., "social tasks"), one should select team members who are high on the personality dimensions of adjustment, sociability, and likability. This schema represents a major integration of relevant findings in this area. It is recommended as a guide for selecting team members on the basis of personality and as a framework for designing future investigations of the performance effects of personality in teams.

Differences in General and Task-Relevant Abilities

Another group of individual-difference variables that are important to team performance are those relating to the general abilities and the specific task-relevant performance abilities of team members. General abilities are usually defined in terms of objective measures such as intelligence test scores, and military and/or academic course grades, or subjective measures such as peer ratings of intelligence and competence (Hill, 1982; McGrath & Altman, 1966). Several variations of such measures have been used in order to derive general ability scores that are predictive of team performance. Among the most commonly used scores are the ability of the least able member, the ability of the most able member, and the mean ability of members (Kahan et al., 1985).

In summarizing the results of prior investigations, Tziner and Eden (1985) noted that the general abilities of team members can produce one of three different effects on group performance: (a) the individual abilities of different team members might be combined in an additive fashion so that performance is increased in proportion to the ability levels of the team members (e.g., Bouchard, 1972); (b) abilities might be combined in ways that result in an overall loss of team efficiency (e.g., the "process loss" of Steiner, 1972); or (c) abilities might be combined synergistically so that team performances are higher than the levels predicted on the basis of simple additivity (e.g., Rohrbaugh, 1981). Tziner and Eden (1985) examined these effects in three-person tank crews by varying crew composition across all possible combinations of (high and low) levels of individual ability and motivation. Their results indicate that abilities seemed to have an additive effect in teams that were heterogeneous with respect to ability. On the other hand, teams that were uniformly high in ability performed considerably better, and teams that were uniformly low in ability performed considerably worse, than anticipated on the basis of team member abilities. Thus, they concluded that the ability of a given team member "influenced crew performance effectiveness differently depending on the ability levels of the other two members" (Tziner & Eden, p. 91). These findings suggests that, in complex interactive tasks, combinations of team members with uniformly low ability levels should be avoided, and that maximum performance can be expected when all team members are selected to have high ability levels.

It should be noted, however, that the effects of general ability are moderated by a number of other variables. For example, although general ability is considered to be distinct from task-relevant ability, the strength of the relationship between general ability and team performance appears to depend on the characteristics of the task being performed by the team (Kabanoff & O'Brien, 1979; O'Brien & Owens, 1969). For example, based upon the organizational structure of tasks, O'Brien and Owens (1969) defined *coordinated* tasks as ones in which separate subtasks are performed by different team members whose efforts are combined in some systematic fashion to determine team performance, and *collaborative* tasks as ones in which all team members must work together interactively in order to complete an overall team assignment. Using data from other studies, O'Brien and Owens (1969) examined correlations between three general ability measures (scores on intelligence tests for the least able member, most able member, and the sum of these scores for all team members) and team performances on collaborative and coordinated tasks. These results indicated that general ability accounted for up to 33% of the variation in team performance scores in coordinated tasks, but no significant relationship was found between general ability and team performance in collaborative tasks. O'Brien and Owens (1969) speculated that, in coordinated tasks, each team member contributes significantly and systematically to task completion, regardless of ability. Thus, the individual abilities of members were reflected in, and predictive of, team performance. In performing collaborative tasks, however, teams could interact in a number of different ways in order to perform the task at hand. Different teams might select different performance strategies, depending on their unique composition of high- and low-ability members. This could dilute the relationship between individual ability and team performance in these tasks.

It should also be noted that investigations of the relationship between general ability and team performance in military teams have generally produced results that appear to differ from those obtained in civilian research. Specifically, while studies of civilian populations have produced positive relationships, most military studies have reported very weak relationships at best (Kahan et al., 1985; the results of Tziner & Eden, 1985, represent a major exception to this generalization). This difference seems to have resulted, in part, from the fact that military studies have been based almost exclusively on the field measurement of cognitive, spatial, and physical performances in tasks that possess very high saliency for the participants. On the other hand, civilian studies have employed tasks that measure cognitive performances in controlled laboratory environments where the tasks have little intrinsic value for the participants and other confounding variables can be controlled so that they do not interfere with performance. Thus, it is likely that task and situational factors that are free to operate in military environments have tended to obviate the effects of general ability on team performance in those operational environments (Kahan et al., 1985).

Studies of the relationship between the task-relevant abilities of team members and team performance usually assess the task proficiency of individuals (or train them to a specified level of proficiency), select and assign team members so as to compose teams with different levels of proficiency, then assess and compare the performances of the different teams. The results of these studies generally indicate that team performance is improved through the selection of individuals with high levels of task specific skills. However, these results have been somewhat inconsistent with respect to the exact nature of this relationship (e.g., see Comrey, 1953; Comrey & Staats, 1955; Gill, 1979). For example, in his study of motor skill ability, Gill (1979) found that the pretask proficiency of the least able member correlated significantly with the team's performance, but no such relationship was found for the most able member. On the other hand, Comrey (1953; Comrey & Staats, 1955) reported significant correlations between team performance and all three task proficiency measures (least able member, most able member, and the sum of proficiency scores for all team members). These differential patterns of results are rather typical of the research in this area. However, it would seem that the differential nature of the tasks performed by different teams might account for some of the inconsistent findings. Specifically, for coordinated tasks (where team members contribute independently to the team's performance of the task), the ability of the least able member seems to predict the team's performance. For collaborative tasks, on the other hand, the task proficiency of the most able member and/or the sum of team member task proficiencies seem to predict team performance best. If a collaborative task can be successfully completed on the basis of the proficiency of the most able member, then the proficiencies of the other team members might not correlate with the team's performance (Kahan et al., 1985). This reinforces the importance of selecting high-ability team members so that team performances will be optimized even in cases where team performance might not be highly correlated with individual levels of proficiency.

Leadership Differences

Three broad areas of investigation are primarily relevant to the current discussion of the effects of leadership on team performance. These areas include studies of the effects of the leader's personality characteristics, skills and abilities, and leadership style. Research from each of these three areas is summarized below.

Several personality traits of leaders have been examined for possible links to team performance. For example, Hewett, O'Brien, and Hornik (1974) investigated the relationship between orientation of the leader (i.e., whether the leader was task oriented or person oriented) and team performance. Results indicated that this personality dimension (orientation) was not related to team performance. Similar results have been reported with respect to other personality dimensions. It should be noted, however, that a possible reason for the lack of consistent evidence linking leader personality and team performance is that many studies have been based upon a rather weak manipulation of leadership. That is, in most cases, particularly in laboratory studies, the leader's position has been relatively temporary in nature, and the leader has been given little real authority with which to impact the behavior of team members. In operational settings, where leadership is relatively enduring and the leader possesses the authority to actually control team processes, the effects of the leader's personality tends to have a greater influence on team performance (Kahan et al., 1985).

Findings from studies of the effects of leader ability (both general and task-related ability) on team performance have been somewhat inconsistent. For example, O'Brien and Owens (1969) found no significant relationship between the leader's general ability and team performance. However, Shaw (1976) concludes that the general ability of leaders accounts for only about 10% of the variance associated with leadership performances. Fiedler and Leister (1977) reported a positive relationship between leader intelligence (a general ability) and team performance, but this relationship was mediated by the leader's level of stress, motivation, and experience. In general, the higher the level of stress, the weaker the relationship between intelligence and performance. On the other hand, the higher the level of motivation and experience, the stronger the relationship. Apparently, stress reduces the leader's ability to apply his or her intelligence to the enhancement of team performance, whereas motivation and experience tend to increase the utility of this general ability in terms of its impact on team performance.

Within the large literature concerning leadership style, several comparisons have been made of the effects of different leadership styles. However, the two dimensions that appear to have produced the greatest effect on team performance are: (a) autocratic versus democratic leadership (e.g., Morse & Reimer, 1956; Shaw, 1955), and (b) high versus low social distance between the leader and other team members (Kahan et al., 1985). Generally, teams with autocratic leaders perform better than teams with democratic leaders, although team members in democratic teams tend to react more positively to their team. Similarly, teams with greater social distance between leaders and followers usually perform better than teams where this social distance is smaller.

Fiedler's (1978) contingency model of effective leadership style is based on the favorableness of the group-task situation. This favorableness is determined by three dimensions: the task structure, the power of the leader, and the affective relationships between the leader and the other team members. According to this model, leaders are predicted to be more effective when there is an appropriate match between the orientation of the leader and the amount of situational control (or favorableness) provided by the group-task environment. Although a meta-analysis of 178 investigations provides fairly strong support for Fiedler's general approach (see Strube & Garcia, 1981), the interactions between leadership style and favorableness conditions are complex (see Fiedler, 1978, for a complete discussion), and not all of the predictions from Fiedler's model have been supported by research results. Furthermore, it is often impossible to apply Fiedler's model to the selection of leaders because of the dynamics of group-task conditions and the practical difficulties involved in making the required matches between leaders and conditions.

For many team situations, a more practical framework for selecting leaders is provided by Blake and Mouton's (1978) managerial grid. This model assumes that leaders (managers) can be categorized in terms of their relative concern for people (person or group orientation) and performance (task orientation). Individuals who exhibit high levels of concern for both people and performance are considered to be the best leaders. Some validation for this notion with respect to aircrews was provided by Helmreich (1982) who found that both group and task orientations were significant predictors of crew coordination in air carrier pilots. Additional research is needed to validate the use of this framework for selecting effective leaders.

In summary, available data indicate that team performances may be impacted by leadership personality, ability, and/or style. The exact nature of these effects, however, are difficult to predict, the relationships are often complex, and there is little framework for organizing the available findings. Reasons for this situation include the fact that numerous definitions of leadership have been used, results have been compromised by weak leadership manipulations and other methodological problems, and leadership variables have been found to interact with task characteristics and the social climate of the team (Kahan et al., 1985). Thus, there is little systematic basis for recommending the selection of team leaders. Nevertheless, the models of Fiedler (1978) and Blake and Mouton (1978) can be recommended as providing the most structured guidelines for such selection. Finally, it should be noted that a great deal more research is needed concerning these issues.

TEAM-DIFFERENCE VARIABLES

As indicated above, the use of selection strategies as a basis for enhancing team training and performance is ultimately a matter of identifying individuals who can make the appropriate contributions to the accomplishment of the team's mission. Team performances, however, are determined not only by the actions of individuals, but also by the interactions of those individual actions with the actions of other team members and the demands of the situation in which they occur. For example, the results of the review by Kahan et al. (1985) suggest that a sizable proportion of the variation in team performance must be accounted for in terms of "other factors, including . . . combinations of characteristics ᵤ₁ groups" (p. 23). Therefore, in addition to considering the individual-difference variables for selecting individuals, it is also important to consider strategies for combining those individuals into effective units. Therefore, the current section will discuss the impact of several team-level factors on team processes and performances. These team-difference variables include factors that cannot be accounted for in terms of a single individual, but that require the interaction of two or more team members. To the extent that they affect the behavior of teams, these factors must be considered in assigning the proper mix of individuals to a given team, or as a basis for selecting among a variety of teams or team conditions.

Four major classes of team-difference variables are discussed here. The first is team size, which will be discussed in terms of its effects on member participation, member conformity and consensus, team performance, and leadership. The second class of variables deals with team structure and organization. The discussion of these variables will focus on the effects of assembly, the working environment, task demands, and team member position within the team. The third class of variables deals with compatibility issues, specifically those concerned with homogeneity versus heterogeneity of certain team member characteristics, and how the composition of these characteristics across members of a team affect the team's performance. The characteristics discussed here include personality traits, abilities, attitudes, and creativity. The final set of variables deals with the effects of team cohesion on team member interactions, satisfaction, and team productivity and performance.

Team Size

The number of individuals that constitute a team is an important consideration in the composition of teams. Although optimum team size should be determined by the demands of the task(s) performed by the team (Bass & Ryterband, 1979), the size of the team has been found to have several important effects on the process and outcome of team performance (Steiner, 1966). A few of these effects are discussed below.

Obviously, the overall pool of performance resources increases as individuals are added to a team (Shaw, 1976). Perhaps as a result of these increased resources, larger teams (within limits) have been found to process a wider variety of information and attain higher levels of skill (Cattell, 1953). On the other hand, as team size increases, coordination among team members can become more difficult because of the increasing number of potential team member interactions (Bass, 1982). This increase in the volume of interactions can result in an increase in communicative errors and longer performance times. In a study of individual and team performances during illness, this relationship between performance and team size was noted to have offset the effects of illness on team (but not individual) performance (Morgan, Coates, & Rebbin, 1970). It was reported that, in some cases, team performance was improved during periods of illness when a team member was missing from the five-man team. Because of this, it was concluded that the expected decrements in team performance were not observed because "coordination among four crew members should have been easier than among five" (p. 18).

Thus, increases in team size tend to increase the coordination demands or communication workload of the team, and it is possible for these demands to offset gains due to an increase in task-related resources associated with increases in team size (Shaw, 1976). On the other hand, it has also been found that there tends to be a general decrease in the overall participation of team members as the size of the team increases. For example, in an investigation of three organizations, Indik (1965) found that as organizational size increased, the overall amount of communication decreased. This finding might result from the fact that increases in the size of the team reduces the amount of time that each member has to participate in the team's activities (unless overall performance times are increased; see Indik, 1965; Shaw, 1976).

Gerard, Wilhelmy, and Conolley (1968) also found that increases in team size reduced the participation of some team members in the team's efforts to complete its tasks. Thus, not only does overall participation tend to decrease with increasing team size, but the distribution of participation sometimes also varies with team size. As size increases, differences in the levels of participation between the most active team members and less active members have been found to increase to a point where relatively few members dominate the team's activities (Bales, Strodtbeck, Mills, & Roseborough, 1951). It has also been found that, as the size of the team increases, members report feeling a greater inhibition to participate (Gibb, 1951). Presumably, the increased complexity and difficulty of communication, and the concomitant changes in social structure, can cause some people to decrease their involvement in team communications.

These forces have also been found to affect the emergence of a leader in initially leaderless teams. In general, the larger the team, the more likely it becomes that a leader will emerge (Bass & Norton, 1951). This is, in part, a result of the fact that (as indicated above), as the team becomes larger, there is a shift in communication patterns among team members such that a few members begin to dominate the team's activities (Bales et al., 1951). Taken to the extreme, these few individuals tend to monopolize communication and control team activities until a single team member emerges and increasingly assumes the leadership role (Hemphill, 1950).

Shifts in communication patterns due to increasing team size seem to be related to the increased conformity that emerges among team members as size increases. There is general agreement that conformity, or the extent to which a team member's behavior corresponds to the norms of the team, tends to increase as the size of the team increases (Shaw, 1976). However, the exact nature of this relationship seems to depend upon other task or situational demands. For example, both linear (Gerard, Wilhelmy, & Conolley, 1968) and curvilinear (Rosenberg, 1961) relationships have been reported to exist between team size and conformity. Whatever the shape of the function, there is little doubt that conformity does increase as team size increases. Thus, it might be argued that the forces which tend to inhibit and redistribute the general participation of team members also cause members to conform more readily. It is also important to note that increases in conformity might result in more efficient performances in some simpler and more structured team tasks, whereas tasks involving creativity are likely to be affected negatively by conformity.

As suggested by this discussion and noted earlier by Bass (1982; Bass & Ryterband, 1979), increasing the size of a team pits two forces against each other. On one hand, larger teams have more resources available to them, and this can lead to increased creativity, variety of information processing, and effectiveness in team performance. On the other hand, larger teams face more problems associated with increased team member interactions, difficulty in coordination, and decreased member participation, all of which can negate the advantage of having more resources. The effects of these forces depend largely on the demands of the tasks that teams are required to perform. Tasks that require team members to follow a routine and structured set of procedures (i.e., "coordinated"— O'Brien & Owens, 1969; or "established"—see Boguslaw & Porter, 1962, tasks) might benefit from a general reduction of participation, with a relatively few members controlling the activity. Tasks that require flexibility and creativity (i.e., "collaborative," O'Brien & Owens, 1969, or "emergent," Boguslaw & Porter, 1962, tasks), however, are likely to be adversely affected by these processes. Steiner (1966, 1972) identified three general types of team tasks: additive, disjunctive, and conjunctive. In additive tasks, the individual performances of all team members are summed to produce the team product. The team's performance on disjunctive tasks depends on the performance of the team's most competent member. Performance on conjunctive tasks requires team members to perform similar functions, but the team's performance depends on its least competent members. Steiner reports that increasing team size has a positive effect on performance in additive and disjunctive tasks, but a negative effect on conjunctive tasks (Steiner, 1972).

Thus, it is apparent that team processes and performances are significantly affected by team size. However, these effects are modified by the demands of the task requirements and a number of other variables. The discussion now turns to some of these other variables.

Team Structure and Organization

One of the factors that is known to modify the effects of team size has been called "the assembly effect," which refers to the variability in team performance that results from the particular combination of members in the team, aside from any effects that could be caused by traits or characteristics of the team members (Shaw, 1976). The impact of the assembly effect was investigated in a landmark study by Rosenberg, Erlick, and Berkowitz (1955), which assessed the relative contributions of individuals as a function of the combination of other individuals assigned to the team. The results of this study indicated that individuals performed differently, depending on which other individuals comprised the team.

The subtle impact of the assembly effect has often been overlooked in team research. However, recent findings from Gersick (1988) might suggest a cause for this effect. Gersick reports that a framework of behavioral patterns and assumptions that guide the interactions and performances of a team are established very early during the first meeting of the team members. If different groups of individuals develop different interaction patterns (and they have been found to do so; cf. Gersick, 1988, Glickman et al., 1987), this could account for the differential team performances that constitute the assembly effect.

Conditions imposed upon the team by the job or organizational environment also have implications for team composition and team performance. For example, Pugh, Hickson, Hinings, and Turner (1968) note that the degree of formalization in an organization (or team) has profound effects on performance. According to these authors, organizational formalization involves standard operating procedures, plans of action, and other rules and roles to be followed in order to insure maximal team effectiveness. If the team structure contains a high degree of such formalization, then performance tends to be much more proceduralized and routinized. This type of organization is best for performing routine tasks that require little creativity and for which rules of engagement are well established (coordinated or established tasks). As suggested above, larger teams are more likely to perform better under these conditions. If the team structure contains less formalization so that team member interactions are more flexible (or "organismic"; see Alexander & Cooperband, 1965), teams are able to respond more effectively to situations that are less stable or predictable (collaborative or emergent tasks). Smaller teams are more likely to perform better under these conditions.

The relative position, rank, or status of an individual within a particular team has also been shown to affect both that member's performance in the team and the performance of the team as a whole. Bass and Wurster (1953) reported a strong relationship between the status of team members in initially leaderless teams and subsequent leadership behavior. In studies involving communication networks, Shaw (1954) found that team members in central network positions exerted more influence on peripherally placed members than vice versa. Team members can be equally ranked to form a single level team, or they can be distributed into several levels or hierarchies. Different rank structures impose different interaction requirements upon team members, and this can produce important effects on team performance. For example, Foushee and Helmreich

(1988) report that "the strong role structure (chain of command) of the flight deck is . . . a powerful predictor of flight crew interaction" (p. 205). Because of the strongly ingrained "chain of command" within the cockpit, subordinates are reluctant to question superiors or assume control of the aircraft, and this has been shown to have disastrous results (Foushee & Helmreich, 1988; Harper, Kidera, & Cullen, 1971).

However, not only is rank within the team important, but the rank of the team in relation to other teams in the organization can influence team performance. For example, Ronan (1963) found that industrial teams performing low-status jobs were much less aggressive in their interactions with management, the union, and other organizational units than were teams performing high-status jobs. This suggests that the team's perception of its own role, status, and value to the organization can be an important factor in determining the way the team interacts and performs.

Compatibility Among Team Members

One of the most important considerations in team composition is the compatibility of team members. This property of a team is important above and beyond the combined talents and abilities of its members. Even high-ability teams that contain incompatible members may experience difficulty in achieving team goals, maintaining adequate communications, and dealing with team member interactions (Bass, 1982). However, a mixture of various backgrounds, interests, abilities, and so on, (i.e., a heterogeneous team) is often necessary in order for the team to accomplish its mission. Therefore, it is necessary to understand the effects of compatibility (or incompatibility) on team behaviors and performances.

A considerable amount of research has investigated the effects of homogeneity and heterogeneity of team composition on team performance. One heavily studied area deals with the mix of personality traits within teams. It has been found that the combination of personalities on a team can exert a strong influence on the team's performance, both as a direct input variable and by its interaction with team processes (Hackman & Morris, 1975; Driskell et al., 1987). For example, teams whose members are homogeneous with respect to certain personality trait dimensions (i.e., dependence, assertiveness, and personalness) have been found to be more productive than teams that are heterogeneous with respect to these dimensions (Schutz, 1955). Altman and Haythorn (1967) investigated the performance of teams that were homogeneous or heterogeneous in terms of need achievement, need affiliation, and need dominance. Their results indicated that only teams that were homogeneous with respect to need affiliation performed better than their heterogeneous counterparts. Hoffman (1959; Hoffman & Maier, 1961) investigated the effects of homogeneity versus heterogeneity of personality profiles of team members on problem-solving tasks and found that heterogeneous teams produced better solutions. Results from these studies tend to suggest that, in general, it is better to staff teams with homogeneous personalities. However, these results aren't very clear with respect to the specific composition of team member personalities that will result in better team performance.

Unlike studies on personality traits, studies of the effects of the homogeneity/heterogeneity of team member abilities on team performance are more straightforward. For example, Laughlin, Branch, and Johnson (1969) found that three-person teams heterogeneous in ability (as determined by scores on an intelligence test) performed better than three-person homogeneous teams on a "team" retake of a parallel version of the same test. Goldman, Dietz, and McGlynn (1968) found that teams heterogeneous with respect to wrong response tendencies and patterns of interaction performed better than an individual, and that teams homogeneous in these regards performed worse than an individual. Similar results have been found regarding the homogeneity/heterogeneity of attitudes within a team. For example, teams that are heterogeneous in attitudes have been found to produce better problem solutions than homogeneous teams (Campbell, 1960; Hoffman, 1959; Hoffman & Maier, 1961).

One additional factor—namely, the demands of the tasks being performed by the team—must be considered in interpreting the findings with respect to the effects of the homogeneity/heterogeneity of team composition. Specifically, if smooth and timely team member interactions are important to team performance, then homogeneity of personalities, abilities, attitudes, and so on, will result in better team performance. Such concordance will result in less conflict and effort invested in interpersonal issues (Byrne, 1971). On the other hand, if time is not essential, and the task is relatively complex and/or requires a creative solution, a heterogeneous team is more likely to perform better than a homogeneous one. Heterogeneous teams may start more slowly toward task completion, but the end result is often better (Bass & Ryterband, 1979). The high degree of similarity of members in homogeneous teams often acts as an obstacle to creative and thorough solutions because of the team's relative lack of breadth and variety of resources. In general, the more heterogeneous the team, the more likely it is to possess the required abilities, resources, and so on, to complete the task effectively.

Team Cohesion

The final team-difference variable to be discussed here is team cohesion, or the degree to which team members are motivated to remain in the team (Shaw, 1976). Highly cohesive teams tend to have members who: (a) are greatly involved in the team's activities; (b) have less tendency toward absenteeism; and (c) display high levels of coordination during team tasks. The effects of team cohesion have been related to several team process variables, the major ones being team member interactions, satisfaction, and team performance (Shaw, 1976).

For example, Lott and Lott (1961) have shown that team cohesion is related to team member interaction. These investigators studied the relationship between cohesion and communication level among team members. A significant positive correlation was found between these two variables, even when the opportunity for interaction was the same for all groups. Reasons for increased interactions in highly cohesive teams include the facts that: (a) members are more motivated to respond in a positive way to other members (Shaw, 1976); and (b) cohesion facilitates interaction through the reduction of inhibitions to communicate (Moran, 1966).

A relationship between team cohesion and team member satisfaction has also been reported. For example, Manning and Fullerton (1988) report that members of highly cohesive Army units rated their jobs higher with satisfaction than their counterparts in units characterized by low levels of cohesion. In general, members of cohesive teams are more satisfied with their jobs and team situations.

The notion that team cohesion is strongly related to team performance is generally accepted, although there are some detractors (e.g., Stogdill, 1972). It is generally believed that high team cohesion enhances team performance (Shaw, 1976), although the reverse relationship has also been shown. For example, in task-oriented teams, cohesion can increase when teams are more successful (Anderson, 1975). Similarly, Bakeman and Helmreich (1975) found that teams that spent more time performing their duties developed higher cohesion than teams that devoted most of their time to interpersonal interaction.

SUMMARY AND CONCLUSIONS

Perhaps the most obvious conclusion to be drawn from the current review is that optimum strategies for the selection of team members cannot be developed solely on the basis of individual- and team-difference variables such as those discussed here. Although several factors such as biographical differences (e.g., McGrath & Altman, 1966), and team size (e.g., Bass, 1982) have been found to influence team processes and performances, the exact nature of those effects are often unclear. In almost every case, these variables have been found to interact with other task and/or situational variables so as to produce rather complex relationships. For example, team performance is predicted by general team member ability in coordinated tasks but not in collaborative tasks (O'Brien & Owens, 1969). The consistency with which these interactions occur clearly indicates a need to include these moderating variables in efforts to select team members. Specifically, selection paradigms must begin with a careful definition of the conditions and purposes for which the selections are to be made.

Traditional personnel selection systems are built upon strong front-end analyses of the target job. They begin by defining the requirements of the job in terms of the capabilities and behaviors of the worker and/or the nature and objectives of the work itself (cf. Dunnette, 1966). It would seem to be rather obvious that the staffing of teams should also begin with a task analysis to define the requirements of the team's job. However, traditional job analysis procedures are inadequate and inappropriate for analyzing team requirements on at least two counts. Specifically, they fail (a) to account for the interaction and coordination behaviors required for successful team performance, and (b) to identify the situational and organizational factors that influence team processes and performances. These inadequacies represent an area of obvious need. Research is needed in order to develop adequate procedures for identifying the job-requirement variables that are predictive of team processes and performances. The recent efforts of Levine, Brannick, Coovert, Llobet, and Salas (in preparation) seem to be promising in this regard.

As indicated in the earlier discussion, the most salient factor that tends to interact with individual- and team-difference variables is the nature of the task performed by the team. A clear taxonomic structure for categorizing team tasks is needed to guide future investigations of these interactions. The most complete typology of team tasks has been provided by McGrath (1984). After reviewing several earlier formulations (e.g., Hackman, 1968; McGrath & Altman, 1966; Steiner, 1972), McGrath proposes a circumplex of eight types of group tasks. According to his two-dimensional representation, the horizontal dimension represents the nature of the performance required of team members (intellectual versus behavioral), whereas the vertical dimension represents the nature of the relationships among team members (cooperation versus conflict). McGrath (1984) contends that "the eight types [of team tasks] can accommodate virtually all tasks used in group research" (p. 66). However, all of the available typologies, including McGrath's, fail to incorporate a dimension which reflects the amount of interaction or coordination required by team members in the performance of their duties. It is recommended that efforts be made to develop a schema which represents two orthogonal dimensions as follows: One dimension should quantify the nature of the required task performance (such as McGrath's, 1984, horizontal dimension or Driskell et al.'s, 1987, classification), and the other dimension should represent the amount of interaction involved in the task's performance (such as O'Brien & Owens's, 1969, collaborative versus coordinated dimension).

The current authors agree with the recent observation of Foushee and Helmreich (1988) that "altering the group's composition may be the most effective and perhaps the most difficult means for improving group effectiveness" (p. 222). However, it is clear from the current review that a much better understanding of group interaction, development, and performance is needed to guide the optimization of team composition for different situations and missions.

Therefore, there is a great need for additional research in this area. Efforts are needed to develop adequate task analysis procedure for teams, to develop an adequate team task taxonomy, and to further investigate the prediction of team processes and performances from input variables such as those discussed here. Further specification of guidelines for selecting team members must be based upon a systematic program of research designed to investigate the effects of team composition on team processes and performances. A promising methodology for such a research program has been described by Morgan and Salas (1988; Morgan, Lassiter, & Salas, 1989). They recommend the use of a network of computer workstations to present a low-fidelity battery of time-shared team performance tasks that will provide reliable, real-time measures of team processes and performances. This approach seems to provide an ideal test-bed for investigating the effects of individual- and team-difference variables (and their interactions) on team effectiveness. Innovative approaches such as this are recommended as a basis for generating additional guidelines for the enhancement of team processes and performances through the selection and staffing of teams.

REFERENCES

Alexander, L. T., & Cooperband, A. S. (1965). *System training in team behavior* (Tech. Memo No. 2581). Santa Monica, CA: System Development Corporation.

Alluisi, E. A. (1977). Lessons from a study of defense training technology. *Education Technology Systems, 5*(1), 57–76.

Altman, I., & Haythorn, W. W. (1967). The effects of social isolation and group composition on performance. *Human Relations, 20*, 313–340.

Anderson, A. B. (1975). Combined effects of interpersonal attraction and goal-path clarity on the cohesiveness of task oriented groups. *Journal of Personality and Social Psychology, 31*, 68–75.

Bakeman, R., & Helmreich, R. (1975). Cohesiveness and performance: Covariation and causality in an undersea environment. *Journal of Experimental and Social Psychology, 11*, 478–489.

Bales, R. F., Strodtbeck, F. L., Mills, T. M., & Roseborough, M. E. (1951). Channels of communication in small groups. *American Sociological Review, 16*, 461–468.

Bass, B. (1982). Individual capability, team performance, and team productivity. In E. A. Fleishman & M. D. Dunnette (Eds.), *Human performance and capability: Human capability assessment.* Hillsdale, NJ: Erlbaum.

Bass, B. M., & Norton, F-T. M. (1951). Group size and leaderless discussion. *Journal of Applied Psychology, 35*, 397–400.

Bass, B. M., & Ryterband, E. (1979). *Organizational psychology* (2nd ed.). Boston: Allyn and Bacon.

Bass, B. M., & Wurster, C. R. (1953). Effects of the nature of the problem on LGD performance. *Journal of Applied Psychology, 37*, 96–99.

Birren, J. E., & Schaie, K. W. (Eds.). (1977). *Handbook of the psychology of aging.* New York: Van Nostrand Reinhold.

Blake, R. R., & Mouton, J. S. (1978). *The new managerial grid.* Houston, TX: Gulf Publications.

Boguslaw, R., & Porter, E. H. (1962). Team functions and training. In R. M. Gagne (Ed.), *Psychological principles on system development.* New York: Holt, Rinehart, & Winston.

Bouchard, T. J., Jr. (1969). Personality, problem-solving procedure, and performance in small groups. *Journal of Applied Psychology, 53,* 1–29.

Bouchard, T. J., Jr. (1972). Training, motivation, and personality as determinants of the effectiveness of brainstorming groups and individuals. *Journal of Applied Psychology, 56,* 324–331.

Briggs, G. E., & Naylor, J. C. (1965). Team versus individual training, training task fidelity and task organization effects of transfer performance by three-man teams. *Journal of Applied Psychology, 49,* 387–392.

Butler, M. C., & Burr, R. G. (1980). Utility of a multidimensional locus of control scale in predicting health and job-related outcomes in military environments. *Psychological Reports, 47,* 719–728.

Byrne, D. (1971). *The attraction paradigm.* New York: Academic Press.

Campbell, D. T. (1960). Blind variation and selective retention in creative thought as in other knowledge processes. *Psychological Review, 67,* 380–400.

Cattell, R. B. (1953). On the theory of group learning. *Journal of Social Psychology, 37,* 27–52.

Chidester, T. R. (1987). Selection for optimal crew performance: Relative impact of selection and training. In R. S. Jensen (Ed.), *Proceedings of the Fourth International Symposium on Aviation Psychology.* Columbus, OH: Ohio State University.

Chidester, T. R., Helmreich, R. L., Gregorich, S., & Geis, C. E. (1991). Pilot personality and crew coordination: Implications for training and selection. *Journal of Aviation Psychology, 1*(1), 23–42.

Coates, G. D., & Kirby, R. H. (1982). Organismic factors and individual differences in human performance and productivity. In E. A. Fleishman (Ed.), *Human performance and productivity: Stress and performance effectiveness.* Hillsdale, NJ: Erlbaum.

Comrey, A. L. (1953). Group performance in a manual dexterity task. *Journal of Applied Psychology, 37,* 207–210.

Comrey, A. L., & Staats, C. K. (1955). Group performance in a cognitive task. *Journal of Applied Psychology, 39,* 354–356.

Denson, R. W. (1981). *Team training: Literature review and annotated bibliography* (Tech. Rep. AFHRL-TR-80-40). Wright Patterson Air Force Base, OH: Logistics and Technical Training Division, Air Force Human Research Laboratory.

Driskell, J. E., Salas, E., & Hogan, R. (1987). *A taxonomy for composing effective Naval teams* (Tech. Rep. No. TR87002). Orlando, FL: Naval Training Systems Center.

Dunnette, M. D. (1966). *Personnel selection and placement.* Monterey, CA: Brooks/Cole Publishing Company.

Dyer, J. (1984). *State-of-the-art review on team training and performance.* Fort Benning, GA: Army Research Institute Field Unit.

Exline, R.V., Gray, D., & Schuette, D. (1965). Visual behavior in a dyad as affected by interview content and sex of respondent. *Journal of Personality and Social Psychology, 1,* 201–209.

Fenelon, J. R., & Megargee, E. I. (1971). Influence of race on the manifestation of leadership. *Journal of Applied Psychology, 55,* 353–358.

Fiedler, F. E. (1978). The contingency model and the dynamics of the leadership process. In L. Berkowitz (Ed.), *Advances in experimental social psychology* (Vol. 11). New York: Academic Press.

Fiedler, F. E., & Leister, A. F. (1977). Leader intelligence and task performance: A test of a multiple screen model. *Organizational Behavior and Human Performance, 20,* 1–14.

Foushee, H. C., & Helmreich, R. L. (1988). Group interaction and flight crew performance. In E. L. Weiner & D. C. Nagel (Eds.), *Human factors in aviation* (pp. 189–228). San Diego: Academic Press.

Gerard, H. B., Wilhelmy, R. A., & Conolley, E. S. (1968). Conformity and group size. *Journal of Personality and Social Psychology, 8,* 79–82.

Gersick, C. J. G. (1988). Time transition in work teams: Toward a new model of group development. *Academy of Management Journal, 31,* 9–41.

Gibb, J. R. (1951). The effects of group size and of threat reduction upon certainty in a problem-solving situation. *American Psychologist, 6,* 324.

Gill, D. L. (1979). Prediction of group motor performance from individual member abilities. *Journal of Motor Behavior, 11,* 113–122.

Gladstein, D. L. (1984). *Groups: Interactions and performance.* Englewood Cliffs, NJ: Prentice-Hall.

Glickman, A. S., Zimmer, S., Montero, R. C., Guerette, P. I., Campbell, W. J., Morgan, B. B., Jr., & Salas, E. (1987). *The evolution of teamwork skills: An empirical assessment with implications for training* (Tech. Rep. No. NTSC 87-D16). Arlington, VA: Office of Naval Research.

Goldman, M., Dietz, D. M., & McGlynn, A. (1968). Comparison of individual and group performance related to heterogeneous wrong responses, size, and patterns of interaction. *Psychological Reports, 23,* 459–465.

Gregorich, S., Helmreich, R. L., & Wilhelm, J. A. (in press). The structure of cockpit management attitudes. *Journal of Applied Psychology.*

Hackman, J. R. (1986). Effects of task characteristics on group products. *Journal of Experimental Social Psychology, 4,* 162–187.

Hackman, J. R. (1983). *A normative model of work team effectiveness* (Tech. Rep. No. 2). New Haven, CT: Yale School of Organization and Management.

Hackman, J. R., & Morris, C. G. (1975). Group tasks, group interaction process, and group performance effectiveness: A review and proposed integration. In L. Berkowitz (Ed.), *Advances in experimental psychology* (Vol. 8, pp. 45–49). New York: Academic Press.

Hare, A. P. (1972). Bibliography of small group research: 1959–1969. *Sociometry, 35,* 1–150.

Harper, C. R., Kidera, G. J., & Cullen, J. F. (1971). Study of simulated airline pilot incapacitation: Phase II, subtle or partial loss of function. *Aerospace Medicine, 42,* 946–948.

Haythorn, W. (1953). The influence of individual members on characteristics of small groups. *Journal of Abnormal and Social Psychology, 48,* 276–284.

Haythorn, W. W. (1968). The composition of groups: A review of the literature. *Acta Psychologica, 28,* 97–128.

Haythorn, W. W., Couch, A., Haefner, D., Langham, P., & Carter, L. F. (1956). The effects of varying combinations of authoritarian and equalitarian leaders and followers. *Journal of Abnormal and Social Psychology, 53*, 210–219.

Helmreich, R. L. (1982, August). *Pilot selection and training.* Paper presented at the American Psychological Association, Washington, DC.

Helmreich, R. L. (1984). Cockpit management attitudes. *Human Factors, 26*, 583–589.

Helmreich, R. L. (1987). Exploring flightcrew behavior. *Social Behavior, 2*, 63–72.

Hemphill, J. K. (1950). Relations between the size of the group and the behavior of "superior" leaders. *Journal of Social Psychology, 32*, 11–22.

Hewett, T. T., O'Brien, G. E., & Hornik, J. (1974). The effects of work organization, leadership style, and member compatibility upon the productivity of small groups working on a manipulative task. *Organizational Behavior and Human Performance, 11*, 283–301.

Hill, G. W. (1982). Group versus individual performance: Are $N + 1$ heads better than one? *Psychological Bulletin, 91*, 517–539.

Hoffman, L. R. (1959). Homogeneity of member personality and its effect on group problem-solving. *Journal of Abnormal and Social Psychology, 58*, 27–32.

Hoffman, L. R., & Maier, N. R. F. (1961). Quality acceptance of problem solutions by members of homogeneous and heterogeneous groups. *Journal of Abnormal and Social Psychology, 62*, 401–407.

Hogan, J., & Hogan, R. (1989). Noncognitive predictors of performance during explosive ordinance disposal training. *Military Psychology, 1*(3), 117–133.

Indik, B. P. (1965). Organizational size and member participation: Some empirical tests of alternatives. *Human Relations, 18*, 339–350.

Johnston, W. A. (1966). Transfer of team skills as a function of type of training. *Journal of Applied Psychology, 50*, 102–108.

Kabanoff, B., & O'Brien, G. E. (1979). Cooperation structure and the relationship of leader and member ability to group performance. *Journal of Applied Psychology, 64*, 526–532.

Kahan, J. P., Webb, N., Shavelson, R. J., & Stolzenberg, R. M. (1985). *Individual characteristics and unit performance* (Rep. No. R-3194-MIL). Santa Monica, CA: Rand Corporation.

Kent, R. N., & McGrath, J. E. (1969). Task and group characteristics as factors influencing group performance. *Journal of Experimental Social Psychology, 5*, 429–440.

Laughlin, P. R., Branch, L. G., & Johnson, H. H. (1969). Individual versus triadic performance and undimensional complementary task as a function of initial ability level. *Journal of Personality and Social Psychology, 12*, 144–150.

Levine, E. L., Brannick, M. T., Coovert, M. D., Llobet, J. M., & Salas, E. (in preparation). *Job/task analysis methodologies for teams: A review and implications for team training* (Tech. Rep. No. NTSC 88-019). Orlando, FL: Naval Training Systems Center.

Lott, A. J., & Lott, B. E. (1961). Group cohesiveness, communication level, and conformity. *Journal of Abnormal and Social Psychology, 62*, 408–412.

Mann, R. D. (1959). A review of the relationships between personality and performance in small groups. *Psychological Bulletin, 56*, 241–270.

Manning, F. J., & Fullerton, T. D. (1988). Health and well-being in highly cohesive units of the U.S. Army. *Journal of Applied Social Psychology, 18*, 503–519.

McGrath, J. E. (1964). *Social psychology: A brief introduction.* New York: Holt.

McGrath, J. E. (1984). Groups in context: A model of task group effectiveness. *Administrative Science Quarterly, 29,* 499–517.

McGrath, J. E., & Altman, I. (1966). *Small group research: A synthesis and critique of the field.* New York: Holt.

Modrick, J. A. (1986). Team performance and training. In J. Zeidner (Ed.), *Human productivity enhancement, Vol. 1: Training and human factors in systems design.* New York: Praeger Publishers.

Moran, G. (1966). Dyadic attraction and orientational consensus. *Journal of Personality and Social Psychology, 4,* 94–99.

Morgan, B. B., Jr., Coates, G. D., & Rebbin, T. J. (1970). *The effects of Phlebotomus fever on sustained performance and muscular output* (Interim Tech. Rep. No. ITR-70-14). Louisville, KY: University of Louisville.

Morgan, B. B., Jr., Glickman, A. S., Woodard, E. A., Blaiwes, A. S., & Salas, E. (1986). *Measurement of team behaviors in a Navy environment* (Tech. Rep. No. NTSC TR-86-014). Orlando, FL: Naval Training Systems Center.

Morgan, B. B., Jr., Lassiter, D. L., & Salas, E. (1989). Networked simulation application for team training and performance research. In R. Gilson, J. P. Kincaid, & B. Goldiez (Eds.), *Proceedings: Interactive networked simulation for training* (pp. 16–21). Orlando, FL: Institute for Simulation and Training.

Morgan, B. B., Jr., Salas, E., & Glickman, A. S. (in preparation). *A model of team evolution and maturation.*

Morgan, B. B., Jr., & Salas, E. (1988). A research agenda for team training and performance: Issues, alternatives, and solutions. *Proceedings of the 10th Interservice/Industry Training Systems Conference.* Washington, DC: National Security Industrial Association.

Morris, C. G. (1966). Task effects on group interaction. *Journal of Personality and Social Psychology, 4,* 545–554.

Morse, N. C., & Reimer, E. (1956). The experimental change of a major organizational variable. *Journal of Abnormal and Social Psychology, 52,* 120–129.

O'Brien, G. E., & Owens, A. G. (1969). Effects of organizational structure on correlations between abilities and group productivity. *Journal of Applied Psychology, 53,* 525–530.

Oser, R. L., McCallum, G. A., Salas, E., & Morgan, B. B., Jr. (1989). *Toward a definition of teamwork: An analysis of team behavior* (Tech. Rep. No. TR89-018). Orlando, FL: Naval Training Systems Center.

Pugh, D. S., Hickson, D. J., Hinings, C. R., & Turner, C. (1968). Dimensions of organization structure. *Administrative Science Quarterly, 13,* 66–105.

Reitan, H. T., & Shaw, M. E. (1964). Group membership, sex-composition of the group, and conformity behavior. *Journal of Social Psychology, 64,* 45–51.

Rohrbaugh, J. (1981). Improving the quality of group judgment: Social judgment analysis and the nominal group technique. *Organizational Behavior and Human Performance, 28,* 272–288.

Ronan, W. W. (1963). Work group attributes and grievance activity. *Journal of Applied Psychology, 47,* 38–41.

Rosenberg, L. A. (1961). Group size, prior experience, and conformity. *Journal of Abnormal and Social Psychology, 63,* 436–437.

Rosenberg, S., Erlick, D. E., & Berkowitz, L. (1955). Some effects of varying combinations of group members on group performance measures and leadership behaviors. *Journal of Abnormal and Social Psychology, 51,* 195–203.

Salas, E., Blaiwes, A. R., Reynolds, R. E., Glickman, A. S., & Morgan, B. B., Jr. (1985). Teamwork from team training: New directions. *Proceedings of the 7th Interservice/Industry Training Equipment Conference and Exhibition.* Orlando, FL: American Defense Preparedness Association.

Salas, E., Dickinson, T. D., Tannenbaum, S. I., & Converse, S. A. (in preparation). *A meta-analytic review of the team training and performance literature* (Tech. Rep. No. TR87-033). Orlando, FL: Naval Training Systems Center.

Schutz, W. C. (1955). What makes groups productive? *Human Relations, 8,* 429–465.

Shaw, M. E. (1954). Some effects of problem complexity upon problem solution efficiency in different communication nets. *Journal of Experimental Psychology, 48,* 211–217.

Shaw, M. E. (1955). A comparison of two types of leadership in various communication nets. *Journal of Experimental Psychology, 50,* 127–134.

Shaw, M. E. (1976). *Group dynamics: The psychology of small group behavior.* New York: McGraw-Hill.

Spence, J. T., & Helmreich, R. L. (1978). *Masculinity and femininity: Their psychological dimensions, correlates, and antecedents.* Austin, TX: University of Texas Press.

Spence, J. T., Helmreich, R. L., & Pred, R. S. (1987). Impatience versus achievement strivings in the Type A pattern: Differential effects on students' health and academic achievement. *Journal of Applied Psychology, 72,* 522–528.

Steiner, I. D. (1966). Models for inferring relationships between group size and potential group productivity. *Behavioral Science, 11,* 273–283.

Steiner, I. D. (1972). *Group process and productivity.* New York: Academic Press.

Stogdill, R. M. (1948). Personal factors associated with leadership: A survey of the literature. *Journal of Psychology, 25,* 35–71.

Stogdill, R. M. (1972). Group productivity drive, and cohesiveness. *Organizational Behavior and Human Performance, 8,* 26–43.

Strube, M. J., & Garcia, J. E. (1981). A meta-analytic investigation of Fiedler's contingency model of leadership effectiveness. *Psychological Bulletin, 90,* 307–321.

Swezey, R. W., & Salas, E. (1987). Development of instructional design guidelines for team training devices. *Proceedings of the Human Factors Society 31st Annual Meeting.* Santa Monica, CA: Human Factors Society.

Tziner, A., & Eden, D. (1985). Effects of crew composition on crew performance: Does the whole equal the sum of the parts? *Journal of Applied Psychology, 70,* 85–93.

Wyer, R. S., & Malinowski, C. (1972). Effects of sex and achievement level upon individualism and competitiveness in social interaction. *Journal of Experimental Social Psychology, 8,* 303–314.

$$5$$

Can You Study Real Teams in Contrived Settings? The Value of Small Group Research to Understanding Teams *

James E. Driskell and Eduardo Salas

Small groups have been a major focus of study in the behavioral sciences since the early part of this century. The work of Triplett (1898), Ross (1908), and Durkheim (1893) represents some of the earliest attempts to study group phenomena. While interest in the small group has waxed and waned over the past 100 years, there are few areas that have been the subject of such intense and continued scrutiny, and few areas that have generated as much valuable research and application. On the other hand, there are few areas of scholarship that are as wrought with such self-doubt, despair, and general pessimism. Reviews of group research invariably note a lack of progress in the field, and many authors have

* The views expressed in this chapter are those of the authors and do not reflect the official position of the Department of the Navy, Department of Defense, or the U.S. Government. We would like to thank Janis Cannon-Bowers for a thoughtful review of an earlier draft of this chapter.

questioned the basic value of group research. If General Motors sold cars the way group researchers promote the value of their research, our roads would not be nearly as congested.

We believe that small group research has made and continues to make substantial contributions to our understanding of groups and teams. Yet there is no doubt that the relevance of much small group research has been questioned, often by those who work in real-world settings and are faced with real-world problems. Critics bemoan the fact that the small group research setting is often sterile and artificial, results are unique and not generalizable to the real world, the theories and concepts are too abstract, and that research conducted is often simply common sense and of questionable practical value. We maintain that these statements on their face are correct—most small group research is indeed artificial, not directly generalizable to real-world settings, abstract, and common sense. However, as a critique of small group research (the implication being that small group research of this nature is of limited utility), we believe that these statements are misleading and inaccurate. We base this claim on several points. The first is that people conduct research for differing purposes, including that of testing theory, applying knowledge to the real world, and predicting real-world phenomena. Second, we claim that most small group research is in fact experimental laboratory research conducted for the purpose of testing theory. Third, we argue that the above criticisms are without substance when applied to research that is conducted for the purposes of testing theory, for the (not-so-simple) reason that this type of research is not meant to be otherwise.

This position implies that criteria that are used to judge the value of applied research (i.e., that the research setting mirror the real-world setting) or survey research (i.e., that the results can be directly generalized to a specific population) often do not apply to research conducted for the purpose of testing theory. For example, the recent emphasis on research conducted in "naturalistic" settings suggests an implicit naturalistic/artificial, good/bad dichotomy. That is, research conducted in natural settings is valuable, while research conducted in artificial settings is suspect. This approach has obscured the fact that, for certain purposes such as theory testing, the "artificial" laboratory is the *most* appropriate environment in which to conduct research. In fact, we intend to argue that, for the goal of testing theory, the more artificial the research setting, the better.

Because these common criticisms invariably surface in a discussion of small group research, they serve to shake our faith in the value of this work. But more importantly, we feel they indicate a misunderstanding of basic experimental research. In this chapter, we will examine the relationship of small group research to understanding teams. We will do this, not by reviewing the contributions of the small group literature to team performance, but by examining the role and nature of small group research. What is the value of small group research for those interested in real-world teams? In addressing this issue, we hope to illustrate the value of small group research in generating basic scientific knowledge as well as guiding practical applications.

SMALL GROUP RESEARCH

Small group research is often equated with the experimental method, and more precisely, with laboratory experimentation. This is of course an overgeneralization; some of the classic studies of small groups have taken place in the field. Nevertheless, it would not be inaccurate to say that the principal setting for small group research has been the experimental laboratory. And herein lies some of the major objections to and misunderstandings of most small group research.

Small group research is frequently faulted because (a) it is artificial, (b) results cannot be generalized outside of the laboratory, (c) it is too abstract, and (d) most findings are commonsense. To summarize the first objection, the standard criticism is that most small group research takes place in artificial and unusual laboratory settings, atypical of most real-world settings. If by "artificial" we mean that the laboratory setting of most small group research is unlike any that is found in the "real world," we agree. Second, some have argued that we cannot generalize from the college sophomores and laboratory tasks of the typical research study to any concrete real-world setting. If by "nongeneralizable" we mean that the concrete features and results of any one laboratory study are not directly generalizable to a particular real-world setting, we agree. Third, many argue that small group research is unnecessarily abstract, examining concepts such as stress or status, but telling us little about any one specific task situation. If by "abstract" we mean that the concepts and variables studied in small group research often do not describe any particular concrete situation, we again agree. Finally, small group research has been faulted for belaboring the obvious; uncovering or documenting obvious or trivial phenomena. If by "common sense" we mean that small group research often tests what we think we already know, we again are in total agreement.

By agreeing with the above statements, we do not lend credence to the criticisms from which they stem. For example, while we agree that the laboratory setting of most small group research is indeed artificial, we do not agree that this represents an inherent weakness of this approach. In fact, we intend to argue that artificiality is a virtue of the experimental method, and that most pleas to make the laboratory more representative of the "real world" are misguided.

We believe that attempts to dismiss the results of small group research on the basis of these common arguments represent a basic misunderstanding of the purpose and goals of laboratory research. Because these objections are so widespread, and because an understanding of the role of laboratory research is fundamental to evaluating the value of small group research, we intend to address each of these issues in the following sections.

THE ARTIFICIALITY OBJECTION

"The major disadvantage of experimentation [involves] basing conclusions on contrived groups that have no parallels among naturally occurring groups" (Forsyth, 1990, p. 46).

Perhaps the most common objection to research conducted in the experimental laboratory is its artificiality. One can hardly pick up a textbook on research methods that does not note authoritatively that the greatest weakness of laboratory experiments is that they are artificial. In most discussions of this point, the disadvantage of artificiality is viewed as a tradeoff that the experimental researcher accepts in order to gain greater control of variables. The problem, as Forsyth (1990) concludes, is that researchers may "end up studying closely monitored but artificial group situations" (p. 45). The implication is simply that artificiality is an inherent defect of the experimental method, but it is a liability that we often accept because of other advantages that the experimental laboratory provides.

Let's attempt to define in general terms what we mean by "artificial." Certainly, we do not mean to imply "unreal"; behavior in the laboratory is real human behavior—as real as behavior in the cockpit of an airplane. It is likely that what we mean by artificial in this context is that the setting is unique or uncommon, and designed by human hands rather than nature. Indeed, the laboratory contains a number of uncommon conditions that are rarely found outside of this setting: one-way mirrors, data entry consoles, strange laboratory tasks, and a newly formed group of strangers with which to work. Certainly, no one but a college sophomore is likely to encounter this type of situation in his or her everyday life. Furthermore, the laboratory incorporates few of the rich array of personal, social, and environmental characteristics that make a real-world setting unique.

Therefore, according to the artificiality objection, anything that takes place in the laboratory setting is unique to that setting and thus can tell us little about how people act under natural conditions. Some critics take a hard-line approach and conclude that this type of research has little relevance to the real world. For example, Mackie (1987), conducting an evaluation of several research studies on stress and performance, rated each study according to the criteria of whether the experimental conditions corresponded to real-world settings. Implicit in this approach is an assumption that an experiment that does not realistically mimic a real world setting has little value. These critics often call for greater representativeness or realism in experimental research by conducting research in as naturalistic a setting as possible. While this perspective is intuitively pleasing (who would argue against "representative" research?), we believe it is based on a gross misunderstanding of the role of experimental research in science.

It is important at this point to note that all research does not fall into any one type. We may draw a distinction between three different types of research which involve different goals: (a) research that attempts to predict real-world behavior, (b) research that attempts to test hypotheses about the real world, and (c) research that attempts to apply hypotheses to the real world.

The first type of research endeavor attempts to predict real-world behavior in a specific setting. For example, a chemist may study isolated chemical reactions in a laboratory in order to predict their behavior in an external environment. An agricultural researcher may study the rate of seed germination in the laboratory to predict performance in the farmer's field. However, we maintain that this type of research is seldom a goal of the experimental social psychologist. We believe, instead, that most of the research in the behavioral sciences is conducted to test hypotheses about the real world, our second type of research activity. The authors recently conducted a study that illustrates this type of research goal (Driskell & Salas, 1991). In this study, we formed teams that included high-status (team leaders) and low-status (team members) members. Some teams performed a decision-making task under normal conditions, and some teams performed this task under stress. Since our subjects for this study were military recruits, we were able to manipulate stress in the "high-stress" experimental conditions by informing these subjects that they would be performing the task under conditions similar to those of a military "tear gas" drill.[1] According to the threat-rigidity thesis offered by Staw, Sandelands, and Dutton (1981), organizations (as well as societies) often respond to stress or threat with a constriction of control, or centralization of authority in higher levels of the organizational hierarchy. Extending this hypothesis to the group or team level, we predicted that, if stress results in a constriction of control, then team members should be more likely to defer decision making to team leaders when under stress. This, in fact, occurred in our study.

On the basis of this study, we could have concluded that: "Threat of tear gas caused military recruits to depend more on team leaders to make decisions in this setting. Therefore, it probably would have the same effect in a similar real-world setting." This would be a seemingly legitimate conclusion, yet extremely trivial. Even the most wayward recruit is not likely to be tear gassed with any regularity in the real world. This conclusion was obviously not our objective. Or, we could have concluded that: "Threat of tear gas caused military recruits to depend more on team leaders to make decisions in this setting. Therefore, stress causes people to defer more to authority in normal situations." We believe that this type of conclusion more accurately reflects the "common" view of how research studies are generalized, but to make this type of statement was not the objective of this

---

[1] This drill is a military exercise involving tear gas that the recruits had recently completed, and which is a very aversive experience for almost all involved. For the high-stress conditions of our study, subjects were instructed that, during the task, a similar drill would be implemented. The experimental setting was designed so that this threat was believeable; however, we of course did not actually fulfill this threat. It turned out to be a very effective stress manipulation.

study. And as Mook (1983) notes, to make this type of real-world prediction on the basis of laboratory results is not only risky, but foolhardy. The position that we took on the basis of our results was that: "Stress caused team members to defer more to authority under these conditions. Therefore, the threat-rigidity hypothesis, which predicts that this would occur, is supported on this point when it is extended to the team level."

The critical point here is that we did not attempt to generalize the concrete results of this particular study from the laboratory to the real world. Our goal was not to predict real-world behavior directly from lab results. What the laboratory setting allows the researcher to do is to *test hypotheses about the real world*. In other words, the purpose of this research was to test theory, and *it is the theory that is applied to the real world*.

At this point, we may consider a third type of research activity, that which relates theory to the real world. A researcher often wishes to apply theory to a particular real-world setting. For example, investigations of airline accidents have noted a number of instances in which first officers have deferred decision-making responsibilities to the flight captain, even when the first officers had correct and often critical information. Let's assume that we are interested in applying what we know about stress and decision making to the cockpit, with the eventual goal of designing interventions to overcome these sometimes detrimental patterns of interaction. This research involves a different type of goal and a different type of research activity than that of testing hypotheses in the laboratory; the purpose here is to *relate theory to a real-world setting*. This type of applied research not only serves the function of "grounding" theory to the real world, but serves to define the applicability of a specific theory in a specific setting.

Thus far, we have briefly described three types of research activity; (a) research that attempts to predict real-world behavior, (b) research that attempts to test hypotheses about the real world, and (c) research that attempts to apply hypotheses to the real world. Our intention was to make several simple points. First, while each type of research is a legitimate method of scientific endeavor, each method serves a different purpose or goal. The primary goal of survey research differs from that of theory testing, which differs from applied research. Further, the means to achieve these goals differ; the most efficient procedure for testing theory may differ from the setting and methods we use to apply theory. Second, while these types of research are distinct, in practice there is a crucial interplay, particularly between theoretical research and applied research. Theoretical research that is not tested through real-world applications is at best incomplete, while applications that are not grounded in theory are, at worst, random.

The third point we wish to make is that it is the second type of research, the hypothesis-testing approach, that represents most small group experimental research. And for this type of research, the criticism of artificiality and the call for more realism is simply wrong. In the following, we argue that (a) most psychological experimental research is conducted to test hypotheses about the real world rather than to predict real-world behavior, and (b) if our purpose is to test theory, then the fact that the laboratory is an artificial environment is irrelevant.

Most research in the small group field and in the social and behavioral sciences is conducted to test hypotheses, rather than to generalize a result from one setting to a similar setting. As Mook (1983) notes, in most of our research, we are not *making* generalizations about the real world, but *testing* them. There are certainly instances in which our goal is to predict behavior in a concrete setting, such as predicting the likely crowd response at the 1994 World Cup, but this is a relatively rare goal in psychology, and the information it provides is limited to that instance.[2] The group researcher is more likely to be interested in the question of what determines crowd rioting, and he or she is likely to approach this problem by testing a theory that explains rioting behavior. If the theory is supported, then it is the theory that guides applications in the real world. The researcher is then able to make specific recommendations for limiting the occurrence of mob violence, not only at the 1994 World Cup, but at other sporting events as well as other situations that fit within the domain of that theory. (And note that it is the results of this *application* that allow the researcher to refine or revise the theory—illustrating the reciprocal relationship between theory and application.)

A second example may further illustrate this point. On July 3, 1988, the USS Vincennes mistakenly shot down an Iranian airliner over the Persian Gulf. Post-incident investigations found that a primary cause of this tragedy was a breakdown in the performance of the crew, who were faced with a novel, extremely stressful task situation. As a result of this incident, the military services subsequently have placed an increased emphasis on research to examine team performance under stress, in order to lessen the likelihood of a similar occurrence in the future (see Driskell & Olmstead, 1989). How would we describe the goal of such a research problem? It is likely that the military is interested, on one hand, in *predicting performance aboard the USS Vincennes.* They certainly would want to know why this episode occurred aboard the Vincennes and how to prevent this specific outcome in the future. If we were to conduct research to pursue this goal in the laboratory, we would be rightfully concerned with making the laboratory resemble as closely as possible the USS Vincennes. If our research was successful, we would end up knowing a great deal about the USS Vincennes. This research strategy is reasonable and commendable.

---

[2] Note that we are claiming that predicting the behavior of a specific target population is not a common purpose of most social psychological *experimental* research. There are certainly many other instances in which this is a goal. These include survey research, in which making generalizations from one sample population to another *is* a primary goal, as well as certain applied research that takes place in organizational settings.

But in a much more important sense, the military would also want to know how to prevent the detrimental effects of stress on team performance in other ships, other settings, and other situations. That is, not only are we interested in the effects of the specific stressors faced by the Combat Information Center crew of the USS Vincennes, but we are also interested in other teams that perform different but no less critical functions, teams on other ships that are not similarly outfitted, and on teams that may face a different array of stressors. In this case, our research strategy is not (a) to predict behavior in a concrete setting, but (b) *to test hypotheses about the effects of stress on team performance*. In other words, the group researcher is likely to be interested in testing theory to define the relationship between stress and team performance, not in predicting behavior aboard the USS Vincennes per se.

Zelditch (1968) makes the point that the experimental group researcher seldom attempts to study a small group in itself. That is, the experimental researcher rarely attempts to study a specific real-world group *in the laboratory*. If that is our purpose, then the groups formed in the laboratory setting are indeed so artificial that they are unlike any other groups we are likely to encounter. But if the purpose of experiments is not to study the types of groups found in natural settings, then what is their purpose? Zelditch notes that the answer is deceptively simple: "The purpose of the laboratory experiment is to create certain theoretically relevant aspects of social situations under controlled conditions" (p. 532). In other words, the purpose of the laboratory is to create conditions conducive to testing a particular theory. Thus, this type of research should model relevant theoretical processes, not the natural setting.

If the researcher chooses to test a theory in the laboratory, he or she creates a situation unlike any that exists in the outside world (or else why create it?) that isolates *only* those variables relevant to the theory. The greater the control of extraneous variables, and the greater the artificiality of the setting in terms of isolating only those variables relevant to the hypothesis being tested, then the greater confidence we have that we have provided a clear test of the theory. A theory is tested and refined in this manner. It is the theory that is applied to concrete settings. The theory is then further refined and revised by the results of applied research in the real-world setting. Theories that are robust in their application—that is, their predictions hold in a wide variety of settings—are seen as more useful.[3]

In summarizing recent progress in small group research, Levine and Moreland (1990) note that researchers have begun to develop theories that can account for

---

[3] We imply that a theory that has been shown to apply to a wide range of settings is seen as more valuable. Note that, in some cases, a theory may only apply to very narrowly defined or rare situations, such as panic behavior, yet, because these situations are critically important, the theory has utility.

complex behavior in natural groups. We agree that this is a very positive development; we believe that it is this type of theory development that accounts for most
of the growth of psychology as a science. That is, conducting research to test and
develop theories that apply to a wide range of natural settings is certainly an ideal
goal. It is likely that this goal will be achieved by both the performance of
experimental research to test and build theory and applied research to determine
the limits and applications of theory. However, we believe that the proclamation
made by Levine and Moreland is entirely different from that made by those who
make the blanket call for more naturalistic research. A "naturalistic" research
setting is most often the appropriate setting for applying theory; the "artificial"
laboratory environment is most often the appropriate setting for testing theory.
The criticism that the typical small group laboratory study (designed to test
theory) is not realistic enough is simply nonsensical.

The point that we have emphasized is that the theory-testing or hypothesis-
testing approach represents a large share of experimental small group research.
And, for the research goal of testing generalizations, testing hypotheses, and
testing theory, artificiality is in fact a virtue. The more artificial the setting, in the
sense that it contains only those variables that are relevant to the theory being
tested, the more rigorous is the test of the researcher's hypothesis. As Webster
and Kervin (1971), Mook (1983), and others agree, for these purposes what we
require is *greater* artificiality, not less.

There is a second type of theory-based research strategy for which artificiality
is also required. Henshel (1980) argues that a researcher may use the experimental laboratory, again not to study real-life conditions directly, but to examine
whether a phenomenon "can" occur. Instead of asking whether the phenomena
observed in the laboratory can be observed in a real-life setting, Henshel would
ask the question: Does the research uncover a desirable result that can be explained by theory, even though the phenomena is otherwise nonexistent? If so,
perhaps the researcher can reproduce the desired phenomena in the outside
world. That is, this strategy requires that, instead of asking "What is?", we ask
"What if?"

Therefore, one use of the experimental laboratory is to maximize artificiality
deliberately in order to create conditions that allow a phenomenon to occur that
we would never otherwise observe in the outside world. If the results are desirable, we may attempt to create similar conditions in a real-world setting. This is a
common research approach in engineering and the natural sciences, although it is
used less frequently in social psychology. Henshel (1980) notes that laboratory
studies of unnatural or unusual phenomena are often of this variety; citing Bavelas's study of communication networks as an example (see Bavelas, 1950).
Bavelas's research is often criticized because of the artificiality of the group
structures that he studied. Where do we actually find networks of communication
of the type Bavelas examined (such as the wheel or chain)? But this question

misconstrues this research strategy. Instead of asking where this artificial phenomenon exists outside the laboratory, it is more valuable to question how we can create the desired result in the real world. Therefore, Bavelas's research may be of little value in predicting *existing* real world behavior, in that we probably will find few existing groups organized into a formal wheel pattern. However, this work does provide theoretical guidance (for example, by suggesting the types of communications patterns most efficient for specific types of tasks) that would allow us to engineer desired results in real-world groups.

A second example of the value of this strategy is the development of powered flight. Early researchers attempting human flight conducted numerous experiments with flapping-wing type machines. If researchers had been simply content to mimic in their laboratories real-world behavior, we would still be watching newsclips of well-meaning but frustrated researchers flapping vigorously in a futile attempt to defy gravity. The Wright brothers, on the other hand, created a set of unnatural conditions, testing a rigid wing as an airfoil, that had no real-world analog (although a number of birds do glide, none use this method as a primary source of propulsion). The Wright brothers succeeded, whereas the flapping machine proponents failed, because of their strategy. Rather than model in the laboratory only what exists in the real world, they deliberately examined conditions in the laboratory that had little "realism" but produced a desirable result. In other words, they created artificial conditions in the laboratory to test a theory of flight. They then applied their newly tested theory of aerodynamics to the real world.

In summary, we agree that the setting for most experimental small groups research is artificial. There is no doubt that the experimental laboratory is an extremely unusual situation. This has moved some critics to call for experimental settings to be made more natural and realistic. We believe that this represents a misunderstanding of the goals of this type of research. For the purpose of testing hypotheses about the real world, we design experimental conditions in the laboratory to enact only those conditions relevant to testing the theory. The fact that these conditions do not mirror the real world is simply irrelevant. The primary criterion for designing an empirical setting to test theory is that it provide a clear and robust test of that theory, not that it resemble the outside world. However, when we attempt to apply the theory to a real-world setting, then the realism of the setting in which the application or intervention is conducted is critical.

To make the blanket criticism that most experimental research is artificial and thus suspect ignores the fact that there are different types of research activities that pursue different goals. As Orne (1969) has stated: "We cannot afford to give up either laboratory research or observation in a naturalistic setting. Both kinds of data are an integral part of behavioral research" (p. 177). We simply do not apply the same criteria (i.e., that research should mimic the real world) to all types of research.

GENERALIZABILITY

"One of the great criticisms of laboratory research by organizational psychologists is that the research is frequently conducted on college sophomores and then generalized to adult members of the workforce" (Ilgen, 1986, p. 259).

There are actually two versions of the artificiality objection. The first deals with the *uniqueness* of the experimental situation. We have argued that, when the goal of the researcher is to test generalizations about the real world, this artificiality is in fact a virtue. A second type of "artificiality" objection deals with generalizability of the results based on the population studied.

We commonly use the term *generalizability* to refer to the extent to which findings based on experimental "samples" can be generalized to other populations. This is often termed *external validity*. Campbell and Stanley (1967) state: "External validity asks the question of generalizability: To what populations, settings, treatment variables, and measurement variables can this effect be generalized?" (p. 5). The typical form of this generalizability objection, which is often based on statistical grounds, claims that the population studied in the experimental laboratory is so atypical of any external real-world population that results from this setting cannot be applied to any other setting. Henshel (1980) notes that the rationale for this objection is often blurred with the artificiality objection, and poses a seemingly grave dilemma for the experimental researcher: If the purpose of experimentation is to predict real-world behavior, but the research setting is artificial and the sample population is college sophomores, then the results are only weakly generalizable to any external setting.

This simply represents one mistake placed on top of another. First is the statement that "the purpose of experimentation is to predict real-world behavior." We have argued that the primary use of experimental research in psychology is *not* to predict the real world, but to test hypotheses. Mook (1983) calls this misperception a consequence of the agricultural model of research. The research context from which sampling theory was derived was agricultural research, in which the laboratory researcher may have been interested in relating the germination rate of hybrid corn seed in the laboratory directly to the field. In this case, the results of a particular experiment were intended to be generalized directly to a similar real-world setting. We have claimed that this type of study is very rare in social psychology.

In the laboratory study carried out for the purposes of theory testing, the results of any one experiment are never meant to be generalized to an external setting. It is the theory which is the subject of the empirical test (and which is either supported or delimited by the experimental results), and it is the theory that is applied to the external world. This is a critical point. Given that most small group experimental research is not conducted in order to generalize directly to the real world, then the "sampling theory" notion of generalizing from a sample to a population is inaccurate and misleading.

Zelditch (1968) observed that the term *generalizability* is typically used to refer to the extent to which we can equate concrete features of the experiment with concrete features of the natural setting. Let's use Higgins and Marlatt's (1973) study of alcohol consumption (cited in Mook, 1983) to examine this common conception of generalization. In this study, researchers manipulated anxiety in subjects through the threat of shock. According to the tension-reduction hypothesis, if alcohol reduces tension and people drink to reduce tension, then highly anxious subjects should drink more. This did not occur. The threat of shock did not cause subjects to drink in this study, and the tension-reduction hypothesis, which predicts that it should have done so, was not supported. In terms of generalizing the results of this study, we may ask if we are likely to see the same behavior in a bar as we observed in the experimental laboratory. Of course not. How often are we likely to see college sophomores vary their drinking consumption based on the threat of electrical shock? The purpose of this study was not to predict directly real-world behavior. The experimental researchers were not "sampling" a population to make generalizations about how they would behave in a representative external setting. The researchers were testing a theory.

The primary use of the experimental laboratory is to test hypotheses about the real world based on a theory of how the real world operates. In this situation, there is no intention to predict real-world behavior directly. As Mook (1983) observes, the intention of the experimental researcher is to predict behavior *in the laboratory*. What does this mean? The experimental researcher can make a very precise test of a theory by use of the artificial laboratory setting—it includes only those variables relevant to the theory. Therefore, the theory should predict exactly what occurs *in the laboratory*. We test our hypotheses in the laboratory and modify the theory accordingly. The conclusion drawn from this type of experimental research is not a probabilistic statement about a specific population (that we are 95% confident that college drinkers will not respond to threat of shock by increasing alcohol consumption), but the conclusion is about a theory (the results suggest that the tension-reduction theory of alcohol consumption should be modified).

What then, is the relationship between the laboratory and the real world? It is not the generalization of subject responses, as is implied by the common form of the generalizability objection. The link between the laboratory and the real world is theory. Zelditch (1968) refers to theory as a bridge spanning the laboratory and the natural setting. It is not necessary that the two settings be identical in terms of concrete features such as the task or population, only that the theory implies both settings.

Stated differently, how do we apply the findings of experiment A to the real world? We do not. The task, the setting, the specific subject group have no real-world equivalent. Therefore, the goal of experiment A is not to predict behavior in setting X. The goal of experiment A is to test and refine theory A. However, we do apply the theoretical knowledge that we have gained from experiment A. Plus, and this is not a trivial point, our new-found knowledge applies potentially to setting X, setting Y, setting Z, and *any setting to which the theory applies* (the limits are often defined, as we note below, by applied research).

For these reasons, we maintain that the differences between the laboratory and the real world, in terms of the setting and the population studied, do not determine the generalizability of experimental research. Experimental research is generalized on the basis of the theoretical relationships that are tested, not through the concrete results of a single study.

However, the differences between the laboratory and the real world must be acknowledged in the *application* of the theory. One way in which the relationships tested and defined in the laboratory are tied to the real world is through applied research. In other words, we do not expect to find the velocity of a falling object to be $(1/2) gt^2$ very often outside the laboratory; real-world settings contain a number of factors (such as air resistance) that are not addressed by the theory (Webster & Kervin, 1971). The drinking behavior of adults is influenced by numerous factors other than tension reduction, such as peer pressure.

The point is, a well-supported theory should apply, or make accurate predictions, in the laboratory as well as in natural settings. It is one function of applied research to determine the limits of that application. In this sense, no amount of experimental support for a theory is sufficient to ensure its exact applicability to a particular setting—experimental research must be coupled to applied research in the target setting in order to relate the theory to a concrete setting. In other words, theory is grounded through application. However, the purposes of theory testing in the experimental laboratory and applied research in a target setting differ.

Thus, the "sampling notion" of generalizability is misapplied when applied to experimental research that is conducted for the purposes of theory testing. A theory can be appropriately tested in any situation that fits within its scope. If college sophomores are available, the theory should be able to make accurate predictions about their behavior, and thus they would constitute a fair test of the theory. The confusion arises when critics assume that the experimental researcher intends to generalize directly from the laboratory subjects to a target population, or from the concrete laboratory results to an external setting. Direct generalizability of results is a crucial issue for research for which that is a goal, including survey research. For other purposes, such as that represented by most small group research, it is simply not relevant.

Vancouver and Ilgen (1989), in a laboratory study of the effects of interpersonal orientation and other variables on the preference to work alone or in groups, provide a concise summary of this point:

> Questions are always raised when research conducted in one setting with one sample of individuals is used to draw conclusions about behavior in another setting

with another sample, particularly if those settings differ as much as the laboratory from the workplace. However . . . our task was not to predict employees' choices; rather, it was to discover the effects of interpersonal orientation . . . on the decision to work alone and in groups. Once these effects have been demonstrated to exist in one setting, we can speculate about the functions of these variables in other settings. (p. 933)

THE ABSTRACT NATURE OF THEORY

Small group research is often faulted for being too "abstract." The concepts are broad (organizational rigidity, status, decision making), and the theoretical assumptions are exceedingly general (i.e., "the higher the relative status of person A to person B, the higher A's position in terms of power and prestige"). Why isn't the theory that is developed in the laboratory framed in terms of specifics?

A theory strives to be general. A theory includes concepts that, in principle, apply to a variety of settings. The more a theory tells us about the USS Vincennes, the less it tells us about any other setting, because each concrete setting is unique.

Let's consider the hypothesis that "the higher the stress, the more likely that the individual will relinquish decision making to others." This is a general theoretical statement; the concepts of stress and decision making apply to any number of concrete settings, of which the USS Vincennes is one example. Let's consider a more specific theoretical statement: "the higher the time pressure, the less likely a Navy Combat Information Center team member will critically evaluate each decision input from others." This statement is more specific in terms of the properties of a particular concrete setting: the concept "stress" has become "time pressure," and the concept "decision making" has become an "anti-air warfare" task. This type of theoretical statement is less abstract, yet at the same time it is less informative—it applies only to one specific setting. A theory that is developed at this level may only apply to those concrete features of that particular setting. It would say nothing about, for example, sonar performance aboard a submarine, or decision making in the cockpit.

Zelditch (1968) provides another example of the generality of theory. Consider two Air Force airmen in an experimental laboratory. They sit in isolated cubicles. Their task is to make a series of binary choices on a standard laboratory task. One airman is appointed leader of the group. During the task, a loud noise is present. Data are gathered on how the airmen resolve disagreements on the decision task. Zelditch notes that what is being studied is no more like an actual Air Force crew than it is like an Air Force jet. In other words, what is being studied in this example is not the concrete features of the setting, but the concepts of "stress" and "decision making." It is theoretical concepts that are tested in the laboratory. These must be abstract in order to apply to other settings.

Therefore, we do not study *the Air Force* in the laboratory; we study properties of the Air Force. The theory defines the relationships between these properties or concepts, such as between stress and decision making. We test these relationships in the laboratory. The theoretical understanding that we gain in the laboratory should apply, not only to the Air Force, but to the Army, Navy, and General Motors as well. Thus, theory is abstract because of its desire to be general. And, as we noted earlier, it is the theoretical understanding of how these factors operate that is generalized to the real world.

MAKING SENSE OF COMMON SENSE

The results of small group research are often met with a resounding "So what?" The consumers of small group research—other professionals, practitioners, and the general public—are apt to respond to a particular journal article, or a professional presentation describing a group research study, with a feeling that the study results are trivial, they are little more than common sense, and they tell us little more than what we already know. To understand this position, let's examine some of the more well-documented small group findings.

1. Teams under stress experience a constriction in control or authority, with team leaders consolidating authority for decision making. (The tendency for organizations as well as nations to become more centralized and place authority in the hands of a few when under threat has been well documented.)

2. Highly cohesive groups are more productive than less cohesive groups. (It is not surprising that groups whose members have a higher degree of esprit de corps or attraction to the group outperform less closely knit groups. The military has known this for years.)

3. Allowing team members to generate problem solutions in an open, uncritical manner in a group setting results in greater variety and creativity of responses. (A task group in an advertising agency generating slogans for a product is a common example of this practice. The business community has used this technique to its advantage for years.)

This short list of findings illustrates the argument that the results of small group research is often little more than just simple common sense. Furthermore, these conclusions should be self-evident to most anyone, even the small group researcher. However, as the astute reader has probably guessed by now, each of the above statements is also wrong (or is inaccurate and must be qualified to a significant degree).

To illustrate how things that often seem common sense are not, let's briefly examine each of the above claims.

Team Decision Making Under Stress

We began this section with the statement that decision-making authority becomes centralized in the hands of a team leader when under stress. We now make the claim that this is inaccurate. This is a particularly apt illustration of how intuitively reasonable claims are often qualified in a substantial manner by the results of experimental research.

We introduced the study earlier in this chapter conducted by the authors (Driskell & Salas, 1991) to test the threat-rigidity hypothesis. According to this theory, organizations respond to threat by a constriction in control, whereby authority becomes increasingly centralized in the hands of a few individuals at the top of the organizational hierarchy (see Staw, Sandelands, & Dutton, 1981). At a societal level, Hertzler (1940) found that people are often willing to give away decision-making rights to a central authority in times of stress. Drawing on an historical analysis, he found that practically every dictatorship examined, from Caesar to Cromwell to Napoleon, was preceded by periods of stress or emergency. Hertzler noted that a "mass, in time of crises is nearly always ready . . . to give control to anyone who gives evidence of ability to wield it efficiently" (p. 160).

There is some empirical support to suggest that this process also operates at the team or group level. For example, Worchel, Andreoli, and Folger (1977) found that members of groups in competition identified fewer members as leaders than did members of cooperative groups, suggesting a centralization of authority under stress. Foushee and Helmreich (1988) have suggested that flight crews experience a similar increased dependence on the crew captain under stress conditions, whereby crew members place more responsibility for task performance on the leader. Therefore, we predicted that members of decision-making groups would experience a similar constriction of control. In effect, the team hierarchy would become more centralized, with team members more likely to defer decisions to the team leader, and the team leader more likely to reject decisions from other team members. In other words, the team members become more subordinate, while the team leader becomes more in command.

We formed teams in the laboratory to test this hypothesis. The decision-making task required each team member to make an initial choice on a series of problems, exchange information with other team members, and then make a final "team" choice. The data indicated that team members were much more likely to defer to the team leader's choice when under stress. This is consistent with the threat-rigidity hypothesis—that there is a centralization of control in groups under stress. However, the data further indicated that the team leader was *also* more likely to defer more to other team members when under stress. This suggests a process quite different from that predicted by the threat-rigidity hypothesis. In other words, our data suggested that what may occur in teams under stress is not that team members defer more to the team leader to make decisions, while at the same time the leader increasingly ignores the team members' inputs. Our data showed that team members are indeed more likely to defer more to the leader's task inputs, but that the leader is also more likely to accept input from other team members when under stress. Rather than a strengthening of the team leadership hierarchy, we observed a flattening of this hierarchy.

What does this research imply? First, this study suggests that the threat-rigidity hypothesis requires further qualification when applied to team performance. Second, recall that investigations of airline incidents often find a reluctance of flight crew members to question superiors during emergency situations (see Foushee & Helmreich, 1988). Our data suggest one theoretical explanation for this phenomena; that those in low-status team positions are even more likely to defer team decisions to high-status members when under stress. However, based on the additional knowledge gained from this study, particularly in terms of leader behavior, we would suggest quite different training interventions to overcome dysfunctional decision making in the cockpit than that based on the general threat-rigidity hypothesis. Third, this study illustrates that things are frequently not as simple as they seem. We often find that, even when starting with an intuitively reasonable hypothesis, data from careful experimentation can modify our understanding of theoretical processes in a substantial manner.

Team Cohesiveness and Productivity

The concept of cohesiveness has occupied a central position in the small group literature, certainly since the work of Lewin and his colleagues in the 1940s and 1950s. Golembiewski (1962) considered cohesiveness to be "the essential small group characteristic" (p. 149) and further noted that the potency of cohesive groups is "the elemental law of small group physics" (p. 164). Group cohesiveness is intuitively easy to describe: At one extreme of this dimension are the close-knit, well functioning set of individuals that embody the concept of a "team," and at the other extreme are a set of disparate individuals in a group context who are perhaps more properly termed a collective. The effects of cohesiveness on group performance are also intuitively apparent; it is generally believed that cohesive task groups are more productive, both in the laboratory and applied settings. However, a recent National Research Council report concluded that, of the topics studied, "none shows a larger discrepancy between what we think we know and the existing evidence than that of cohesion" (Druckman & Swets, 1988, p. 133).

The cohesiveness of groups has been shown to be consistently linked with several aspects of group interaction. In the first place, it seems that positive interpersonal relationships in a group may be socioemotionally pleasing; a number of studies have revealed a positive relationship between cohesiveness and satisfaction with the group (Exline, 1957; Marquis, Guetzkow, & Heyns, 1951). Second, group cohesiveness is shown to be positively related to the amount of influence group members exercise over one another (Berkowitz, 1957; Festinger, Schachter, & Back, 1950; Lott & Lott, 1961). Finally, the cohesiveness of a group tends to be related to the amount and quality of interaction within the group. Back (1951) found that cohesive groups interacted more, and that interaction was distributed more equally across group members, while Curtis and Miller (1986) found that positive interpersonal relations led to less disagreement and more positive affect in discussion groups. Thus, cohesive groups tend to interact more, agree more readily, and engender greater satisfaction. However, the degree to which cohesiveness determines actual task group productivity is less apparent.

Van Zelst (1952) reported that work teams of carpenters and bricklayers were more effective if they were grouped according to sociometric choice. Strupp and Hausmann (1953) reported a positive correlation between cohesiveness and the productivity of aircraft maintenance crews, while Hemphill and Sechrest (1952) reported a significant relation between sociometric ratings and actual bombing accuracy of B-29 air crews. However, Tziner and Vardi (1982) found no relationship between cohesiveness and the effectiveness of military tank crews. Terborg, Castore, and DeNinno (1976) had groups perform a three-person land surveying task and found that liking had no effect on group performance. Lodahl and Porter (1961) observed no relation between cohesiveness of airline maintenance shop crews and productivity. Some studies indicate that cohesiveness may even degrade group performance. Weick and Penner (1969) found interpersonal attraction to be inversely related to performance of laboratory teams. Finally, Roby (1952) reported sociometric ratings to be negatively related to performance scores of military crews.[4]

Two conclusions may be drawn from the preceding studies. First, the results are a maze of inconsistent findings. Even this brief review indicates that there is a discrepancy between what is intuitively assumed to be the case regarding cohesiveness and performance and what is empirically supported. Second, almost all studies use some measure of positive sentiment toward others in the group, or toward the group itself, as the index of cohesiveness.

One reason for the inconsistency of results in this area is the fact that cohesiveness is not a unitary concept, as it has at least in practice been treated (i.e., as interpersonal attraction). Feldman (1968) and others have lent empirical support to the notion that there are at least three major separate, identifiable dimensions of cohesiveness. Feldman distinguished between interpersonal integration (representing liking or attraction), functional integration (coordinated or interdependent task behavior), and normative integration (shared beliefs or normative consensus). Other researchers have identified similar dimensions; for example, Newcomb, Turner, and Converse (1965) identified these dimensions as mutual attraction, structural integration, and normativeness (see also Kanter, 1968; Tziner, 1982).

Furthermore, Ridgeway (1983) has argued that the type of group will determine which of these dimensions of cohesiveness is most relevant in terms of contributing to attainment of the group goal. For primary or social groups,

---

[4] Cohesiveness may also have negative effects when group norms do not support productivity, or when there is too much cohesiveness, (i.e., groupthink).

interpersonal integration will be most salient; for ideological or interest groups such as religious or political organizations, normative integration will be most relevant; and for task groups, functional integration will be most important. In fact, in a partial test of this hypothesis, Driskell and Salas (in press) found that functional integration (which they termed collective orientation—the degree to which group members are interdependent) determined task group productivity, while interpersonal attraction was unrelated to group effectiveness.

This view has two implications. First, cohesiveness is most accurately defined as a group property that binds members to the group, and which has three primary bases: mutual attraction, coordinated or interdependent behavior, and shared beliefs. Failures in past research to find a consistent relationship between cohesiveness and group performance stem, in part, from the failure to operationalize these other relevant dimensions of group cohesiveness. Second, in applying the concept of cohesiveness to groups, we must specify, not only the "type" of cohesiveness, but also the type of group. For some groups that encompass broad goals, such as military units, it is critical that all of these dimensions be emphasized. For example, a military team manager must be concerned with promoting positive interpersonal affect, ensuring collective or interdependent task behavior, and building normative consensus. For other task groups, such as the typical short-term, task-oriented, instrumental work teams, functional integration is likely to be more predictive of team effectiveness.

Brainstorming and Productivity

A. F. Osborn, an advertising executive, proposed the method of brainstorming as an effective means of enhancing the quantity and quality of ideas generated in groups (Osborn, 1957). The brainstorming technique requires group members to (a) express any idea that comes to mind, (b) not critically evaluate any ideas, (c) generate as great a number of ideas as possible, and (d) combine and revise these ideas to build new and creative solutions. According to Osborn, brainstorming groups had the potential to generate twice as many ideas as could be generated individually.

Since Osborn's proposal of the brainstorming technique, a number of studies have examined the hypothesis that brainstorming groups will outperform individuals. The consensus of researchers in this area is that brainstorming groups actually perform more poorly than a similar number of individuals working alone (e.g., Diehl & Stroebe, 1987; Casey, Gettys, & Pliske, 1984). The consensus among researchers notwithstanding, the popularity of brainstorming in government, business, and industry is anectdotally apparent to anyone who has ever served in the consultant's role outside academia. This robust, if misguided, popularity of brainstorming techniques in the applied community highlights the importance of determining the conditions that contribute to productivity loss in brainstorming groups.

Mullen, Johnson, and Salas (1989) have provided a meta-analytic integration of productivity loss in brainstorming groups, providing unequivocal evidence that nominal groups (composed of noninteracting individuals) do in fact outperform brainstorming groups. Further, they examined several likely mechanisms for this productivity loss in brainstorming groups. Mullen et al. identified three independent plausible classes of explanatory mechanisms for productivity loss in brainstorming groups. *Procedural* mechanisms derive from the nature of the procedure itself; for example, an individual may not be able to propose a good idea because of the high level of communication activity occurring in the brainstorming group (Lamm & Trommsdorf, 1973). *Social psychological* mechanisms are basic social processes engaged by the presence of the other people, such as drive-arousal (Zajonc, 1965; Geen & Bushman, 1987) or self-attention (Carver & Scheier, 1981; Mullen & Baumeister, 1987). Finally, *economic* mechanisms represent an intentional withdrawal of effort, such as social loafing (Latane, Williams, & Harkins, 1979). Results of the Mullen et al. meta-analysis were entirely inconsistent with economic mechanism explanations, marginally consistent with procedural mechanism explanations, and highly consistent with social psychological mechanism explanations. Therefore, the evidence indicates that social psychological mechanisms account for productivity loss in brainstorming groups to a greater degree than procedural or economic mechanisms.

In sum, this and other research disconfirms the "folk wisdom" that brainstorming is a productive means of generating creative ideas. However, given that the "brainstorming team" seems to be an ingrained tool in the business community, this research also suggests ways to make brainstorming more efficient. Imagine that we wish to maximize the effectiveness of brainstorming groups. The Mullen et al. results suggest that the operation of social psychological processes such as drive-arousal and self-attention account for most of the productivity loss in brainstorming groups. The applied researcher may be less successful if he or she were to implement an intervention in these groups to get members to work harder (an economic mechanism) or to communicate more efficiently (a procedural mechanism), than if he or she were to develop an intervention to lower the effects of arousal level or to increase self-attention (social psychological mechanisms). Further research is required to evaluate the effectiveness of these measures.

In sum, we have examined three areas in which small group research has served to clarify common, yet inaccurate "folk wisdom." Our purpose in briefly reviewing these topics is to illustrate the point that, while some research may indeed be trivial, in many cases research that addresses areas of seemingly common knowledge serves to revise or correct what we "know."[5] Because what

---

[5] We do not mean to imply that small group research provides an infallible path to the truth, or that all laboratory research functions to correct misperceptions. Indeed, in almost all research domains (such as the brainstorming literature), studies exist that demonstrate alternative and conflicting results, some claiming one type of outcome and some claiming another.

we intuitively believe to be the case often is not, these studies illustrate the value of examining the "obvious."

SUMMARY

In this chapter, we have attempted to examine the role of small group research in understanding real-world teams. In doing so, we have not attempted to catalog findings in the small group literature that are applicable to teams, but have tried to address the nature of small group research and the role of small group research in generating knowledge about teams. We have argued that the function of the typical experimental small group study is to test theory. This goal differs from that of research that attempts real-world applications or attempts to predict real-world behavior. Furthermore, criteria that are used to judge the value of applied research (i.e., that it mimic the real-world setting) often do not apply to small group research designed to test theory.

This is not meant to imply that the experimental small group researcher has carte blanche in the laboratory. There are a number of factors, such as experimenter effects, that limit the usefulness of this type of research. The experimenter is not exempt from the necessity of careful research design, precise measurement, and appropriate analysis of data. However, we maintain that the common complaints leveled at small group research are in most cases unfounded and based on a misunderstanding of the purposes of experimental research.

First, the laboratory is indeed a uniquely artificial environment. The laboratory does not even remotely resemble *any* real-world setting of which we are aware. Yet, for the purposes of testing theory, there is no setting more appropriate or well suited.

Second, because of the uniqueness of the laboratory situation, we agree that one cannot generalize the results of most small group research directly to the real world. However, we have argued that the proper role of this type of research is not to generalize to a concrete real-world setting, but to test and build theory. It is the theory that is applied to the real world, not the results of any particular study. It is one critical function of applied research to revise and refine the theory through the results of applications in real-world settings.

Third, small group research is abstract because it tests theories that are meant to be general. A theory of status and decision making does not apply only to the Navy; it may apply to any "hierarchically structured" organization. Again, it is one function of applied research to determine the limits of the theory and its applicability to the Navy environment.

Finally, small group research often belabors the obvious; however, this research sometimes results in small yet significant increments in our understanding of how groups and teams perform.

In sum, one type of research activity, which we believe represents the bulk of small group research, is to test hypotheses about the real world. However, the value of this research is often questioned because it is too artificial, results are not directly generalizable to real-world settings, it is too abstract, and findings are often commonplace. We have argued that these objections are in most cases misguided. To fault the researcher who performs this type of research because the laboratory setting in which it is conducted is artificial is tantamount to faulting a bullfrog because it cannot fly. The experimental small group researcher in most cases does not intend to create a "realistic" laboratory setting, no more than a bullfrog intends to sprout wings. Further, there is no one type of research or research strategy that holds the answer for understanding teams. We feel that advances in understanding team performance are most likely to result from the dynamic interplay between theory, research that tests theory, and applications.

REFERENCES

Back, K. W. (1951). Influence through social communication. *Journal of Abnormal and Social Psychology, 46*, 9–23.

Bavelas, A. (1950). Communication patterns in task-oriented groups. *Journal of the Acoustical Society of America, 22*, 725–730.

Berkowitz, L. (1957). Liking for the group and the perceived merit of the group's behavior. *Journal of Abnormal and Social Psychology, 54*, 353–357.

Campbell, D. T., & Stanley, J. C. (1967). *Experimental and quasi-experimental designs for research.* Chicago: Rand McNally.

Carver, C. S., & Scheier, M. F. (1981). *Attention and self-regulation: A control theory approach to human behavior.* New York: Springer-Verlag.

Casey, J. T., Gettys, C. F., & Pliske, R. M. (1984). A partition of small group predecision performance into informational and social components. *Organizational Behavior and Human Performance, 34*, 112–139.

Curtis, R. C., & Miller, K. (1986). Believing another likes or dislikes you: Behaviors making the beliefs come true. *Journal of Personality and Social Psychology, 51*, 284–290.

Diehl, M., & Stroebe, W. (1987). Productivity loss in brainstorming groups: Toward the solution of a riddle. *Journal of Personality and Social Psychology, 53*, 497–509.

Driskell, J. E., & Salas, E. (1991). Group decision-making under stress. *Journal of Applied Psychology, 76*, 473–478.

Driskell, J. E., & Salas, E. (in press). Collective behavior and team performance. *Human Factors.*

Driskell, J. E., & Olmstead, B. (1989). Psychology and the military: Research applications and trends. *American Psychologist, 44*, 43–54.

Druckman, D., & Swets, J. A. (Eds.). (1988). *Enhancing human performance: Issues, theories, and techniques.* Washington, DC: National Academy Press.

Durkheim, E. (1893). *The division of labor in society.* New York: Macmillan.

Exline, R. V. (1957). Group climate as a factor in the relevance and accuracy of social perception. *Journal of Abnormal and Social Psychology, 55*, 382–388.

Feldman, R. A. (1968). Interrelationships among three bases of group integration. *Sociometry, 31,* 30–46.

Festinger, L., Schachter, S., & Back, K. (1950). *Social pressures in informal groups.* New York: Harper.

Forsyth, D. R. (1990). *Group dynamics.* Pacific Grove, CA: Brooks/Cole.

Foushee, H. C., & Helmreich, R. L. (1988). Group interaction and flight crew performance. In E. L. Wiener & D. C. Nagel (Eds.), *Human factors in aviation* (pp. 189–227). San Diego: Academic Press.

Geen, R. G., & Bushman, B. J. (1987). Drive theory: Effects of socially engendered arousal. In B. Mullen & G. R. Goethals (Eds.), *Theories of group behavior.* New York: Springer-Verlag.

Golembiewski, R. T. (1962). *The small group: An analysis of research concepts and operations.* Chicago: University of Chicago Press.

Hemphill, J. K., & Sechrest, L. (1952). A comparison of three criteria of air crew effectiveness in combat over Korea. *American Psychologist, 7,* 391. (Abstract)

Henshel, R. L. (1980). The purposes of laboratory experimentation and the virtues of deliberate artificiality. *Journal of Experimental Social Psychology, 16,* 466–478.

Hertzler, J. O. (1940). Crises and dictatorships. *American Sociological Review, 5,* 157–169.

Higgins, R. L., & Marlatt, G. A. (1973). Effects of anxiety arousal on the consumption of alcohol by alcoholics and social drinkers. *Journal of Consulting and Clinical Psychology, 41,* 426–433.

Ilgen, D. R. (1986). Laboratory research: A question of when, not if. In E. A. Locke (Ed.), *Generalizing from laboratory to field settings.* Lexington, MA: Lexington Books.

Kanter, R. M. (1968). Commitment and social organization: A study of commitment mechanisms in utopian organizations. *American Sociological Review, 33,* 499–517.

Lamm, H., & Trommsdorf, G. (1973). Group versus individual performance on tasks requiring ideational proficiency (brainstorming). *European Journal of Social Psychology, 3,* 361–387.

Latane, B., Williams, K., & Harkins, S. (1979). Many hands made light the work: The causes and consequences of social loafing. *Journal of Personality and Social Psychology, 37,* 822–832.

Levine, J. M., & Moreland, R. L. (1990). Progress in small group research. *Annual Review of Psychology, 41,* 585–634.

Lodahl, T. M., & Porter, L. W. (1961). Psychometric score patterns, social characteristics, and productivity of small industrial work groups. *Journal of Applied Psychology, 45,* 73–79.

Lott, A. J., & Lott, B. E. (1961). Group cohesiveness, communication level, and conformity. *Journal of Abnormal and Social Psychology, 62,* 408–412.

Mackie, R. R. (1987). Vigilance research-Are we ready for countermeasures? *Human Factors, 29,* 707–723.

Marquis, D. G., Guetzkow, H., & Heyns, R. W. (1951). A social psychological study of the decision-making conference. In H. Guetzkow (Ed.), *Groups, leadership, and men* (pp. 55–67). Pittsburgh: Carnegie Press.

Mook, D. G. (1983). In defense of external invalidity. *American Psychologist, 38,* 379–387.

Mullen, B., & Baumeister, R. F. (1987). Group effects on self-attention and performance: Social loafing, social facilitation, and social impairment. In C. Hendrick (Ed.), *Review of personality and social psychology.* Beverly Hills, CA: Sage.

Newcomb, T. M., Turner, R., & Converse, P. E. (1965). *Social psychology: The study of human interaction.* New York: Holt.

Orne, M. T. (1969). Demand characteristics and the concept of quasi-controls. In R. Rosenthal & R. Rosnow (Eds.), *Artifact in behavioral research.* New York: Academic Press.

Osborn, A. F. (1957). *Applied imagination.* New York: Scribner.

Ridgeway, C. L. (1983). *The dynamics of small groups.* New York: St. Martin's.

Roby, T. B. (1952). The influence of subgroup relationships on the performance of group and subgroup tasks. *American Psychologist, 7,* 313–314. (Abstract).

Ross, E. A. (1908). *Social psychology.* New York: Macmillan.

Staw, B. M., Sandelands, L. E., & Dutton, J. E. (1981). Threat-rigidity effects in organizational behavior: A multi-level analysis. *Administrative Science Quarterly, 26,* 501–524.

Strupp, H. H., & Hausman, H. J. (1953). Some correlates of group productivity. *American Psychologist, 8,* 443–444.

Terborg, J. R., Castore, C., & DeNinno, J. A. (1976). A longitudinal investigation of the impact of group composition on group performance and cohesion. *Journal of Personality and Social Psychology, 34,* 782–790.

Triplett, N. (1898). The dynamogenic factors in pacemaking and competition. *American Journal of Psychology, 9,* 507–533.

Tziner, A. (1982). Differential effects of group cohesiveness types: A clarifying overview. *Society for Personality Research, 10,* 227–239.

Tziner, A., & Vardi, Y. (1982). Effects of command style and group cohesiveness on the performance of self-selected tank crews. *Journal of Applied Psychology, 67,* 769–775.

Van Zelst, R. H. (1952). Sociometrically selected work teams increase production. *Personnel Psychology, 5,* 175–186.

Vancouver, J. B., & Ilgen, D. R. (1989). Effects of interpersonal orientation and the sex-type of the task on choosing to work alone or in groups. *Journal of Applied Psychology, 74,* 927–934.

Webster, M., & Kervin, J. B. (1971). Artificiality in experimental sociology. *Canadian Review of Sociology and Anthropology, 8,* 263–272.

Weick, K. E., & Penner, D. D. (1969). Discrepant membership as an occasion for effective cooperation. *Sociometry, 32,* 413–424.

Worchel, S., Andreoli, V. A., & Folger, R. (1977). Intergroup cooperation and intergroup attraction: The effect of previous interaction and outcome of combined effort. *Journal of Experimental Social Psychology, 13,* 131–140.

Zajonc, R. B. (1965). Social facilitation. *Science, 149,* 269–274.

Zelditch, M. (1968). Can you really study an army in the laboratory? In A. Etzioni (Ed.), *Complex organizations: A sociological reader.* New York: Holt.

Part II
THE RESEARCH BASE

6

Cognitive Complexity and Team Decision Making

Siegfried Streufert and Glenda Nogami

SCIENTIFIC ANALYSES OF TEAM DECISION MAKING

Many important decisions are made by teams, that is, by groups of goal-oriented and motivated individuals that are assembled to deal with a specific problem or a specific range of problems. Organizations use teams to decide on new products, new employees, new marketing strategies. Military organizations use teams to plan, initiate, and coordinate battles. Presidential teams make decisions or provide decision options that determine reactions to international crises. Teams vary in their composition, in their expertise, in their freedom to act, their goals, and more; yet all tend to prepare or make decisions. Some decisions are later classified as excellent. Others result in utter failure or, at least, in undesirable consequences. Yet others allow the organization to "get by."

Decisions are often delegated to teams because those responsible believe that team decisions have advantages over individual decisions. In other cases, teams of advisers are provided for individual decision makers. Appointment of a team reflects the "hope" that the team will be better equipped to handle difficult tasks than any one individual would be. Why, then, are some teams so utterly ineffective? Despite thousands of studies on group or team performance (cf. reviews by Finstuen, 1983; Hare, 1972; McGrath & Altman, 1966), we are not yet sure. Should we be pessimistic? Some writers would argue that pessimism is premature. For example, Hackman and Morris (1983) believe that more optimal team decision making might be achieved by procedures designed to improve the interaction process in group functioning. Streufert and Swezey (1986) have suggested improvements based on a complexity theory approach to decision making. These, as well as some other writers, have pointed toward a range of techniques that might aid us in a better understanding of team decision making.

The present chapter focuses on one of these techniques: the application of complexity theory to the analysis, prediction, and training of team decision making. First, however, we will examine some more basic questions about team functioning. Are we, with today's knowledge, able to understand the processes underlying team decision making? Do we need teams, or should decisions be made by individuals or by computers? The answers to questions of this kind provide a few of the various reasons why a complexity-based approach to team decision making has considerable value.

The Level of Analysis

Before we can generate major improvements of team decision making in today's complex world, we need to better understand how groups function. We also need to know more about decision-making processes, especially those involving high levels of problem complexity. The vast majority of controlled research efforts employing designs that assure accuracy of interpretation have focused on relatively simple team functions. Others, sometimes involving more complex task settings, have restricted their views to a minimum number of variables. In contrast, observational procedures have provided a rich source of data that, however, rarely aid us in inference of causality (Streufert & Streufert, 1969, 1981).

Ideally, we would want researchers and theorists to predict in advance what kind of team characteristics would produce optimal decisions. We want to be certain that the data on which we base our predictions have been obtained by the best means our science has to offer. Based on those data, we would tell practitioners in government, in industry, in the military, and elsewhere *how* to approach decision-making situations. Clearly, we are not yet able to attain such a goal with today's knowledge. But will our science ever allow us to achieve such a lofty goal?

Scientists tend to prefer neat and simple explanations of phenomena under their investigation. That desire for simplicity is often thwarted by the object of interest: Unfortunately, the world under scrutiny is anything but simple. Of course, one can make the assumption that the apparent complexity is merely the sum of simple interrelationships among specifiable variables. However, even if, in the final analysis (if we are capable of it), all complex events would turn out to be orderly and would reflect joint effects of multiple but nonetheless simple variable relationships; even if we discovered the specific numerical values and formulas that would control multiple interrelationships, we may still lack the capacity to make reliable recommendations. Our understanding may be limited by the sheer number of variable interactions involved.

Our inability to comprehend complexity has led to a desire for simplicity of scientific statement. Some years ago, this desire produced a movement toward "infinite regress." Fortunately, we are no longer searching for utter simplicity. Nonetheless, where observed complexity suggests that multiple factors contribute to specific phenomena of interest, we still tend to limit our views to only a few antecedents and consequences of phenomena under study. In some cases, we attempt to overcome these limits by developing contingency theories (e.g., Fiedler, 1964); in others we tend to ignore many variables which may have distinct effects upon the phenomenon under study.

Organizations and their teams function in a myriad of (even if only slightly) different ways and generate a diversity of outputs (products, services, communications, implicit and explicit aggressive and cooperative actions, and much more). Individuals and teams inside and outside the organization are variously affected by the functioning and the "actions" of these organizations. Can we capture the many aspects of organizational and team behavior in reliable scientific statements? To what extent (up to what level) could we hope to conceptualize, understand, and communicate the potential complexity of those statements? If we could comprehend the complexity, would such statements hold only "now" and be obsolete tomorrow (cf. Gergen, 1973)? Without question, the limits of our present understanding continue to hamper us as we attempt to understand and communicate about the functioning of organizations and their components, including the functioning of organizational decision-making teams.

MODELS OF TEAM DECISION MAKING

If we don't know how to do something, we tend to search for someone who can. Someone else does the serious plumbing in our homes; another person may take care of electrical problems, fix the roof, and so forth. It is not different where our concerns focus on scientific analysis. If we don't comprehend some phenomenon in our science, we try to find someone who does. If we don't understand the multiple interactions among variables that represent the functioning of decision making in teams, to whom can we turn? Some believe that the solution can be found in a model of the system under study, often a model played out on a computer.

Indeed, it would be nice if we could "model" and, consequently, predict future team decisions on the basis of parameters generated by an understanding of the team's past decisions (or, better, decisions made by multiple generic teams). It may be even better if decisions of individuals and teams could be accurately described by some mathematical model (for example, one that could be simulated on a computer, e.g., Keen & Scott-Morton, 1978). Of course, we can build such models, and we can construct associated computer simulations. Several theorists and researchers have chosen this approach. However, despite valiant efforts, the predictive capacity of computer-based models continues to remain limited. In part, the limits may reflect the hardware restrictions of most current computer systems and their available software: Human decisions are not restricted to the binary choices generally made by computers. Rather, human cognitive efforts and their consequences often reflect comparisons among the magic "seven" options (Miller, 1956; Streufert & Swezey, 1986). In another part, the limitations of existing computer software may be due to our inability to specify the joint impact of all of the salient variables in all relevant situations for different kinds of organizations.

We *might* be able to construct computers which better emulate human functioning in the future. We may even be able to build software systems that make optimal use of that hardware. However, even then our models will likely be restricted in their depth. There are at least two reasons: (a) we would find it difficult to identify each event that may contribute to organizational or team functioning and, because of our own cognitive limitations, we may find it impossible to transmit the high-level interactions among team decision phenomena to the software that has to operate the computer simulation; (b) the direction of fluidity (change) in the system to be modeled may not be predictable in advance. In other words, it remains in question whether the kind of "scientific" order that we assume to prevail at any one point in time is subject to change over time.

In conclusion, when we wish to predict team decision making in organizations, we are attempting to deal with an extremely complex phenomenon. Despite volumes of research on groups and teams, we still possess insufficient knowledge about team decision making. There seems to be relatively little hope that we can attain a complete understanding in the very near future. If meaningful applications are to be achieved, they will have to depend on a somewhat different approach to the problem at hand.

A FOCUS ON COGNITIVE STRUCTURE: THE EFFECTS OF COMPLEXITY

If model building is not (yet) helpful, it may be necessary to explore in greater detail "what" and "how" human decision makers think and how these thought processes affect team functioning. Any future model, whether or not played out on some computer system, may have to incorporate the processes we would discover.

Even a cursory consideration of teams points to a wide array of phenomena that likely affect team functioning. For example, there are interpersonal attitudes, attributions, task characteristics, stressor levels, leadership styles, group composition factors, environmental variables, satisfaction, and on and on and on.

The reader of a handbook on organizational effectiveness, of a volume on group dynamics, of organizational psychology or sociology, of management styles, and of the wide range of popular books written for managers during the last decade will find a multitude of concepts that relate to team decision making. Indeed, some of those concepts duplicate each other or use different names for the same phenomenon; other concepts may overlap to some extent. There are many clearly and some not quite so clearly defined variables which have some interactive impact upon team decision making. How can we, as scientists who wish to understand causal relationships, achieve a better understanding of team functioning?

One path toward a solution is a change in approach. Prior efforts have generally limited the number of variables under investigation. For example, some researchers have studied satisfaction with team decisions, others have considered attitudes among team members, yet others have focused on the decision outcome, and so forth. Rather than a focus on only a few "content" components of the team decision making process, we might employ a structural basis for our efforts. Where *cognitive structure* is concerned with *how* information is processed, *content* refers to *what* decision makers think, what specific actions they engage in, and so forth (Streufert & Swezey, 1986).

Analyses based on cognitive structure were initially applied to cognitions of individuals (cf. Messick & Associates, 1976); i.e., the analyses focused on their characteristic manner of organizing and processing human experience (e.g., thoughts, information, actions, and so forth). In the application to groups and teams (cf. Streufert & Swezey, 1986), one structural approach based on complexity theory considers *how* the team processes information, i.e., how existing views and conceptions of a team interact with input toward a greater understanding, toward the development of modified or new conclusions and actions. A major advantage of a complexity-based analysis is the ability to *simultaneously* consider a large number of different aspects of team functioning. The complexity approach achieves this capacity because of a different level of analysis. For example, rather than evaluating team competence in some relevant domain, or rather than delving into the beliefs the team has about competitors, complexity-based analysis might consider how existing beliefs control aspects of competence that are utilized to counter the actions of competitors. In other words, the analysis avoids a focus on the specific content of team functioning (e.g., it will only be indirectly concerned with attitudes, leadership role, attributions of intent, and the many other phenomena that are part of the interaction among team members or are part of the functioning of the team as a whole).

The complexity approach to team decision making considers how the team uses many content factors as it engages in the task effort. Structural complexity includes process variables but is not limited to them. The complexity approach is greatly concerned with the *impact* of decisions made by the team, the interplay of decisions, the consequences of these decisions, *and* the team processes that follow the receipt of resulting (subsequent) information (e.g., the team's view of its impact upon the task environment).

To focus on complexity variables, we need not leave our understanding of "content" knowledge behind. For that matter, content (specific actions, attitudes, etc.) remains important; for example, the complexity approach would consider how the content of an attitude is used (but not, for structural purposes, what that content might be). This shift in orientation allows us to focus upon multiple "content" variables within a single framework; i.e., we need not study each of them separately.

The complexity approach to human functioning is by no means new. Earlier theorists (including Harvey, Hunt, & Schroder, 1961; Schroder, Driver, & Streufert, 1967; Scott, Osgood, & Peterson, 1979; Streufert & Streufert, 1978) have formulated various versions of a "complexity theory" that employs variables based on cognitive structure as predictors of human and group (team) functioning. Many writers of organizational theory have (often unknowingly) employed concepts inherent in complexity theory in the past. In a multidimensional analysis of organizational terminology, Swezey, Streufert, and Mietus (1983) found that the largest factor describing relevant phenomena (as reflected in organizational terminology) is relevant to structural complexity rather than to content. While lower order factors emphasized terms that involve content variables (e.g., components of leadership, of power, communication, conflict, and so forth), the highest order factor was defined by terms such as *integration, complexity, differentiation, decision making, information, input, sensing, simplicity,* and *environment.* These descriptors represent, in effect, defining components or primary variables employed by the complexity theories, i.e., theories that emphasize the study of "how" a decision-making team functions rather than "what" decisions the team makes (Streufert & Streufert, 1978; Streufert & Swezey, 1986).

WHY TEAM DECISION MAKING?

Before we delve into a complexity-theory-based analysis of team decision making, we should ask ourselves whether the effort will be worth our while. Should we be concerned with team decision making? Should decisions be made by teams in the first place? Should we replace the team with something that can do the job better, whatever that something may turn out to be? More precisely, should decisions be left to individuals or even to computer systems?

Computer-Aided Decision Making

Let us initially consider the easier of the two questions: can we replace the team with a computer that would assist an "optimal" individual or could the computer even replace the entire team? We have already considered computer modeling and have found the approach lacking, at least for the present. However, teams are prone to errors, just as computer models are not yet perfect. Which of the two would be preferable?

There certainly have been theorists and researchers who were quite enamored of computer-based decision making, both at the level of the individual and at the level of the team. Since teams are made up of individuals, let us first consider whether a computer might be able to accurately simulate (or, ideally, improve upon) the functioning of an individual decision maker. Certainly the computer is (unless there is a brown-out or an error in a circuit board) not going to be irrational, something the decision maker may well be. Nonetheless, until computers can, at least, reliably beat chess masters at their game, we cannot yet hope for much computer-based improvement upon human functioning. But can a computer at least parallel the actions of a superior human decision maker?

Modeling individual decision making. Simulating the performance of an individual may be difficult: As research by M. B. Jones at Pennsylvania State University College of Medicine (personal communication, October 16, 1989) has pointed out, the performance of any individual is characterized by a great deal of (apparent) error variance; that is, a simulation of that person's performance would involve a reasonable amount of variable error. This variable error may, however, not necessarily be error in the true sense (e.g., variable faulty behavior). Rather it may reflect error of measurement because the observer is unable to interpret (know) the meaningfulness of the action(s) involved. Such "errors," especially if they reflect salient but unknown meaningful (or even "rational") functions, make the construction of a predictive computer decision model difficult or impossible.

Moreover, as Streufert and Swezey (1986) have pointed out, computer-based models do not and cannot (at present) represent human or team functioning whenever decision making does not follow the supposed "rational" and/or the "dialectic choice" systems that are typically used by computer-based decision processes. Computer systems and software existing today are generally built to pick alternative (and possibly interactive) decision sequences from given alternatives. However, the real-world options among which choices must be made are often unknown in advance, resulting in levels of discontinuity and uncertainty that are not represented in concurrent computer systems (cf. Wohl, 1981) and their software.

By taking change into account (i.e., via the development of new concepts that interact with incoming information), decision makers tend to stay abreast of changing task demands. From the vantage point of standard computer based technology which operates on preexisting options, these decision makers or decision-making teams are *not* functioning rationally. On the basis of similar observations, Peters and Waterman (1982) have concluded that human decision makers tend to be "irrational" but that irrationally led organizations tend to perform better than rationally led organizations.

At first view, terms like *error variance* or *irrationality* tend to suggest poor performance. Indeed, such a negative evaluation of observed irrationality may be quite inaccurate. Part of the reason why scientists refer to unexplained behaviors as "error variance" and "irrationality" may be due to a lack of prior research emphasis on structural complexity variables. Approaches inherent in complexity theory tend to predict a range of previously unexplained variations in behavior. Based on the tenets of complexity theory, Peters and Waterman would no longer have to classify many successful decision makers as "irrational." Their behavior, in many cases, now makes excellent sense.

For example, where diverse sets of information are *integrated* in ways that are not emulated by computer systems, they may produce conclusions that cannot be directly deduced from that information. A form of "induction" or "integration" has replaced deduction. To the computer system, the obtained conclusions would appear irrational (we will deal with the effects of integration as part of structure in greater detail below).

Modeling group or team decision making. Computer modeling of group functioning has not fared much better than modeling of individuals. Part of the difficulties are generated by the typical approach chosen by those interested in modeling (which again tends to fit the capacity of computer systems but not necessarily the characteristics of teams, i.e., the assumed choice among discrete consecutive options following a dialectic tree path toward one or several goals). Poole (1983) has argued persuasively that such traditional models of group decision making are inadequate. In that author's view, earlier attempts should be replaced by more complex models of "continuously developing threads of activity." Effective computer models representing such an approach are, however, not yet available.

Computer-assisted decision making. Of course, a computer system might be used to *assist* a decision maker or a decision team in arriving at a more appropriate selection of options. Such systems have been designed to represent the prototypical management consultant (Holt, 1988), to enhance communications among team members (Barefoot, Wiggins, Harper, & Peterson, 1985), or to assist military commanders in battlefield settings (Bowyer, 1983). They may operate at a rather simple level of information retrieval or at a much more complex level (e.g., make action recommendations). At their present stage of development, however, computer-assisted decision aids tend to be more useful as simple tools; their capacity to aid a decision-making team in a complex and fluid environment has yet to be proven. Research has generally shown that decisions made with the aid of a computer "assistant" are not appreciably different from those made by teams which had not been provided with computer assistance (e.g., Bowyer, 1983; Driscoll & King, 1988; Hugues & Webb, 1987). Obviously, considerable additional research and development is needed before computers will be sufficiently helpful (Weisband, Linville, Liebhaber, Obermayer, & Fallesen, 1988) or, for that matter, before we can decide whether the computer system will be adaptable to the team decision making task. For the present, at least, computers are not able to develop the "cognitive complexity" that aids individuals and teams in their decision making task.

Team or Individual?

Another question involves the team vs. the individual. When do teams make better decisions? When would individuals do equally well or better? In many situations, of course, the sheer volume of effort inherent in a decision-making task requires the simultaneous and coordinated action of many individuals. In some cases, we could not even do without teams if we tried. If our organization represented a football team, we could hardly expect a single player on our side to take on the entire team on the other. But, if single decisions are to be made and if these decisions need not be made under time pressure, does one need a team, or would an individual do a better job?

Early theorists and researchers generally accorded group solutions a higher value than individual solutions (e.g., Shaw, 1932). After all, if an identifiably "correct" solution is sought, the probability of a group-based solution is greater, since only one team member needs to discover the appropriate answer to the problem (Taylor, 1954; Lorge & Solomon, 1955; later referred to as "truth wins" by Steiner, 1972). The larger the team, the more likely it will be that someone will come up with the insight that represents the "truth." However, not all task situations fit the "truth wins" paradigm. Interestingly enough, even if they do, the group does not always do a better job (Davis, 1969).

The research literature from group dynamics and from management would suggest that team decisions tend to be generally better than individual decisions, *but* that team decisions are often less good than decisions made by the *best* team member (Tindale & Davis, 1983). Then why not hire the optimal person and let him or her do the job?

If we wished to proceed in that direction, would we know who the best person for the job might be? On what basis could we make such a choice? Certainly we would have to consider both content *and* complexity variables. We would want to assure that adequate knowledge exists, that the person's views of the task environment are appropriate, and so on; we would want to make sure that the content of the individual's thought or functioning is appropriate. We also would want to make sure that the decision maker is maximally capable of processing all relevant information in the most optimal way, for example, strategically where appropriate or decisively where decisions must be made immediately. In other words, we would want to make sure that adequate competence in the realm of structural complexity exists.

Some multiple competencies might be carried out by a single person. But for others we might need several team members. Situational demands do not necessarily remain constant and stable. Any decision-making task that can be easily handled by one individual at one point in time may overwhelm the same individual as load, task complexity, uncertainty, and fluidity increase. Another individual, or a set of individuals functioning as a team, may be more adequately equipped to deal with the changed task environment.

Dealing with greater load, with multiple task complexity, with increasing uncertainty and fluidity (discontinuity), requires more than any fixed "rational" system can accomplish, no matter whether that system is a computer or whether it is the best trained, most motivated and highly intelligent decision maker. We must make sure that enough capacity is present to handle the potential task complexity. In such situations, we may need a team rather than a single individual. Without question, we need an individual or, better, a team that can function along the principles described by complexity theory. Let us focus on some of the tenets of that theory at this point. Subsequently, we will consider how complexity-based training can improve effectiveness of decision-making teams.

COMPLEXITY THEORY

We are concerned with decision making by individuals and teams, such as, task-oriented small groups. To clearly understand their functioning, we need to know and understand actors' motives, their intent, and their goals. Secondly, we need to come to grips with the information an individual or a team has available, that is, with the (developing) comprehension of a problem at hand. We should know the decision makers' attitudes, the cognitive style they are using to deal with problems, and more.

Typically, research or observational efforts can approximate an understanding of some of these phenomena, yet we most often will find it difficult to gain a complete overview. As Brehmer (1984) has pointed out: We are attempting to resolve a single equation with several unknowns.

Our explanatory and predictive views of individual or team behavior tend to assume orderliness of the underlying scientific logic in the relationships among elements, in flux across time, and in rationality of human (or team) functioning (cf. Allison, 1971). Rationality, in turn, assumes (as discussed earlier) that behavior functions in a predictable way (e.g., that a team would behave in the future as it has in the past, or as other teams have behaved, and that the team would optimize its outcomes in some mathematically calculable fashion). Such optimizations would, of course, require that meaningful predictions of future events or outcomes are possible, that uncertainty is minimized, and that the complexity of a task environment (and its important elements) does not exceed the mental processing capacities of (co-acting and/or interacting) team members. Unfortunately, all of these conditions for a perfect theory of team decision making cannot be satisfied. Both limitations in the functioning of the team (and its members) and in the capacity of the observers stand in the way.

We have learned to understand that human and team judgments based on probabilistic functioning do not follow the rules of probability (Tversky & Kahneman, 1974). We know that people are "satisficers" and not "optimizers" (Simon, 1953). An even cursory review of political history tells us that decision-making teams, even in the presence of all the relevant information, often fail to make optimal decisions. In other words, we must share the problems the mathematical modelers have encountered when they tried to develop paradigms: People and teams simply don't behave like they "should" behave.

Indeed, we may be able to predict a team's decisions where a problem is exceedingly simple. We often (but not always) can assume that a team would prefer to make a decision involving low risk that is associated with potentially highly favorable consequences rather than a high-risk decision that might produce only mildly favorable outcomes. However, as the team's task situation becomes more and more complex and uncertain, as risk to gain ratios become smaller, as actions may result in mixed gains and losses, our rationality-based assumptions often turn out to be faulty. What should we do?

Our prediction (even if it is imperfect) of team decision making must have a somewhat different point of departure. Obviously it is not possible (at this juncture) to predict a multitude of isolated events in the life of a decision-making team. We might try to approach the problem of team decision making from a somewhat different point of view. A number of prior attempts in that direction have been published. For example, Dawes (1976) argued that prediction can be based on a "shallow psychology of cognitive processes." Brehmer (1984) developed an alternate view from Hammond, Stewart, Brehmer, and Seinmann's (1975) social judgment theory. The present chapter approaches the problem in yet a different way, one that might be considered 90 degrees shifted from most prior attempts to understand and predict each decision that would be made by a team. Based on complexity theory, we intend to view the team as a structural system which interacts with team members, with information, with prior decisions, with their consequences, and more.

Yet before we delve into the complexity-based analysis of team decision making, we should be aware of some special (peculiar?) characteristics of groups and teams. Unlike early writers like Durkheim (1898), we will not invest the team with a personality that is different from that of its members. Allport (1924) has already shown that the group will not do what its individual members cannot do. Nonetheless, there are characteristics of an interacting assembly of persons that influence what the group or team may do. Some of the consequences may be valuable; others can be undesirable.

A number of distinct "team"- or "group"-based behaviors that are not (or rarely) measured in individuals have been observed. To save space, we will mention only two examples: *choice shift* and *group-think*. Indeed, the choice shift phenomenon no longer has the stature of a major discrepancy between group and individual functioning (since Pruitt, 1971a,b, demonstrated measurement confounds). Nonetheless, there is still some evidence of meaningful choice shifts toward greater riskiness that cannot be explained as artifact. At the minimum, interaction among team members allows behaviors (and decisions) to emerge that might otherwise be dormant. A related example of a unique group effect is defined as *group polarization* (e.g., Burnstein & Schul, 1983). However the most interesting phenomenon which appears to emerge *only* with the existence of a group or team may be group-think.

Janis (e.g., 1972, 1983) has written extensively about group-think, a failure of the group or team to arrive at adequate decisions. Apparently the phenomenon originates in good part because consensus (*concurrence-seeking*) can become sufficiently important to the team to diminish adequate functioning in the decision-making realm. Janis provides a number of examples from the (rather easily observable) political field, where groups of advisors have failed to provide reasonable suggestions to central decision makers in the past. Among the examples are teams that recommended such decisions as England's appeasement of Hitler in the 1930s, Truman's escalation of the war in Korea, Kennedy's Bay of Pigs invasion, and Johnson's escalation of the war in Vietnam. One might add Japan's decision to meet the American fleet near Midway. In all cases, advisors disregarded salient information that predicted failure.

The group-think views of Janis have, at least, received partial support from data in a number of research publications based, generally, on small group functioning in the laboratory (e.g., Callaway & Esser, 1984; Hensley & Griffin, 1986; Moorhead & Montanari, 1986). Stress experience may further increase group-think: Members of a threatened group may attempt to recreate a sense of normalcy by even greater emphasis on "getting along (i.e., agreeing) with each other."

Janis (1983) suggests that a number of conditions must hold for decision-making teams to function optimally (and avoid group-think): A number of alternative actions must be considered; the needed range of objectives and their values should be assessed; costs, risks, and potential consequences of each decision alternative must be evaluated; new relevant information should be obtained; additional information must be considered and, where useful, utilized, even if it disagrees with extant views; and potential positive and negative consequences of all options must then be reexamined in the light of new information, even those rejected earlier. Finally, implementations and contingencies in case of undesirable consequences must be included in plans. While Janis is not phrasing these "ideals" in the terminology of complexity theory, many of them reflect or, at least, represent consequences of team information processing described by that theory. As was evident in the multidimensional analysis of terminology from organizational psychology (Swezey et al., 1983), the complexity-based approach appears to be a quite powerful predictor of optimal team functioning. In contrast, the "simplification" of team information processing generated by choice shifts or group-think tends to diminish team effectiveness.

In other words, an implementation of suggestions for more optimal team decision making suggested by various authors such as Hackman and Morris (1983) or Janis (1983) can, in good part, be achieved through a complexity-based approach. Complexity theory is relevant to both individuals (Streufert & Streufert, 1978) and to their purposeful associations, that is, to teams and organizations (Streufert & Swezey, 1986). True, the "cognition" of individuals is not the same as group-based verbal or written interaction among team members who may be presenting ideas for discussion or implementation. Nonetheless, similar principles are at work (cf. Streufert & Swezey, 1986). While this chapter is insufficient in length to describe all aspects of the complexity approach to cognitive structure, some of the concepts and their applications will be briefly reviewed.

The two most basic relevant components of team functioning are "differentiation" and "integration." Both apply to the information acquisition process, to team interaction, to information processing by the team, and to decision making, decision monitoring, and adjustment of prior actions following outcome feedback. Other concepts included in the complexity approach to team decision making include adaptive flexibility, capacity for both closure and openness, creativity, and more. Since more extensive definitions of the relevant terms can be found in Streufert and Swezey (1986), only a short description will be provided here. The interested reader who needs greater detail is referred to the prior book.

Differentiation. The term reflects the process of dividing the conceptual space of the team (or of team members) into two or more orthogonal or oblique bipolar dimensions, systems, or subsystems. Ordering requires relative intransitivity. For example, the team may view an opponent organization's strategy separately from the primary intent of that opponent. Both may be responded to disparately.

Dimension. The term implies a conceptual bipolar scale employed by the team (or team members). Dimensions allow the ordering of information, ideas, attitudes, concepts, events, etc. along points of a bipolar continuum. The location of, for example, an attitude on an evaluative dimension would reflect the (attitudinal) content orientation of the individual (or group of team members) involved. If differentiation occurs, ordering of the same information will differ from dimension to dimension. A differentiated (and potentially integrated) view may be described as "multidimensional."

Integration. Integrative functioning implies diversely organized (interrelated) differentiated stimulus configurations which had been (partially) represented on at least two or more intransitive dimensions in the cognitive space of a team (or any of its members). Joint (interactive) consideration of multiple dimensions would (interactively) produce conclusions, outcomes, or other group (or group-member) generated events that combine the impact of two or more content-based views or orientations. Integration must be preceded by differentiation (although the differentiative effort might have been achieved by another person or team). For example, a team (see above) which viewed a competitive organization's strategy as separate from intent might not just have responded to each of the two separately. Rather (via the integrative process), they might have considered to what extent the opponent's strategic actions did reflect intent, and whether, responding in a specific way, they might adjust the opponent's intent (e.g., by allowing that opponent to "save face") to achieve a satisfactory outcome for both parties.

Flexible integration. Integration can be either flexible or hierarchical. The term *flexible integration* implies a varied and, from time to time, changing (fluid) relationship among dimensions and their component information, ideas, concepts or events. As events change, as new information becomes available, as team conceptualizations or needs are modified, information, etc., can be *re*integrated to permit *new* (changed, more adaptive) functioning. Flexible integration is of particular value in complex, fluid situations where outcomes are uncertain and outcome monitoring with associated decision adjustment may be required.

Hierarchical integration. Here the relationship among dimensions and their components, once established, remains fixed. As a result, specific stimuli, events, team member actions, etc., if repeated, would be interpreted identically (on the basis of the joint impact of multiple differentiated dimensions) and, consequently, would always affect team functioning in the same way.

Strategic capacity. The capacity to employ differentiation and integration in the pursuit of team goals. Team decisions would likely address relatively well-defined short-term goals, which, in turn, would provide the preconditions for the accomplishment of more vaguely defined longer term goals, and so forth. Higher levels of strategic capacity imply (where needed) a *stepwise* and generally *multiple* complex of actions toward intended outcomes that are less and less specifically stated the more distant their intended achievement is placed into the future. Higher levels of strategic capacity tend to require higher levels of flexible integration.

Capacity for closure. An ability to adapt action(s) to situational demands of the moment, for example, to engage in strategic planning where adequate time is available, but to close for decisive action when immediate responding to events is required to avert serious problems. This capacity includes the ability to "reopen" for strategic planning as problem situations have been resolved.

THE APPLICATION OF COMPLEXITY VARIABLES TO TEAM DECISION MAKING

Complexity theory variables provide much of the basis for effective team functioning. As already suggested, Janis's (1983) list of requirements for optimal team functioning includes several aspects that are furthered by differentiation, integration, and so forth. Janis argues that the team should canvass a wide range of alternatives and weigh the costs, drawbacks, and risks generated by each alternative. Such processes, to be optimal, require differentiation among alternatives. On another point Janis states that the team should consider new information or expert judgment—even if it conflicts with previously established views. In this case, both openness and integration are required. Closure, even if temporary, is subsequently required to make decisions; the reestablishment of openness is needed to monitor the impact of prior decisions (and allow for adjustments or revisions of previous actions).

Similarly, when Hackman and Morris (1983) speak of the coordination of member efforts, differentiation and integration are likely involved. But is the fact that these "optimal" team behaviors are described by a complexity approach reason to apply that theory to team decision making and to the training of teams toward better decisions?

On the surface, it might appear reasonable merely to state that certain specific *procedures* (including those derived from complexity theory) could be employed to improve team functioning. For example, most members of decision-making teams might well applaud the suggestion that a wide range of alternatives should be considered and that the advantages, drawbacks and multiple consequences of each alternative should be analyzed in depth. However, even if such recommendations are viewed positively by team members, implementation is a quite different matter from the acceptance of the idea.

In some cases, the simple implementation of a concept provided by complexity theory is not possible unless a more detailed understanding of the theory and its implications is communicated. For example, team members need to understand when an *adequate* number of relevant alternatives have been considered. Should one go on forever as long as there are alternatives left? Are two alternatives enough, or maybe eight? Complexity theory and associated research shows that optimal levels of alternatives and optimal sequencing of their consideration exist (see below).

Moreover, without an understanding of the theoretical tenets, many complexity-based recommendations for improvement of team functioning would appear quite unrelated to each other. As long as these multiple recommendations are viewed independently, only a few would likely be put into practice.

Actually many suggestions for the improvement of team functioning advanced by previous writers (e.g., those of Janis, or of Hackman and Morris) have much in common if they are viewed from the vantage point of the complexity approach. Many tend to focus on *how* the team functions, on how the team members think and contribute; fewer dwell on *what* the team does. A greater understanding of the commonality of these suggestions (from the basis of the complexity approach) would help team members "make sense" of these otherwise disparate views and will help them to implement the recommendations in a consolidated, integrated manner.

To this end, the team as a whole (or at least some of its members) should be trained to understand the impact of cognitive complexity and should be encouraged to employ differentiation, integration, and other components of structurally oriented functioning as part of the team's decision-making repertoire. To accomplish that task, for example, to understand the interrelationships among the various recommendations, team members need to grasp the concepts involved in structural complexity theory. They need to distinguish between *how* they think or *how* their team functions from *what* their team is doing. That distinction, as research (Streufert & Streufert, 1978) has shown, is difficult to achieve *unless* specific training is provided.

The problem is complicated by the fact that most team members are quite unfamiliar with the *how* of their own thinking and with the *how* of their team's functioning. This holds true even if team members themselves are capable of some differentiation, integration, and so on, at least within some domain of their personal experience. People generally are not aware of their own use of the various processes involved in cognitive complexity. And, since they tend not to be aware of their own use of cognitive complexity, they would hardly be aware of the application of complexity by teams of which they are members. Obviously, some training, including reorientation to include the "how" of thinking and functioning, is needed.

TRAINING FOR STRUCTURAL EFFECTIVENESS

Assume for a moment that we would wish to train team members in the "how" of functioning, that is, toward an understanding of the concepts involved in cognitive complexity to achieve both greater personal effectiveness and toward greater effectiveness of teams. Can such a goal be achieved? Fortunately, individual and team functioning mediated by complexity-based variables can be reliably assessed. Measurement validity has been established (Streufert, Pogash, & Piasecki, 1988). Equally important for present purposes, however, is the fact that personnel can be *trained* in more optimal functioning (Streufert, Nogami, Swezey, Pogash, & Piasecki, 1988). What kind of improvements in team behavior, especially in team decision making, might we achieve?

Let us consider three examples of how team functioning might be improved via training based on complexity variables. To discuss an even larger number of decision team functions would go beyond the focus (and length) of a single chapter. To be representative of decision team efforts, we have selected one example reflecting input to the team (how the team deals with information), one example which considers the process of team interaction (communication among team members), and finally one example of team output (strategic decision making). Basic to the handling of information and to the decisions that a team will make is, of course, the interaction among team members. We will, therefore, begin with a consideration of communication as part of team interaction.

Communications among Team Members

The interpersonal functioning of a team toward one or more (hopefully common) goals is, of course, determined by a number of factors. Among them are team composition, distribution of expertise, leadership, communication effectiveness, and many more. We will here consider only one aspect of team interaction: communication, especially among the members of a team.

On the surface, communication is merely the transmission of information from one individual (or team) to another. It is evident that communication does not work well where two individuals or groups cannot speak a common language. Yet two communicators may, in effect, use identical words but still fail to transmit the intended information. Such difficulties occur when the dimensions on which communicated content is placed do not match between communicator and recipient.

For example, if one team member argues that the price of a product should not be raised, thinking that too many product shares would be lost, and another team member agrees, thinking that the communication by the first team member was based on a belief that profit margins will increase anyhow due to lower production costs, they may have arrived at a decision that is untenable. It is possible that both would have had valid counterarguments to the other's assumption, arguments that were not even considered because of dimensional *mis*communication.

This rather simple example assumes, of course, that the communicators are cooperative in their orientation. If, on the other hand, their relationship is competitive, they may not even wish to share their own dimensional conceptualizations with one another. Tjosvold and Deemer (1980) have shown that competitive orientations among team members tend to generate insecurity, closed-mindedness, knowledge, but little interest in the position of another. The result can be failure to reach agreement or, where a decision must be made, actions taken on the basis of only parts of the relevant information. In contrast, teams that avoid controversy are more open to the views of others. Whether or not team members are, however, interested in those views and gain adequate knowledge of those views depends on the degree to which cognitive complexity determines the functioning of their group.

Competitive orientations among team members, where information may be withheld for the sake of personal power, should not be confused with controversy among team members. Structural integration of ideas toward an optimal decision can only be effective where (multiple) differentiation of ideas (and events, etc.) has taken place. Alternate points of view expressed by various group members may generate "friendly" controversy (those with knowledge of Latin might wish to call it *ergaversy*). Such a process (involving openness to alternate conceptualizations) may aid the various team members in an understanding of both the "facts" of the situation and of the various conceptual and informational dimensions that might be applied to these facts. Such a differentiative process can then lead to an integrative effort designed to generate higher levels of (possibly more complex) strategy. For example, Smith, Peterson, Johnson, and Johnson (1985) have shown that controversy can result in factors that are basic to strategy development: higher level reasoning in the decision making process, greater epistemic curiosity, greater personal efficacy, and more commitment to the joint decision. All these values are achieved without damage to the relationship among team members (Smith et al., 1985).

Communicating appropriately on multiple relevant dimensions is, of course, not achieved without effort. It is rare that all persons who make up a team "naturally" hold the same multiple dimensions and/or conceptualizations of the situation at hand. It is rare that all have the capacity to integrate. Effective communication despite a mismatch in dimensionality requires, first of all, an understanding by all communicators of the dimensionality concept. Secondly, it requires a willingness toward "empathy" from the recipient of a message and, of course, the capacity and willingness to approach problems at hand in a multidimensional fashion.

Can multidimensional communication which provides one of the bases of the cognitive complexity approach to team functioning be trained? It can, even if not in all individuals. It is well known that some persons are able to be empathic and others are not. Empathy, "putting oneself in the other person's shoes," requires (where more than one dimension is present) an understanding of informative content *within the dimensional cognitive framework of another*. To consider another person's dimensional content, one needs, first of all, an understanding that dimensions as well as the location of content on these dimensions can *legitimately* differ from one person to another. That acceptance implies at least the rudiments of a capacity for perceptual differentiation. The next step involves duplicating, to the extent that information is available and sufficiently complete, the dimensionality of the other in one's own mind, even if that dimensionality clashes with one's own. Perceptual differentiation has now been achieved; possibly some hierarchical integration as well. The final step on the perceptual end of communication involves reintegration: combining one's own (or the team's prior) conceptualizations (dimensionality) with the newly obtained understanding of another's dimensional views.

However, communication is bidirectional. One must also be able to communicate one's own dimensional view to another who does not hold the same view. Again, it is necessary for the recipient to accept the legitimacy of alternate conceptualizations. Communication would then have to proceed dimension by dimension, indicating how and why certain content is placed at particular locations on each dimension. With that set of communications, differentiation has been clarified. Finally, the integrative interrelationship among dimensions (e.g., toward some goal(s) or other intended consequences) might be communicated.

Training to achieve such communication (on both the part of the communicator and the recipient) requires, first of all, some capacity for multidimensional (differentiative and integrative) thinking on the part of all or at least most team members. It requires, as already stated, the acceptance that alternate dimension-ality is legitimate and that partial views of several team members might be joined in some higher order integrative effort. It also requires an acceptance that one's own dimensionality might not win out intact or, for that matter, might even lose out altogether. Beyond training for an understanding of structural variables and training for dimensional openness, training people to communicate dimensional information appropriately is required. Optimal procedures for this purpose make excellent use of examples describing situations where unidimensional and fixed thinking failed and where adaptive multidimensionality aided greatly in the achievement of success.

Information and Team Functioning

As Katzell, Miller, Rotter, and Venet (1970) have stated, the number of factors that affect group or team functioning is so great that managing more than a few at any one time, conceptually or experimentally, is hardly possible. Many of these factors are concerned with "information:" for example, instructions about a task, ongoing events, opinions of team members, feedback from the environment, and more. Such information results in "load" on the team. Prior research has shown that load levels can be both suboptimal and superoptimal (Streufert, 1970). What is an optimal load level?

Optimality depends on what the team is supposed to accomplish. If the team was established to push appropriate buttons at the appropriate time, i.e., if simple preconditions for pushing the right button can be established, load can be very high without much loss to the quality of team functioning. Task demands can approach the physical capacity for recognizing stimuli and responding to them (cf. Streufert, Driver, & Haun, 1967). However, in general, team tasks are *not* so simple.

Where tasks are complex, where multidimensional information must be taken into account, where situations are in flux, and so forth, optimal conditions for differentiation and integration are required whenever the development and imple-mentation of strategic thought and action are important. Many managers of teams, and many team members, consider it optimal to receive as much relevant information as possible. Unfortunately, their view of informational antecents for success is seriously flawed. Information overload, no matter how relevant the obtained information might be, can lead to failure.

Prior research has shown that optimality in highly *complex* decision-making settings is achieved as information arrives at a rate of approximately one item per 3-minute period (Streufert, 1970) and/or at levels of about seven items of infor-mation that must be handled at any one time (Miller, 1956). If information arrives at a much lower rate, it produces underload and may contribute to deci-sions that are partly based on irrelevant information (Streufert & Streufert,

1970). Much higher levels of information than those described as optimal may result in decisions that represent snap judgments based on limited (even if relevant) input to the team (Streufert & Schroder, 1965). Both underload and overload conditions tend to produce less utilization of the team's capacity to differentiate or integrate and, as a result, less application of strategy to the task at hand. Optimally functioning teams faced with complex tasks in uncertain settings are able to limit themselves to information levels that allow them to operate at their best, yet to include as much relevant (and strategically useful) information in their deliberations as possible.

One way to achieve optimal loads (assuming that time pressure is not high) is the sequential processing of information that Isenberg (1984) has observed in superior executives. If a team can take the necessary time to consider about seven items of information (or concepts, etc.) at one time and integrate the information into fewer (e.g., three or four) concepts, new items might be introduced for the next processing cycle. However, it will be necessary to reevaluate previously integrated items in terms of any new integration to avoid what Streufert and Swezey (1986) have termed *integration error*.

How can appropriate handling of information be trained? The procedures are, in their basis, not dissimilar from those described in the last section. Again, an understanding of multidimensional functioning, especially of differentiation and integration, is required. Training generally begins with providing individuals or teams with information at optimal, suboptimal, and superoptimal levels. Teams are then asked to form policy and/or to make decisions. They are subsequently reminded of the various items of information (both task relevant and irrelevant) to which they had been exposed. The part played by any one item of information (and, in the case of underload, of spurious determinants of action) in prior deliberations and decisions is examined with their cooperation. Such a procedure quickly clarifies that only "optimal" information tends to generate a high quality of, for example, strategic decision making.

With an understanding of optimality given, training procedures can be extended to include responses to the "magic number seven," that is, limiting one's search to a load of no more than seven items at any one time (and to the avoidance of integration error discussed by Streufert & Swezey, 1986). Included in this form of training is the emphasis on stepwise processing of information as described by Isenberg.

Decision Making: Allocations of Strategy toward Goals

Let us assume that a team is able to hold load at an optimal or near optimal level. Let us further assume that the communication among team members has been multidimensional, and that "matching" dimensions were used or communicated and understood. In observing events and in communicating, the team has at least reached the level of differentiation. Multiple options may have been generated. What about decisions that would, and typically should, be the product of this group process?

Decision making involves the bringing together of preintegrated information about the task, observed events, external forces, member and team preferences, goals, and more to produce an action. Certainly that action need not be restricted to a single team "output." In many cases, teams are able to "test the waters" with partial or preliminary decisions. In other cases they can "read" feedback from prior actions to adjust subsequent decisions. In yet other cases, decision making is a lengthy process where *sequential* actions are intended to lead to more or less specific overall goal(s). To save space, we will only consider training procedures toward the latter of these three intents.

Clearly, decision making in uncertain, complex, and fluid task settings is difficult to translate into a simple, quick, and "cute" training procedure. Many prior attempts toward achieving such a goal have failed. The most optimal training for this purpose would probably be carried out in a team's actual work setting. However, that setting is not under control of the trainer, and events that would aid in the training procedure may or may not occur. A solution is found in the construction of an equivalent task setting which contains all the needed elements of task complexity, information load, goal orientation, stress, team structure, and so forth that are found in the team's "real" world. It is a setting that permits ample opportunity for the trainer to introduce challenges and events that allow assessment and training of decision performance. A quasiexperimental simulation technique developed by Streufert and associates has proven quite useful for this purpose.

Participants who might be either teams or individuals spend an evening familiarizing themselves with a task. Task characteristics are sufficiently familiar to appear quite reasonable but have not been part of the direct prior experience of team members. The team spends the entire next day making decisions in a complex and well-equipped task setting. Feedback (partially preprogrammed) is generated by a computer program which also scores team performance on some 40 to 60 measures that load on about 8 to 12 reliable orthogonal dimensions. Scores predict managerial success, for example, promotions, income at age, job level at age, and number of persons supervised (Streufert et al., 1988). In addition, the computer provides a graphic feedback of team or participant functioning that is easily understood and easily compared with graphic data obtained from other more or less able prior participants.

Training is based on comparing a team's performance with that of other teams, on discussions of specific shortcomings, and on discussions of excellent performance generated by prior teams. Validated measurement systems based on complexity theory concepts are employed. For training to be effective, an understanding of differentiation, integration, and other complexity-theory-based concepts must again be generated. Emphasis is placed upon the application of these concepts in strategy development and planning toward sequential goals. As training proceeds, participants are encouraged to "take over" in the analysis of their own prior performance to assure that an adequate understanding is gained. Finally, teams or individuals are able to repeat their task participation by engaging in another simulation task with quite divergent content but highly similar demands. The second set of scores provides a check on improvement following training. Training with this methodology is now used by Vector Management of Sarasota, Florida, and DISCE GMBH, Gütersloh, Germany for the benefit of major corporations.

Earlier we stated that training teams by emphasizing one recommendation at a time (i.e., in the absence of an understanding of cognitive complexity and its implications) may not result in pervasive improvement. The data from our laboratory suggest that an understanding of structural concepts and their wider application appears much more advantageous. The simulation technique has demonstrated great value for this purpose. It parallels real-world functioning demands upon decision makers and decision-making teams. Since the simulation system measures *multiple* aspects of team functioning, the interrelationships among various impacts of complexity-based variables upon a range of functions can be measured and demonstrated to trainees. In most cases, demonstrably improved functioning after completion of training procedures can be observed.

REFERENCES

Allison, G. T. (1971). *Essence of decision.* Boston: Little, Brown and Co.

Allport, F. H. (1924). *Social psychology.* Boston: Houghton Mifflin Co.

Barefoot, J., Wiggins, B., Harper, J., & Peterson, B. (1985). *Increasing productivity through social structure: An examination of social loafing in a computer-mediated environment.* Final Report # 7 to the Office of Naval Research. Chapel Hill, NC: University of North Carolina Institute for Research in Social Science.

Bowyer, B. J. (1983). *Toward a theory of military decision making* (Rep. No. 103P). Monterey, CA: Naval Postgraduate School.

Burnstein, E., & Schul, Y. (1983). Group polarization. In H. H. Blumberg, A. P. Hare, V. Kent, & M. Davies (Eds.), *Small groups and social interaction* (Vol. 2). New York: Wiley.

Brehmer, B. (1984). The role of judgment in small-group conflict and decision making. *Progress in Applied Social Psychology, 2,* 163–183.

Callaway, M. R., & Esser, J. K. (1984). Groupthink: Effects of cohesiveness and problem solving procedures on group decision making. *Social Behavior and Personality, 12,* 157–164.

Davis, J. H. (1969). *Group performance.* Reading, MA: Addison-Wesley.

Dawes, R. M. (1976). Shallow psychology. In J. S. Carroll & J. W. Payne (Eds.), *Cognition and social behavior.* Hillsdale, NJ: Erlbaum.

Driscoll, J. P., & King, J. A. (1988). *An empirical experiment evaluating the effectiveness of group decision support systems* (Rep. No. AD-A201-864). Monterey, CA: Naval Postgraduate School.

Durkheim, E. (1898). Representations individuelles et representations collectives. *Revue de Metaphysique, 6,* 274–304.

Fiedler, F. (1964). A contingency model of leadership effectiveness. In L. Berkowitz (Ed.), *Advances in experimental social psychology* (Vol. 1, pp. 149–190). New York: Academic Press.

Finstuen, K. (1983). *The iterative decision method (IDM).* Small Group Decision Making and Problem Solving Bibliography (Final Report). Fort Sam Houston, TX: Academy of Health Sciences.

Gergen, K. J. (1973). Social psychology as history. *Journal of Personality and Social Psychology, 26,* 309–320.

Hackman, J. R., & Morris, C. G. (1983). Group tasks, group interaction process and group performance effectiveness. In H. H. Blumberg, A. P. Hare, V. Kent, & M. Davies (Eds.), *Small groups and social interaction* (Vol. 1). New York: Wiley.

Hammond, K. R., Stewart, T. R., Brehmer, B., & Seinmann, D. O. (1975). Social judgment theory. In M. Kaplan & S. Schwartz (Eds.), *Human judgment and decision processes in applied settings.* New York: Academic Press.

Hare, A. P. (1972). Bibliography of small group research. *Sociometry, 35,* 1–150.

Harvey, O. J., Hunt, D., & Schroder, H. M. (1961). *Conceptual systems and personality organization.* New York: Wiley.

Hensley, T. R., & Griffin, G. W. (1986). Victims of groupthink: The Kent State University Board of Trustees and the 1977 gymnasium controversy. *Journal of Conflict Resolution, 30,* 497–531.

Holt, J. R. (1988). *An expert system model of organizational climate and performance* (Report AFIT/CI/Nr. 88-15). Wright-Patterson Air Force Base, OH: Air Force Institute of Technology.

Hugues, A. L., & Webb, D. H. (1987). *A comparative study of group decision support system use: Empirical evidence and model design* (Report AD-A186-308). Monterey, CA: Naval Postgraduate School.

Isenberg, D. J. (1984, November–December). How senior managers think. *Harvard Business Review,* pp. 80–90.

Janis, I. L. (1972). *Victims of Groupthink.* Boston: Houghton-Mifflin.

Janis, I. L. (1983). Groupthink. In H. H. Blumberg, A. P. Hare, V. Kent, & M. F. Davies (Eds.), *Small groups and social interaction.* New York: Wiley.

Katzell, R. A., Miller, C. E., Rotter, N. G., & Venet, T. G. (1970). Effects of leadership and other inputs on group processes and outputs. *Journal of Social Psychology, 80,* 157–169.

Keen, P. G. W., & Scott-Morton, M. S. (1978). *Decision support systems: An organizational perspective.* Reading, MA: Addison-Wesley.

Lorge, I., & Solomon, H. (1955). Two models of group behavior in the solution of Eureka-type problems. *Psychometrika, 20,* 139–148.

McGrath, J. E., & Altman, I. (1966). *Small group research, a synthesis and critique of the field.* New York: Holt.

Messick, S., & Associates. (1976). *Individuality in learning.* San Francisco: Jossey-Bass.

Miller, G. A. (1956). The magical number seven plus or minus two: Some limits on our capacity to process information. *Psychological Review, 63,* 81–97.

Moorhead, G., & Montanari, J. R. (1986). An empirical investigation of the groupthink phenomenon. *Human Relations, 39,* 399–410.

Peters, J. J., & Waterman, R. H., Jr. (1982). *In search of excellence.* New York: Harper and Row.

Poole, M. S. (1983). Decision development in small groups: III. A multiple sequence model of group decision development. *Communication Monographs, 50,* 321–341.

Pruitt, D. G. (1971a). Choice shifts in group discussion: An introductory review. *Journal of Personality and Social Psychology, 20,* 339–360.

Pruitt, D. G. (1971b). Conclusions: Toward an understanding of choice shifts in group discussion. *Journal of Personality and Social Psychology, 20,* 495–510.

Schroder, H. M., Driver, M. J., & Streufert, S. (1967). *Human information processing.* New York: Holt, Rinehart and Winston.

Scott, W. A., Osgood, D. W., & Peterson, C. (1979). *Cognitive structure: Theory and measurement of individual differences.* New York: Halsted Division, Wiley.

Shaw, M. E. (1932). Comparisons of individuals and small groups in the rational solution of complex problems. *American Journal of Psychology, 44,* 491–504.

Simon, H. A. (1953). *Models of man.* New York: Wiley.

Smith, K. A., Peterson, R. P., Johnson, D. W., & Johnson, R. T. (1985). *The effects of controversy and concurrence seeking on effective decision making* (Report CLC-003 to the Office of Naval Research). Minneapolis: University of Minnesota.

Steiner, I. D. (1972). *Group process and productivity.* New York: Academic Press.

Streufert, S. (1970). Complexity and complex decision making: Convergences between differentiation and integration approaches to the prediction of task performance. *Journal of Experimental Social Psychology, 6,* 494–509.

Streufert, S., Driver, M. J., & Haun, K. W. (1967). Components of response rate in complex decision making. *Journal of Experimental Social Psychology, 3,* 286–295.

Streufert, S., Nogami, G. Y., Swezey, R., Pogash, R. M., & Piasecki, M. T. (1988). Computer assisted training of complex managerial performance. *Computers in Human Behavior, 4,* 77–88.

Streufert, S., Pogash, R., & Piasecki, M. (1988). Simulation based assessment of managerial competence: Reliability and validity. *Personnel Psychology, 41,* 537–557.

Streufert, S., & Schroder, H. M. (1965). Conceptual structure, environmental complexity and task performance. *Journal of Experimental Research in Personality, 1,* 132–137.

Streufert, S., & Streufert, S. C. (1969). The effect of conceptual structure, failure and success on attributions of causality and interpersonal attitudes. *Journal of Personality and Social Psychology, 11,* 138–147.

Streufert, S., & Streufert, S. C. (1970). The perception of information relevance. *Psychonomic Science, 18,* 199–200.

Streufert, S., & Streufert, S. C. (1978). *Behavior in the complex environment.* New York: Halsted Division, Wiley.

Streufert, S., & Streufert, S. C. (1981). Attribution, dimensionality and measurement: How you measure is what you get. In D. Gorlitz (Ed.), *Perspectives on attribution theory and research* (pp. 159–186). Cambridge, MA: Ballinger.

Streufert, S., & Swezey, R. W. (1986). *Complexity, managers and organizations.* New York: Academic Press.

Swezey, R. W., Streufert, S., & Mietus, J. (1983). Development of an empirically derived taxonomy of organizational systems. *Journal of the Washington Academy of Sciences, 73,* 27–42.

Taylor, D. W. (1954). Problem solving in groups. *Proceedings 24 of the International Congress of Psychology.* Amsterdam: New Holland Publishing.

Tindale, R. S., & Davis, J. H. (1983). Group decision making and jury verdicts. In H. H. Blumberg, A. P. Hare, V. Kent, & M. Davies (Eds.), *Small groups and social interactions* (Vol. 2). New York: Wiley.

Tjosvold, D., & Deemer, D. K. (1980). Effects of controversy within a cooperative or competitive context on organizational decision making. *Journal of Applied Psychology, 65,* 590–595.

Tversky, A., & Kahneman, D. (1974). Judgment under uncertainty: Heuristics and biases. *Science, 185,* 1124–1131.

Weisband, S. P., Linville, J. M., Liebhaber, M. J., Obermayer, R. W., & Fallesen, J. J. (1988). *Computer-mediated group processes in distributed command and control systems* (Tech. Rep., AD-A198-140). Alexandria, VA: U.S. Army Research Institute.

Wohl, J. H. (1981). Force management decision requirements for Air Force tactical command and control. *IEEE Transactions on Systems, Man and Cybernetics, SMC 11/9.*

7

Assessment of Team Performance*

Harold F. O'Neil, Jr.
Eva L. Baker
Edward J. Kazlauskas

INTRODUCTION

The purpose of this chapter is to provide analyses of the status of team performance assessment. This area is one of long-standing general interest to education and training constituencies, but in the light of a range of new developments, we anticipate greater needs for developing valid strategies to assess the performance of organized groups. The military, for example, because it is organized in both hierarchical and parallel units comprised of individuals, has been the focus of much of the exploration of unit performance assessment (e.g., Wagner, Hibbits, Rosenblatt, & Schultz, 1977; Scott, 1984; Dyer, 1984; USGAO, 1986; Boldovici, 1987; Shavelson, Winkler, & Stasz, 1985). The need here is to develop measures intermediate to, and predictive of, team performance in times of national emergency. Such measures are assumed to be subsets of complex behavior contributing to the overall organizational goal of defense elements, i.e., winning in combat.

* The research reported herein was supported by the Training Performance Data Center under Subcontract No. EERS-VN-C-88-005 with EER Systems and Advance Design Information, Inc. However, the views, opinions, and/or findings contained in this report are the authors' and should not be construed as an official Department position, policy or decision, unless so designated by other official documentation.

But concern about the performance of groups is spreading rapidly to significant training and education spheres other than the military. For one, the emphasis on international economic competitiveness has pushed American business and industry to revise in part its view of individual, team, and organizational behavior in an effort to adapt approaches that appear to increase our trading partner's productivity (e.g., Ouchi, 1981). Hard on the heels of reorganizing work so that teams and units assume responsibility is the requirement to develop intermediate assessment, that is, before the bottom line of group performance. Almost in parallel, and derived from a social learning perspective, public, precollegiate education is moving towards redefining certain major learning tasks as group rather than as individual endeavors (Slavin, Leavey, & Madden, 1984; Webb, 1982).

In concert with the undeniable rise in investment in achievement measurement for state and national purposes (Elliott, 1989; Baker, 1988), fledgling efforts are underway to develop team and group assessment procedures for use in large-scale testing programs. In fact, Great Britain embarked in 1988 (Burstall, 1989) on a nationwide program to assess children's group performance in schools as part of a national accountability system, a fact which suggests that this move to the attention of group accomplishment is more than an American preoccupation. The implications are significant of this shift in perspective from individual achievement, most frequently measured in paper-and-pencil achievement tests, to team performance assessed in complex cognitive and behavioral situations.

All three of these sectors, the military, business-industry, and public education, have begun to focus attention squarely on the assessment issue—most directly on how to determine the impact of team efforts and how to obtain and analyze data that will contribute to the goals of a wide range of organizations. While each of these sectors varies significantly in the centrality and conceptions of team performance, they nonetheless can profit from systematic analysis of the relevant measurement issues. These questions of team performance assessment will be the larger focus of this chapter.

Human Performance

Fleishman and Quaintance (1984) have codified human performance in terms of classificatory systems focused on behavior descriptions (what people actually do), task requirements (what they are supposed to do), and situational and ability constraints (what they can do). Such analyses focus largely on job performance and are useful to determine the range of performances which might be measured, to create logical clusters for the purpose of measure development, and to allow multiple perspectives on the same problem. Another set of classificatory systems clearly related to team performance in the training and education context are those which focus on learning tasks. These include those developed by Bloom

(1956), Lumsdaine (1960), Carroll (1979), Sternberg (1979), and Gagné (1985). Although with different emphases, these systems attempt to represent the range of human learning processes and are valuable as sources for creating or assessing goals of educational programs. It must be underscored, however, that the focus for each of these learning classificatory systems was the individual learner rather than team or group performance. One obvious question for consideration is how such classifications might be adapted for the group or team context.

Characteristics of Groups and Teams

Part of the problem of assessment is to explicate our notion of group and for its subset, teams, and to identify features that require new approaches to those used in individual assessment. Groups are collections of individuals described or constructed for some purpose. We can describe minimum common characteristics of groups as listed in Table 7.1.

Groups might be composed of volunteers, such as ticket holders to the third game of the World Series; or of individuals designated by an external authority, members of the same platoon or elementary school classroom. Individuals may know they are in a group, such as American Airlines passengers on flight 76, or not know of their group status, such as persons assigned as a high-anxious test taker for the purpose of an experiment. Groups may also be composed of individuals with differentiated functions. These differentiations may be voluntary or assigned. For example, it is common to note individuals in discussion groups who voluntarily adopt functions such as clarifier or summarizer. Or conversely, an authority may assign different functions to individuals in groups, for example, blackboard monitor, for indeterminate periods of time. Groups might be composed of individuals similar on important demographic variables or might vary along these dimensions. An example might be members of a Brownie troop (female, ages 7 and 8), or attendees at a conference of Star Trek devotees or even a Rolling Stones concert. Groups may also vary in terms of their passivity or activity, the extent to which their members perform their functions in isolation or interactively, and the stability versus dynamism of their membership. These dimensions are summarized in Table 7.2 below.

Other attributes include size, status, and influence (Bass, 1982, p. 188).

Table 7.1. Common Characteristics of Groups

- Consist of aggregates of individuals
- Composed for some particular purpose
- Persist for a known period of time
- Pursue individual or collective goals

Table 7.2.   Dimensions of Group
Variability

Voluntary	Assigned
Aware of membership	Unaware
Differentiated Roles	Identical Roles
Heterogeneous	Homogeneous
Passive	Active
Insular	Interactive
Stable	Dynamic

Perhaps the matter of goals structure is among the knottiest problems in the area of group formation and description. Goals differ in terms of their source, their specification, generality, explicitness, commonality, and difficulty (Baker, 1988). For instance, it can be assumed that members of a Great Books Club all want to learn something more about classic literature, but individuals may vary in terms of which book they are most interested in (*The Aeneid* or *Don Quixote*) or whether their purpose is to understand text or force themselves to be exposed to literature they had somehow avoided or missed. Others may look to this group to satisfy social goals, with the literature forming only a backdrop. Clearly, the goals for the group articulated by its literary leader and for the members may differ significantly, as may the stability of given goals over time. Table 7.3 summarizes a few of the dimensions along which goals can vary.

All elements listed in Tables 7.1, 7.2, and 7.3 present anchors to dimensions—dimensions that invariably blur at particular points. Doubtless, the alternative dimensions interact with one another as well, resulting in a relatively complex analytical phenomenon. Let us hasten to add that these group and goal dimensions are presented pragmatically, to provide some scaffolding for the discussion which follows of teams and of the measurement of team performance, and are not intended to reflect or contradict specific sociological or social psychological theory.

Table 7.3.   Dimensions of Group Goal
Structures

Exogenous or Endogenous Source
Autocratic or Democratic Process
Preordained or Emergent Specification
General or Specific Focus
Multiple or Single Topic
Explicit or Implicit Articulation
Common or Differentiated by Member
Challenging or Comfortable

Teams

Teams are a subset of groups, and all the elements in Tables 7.1–7.3 above apply to them. Furthermore, boundary conditions between groups and teams are likely to be problematic to purists. Let us proceed in terms of attributes we can assume to be shared by all teams and then further differentiate our analyses. Teams are composed for specific purposes. Individuals in a team are supposed to accept as preordinate the team's goals as opposed to the individual's goal. Such understanding presupposes some articulation of goals. For example, the college basketball gunner who, instead of passing to an open player, attempts spectacular shots to improve his personal statistics and chance of a professional career, is described as "not a team player." His personal goals overshadow the team goals.[1] An additional feature of teams is that they are organized in some fashion and often have more structure than many other groups. Such structure may be differentiated by task—one team member collects data, and one member analyzes it—or all team members may do about the same thing—run legs of the same relay race. Teams of any duration (other than a pick-up game) typically prepare to do what they do. They practice and attempt to improve their performance. Given common goals, organization, and preparation, it is natural that team membership confers and demands a change of identity. One is a Celtic, or a member of the 2nd Platoon, B Company, first. The internalization of one's membership on a team may be an important interim goal for assessment. An additional context for many teams is competition. Competition may be with parallel groups, such as hockey teams; it may be against a performance standard, such as errorless production in a manufacturing plant; or against a time standard. Competition as an external context is thought to drive internal cooperation, motivation, and performance. Teams can be structured differently, depending upon the heterogeneity of their members, their autonomy, embedded staff hierarchies, and task demands. Obvious differences include teams that have pyramid structures, such as a military unit, contrasted with teams that have flat, differentiated, but mutually dependent structures, such as a baseball team.

A number of authors have pursued functional components of team behavior (Fleishman & Quaintance, 1984; Olmstead & Elder, 1980; also see other chapters in this volume).

Their work is properly mute on issues of structure, task characteristics, dependencies, or authority, although Fleishman reports that attempts to translate his taxonomy to an assessment device have occurred using behavioral check lists.

---

[1] In professional basketball, such behavior may be in fact in service of a team goal, if the operating requirement is to improve fan attendance, but we would not be so cynical to believe this option.

What we have attempted to demonstrate in this introductory section is that the problem of assessing collective action, group or team, has complex definitional, structural, and functional issues embedded within it.

For the next section, we wish to present an extended investigation into the literature of team performance assessment. It was our intention to apply the Performance Assessment Framework, a classificatory system designed to provide access to research literature databases, to the team performance assessment problem (Baker, O'Neil, & Linn, 1991). It was our hope that we would uncover for analysis an extensive literature in the military, business-industry, and public education sectors. Our expectation, however, was that we would have to rely on more specific search strategies for accessing literature, specifically names of team performance measures and names of researchers known to be involved in performance assessment.

LITERATURE REVIEW OF TEAM ASSESSMENT

Two databases were of particular interest, because they were likely to have most content coverage: Educational Resources Information Center (ERIC), and the National Technical Information Service (NTIS). ERIC is produced by the U.S. Department of Education and contains citations and abstracts of journal and report literature dealing with a wide range of topics in education and training. It consists of two files: (a) *Resources in Education*, which contains reports, conference proceedings, etc., and information from 16 clearinghouses with specific topic areas; and (b) *Current Index to Journals in Education*, which abstracts over 750 journals in education and related disciplines. Coverage began in 1966 for research reports and 1969 for journal literature.

NTIS is produced by the U.S. Department of Commerce and contains citations and abstracts of unclassified reports dealing with U.S. and non-U.S. government-sponsored research and development. The documents that are included in NTIS are prepared by U.S. federal, state, and local agencies, their contractors, and grantees. Coverage began in 1964.[2]

First, several key words in performance assessment were searched against the databases, with the result of retrieving thousands of hits or matches with our terms and literature citations. For example, our first results in NTIS are shown in Table 7.4. The 42 abstracts that were retrieved using "performance with human with assessment with military" as a search term were printed and read. However, only 22 (52%) were relevant. This low relevancy percentage suggested the need to improve our search terms. There were several methodological options for

---

[2] Both these databases were accessed from initial date of coverage via Dialog Information Services, Inc. (a Knight-Ridder Company) as a search-and-retrieval vendor of databases produced by a wide array of public and private database developers. The online search facility at the University of Southern California was used.

Table 7.4.   First Pass NTIS

First Pass Results:
- *Performance* with *assessment* terms yielded 1,984 documents
- *Military terms only* yielded 37,036 documents
- *Performance* with *assessment* with *military* terms yielded 100 documents
- *Performance* with *human* terms yielded 8,280 documents
- *Performance* with *human* with *assessment* with *military* terms yielded 42 documents

refining search items: (a) use performance assessment framework terms; (b) use specific Department of Defense (DoD) assessment measures; (c) use names of experts. We decided to explore all three options.

Performance Assessment Framework

Our second tactic was to use the Performance Assessment Framework (Baker et al., in press), a conceptually organized analysis of the area to explore the literature on team performance assessment. The Performance Assessment Framework was developed with assistance from experts in the fields of measurement, assessment, and information science. Three related purposes existed for the design and development of a framework in the performance assessment area. The purpose of the framework or taxonomy was: (a) to facilitate access to existing databases archiving research and development studies related to performance assessment; (b) to define with key words the critical attributes of performance assessment domain for use in the design of a specific DoD-useful database in the area; and (c) to use the structure and terms of the Performance Assessment Framework as a conceptual framework to judge the appropriateness of extant R&D studies, and to plan for new assessment approaches as well as specific examples of performance assessment measures. The Framework is organized into six top levels:

1.0 Performance Assessment Targets—the focus of the assessment (e.g., team job performance).
2.0 Performance Assessment Domains—the substance of what is being assessed (e.g., common tasks).
3.0 Performance Assessment Approaches—the types of assessment and methods and instruments for data collection (e.g., types of tests).
4.0 Psychometrics—the technical issues pertinent to performance assessment (e.g., validity).
5.0 Interpretation and Reporting—how meaning is attached to the data and the formats and users for reports (e.g., norm-referenced).
6.0 Costs—cost considered as an element in performance assessment (e.g., research and development costs).

Table 7.5. Number of Hits in NTIS Using Terms in Performance Assessment Framework

TERM	1.2 Team Performance
RESULT	Performance (142,229); Team (5,334); Team Performance (124)

Within these categories are subdivisions, divided to usually no more than five additional levels. In general, the more specific elements, at levels four and five, are provided as illustration rather than as an exhaustive list. These levels are meant, in part, to provide slots into which additional specific information could be added by either users researchers, or developers.

The results of using selected terms from the Framework to assess team performance assessment are shown in Tables 7.5 and 7.6.

A decision to use terminology from the framework resulted in either broad searches with high retrieval (i.e., many cited documents or hits) but low precision (i.e., few relevant documents), as in Table 7.5, or few hits (see Table 7.6). Given time and other resource limitations, the best strategy for testing the framework's utility to access literature was to use free text searches (of titles and abstracts) based on specific performance measures. Then, once a body of literature had been identified with high precision, terms in the Framework could be applied to that selected body of literature.

Our third approach was to use specific assessment measures as search teams in NTIS and ERIC, specifically performance assessment measures that were used in DoD environments. These measures were ARTEP (Army Training and Evaluation Program), Red Flag, NTC (National Training Center) and MCCRES (Marine Corps Combat Readiness Evaluation System). In addition, a term related to an innovation with potential for performance assessment, SIMNET (Simulation Network), was used. We also included the SQT (Skills Qualification Test), an individual performance measure, to provide a context of rough comparison for the team assessment measures. These measures were used as keywords to search against both the NTIS and ERIC databases. These very specific terms do not

Table 7.6. Number of Hits in NTIS Using Terms in Performance Assessment Framework

TERM	Team Performance Assessment
RESULT	Assessment (49,188); Team Performance Assessment (0)
TERM	Team Evaluation Assessment
RESULT	Evaluation (148,746); Team Performance Evaluation (1)
TERM	Unit Performance Assessment
RESULT	Assessment (49,188); Unit Performance Assessment (1)
TERM	Group Performance Assessment
RESULT	Assessment (49,188); Group Performance Assessment (1)

appear in the ERIC database thesaurus (a source which lists acceptable and unacceptable index words and which shows term relationships and reciprocals). Thus, text searching was performed. This means that the databases were searched against all searchable keyword fields, such as title, descriptors, identifiers, abstract. If the specific assessment measures or name appeared anywhere in these fields, it was considered a hit. The numbers of hits in the NTIS database were: *SQT* (41 hits); *ARTEP* (58 hits); *SIMNET* (5 hits); *NTC* (88 hits); *Red Flag* (10 hits); *MCCRES* (23 hits). Using this method, a high degree of recall (the ratio of relevant documents retrieved to relevant documents in the file) is achieved. Finally, an expert's name in performance assessment (Dr. Robert Glaser) was used, which produced 45 NTIS hits.

Initially, only brief citation information was gathered regarding these searches, i.e., title and document number. The titles were reviewed for relevance. This approach assisted in determining whether the hits were indeed relevant. Terms such as *ARTEP* and *SQT* generated a high level of precision (the ratio of the relevant documents retrieved to the total number of documents retrieved). However, searches on such terms as *Red Flag* did not—*red flag* has various meanings. Likewise, the relevant hits on the term *Dr. Glaser* were low. Although Dr. Glaser is an international expert in performance assessment, he has also written on topics other than performance assessment. Thus, many citations that were retrieved with these search terms were not relevant, and resulted in our dropping the author term search.

Thus, it was decided to continue an in-depth analysis of the citations in NTIS and ERIC on several precise performance assessment measures, for example, *SQT, ARTEP, Red Flag, SIMNET. Red Flag* was retained even though it resulted in low-precision searches to provide an Air Force example. The use of *NTC* as a term was dropped for two reasons: (a) to provide balance among Services; and (b) the Army considers it a unit training measure, not an assessment measure. The specific performance assessment measures as terms were then used to search against the NTIS and ERIC databases, but this time for the purpose of printing full record information.

The number of hits for each term is shown in Table 7.7 and demonstrates that NTIS searches resulted in a large number of hits, whereas ERIC searches did not. For example, there were 58 documents about *ARTEP* that were located in NTIS; none were located in ERIC. There were 23 hits located in NTIS for *MCCRES*, but none were located in ERIC.

These citations were read and categorized as relevant based on the abstract. The relevant number of hits is shown in Table 7.8. For example, using *SQT* as a term resulted in 40 relevant SQT documents in NTIS and 7 relevant documents in ERIC. Likewise, there were 56 relevant documents regarding *ARTEP* in NTIS, but none were found in ERIC (see Table 7.7).

Table 7.9 shows the precision ratios for the performance assessment measures. A *precision ratio* is the number of relevant hits divided by the number of

Table 7.7.   Number of Hits of Performance Assessment Measures

	Army	Hits	Marine Corps	Hits	Air Force	Hits
NTIS	SQT	41	MCCRES	23	Red Flag	10
	ARTEP	58				
ERIC	SQT	7	MCCRES	0	Red Flag	3
	ARTEP	0				

hits converted to a percentage. For example, as may be seen in Table 7.9, the precision ratios for *ARTEP* were 96% for NTIS and Not Applicable (NA) for ERIC. Not Applicable was specified as there were no *ARTEP* hits in ERIC (see Table 7.7).

A similar analysis was conducted for the potential performance assessment measure (i.e., *SIMNET*). These analyses for hits, relevant hits, and precision ratios are found in Tables 7.10, 7.11, and 7.12, respectively. In general, there were no hits in ERIC, and relevance in NTIS was low, as search terms had multiple meanings.

RESEARCH ISSUES

As was stated, one of the purposes of the taxonomy was to use the structure and terms of the Performance Assessment Framework as a conceptual framework to judge the appropriateness of extant R&D studies of performance assessment, the plans for new performance assessment measures, and R&D studies of specific examples of existing performance assessment measures.

Research Gaps Identified from the Qualitative Use of the Framework

We reviewed the ARTEP abstracts to determine the extent to which the Framework offers new areas for systematic research on performance assessment instruments in team training. In this second function, it must be reiterated that our role

Table 7.8.   Number of Relevant Hits of Performance Assessment Measures

	Army	Relevant Hits	Marine Corps	Relevant Hits	Air Force	Relevant Hits
NTIS	SQT	40	MCCRES	23	Red Flag	7
	ARTEP	56				
ERIC	SQT	7	MCCRES	0	Red Flag	0
	ARTEP	0				

Table 7.9.   Precision Ratios for Performance Assessment Measures

	Army	Precision (%)	Marine Corps	Precision (%)	Air Force	Precision (%)
NTIS	SQT	97	MCCRES	100	Red Flag	70
	ARTEP	96				
ERIC	SQT	100	MCCRES	NA	Red Flag	0
	ARTEP	NA				

is not to make judgments about the scientific quality or practical utility of previous efforts. Rather, we are interested in whether the Framework serves the purpose cited by Fleishman and Quaintance (1984, p. 6) of "exposing gaps in knowledge." Our approach suggested that we review the abstracts of the most frequently cited team performance assessment measure, ARTEP.

Our first task was to reread all obtained ARTEP abstracts and then sort them into as many mutually exclusive categories as possible. Fifty-seven abstracts were included in this phase of the study. An initial sort by Dr. Baker was made into four categories: Research and Evaluation; Development and Validation; Descriptions and Guidelines; and Administration and Regulations. A second sort by Dr. O'Neil was conducted, and abstracts were reassigned when appropriate.

We believed that dividing the ARTEP abstracts into these categories would help determine if differences occurred among categories and would assist us in identifying research gaps.

The attributes that differentiate the categories are relatively clear. Category I, the Research and Evaluation category, contains studies that investigate performance on the ARTEP as related to other soldier measures, report feasibility studies on ARTEP, expansion or extension to new problems or contexts, or conduct impact studies on the ARTEP. In addition, some studies focus on other areas and use the ARTEP primarily as a dependent measure for other interventions. Most, but not all, of the work in this category is analytical. Almost all of it is relatively short term and very applied. The relatively few studies in Category II, Development and Validation studies, are divided between heavily empirical studies and descriptions of procedures that should be used in the design of ARTEP or similar instruments. Validation procedures such as psychometric is-

Table 7.10.   Number of Hits of Potential Performance Assessment Measures

	DARPA
NTIS	SIMNET(6)
ERIC	SIMNET(0)

Table 7.11.   Number of Relevant Hits of Potential Performance Assessment Measures

	DARPA
NTIS	SIMNET(4)
ERIC	SIMNET(NA)

sues are rarely discussed. Category III, Descriptions and Guidelines, tends to have a relatively limited empirical base, and its five documents focus on how to implement the ARTEP or descriptions of ideal considerations in the practical development and implementation of the ARTEP. Category IV simply consists of a single document listing Army publications. Regulations and changes thereof that specified procedures for the development and implementation of the ARTEP policies tend not to be catalogued in NTIS.

The distribution of documents to category is presented in Table 7.13.

One purpose of this activity was to review the utility of the Performance Assessment Framework for research and development planning in Team Assessment. This aspect of our work is very speculative, since the overall impact of a classificatory system on research and development planning is likely to be marginal at best when compared to real requirements-driven R & D effort. Nonetheless, in the review of the Performance Assessment Framework in the context of the ARTEP document database, we considered its planning utility.

We reviewed the abstracts, made notes, and discussed opinions. In contrast to previous quasiquantitative sections, this aspect of our work was holistic and speculative. The issue was whether direction could be provided by the Framework. For example, one finding might have been that certain categories were very well represented by the literature. Our inference then would be that the direction setting function was not relevant for these categories.

The overall belief was that the Framework could be very useful in setting directions for R & D in this area. For example, one source for this opinion is the distribution by R & D category of documents in Table 7.13. What was surprising was the relatively small amount of validation work or experimental studies

Table 7.12.   Precision Ratios of Potential Performance Assessment Measures

	DARPA
NTIS	SIMNET(66%)
ERIC	SIMNET(NA)

Table 7.13. Distribution of ARTEP Abstracts by Category of Report

Category	Number of Abstracts
Research and Evaluation	38
Development and Validation	13
Description and Guidelines	5
Administration and Regulation	1

present in the development of the measures themselves. Thus, sections of the Framework, particularly section 4.0 Psychometrics, 5.0 Interpretation and Reporting, and 6.0 Costs, would be sparsely filled if they were based on the ARTEP abstracts alone. In addition, although the largest classification of studies was in the research and evaluation area, these studies often evaluated something else as well, or conducted nondatabased feasibility studies rather than addressing the dimensions included by experts in the Performance Assessment Framework. Clearly, attributes related to section 3.0 of the Framework, that is, the section on Performance Assessment Approaches, could identify other serious issues for attention for research, issues that are driven either by existing policy or that would explore the use of new forms of performance records. These statements are meant to be heavily qualified and are based on reviews conducted without knowing the policy context guiding the development of the documents we reviewed. In sum, however, it would appear that future use of the Performance Assessment Framework might very well stimulate programmatic efforts in validation of newly conceived measures, for example, directed toward technology-based or team assessment innovations.

Research Gaps Identified from the Quantitative Use of the Framework

This section also focuses on the use of the framework to provide a basis for an R&D agenda. However, it focuses on a quantitative approach.

The purpose of this investigation was threefold: (a) to investigate the literature so as to determine the areas of research and publication, and where research gaps exist; (b) to validate the Performance Assessment Taxonomy with a subset of the performance literature; and (c) to examine the retrieval issues associated with a subset of the literature in a specific database.

In order to accomplish the above, a subset of records found in the NTIS database were concatenated with terms from the Performance Assessment Taxonomy. Specifically, the term *ARTEP* was combined with acceptable terms in the structure and, where appropriate, with any related terms (R). For example, a second level taxonomic term, such as *Team Performance* (1.2), was combined with *ARTEP*. If there were any search hits, more detailed terms from that section of the taxonomy were combined for a more detailed search, for example, *ARTEP* and *Team Performance* (1.2) and *Readiness* (1.2.1). In addition, related terms (R), such as *Unit Performance*, were combined with *ARTEP*. Again, if there were any search hits, a more detailed search ensued. In general, there were very few hits. The modal number was zero. As may be recalled, the framework is organized into six top levels. The proportion of number of any hits of a specific term to the number of terms in the Performance Assessment Taxonomy level is as follows: 1.0 Performance Assessment Targets (15/48) (i.e., out of 48 terms at this level in the taxonomy, a total of 15 had at least one hit); 2.0 Performance Assessment Domains (24/53); 3.0 Performance Assessment Approaches (21/98); 4.0 Psychometrics (10/101); 5.0 Interpretation and Reporting (10/56); 6.0 Cost (3/20).

The results of the searches indicate the following: that most of the search hits were at the higher levels of the taxonomy. The interpretation of this is that either the documents did not cover more specific content at the very specific lower levels, such as *Walk-through Test* (3.1.11), or that the title, indexing, or abstracting did not adequately reflect the content of the document. It was also noted that some related terms (R) were used more frequently in the database than the preferred terms, for example, *Unit Performance* (R) and *Group Performance* (R) rather than *Team Performance* (1.1), and *Measurement* (R) rather than *Psychometrics* (4.0). In addition, singular and plural forms of the word could create problems in retrieval. For example, *Common Task* is used rather than the taxonomic term *Common Tasks* (2.1); both *Test* and *Tests* are used in the database—the most general taxonomic term is *Tests* (3.1). Also to be noted is the fact that, in the taxonomy, there are both singular and plural versions of test items names, such as *Psychomotor Tests* (3.1.3) and *Occupational Test* (3.1.8). Further, some of the terms in the taxonomy are too generic to assist in retrieval, for example, *Type of Tests* (3.1). The phrase "Type of" should be eliminated in the taxonomy and in searching. Although there were few Retrieval hits, the taxonomy could be used as a guide to assign titles, write abstracts, and index documents. The assumption is also made that a slight revision of the taxonomy would improve database retrieval performance.

In summary, few of the Performance Assessment Framework terms appear in ARTEP abstracts and, thus, our conclusions regarding research gaps of this quantitative assessment are the same as for the qualitative assessment.

Analyzing the Team Assessment Problem

How should team performance be assessed? Unfortunately, our review of the literature provided few explicit suggestions. Thus, the following section is very speculative. The speculative answer is: in at least three ways. First, team perfor mance can be assessed by looking at their product outputs such as inspecting a car taken at random off a particular assembly line, or judging a cooperatively developed research paper. Performance can also be assessed by looking at records of behavior of the team, such as goals scored, battle damage/loss ratios, or patients treated. Performance processes can also be assessed as they occur, in exercise or simulations. Looking at products, behavioral records, and processes may be wise or foolish, depending upon the goal in view. What is surely foolish is adopting a particular preferred strategy independent of the particular goal. Our analysis of the team assessment problem leads to the following precepts.[3]

Precept one: performance assessment is measured in contexts. What does performance assessment typically mean? As alluded to earlier, performance assessment is seen as a contrast to more standard forms of achievement measurement. Revisionist thinking about the utility of achievement testing is developing for a number of reasons with surprising relevance to team performance assessment. Much of formal testing in kindergarten through 12th grade is decontextualized; that is, the connection between the measurement and the real behavior or construct of interest has been lost. This fact is most directly revealed by investments in test preparation programs (so that higher reading scores will be achieved) rather than teaching the subject matter or skill of interest (reading).

Precept two: performance assessment requires integrated, sensible tasks studied over adequate time periods. Performance assessment suggests the need to collect examples of complex performance over longer periods of time. Unlike measures that focus on molecular segments of tasks, performance assessment should model enough of the relevant performance to allow adequate judgment. Clearly this amount of time depends upon the level of the goal of interest. Target acquisition may require only a relatively brief period, whereas the assessment of medical training may require multiple simulations of many days in length.

Precept three: performance assessment should be reserved for procedural and problem solving tasks. What would a typical performance assessment measure? The answer when we are thinking of cognition seems to be two major categories of performance: (a) the performance of procedures, for instance, team troubleshooting; and (b) the exercise of judgment and knowledge in the application of problem solving. Problem solving may call for problem identification, planning, strategy selection, solution testing, constraint relaxation, and the application of specific knowledge to permit the traversing of these subprocesses. Leadership, when shorn of the impact of charismatic personality variables, may simply be the application of these two categories to affective and motivational problems.

Precept four: do not trade validity for assessment ease. A typical tradeoff in assessment is the ease or convenience of assessment for the assessor and the

---

[3] *Precept*, in this case, is meant as a rule of action or direction.

validity and verisimilitude of the measurement for the inferences at hand. Performance assessment is costly when compared with other measurement approaches. Furthermore, if precepts 1–3 are observed, performance assessment strategies may result in the restriction of the sample of relevant behaviors. For instance, students in high school have been asked to edit paragraphs using multiple choice formats instead of writing prose because it is easier to score such edits and because, in the same period of time, assessors are able to observe the students performance on a range different topics. When we restrict our measurement in this case to a student writing one essay on a particular given topic, we greatly increase the likelihood that we may make mistakes because of inadequate topic sampling. On the other hand, multiple exercises for large teams may not be feasible from a cost perspective. Solutions may reside in matrix sampling models where multiple tasks from a domain related to the goal are performed by various units. Use of simulated environments (e.g., SIMNET) would permit operationalization of such matrix sampling models.

Precept five: specify the domain and scoring criteria using state-of-the art approaches. Assessments of products, behavioral records, or processes depends upon the clarity of the standards for interpreting performance. No one has a problem determining who has won a football game. The standards for interpreting performance are clear. Whereas it is common for us to accept arbitrary point allocations in a game (Why is a safety worth two points?), such allocations are harder to justify in the realm of performance assessment. One practical solution has been sample-dependent scoring, where performance is arrayed best to worst on some sort of a scale, such as five score points. In the public education sector this is comparable in many ways to using norm-referenced measures where half of the distribution is necessarily below the average. This practice has confused the public and confounded policymakers (who want everyone above the average, naturally). It suggests that, in performance assessment, we must develop good descriptions of the domain of interest and adequate scoring criteria to permit the legitimate improvement of all performers. Analyzing the performance of experts, such as the Red Team at the National Training Center on tank tactics, or a master troubleshooter, is a useful way to infer such scoring criteria.

Precept six: invest in trained judges. Because performance samples are likely to be extended and to require the assessment of complex behaviors, for the next few years our only option is to use human raters or scorers of performance or products. Evidence abounds that such raters can be trained through careful procedures to make valid judgments. It is unwise to invest enormous policy capital in the specification of complex tasks and leave it to relatively untrained, unchecked judges to make the assessment. It is similarly faulty to think that such judges, by virtue of experience or rank, know how to, and can, execute objective, valid judgments of particular tasks.

Precept seven: plan assessment procedures so as to minimize potential corruption. Of great concern to the assessment community is the issue of corruptibility of measures. *Corruptibility* simply means attempting to influence success on measures without actually affecting the underlying construct or domain the measure is attempting to assess. If in the public sector, team or individual performance assessment begins to have consequences for groups of individuals, it is likely that attempts to affect directly the measures will occur. For example, there are multiple stories of individuals attempting to circumvent a teacher performance system with portfolios (of teaching plans) prepared by consultants, or by engaging during periods in which instructors are observed in preplanned activity to demonstrate the ability to be "spontaneous" or to discipline students. Even if these stories are apocryphal, the tendency to get around systems is not.

REQUIREMENTS FOR TEAM ASSESSMENT:
A RESEARCH AGENDA

Many of the above precepts can apply equally to individual or team performance. What is unique about the team endeavor that needs measurement? One obvious difference is that the team is usually pursuing an explicit, coordinated goal. Rather than trying to judge capability on microtasks, a larger goal is at hand. In the military that goal is to accomplish "the mission," with the full range of ambiguity of multiple missions, capability, and constraints. Thus, first on the agenda, we must have some overall measure of whether the mission, or major goal is accomplished, looking at the totality of team performance. Closely related to this concern is to determine with some reliability the factors that led to success.

Not enough knowledge exists in the system to specify quantitatively either success factor for team performance (e.g., unit proficiency or combat effectiveness). Thus, in many cases a number-crunch approach has been adopted where everything that could be measured was measured, and inferences about critical attributes came bottom up through the system. Such an approach suffers, obviously, from the correlational fallacy (related events do not necessarily cause observed outcomes). Such data-rich approaches must be supplemented by two alternatives. For example, in military teams we would prefer

1. Systematic assessment of alternative tactics under experimental conditions as the way to develop new doctrine. Such processes are at last feasible because of the rapid advances in simulated systems (SIMNET is one example);
2. Intensive analyses of expert team members' behavior during performance trials, with interviews designed to elicit the reasons used to justify particular decisions. These analyses would result in the description of critical aspects of team performance: for example, communication and coordination.

Additional items for our research agenda include the development of new psychometric models for the analysis of team performance. These analyses probably should be focused on hierarchical and differentiated performance of team members, and should focus on the following topics:

- the development of a theory of team performance
- measuring team competency (see Green & Wigdor, 1988a,b, for individual competency)
- approaches to decomposition of team performance to subgroup and individual performance levels for the purpose of improvement
- development and application of new approaches to content sampling, for instance the exploration of attribute models (see Tatsuoka, 1983) to team performance settings
- explorations of the use of technology for capturing and analyzing team-task relevant behaviors.

Although it is clear from our analysis of the literature that team performance assessment has not been a hotbed of psychometric activity, we are extremely experienced as a discipline in looking at collections of certain types of individual performance—clearly much of the discipline of social science statistics is based on that general task. But our goal now is to look at group performance as more than a simple aggregate of a distribution individuals, with a mean and standard deviation; rather we ascribe some particular meaning to the group entity itself. Here we have some partial methods available to us. When conceiving of groups in hierarchical ways (for instance, children, reading groups, classrooms, grade levels), we confront serious problems resolved only by conducting multilevel analyses of both within and between group data (Burstein, Kim, & Delandshire, 1989). Unfortunately, as Linn (1986) points out, there is still "less understanding of how to match the level of analysis to the question or how best to conduct multilevel analysis" (p. 112). Progress in this area is likely, since a group of strong methodologists is now focused on this problem, for example, Bock (1989), Burstein et al. (1989), Goldstein (1987), Raudenbush and Bryk (1986), and de Leeuw and Kreft (1986). In any case, multilevel analysis is at present a solution for hierarchically nested groups and is not, in its current form, an application that can solve psychometrics of the team performance situation. Thus, the need for articulation and support of a performance assessment research agenda is needed to draw the combined talent of the psychometricians and the psychologists who can help us develop adequate assessments.

Performance Assessment and Evaluation Models

Most, but not all, of this discussion has proceeded as if performance assessment of teams was an end in itself. It is clearly nested in the larger purpose of improving performance of actors of interest, students, workers or military personnel. Assessment is the process by which measures are combined and a judgment is made. That process takes place in larger decision contexts. As a final section, we provide a brief discussion of prevailing evaluation models into which team performance assessment data will be integrated.

Since both quantitative and qualitative approaches to the team training literature provide only limited suggestions to an R&D agenda, this section focuses on integrating constructs from the evaluation literature with the team performance assessment literature. These include discussion of two major types of evaluation and three types of evaluators.

Summative evaluation. Summative evaluation asks the question "Does the intervention work?" In a military environment, a common question is "Has the team training using X approach been effective?" Implicit in that question is comparison. That is, the intervention must be judged either in relation to other existing alternatives, or hypothetically, in terms of other uses for the same set of resources. A second part of the summative evaluation question is "How much does the intervention cost?" Again, comparisons may be explicit to existing or potential options. Third, summative evaluation develops information related to a third critical question: "Should we buy it?" Here, the issues are the confidence in the data, and the validity of the inferences drawn from such data.

Summative evaluation is weak in identifying what to do if a system of intervention is not a total, unqualified success. Given that this is most common for most interventions in early stages of development, comparative, summative evaluations are usually mistimed and may create an unduly negative environment for productivity. Another shortfall of summative evaluations is that they provide almost no help in the development/improvement cycle, which should characterize the systematic creation of team training interventions because they are not designed to pinpoint weaknesses or explore potential alternatives for improvement.

Formative evaluation. Basic literature in formative evaluation was developed by Scriven (1967) and Baker and Alkin (1973). Formative evaluation now represents a major focus of evaluation efforts in the public education sector (i.e., Center for the Study of Evaluation) and permits the integration of a variety of quantitative and qualitative data collection and analysis techniques for program improvement. Formative evaluation is designed to identify success and failure segments, components, and details of programs, rather than solely estimating success against a "control" or comparison group. This approach requires data to be collected in more detail, more intensively, and more frequently in order to permit the continuous improvement and, ideally, the generation of options that have a higher probability of success. What is the relationship between summative and formative evaluation? In the military, these functions have been typically and often artificially separated. However, there are good reasons for partially integrating data sources and inferences from summative evaluations, particularly when comparative studies occur early in the development/implementation cycle in relation to formative evaluation efforts. Formative evaluation may be conducted by project staff or by external groups that maintain "third-party" objectivity, interacting with and understanding deeper program goals, processes, and constraints than summative evaluation terms.

Third-party, formative evaluation is recommended for team training evaluation efforts. Evaluations conducted by the project staff itself are called *first-party evaluations*. One common example is when a developer collects pilot test data to assess and improve the final product. First-party evaluators benefit from an immediate intimate connection and understanding of the project but lack distance, detachment, and objectivity, resulting in a diminished credibility for the findings. Assessment of progress or outcomes by supervising or funding agency is known as *second-party evaluation*. In-Progress Reviews (IPRs) and site visits by sponsoring agencies or governing boards are examples of second-party evaluation. Objectivity may also be a problem with this provider of evaluation because supervising agencies often have a vested interest in the outcome of their assessments. Evaluations conducted by an independent group are called *third-party evaluations*. Most examples of third-party evaluation are summative. For instance, the Government Accounting Office (GAO) performs third-party evaluations for government agencies and projects, although these are not usually formative. Independent contractors reporting to state legislatures, school boards, or school districts in the K-12 educational arena also usually conduct summative evaluations. The intent of the third-party, formative evaluators is to assist their client (either the funding agency or project staff) in using systematic data collection to promote project or program improvement. A variation on this approach is to permit the project staff to conduct evaluations themselves with planning guidance and audit by a third-party independent group.

To optimize knowledge of, and access to, program information and early correction, and the ultimate credibility of the findings, we recommend the use of integrated formative evaluation conducted by third-party teams. In all kinds of evaluation, two major concerns should be (a) the adequacy and appropriateness of criterion measures, and (b) the validity of inferences made from these measures.

SUMMARY

We have attempted to provide an overview of the issues involved in seriously attempting to collect team performance assessment information. We described group and team attributes, provided a detailed and, in outcome, bleak picture of the quantity and quality of the existing research and development literature in this field, created some precepts to guide short-term action, and presented a short but critically important agenda for further research. Finally, we cast this performance assessment enterprise, as we have suggested others do, in the context of evaluation models and decision making.

REFERENCES

Baker, E. L. (1988, April). *Sensitive technology assessment of ACOT*. Paper presented at the annual meetings of the American Educational Research Association and the International Association for Computing in Education for the Symposium "Natural Experiments in Computer Saturation: The Apple Classroom of Tomorrow," New Orleans, LA.

Baker, E. L., & Alkin, M. C. (1973). Formative evaluation in instructional development. *AV Communication Review, 21*(4), 389–418.

Baker, E. L., O'Neil, H. F. Jr., & Linn, R. (1991). A performance assessment framework. In S. J. Andriole (Ed.), *New directions in command and control C² systems engineering*. Fairfax, VA: AFCEA International Press.

Bass, B. (1982). Individual capability, team performance, and team productivity. In M. D. Dunnette & E. A. Fleishman (Eds.), *Human capability assessment* (Vol. 1). Hillsdale, NJ: Erlbaum.

Bloom, B. (Ed.). (1956). *Taxonomy of educational objectives*. New York: McKay.

Bock, R. D. (Ed.). (1989). *Multilevel analysis of educational data*. Cambridge, MA: Academic Press.

Boldovici, J. A. (1987). Measuring transfer in military settings. In S. M. Cormier & J. D. Hagman (Eds.), *Transfer of learning: Contemporary research and applications*. San Diego, CA: Academic Press.

Burstall, C. (1989, October). *Beyond the bubble*. Paper presented at the Conference of the California Assessment Program, San Francisco, CA.

Burstein, L., Kim, K., & Delandshire, G. (1989). Multilevel investigations of systematically varying slopes: Issues, alternatives and consequences. In R. D. Bock (Ed.), *Multilevel analysis of educational data* (pp. 235–276). Cambridge, MA: Academic Press.

Carroll, J. B. (1979). Twenty-five years of research on foreign language aptitude. In K. C. Diller (Ed.), *Individual differences and universals in language learning aptitude*. Rowley, MA: Newbury House.

de Leeuw, J., & Kreft, G. G. (1986). Random coefficient models for multilevel analysis. *Journal of Educational Statistics, 11*(1), 57–86.

Dyer, J. A. (1984). Team research and team training: A State-of-the-art review. In F. A. Muckler (Ed.), *Human factors review: 1984*. Santa Monica, CA: The Human Factors Society.

Elliott, E. (1989, October). *The status of educational indicator systems*. Paper presented at the Taherz Stock Conference, Center for Research on Education, Standards and Student Testing, UCLA, Los Angeles, CA.

Fleishman, E. A., & Quaintance, M. K. (1984). *Taxonomies of human performance: The description of human tasks*. Orlando, FL: Academic Press.

Gagné, R. M. (1985). *The conditions of learning* (4th ed.). New York: Holt, Rinehart and Winston.

Goldstein, H. (1987). Multilevel mixed linear model analysis using iterative generalized least squares. *Biometrik, 73,* 43–56.

Green, B. F., Jr., & Wigdor, A. K. (Eds.). (1988a). *Measuring job competency.* [Available from Committee on the Performance of Military Personnel/Commission on Behavioral and Social Sciences and Education/National Research Council/2101 Constitution Ave., N.W./Washington, DC 20418.] Washington, DC: National Academy Press.

Green, B. F., Jr., & Wigdor, A. K. (Eds.). (1988b). *Analysis of job performance measurement data: Report of a workshop* [Available from Committee on the Performance of Military Personnel/Commission on Behavioral and Social Sciences and Education/National Research Council/2101 Constitution Ave., N.W./Washington, DC 20418.] Washington, DC: National Academy Press.

Kreft, I. G. G., & de Leeuv, J. (1989). *Model-based ranking of schools* (CSE Tech. Rep. No. 297). Los Angeles, CA: Center for the Study of Evaluation, University of California, Los Angeles.

Linn, R. L. (1986). Barriers to new test designs. In *The redesign of testing for the 21st century.* Proceedings of the 46th ETS Invitational Conference, Educational Testing Service, New York, NY.

Lumsdaine, A. A. (1960). Design of training aids and devices. In J. Folley (Ed.), *Human factors methods for system design* (AIR-290-60-FR-225). Pittsburgh, PA: American Institutes for Research.

Olmstead, J. A., & Elder, B. L. (1980, November). *Organizational process performance and unit mission readiness: Training for battalion command groups, Vol. I* (Draft Final Report to U.S. Army Research Institute for the Behavioral and Social Sciences, Contract No. MDA903-78-C-2028). Alexandria, VA: Human Resources Research Organization.

Ouchi, W. G. (1981). *Theory Z: How American business can meet the Japanese challenge.* Reading, MA: Addison-Wesley.

Raudenbush, S. W., & Bryk, A. S. (1986). A hierarchical model for studying school effects. *Sociology of Education, 59,* 1–17.

Scott, T. D. (1984 July). *How to evaluate unit performance* (ARI Research Product 84-14). Alexandria, VA: U.S. Army Research Institute for the Behavioral and Social Sciences.

Scriven, M. (1967). The methodology of evaluation. In R. Tyler, R. M. Gagné, & M. Scriven (Eds.), *Perspectives of curriculum evaluation* (AERA Monograph Series on Curriculum Evaluation, No. 1). Chicago: Rand McNally.

Shavelson, R. J., Winkler, J. D., & Stasz, C. (1985). *Individual characteristics and unit performance: A review of research and methods* (R-3194 MIL). Santa Monica, CA: The Rand Corporation.

Shavelson, R. J., & Salomon, G. (1986). Information technology: Tool and teacher of the mind—Reply to Hawes. *Educational Researcher, 15,* 24–35.

Slavin, R. E., Leavey, M., & Madden, N. A. (1984). Combining cooperative learning and individualized instruction: Effects on student mathematics achievement, attitudes, and behaviors. *Elementary School Journal, 84,* 409–422.

Sternberg, R. J. (1979). The nature of mental abilities. *American Psychologist, 34*(3), 214–230.

Tatsuoka, K. K. (1983). Rule space: An approach for dealing with misconceptions based on item response theory. *Journal of Educational Measurement, 20*(4), 345–354.

U.S. General Accounting Office. (1986, February). *Measuring military capability: Progress, problems and future direction* (Report to the Chairman, Committee on Armed Services, House of Representatives, GAO/NSIAD-86-72). Washington, DC: U.S. General Accounting Office, National Security and International Affairs Division.

Wagner, H., Hibbits, N., Rosenblatt, R. D., & Schulz, R. (1977). *Team training and evaluation strategies: State-of-the-art* (Tech. Rep. No. HumRRO-TR-77-1). Alexandria, VA: Human Resources Research Organization.

Webb, N. M. (1982). Group composition, group instruction and achievement in cooperative small groups. *Journal of Educational Psychology, 74,* 475–484.

8

Mathematical Models of Team Performance: A Distributed Decision-Making Approach *

David L. Kleinman
Peter B. Luh
Krishna R. Pattipati
Daniel Serfaty

INTRODUCTION

In large-scale systems that involve humans, machines, computers, networks, and databases interacting within an organization, problem scope and complexity often require that the decision-making function be *distributed* over several humans. Examples include electric power distribution, military command and control (C^2), air-traffic control, product distribution and supply, management infor-

* This research was made possible through grants N00014-87-K-0707 and N00014-84-C-0577 from the Office of Naval Research, under the Distributed Tactical Decisionmaking program. The authors wish to acknowledge the effort and dedication of their students and ex-students at the University of Connecticut, Linda Bushnell, Cynthia Kohn, Xi-Yi Miao, Dan Sullivan, David Koenig, Greg Burton, and Ranga Mallubhatla, and their colleagues at ALPHATECH, Inc., Elliot Entin and David Castañon, for their assistance in conducting the various experiments and in developing the normative-descriptive models that so excellently replicate the experimental results.

177

mation systems, and so on. A characteristic feature of such systems is the presence of *teams* of human decision makers (DMs) who, while geographically separated, must coordinate to share their information, resources, and activities in order to achieve their goals in what is generally a complex, dynamic, and uncertain environment. The challenge facing the scientific community is to develop and validate theories and models for human decision making in distributed systems—models that could ultimately suggest design modifications to enhance the overall system performance.

For the past several years, Kleinman and his associates (Kleinman, Serfaty, & Luh, 1984; Serfaty & Kleinman, 1985; Bushnell, Serfaty, & Kleinman, 1988; Miao, Luh, Kleinman, & Castañon, 1988; Kohn, Kleinman, & Serfaty, 1987; Koenig, Burton, & Kleinman, 1988; Serfaty, 1990; Mallubhatla, Pattipati, Kleinman, & Tang, 1990; Kleinman & Serfaty, 1989) have collaborated on an interdisciplinary program of experimental and theoretical research involving applied mathematics, experimental psychology, systems and human engineering, and computer science to develop a *normative-descriptive theory* to address problems of team-distributed decision making. Based on this theory, they have developed *empirically validated* normative-descriptive *models* that capture the complexity, dynamicity, and uncertainty of the task environment and, in turn, quantify the resulting team performance, coordination, and decision strategies in specific situations.

The key objectives of this chapter are to present several of these models, to introduce the mathematical tools used to support the modeling activity, to demonstrate the process by which the normative-descriptive theory is applied to generate predictions of actual team performance, and to offer some novel hypotheses on team decision-making behavior and performance. Our long-range objective is to see the normative-descriptive theory developed to the point where it can be used as a tool for *system design*. This is not an unreasonable goal for the not-too-distant future, as the developed models grow in complexity and more experience is obtained with their application.

The purpose of this introductory section is to point out the characteristics of the distributed dynamic decision-making problems that have been addressed, to define the normative-descriptive modeling approach, and to describe a unique research paradigm for distributed decision making that has been used to generate and collect the data to develop and validate the mathematical models.

Characteristics of Distributed Decision Making

Most decision-making activities in large-scale systems and organizations are performed by a team of people who are interconnected by communication networks. As a consequence of decentralization, each DM has only access to a portion of the information available to the team. Moreover, in realistic situations, the total information set may be incomplete and inaccurate due to lax updating, missed detection of events, information whose quality changes with time, and errors in data taking. Hence, team information processing is characterized by a high level of uncertainty with partial overlap of information among DMs. The critical issues in team *information processing* are: who should know what, who should communicate what and with whom, and when people should and should not communicate.

The total decision-making load is generally partitioned among DMs by decomposing functions into specific tasks and assigning these tasks to individual agents who are responsible for their performance. Moreover, an overlap in task processing (wherein two or more DMs share responsibility for a given function) gives the team a degree of freedom to adapt to uneven demand by sharing load. The critical issues in team *task processing* are: what should be done, who should do what, and at what time.

Decision makers are provided with limited resources with which to accomplish their objectives either in information processing or in task processing. The distribution of these resources among DMs, and the assignment of these resources to seek information and process tasks, are key team decisions. The team members must dynamically coordinate their resources to process their individual tasks while assuring that team performance goals are met. The critical issues in team *resource allocation* are: who should own or transfer a specific resource, when, and for how long.

In summary, the type of team decision-making problems that we address are those involving *distributed information processing and dynamic resource allocation under uncertainty*. The term *distributed* implies that the team members may have different information, expertise, resources, responsibilities, and knowledge of their individual subproblems.

The Normative-Descriptive Modeling Approach

A purely *normative* (or prescriptive) approach to develop a theory for team decision making would have the disadvantage of not representing actual human performance. On the other hand, a purely *descriptive* (or data-driven) approach would have the disadvantage of not providing a predictive capability for situations in which there is not directly applicable data. Such a capability is clearly needed for system design. For these reasons we have embraced the *normative-descriptive* approach (Rapoport, 1975) as the basis for building quantitative models for team performance. The key premise of this approach is that motivated expert human decision makers strive for optimality but are constrained from achieving it by their inherent perceptual limitations and cognitive biases. The normative-descriptive approach, which constrains the normative solutions by empirically determined cognitive characteristics, aims to provide *realistic predictions* of human performance.

As illustrated in Figure 8.1, normative-descriptive model building is an iterative process. Typically, one starts with normative mathematical theories (estimation theory, queuing theory, dynamic programming, decision theory, game theory, etc.) that predict "optimal" behavior in certain situations and produce hypotheses and preliminary models to be validated. Model-driven experiments are then designed and operationalized, from which actual human data are collected and analyzed. The normative model predictions of human behavior are compared to the experimental results, and consistent discrepancies are attributed to psychologically interpretable descriptive factors such as human cognitive biases (e.g., recency, confirmation) and other information-processing limitations (e.g., memory, processing rate, planning horizon). These descriptive factors are then quantified and integrated within the normative theories to produce a normative-descriptive model that more closely predicts the experimental results. This process can be repeated if model-vs.-data comparisons are not in agreement.

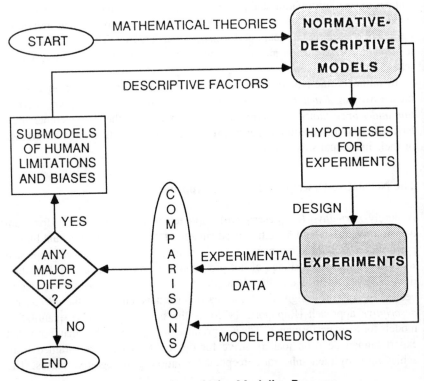

Figure 8.1.   The Normative-Descriptive Modeling Process

Clearly, the identification and quantification of the salient descriptive factors lies at the heart of this modeling approach. Several such biases and limitations, such as anchoring and adjustment, recency, conservatism, and so on, that are pertinent to single human decision making are well known from previous research in cognitive science (Slovic, Fischoff, & Lichtenstein, 1977; Pattipati & Kleinman, 1979). Team-related biases dealing with how an individual interprets and uses the stated judgments of other team members, and how individual choice is affected by the presence of co-acting team members, have only recently begun to receive attention by the research community, and generally require elaboration and quantification via analysis of the experimental results.

The normative-descriptive approach to human modeling has been used with great success in several contexts. In 1971 the Optimal Control Model (OCM) for predicting individual human performance and response behavior in manual control and estimation tasks was developed (Kleinman, Baron, & Levison, 1971). This model, which is now the accepted state of the art in manual control, has since been applied in numerous studies to examine information and display requirements, automatic-vs.-manual control tradeoffs, and effects of environmental stressors. Pattipati, Kleinman, and Ephrath (1983) extended the concepts behind the OCM to dynamic decision problems. The resulting Dynamic Decision Model (DDM) has since been applied to study human decision-making problems in diverse areas such as electric power dispatching under emergency conditions (Pattipati, Entin, Kleinman, & Gully, 1982) and antisubmarine warfare and multitarget tracking (Wohl, Serfaty, Entin, Deckert, & James, 1988). Efforts to apply the normative-descriptive approach to develop models for *multihuman* decision making began in 1984, under the Office of Naval Research's Distributed Tactical Decision Making (DTDM) program. The models to be described in this chapter were developed under the DTDM program. Specifically, we will present results from two modeling efforts in team information processing, and two modeling efforts in team resource allocation.

The Distributed Dynamic Decision Making (DDD) Paradigm

The backbone of our normative-descriptive research is a unique experimental paradigm for studying team decision making and coordination in a controlled laboratory setting (Kleinman, Serfaty, & Luh, 1984; Kleinman & Serfaty, 1989). In the DDD paradigm, multiple tasks with different deadlines, processing times, attributes, and values or priorities, arrive at random. Coacting decision makers must process distributed information to: (a) estimate various task attributes, (b) identify task type, and (c) determine and schedule the resources needed to process any specific task. The DMs can obtain task information from their local/ private databases, from communication exchanges with other team members, or by "probing" to actively seek additional information. A DM may process a task under his or her responsibility by allocating some mix of his or her resources to that task, which are then tied up for a time T_r. Resources can be exchanged or transferred between DMs, but with an attendant time delay. The DMs are required to coordinate their information, their actions, and their resources to process tasks in a timely and accurate manner in order to maximize the total value earned by the team. The DDD paradigm is flexible enough to permit the study of selected team activities, depending on the specific research focus. The richness of the paradigm, however, guarantees nontrivial jobs for the human subjects who must perform them and the scientist who must analyze and model them.

The DDD paradigm is supported by a powerful team-in-the-loop real-time simulator currently implemented on a network of SUN workstations in the University of Connecticut's CYBERLAB. The hardware and software facilities provide real-time control and online data collection, interactive display/interface media, and a computerized intrahuman communications subsystem within which delay can be manipulated. In order to create the experimental environment, the DDD simulation software generates dynamic task scenarios presented to the decisionmakers through a set of graphical and alphanumerical displays. Figure 8.2 shows such a typical configuration. Based upon the distributed information, each "expert" DM decides which task to process, whether to seek more information for situation assessment through probes and/or communication, whether to seek more resources from other DMs, or to allocate resources to process a currently selected task.

A set of "tools" are available to support the decision makers' activities in trying to achieve their team goal: (a) *information* tools—real-time graphical displays showing the geographical distribution of tasks, resources available to the team, estimated attributes, type and time required for each task, actual remaining "strength" of own assets, and so on; (b) *decision* tools—a decision support system (DSS) for resource allocations suggesting amount and type of resources needed to process a given task, which is tuned to the expertise level of the decision maker using it; and (c) *communication* tools—a set of preformatted communication messages for request and transfer of resources, information, and actions between team members. A more detailed description of the DDD paradigm, and the rationale behind its design, can be found in Kleinman et al. (1984), Serfaty and Kleinman (1985), and Serfaty (1990).

The DDD paradigm permits the controlled manipulation of numerous independent variables (Serfaty & Kleinman, 1985). *Internal variables* define the information structure (centralized vs. decentralized), the degree of information overlap in decentralized cases (who "sees" what), overlap and division of task processing responsibility (who "can do" what), the organizational structure (flat vs. hierarchy), etc. In addition, the DDD paradigm can support the manipulation of human-system interface variables such as information presentation, information aggregation, input/output access, and so on (Kleinman & Serfaty, 1989). *External variables* represent conditions that are imposed on the team from the

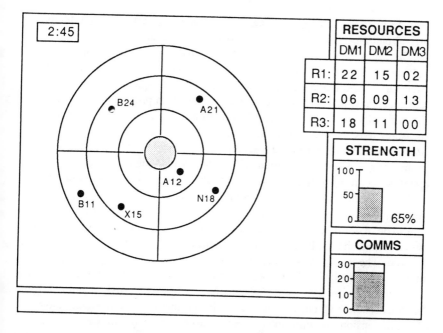

2:45			

RESOURCES

	DM1	DM2	DM3
R1:	22	15	02
R2:	06	09	13
R3:	18	11	00

STRENGTH

65%

COMMS

MESSAGE IN

MSG #1 FROM DM2 TIME 1:27
PLZ SEND RESOURCES 5 0 4

TIME

2:45

MESSAGE OUT

MSG #4 TO DM2 TIME 2:40
SENDING YOU INFO ON TASK 18
TYPE: N ATTRIB: 1.1 4.1

DECISION SUPPORT SYSTEM

TYPE: A   ATTRIBUTES: 3.6 5.1 ⟶   RESOURCES: 4.7 11.2 7.6

TIME	TASK	ATTRIBUTES		PROBE INFO		STATUS	RESOURCES			TR	T.CPL	SCORE
:40	B 11	1.2	*.*	1.3	2.5	OPEN				40		
:52	A 12	3.1	3.9			DONE						89.3%
1:11	A 21	3.6	5.1			ATTK	05	11	08	45	2:50	
1:39	B 24	*.*	*.*			PROBE	02	03	02	40		
2:10	N 18	1.1	4.1			OPEN-U				41		
2:37	X 15	2.2	*.*			OPEN				39		

⟸ ENTER: Attack(A), Probe(P), Update(U), DSS(D), Comm(C#)

Figure 8.2.   An Individual DM's Workstation Display in the DDD Paradigm

outside word and include degree of information uncertainty, task tempo and arrival patterns (input load), team resource scarcity, and so on.

The types of data (i.e., dependent variables or measures) that have been collected and analyzed in the various experiments fall roughly into four, not necessarily disjoint, categories. *Performance* variables deal with reward earned, team accuracy, team timeliness, and effectiveness in processing either information or tasks. Team final strength has been a useful composite performance measure; it is an indicator of how closely the team achieves perfect results. *Strategy* variables describe the mechanisms by which the team attained its performance. These measures are often categorized by individual DM, by task type, by timeline according to when actions were taken, and so on. Thus, these measures include distribution of load among the individual DMs, amount and pattern of resource transfers, resource utilizations, reneging (not performing certain tasks), and so on. *Coordination* variables describe the means by which the team strategy was effected, that is, how the DMs dynamically supported the strategy that they utilized. These measures largely involve communications usage (e.g., resource and/or information requests) and communication patterns among DMs. The subjective *Workload* measures are obtained, using the SWAT technique (Reid, Shingledecker, Nygren, & Eggemeier, 1981), that classify workload along the three dimensions of time load, mental efforts, and psychological stress. The DDD studies have pioneered the use of SWAT to assess team subjective workload in addition to individual workload. At the present time only the first three categories of dependent variables are amenable to mathematical modeling via our normative-descriptive approach.

The Separation Approach in the Modeling of Multihuman Decision Making

The initial efforts in studying team decision making developed and tested the DDD paradigm across a wide range of experimental conditions for a two-person team. The independent variables included: the team information structure, the level of expertise and functional overlap between the team members, task information uncertainty and arrival tempo, resource scarcity, and so on. The results of these experiments generated basic hypotheses for team decision making and defined the directions for follow-on model-based experimentation (Serfaty, 1990).

However, the inherent complexity of developing analytic models for both distributed information processing *and* resource allocation within a single mathematical framework led us to separate our subsequent research into two main thrusts: (a) information processing and situation assessment, and (b) resource allocation and task sequencing. This approach is consonant with the *separation principle* in human decision making (Simon, 1969), wherein, once a DM generates an *estimate* of system status, he or she then uses this estimate as if it were the *true* status. Thus, the following section will describe two modeling efforts that have dealt with the topic of information processing, the first within a dyad, and the next within a three-person hierarchical team. The subsequent section will describe two models in resource allocation/sequencing, the first within a dyad, and the next within a three-person flat organization.

INFORMATION-PROCESSING MODELS

The first applications of the normative-descriptive approach to model team decision making focused on information-processing problems. Recognizing the importance of situation assessment in a large class of naturalistic decision processes, the decision to focus first on team information-processing models was also due to the availability of: (a) a rich set of mathematical models in the area of optimal information processing, (b) extensive psychology results in the area of sequential processing of information, and (c) several successful applications of optimal estimation and filtering theory to develop models of single human information-processing behavior. The information-processing models developed to date consider only static situations, such as those in which the time available to make decisions does not drive the decision-making process.

The Distributed Information-Processing (DIP) Model

The main contribution of this work, which is presented in full detail in Bushnell (1987) and summarized in Bushnell et al. (1988), is the development and validation of a mathematical model that accurately predicts how team members weight and combine sequential information from distributed sources. The model is novel in that it considers the exchange of assessments between team members who may have different quality information sources. The order of the exchange of information, and the quality of the information communicated, are both critical variables affecting the overall team performance.

Problem description. A two-person team is confronted with a series of static targets, the information about which must be processed by both DMs. The team's performance is based on the accuracy with which it estimates attributes (i.e., numerical characteristics) of the target, such as its strength and bearing. In order to make the most accurate estimate of the attributes, the DMs must integrate information from four sources that include: (a) their prior knowledge about the target, (b) initial measurement data, (c) probe data, and (d) communicated data. The initial measurement and probe data are noisy measurements of the target's true attributes, while the communicated information is the partner's current estimate of the attributes. The "expertise" of a DM is directly related to the quality of the information he or she receives. The expertise structure of the team could be either equal (both "high" experts), or differential (one DM is a "high" expert, while the other is a "low" expert). Two different orderings of information sources can also be considered. The "MPC" order (Measure, Probe, Communicate) will be described below. A second order, called "MCP," can also be considered where the DMs exchange their information before probing.

When a target appears on the display screen under the MPC order, initial measurements of the two attributes are presented first to each DM. These measurements have a quality in accordance with each DM's expertise. With this initial data and the prior knowledge of the target, the DMs individually estimate the target's attributes for the first update. Each DM next initiates a probe to gather more information. The probe returns measurements of the attributes with quality in accord with each decision maker's expertise. With this new information about the target, each DM again estimates the target attributes for the second update. Next, the DMs communicate by exchanging their current estimates of the target's attributes. When the DMs receive their partner's data, they each integrate this new data with their previous information to make the final estimate of the target's attributes. Thus, one can analyze the processes of weighting and combining four pieces of information (the prior knowledge about the target, the initial measurement, the probe information, and the communication information), under different orders of information flows within the team, and under different expertise structures.

Normative model formulation. A normative model can be developed to predict the optimal fusion of information in a two-person team. In this analytical approach a decision maker is conceptualized as a sequential information processor who integrates data from initial measurement sources, probes, and communication reports from the other team member with his or her prior knowledge of the target's attributes. Recursive least square theory (Gelb, 1968) provides the mathematical framework for the model. The recursive equation at step k calculates a new estimate $\hat{a}_k$ from the last attribute estimate $\hat{a}_{k-1}$ when a new piece of data z_k with covariance V_k is received. The z_k may represent an initial measurement, a probe, or a communication message, and is a noisy or contaminated replica of the true attribute, a.

When z_k is the initial measurement or a probe the estimate â and its associated error covariance P are updated as:

$$\hat{a}_k = [P_{k-1}^{-1} + V_k^{-1}]^{-1} \times [P_{k-1}^{-1}\hat{a}_{k-1} + V_k^{-1}z_k]; k \geq 1 \tag{1}$$

$$P_k = [P_{k-1}^{-1} + V_k^{-1}]^{-1} \tag{2}$$

The initial conditions on the estimator are the attribute's a priori mean and covariance: $\hat{a}_0 = \mu$, $P_0 = \Sigma$.

MATHEMATICAL MODELS OF TEAM PERFORMANCE 187

When z_k is the communicated information the update equations take the following form:

$$\hat{a}_k = [P_{k-1}^{-1} + V_k^{-1} - \Sigma^{-1}]^{-1} \times [P_{k-1}^{-1}\hat{a}_{k-1} + V_k^{-1}z_k - \Sigma^{-1}\mu]; k \geq 1 \quad (3)$$

$$P_k = [P_{k-1}^{-1} + V_k^{-1} - \Sigma^{-1}]^{-1} \quad (4)$$

The extra term in Eqs. (3)–(4) is needed to remove duplicate use of the same prior information only when the measurement comes from a partner's communication (Willsky, Bello, Castañon, Levy, & Verghese, 1982). It is assumed that each DM starts off with the same prior knowledge about the target.

The initial measurement and the probe data are received via the DM's own information-gathering resources, and each has a variance V_k corresponding to that DM's expertise, where a low expert will have a larger variance than a high expert. When the measurement is from a communication exchange, the variance V_k is equal to the partner's variance on his or here estimate at update step k, namely $V_k = P_{k(partner)}$. Thus, the information received from a partner is weighted by the decision maker's *perception* of how well his or her partner is optimally combining information.

Experimental design and procedure. In order to test the normative model, an experiment was designed to simulate a naval C^2 environment in which team members were required to measure target attributes, and exchange and combine target information among themselves. The resulting distributed information-processing (DIP) experiment was derived from the DDD paradigm and was conducted with two-person teams (dyads). Each subject sat at a workstation consisting of a graphics display and an alphanumeric display. The graphics display showed the position of a static target on a simulated radar screen. The alphanumeric display presented to each subject the target information, the communication messages exchanged (information transferred) between the team members, and an input command line. On each trial the true attribute values were drawn from a normal distribution, $N(\mu, \Sigma)$. The subjects' goal was to estimate the attributes as accurately as possible from their measurements z_0, z_1, z_2.

The experiment was designed using two independent variables that the normative model predicted would affect the information-combining process. The first independent variable changed the relative expertise of the two subjects in the team. In the "differential" expertise case one subject was a high expert (H) and the other was a low expert (L). The "equal" expertise case designated both subjects as high experts. This independent variable yields three cases that can be studied involving the different team expertise structures. These are the points of view of: (a) the high expert in the equal expertise (H-H) team, (b) the high expert in the differential expertise (H-L) team, and (c) the low expert in the differential expertise teams. The second independent variables was the order of information processing. After receiving the initial measurement, a subject received information from either a probe or a communication. The timing of the exchange of data between the subjects in the team was varied by having the subjects communicate either before probing (MCP order) or after probing (MPC order). These two independent variables created four different experimental conditions to be simulated, and resulted in six different subject points-of-view to be observed and analyzed.

The major dependent variables that were recorded were the two-dimensional estimate vectors for each of the three update steps, that is, $\hat{a}_1$, $\hat{a}_2$, $\hat{a}_3$ (for both subjects). These were used to compute the team and individual estimation errors, $e = |a_1 - \hat{a}_1| + |a_2 - \hat{a}_2|$ at each update.

Comparison between model predictions and experimental results. For each of the experimental conditions, a statistical regression analysis was performed on the experimental data. In order to compare the data with the stagewise combining of information as predicted by the normative model, a scalar regression equation that produced the weighting coefficients in a recursive update step was used, such as

$$\hat{a}_k = c_{\hat{a}}\hat{a}_{k-1} + c_z z_k + c_\mu \mu \tag{5}$$

where the update, $\hat{a}_k$, was regressed on the previous (last) estimate, $\hat{a}_{k-1}$, the measurement, z_k, and prior, μ, for each of the three update steps M, P, C. The regression coefficients $c_{\hat{a}}$, c_z, and c_μ in Eq. (5) model how the subjects weighted their information sources when building an estimate of the target's attributes in each of the three update steps. The first step predicted $\hat{a}_1$ from the prior information and initial measurement. The second step predicted $\hat{a}_2$ from the prior information, $\hat{a}_1$, and the probe (MPC order) or communication (MCP order) measurement. The third regression predicted $\hat{a}_3$ from the prior information, $\hat{a}_2$, and the communication (MPC order) or probe (MCP order) measurement. Table 8.1 presents the values of the regression coefficients for each of the three different cases studied, along with the predictions of these weighting coefficients as obtained from the normative model for the MPC ordering.

A comparison of model–data results for the first update shows that the humans underweighed the previous estimate and overweighed the initial measurement as compared to the normative model-predicted weights. When computing the second update, the experts still counted the prior information (which was predicted to have zero weight), overweighed the probe information, and undervalued their previous estimate, as compared to the normative information fusion model. On the third update, the experts did not remove the common prior information as was predicted, and underweighed the communicated information (especially from a lower level expert) as compared to the predictions.

Normative-descriptive model formulation. A normative-descriptive model of the DM's target attribute estimation process was developed by representing the

Table 8.1.   Normative Model vs. Data Weight Comparisons in the MPC Order (from Bushnell, Serfaty, & Kleinman, 1988)

DM Expertise	Data Source	M			P			C		
		$c_{\hat{a}}$	c_z	c_μ	$c_{\hat{a}}$	c_z	c_μ	$c_{\hat{a}}$	c_z	c_μ
H in H-H team	Model	0.00	0.67	0.33	0.60	0.40	0.00	0.55	0.55	−0.11
	Data	0.00	0.95	0.04	0.48	0.46	0.06	0.59	0.38	0.02
H in H-L team	Model	0.00	0.67	0.33	0.60	0.40	0.00	0.83	0.33	−0.16
	Data	0.00	0.92	0.07	0.49	0.48	0.03	0.89	0.12	−0.01
L in H-L team	Model	0.00	0.34	0.66	0.75	0.25	0.00	0.33	0.83	−0.16
	Data	0.00	0.91	0.09	0.42	0.39	0.18	0.19	0.79	0.02

observed human cognitive biases in the normative model. The normative model equations serve as the foundation to calculate the new update, $\hat{a}_k$, as a function of the previous estimate, $\hat{a}_{k-1}$, the new measurement, z_k, and the prior knowledge μ. When z_k comes from the initial measurement or probe data source, the update equations are similar to the normative model update Eqs. (1)–(4), but with the extra "descriptive" parameters of α and γ, namely,

$$\hat{a}_k = [\alpha P_{k-1}^{-1} + V_k^{-1} + \gamma \Sigma^{-1}]^{-1} \times [\alpha P_{k-1}^{-1}\hat{a}_{k-1} + V_k^{-1}z_k + \gamma \Sigma^{-1}\mu] \quad (6)$$

$$P_k = [\alpha P_{k-1}^{-1} + V_k^{-1} + \gamma \Sigma^{-1}]^{-1} \quad (7)$$

with initial conditions $\hat{a}_0 = \mu$ and $P_0 = \Sigma$. When the new information z_k is the communication message received by the decision maker, two more descriptive parameters, β and δ, are introduced to model the cognitive biases that arise due to the combining of this data. These update equations are:

$$\hat{a}_k = [\alpha P_{k-1}^{-1} + \beta V_k^{-1} + (\gamma - \delta)\Sigma^{-1}]^{-1} \times [\alpha P_{k-1}^{-1}\hat{a}_{k-1} + \beta V_k^{-1}z_k + (\gamma - \delta)\Sigma^{-1}\mu] \quad (8)$$

$$P_k = [\alpha P_{k-1}^{-1} + \beta V_k^{-1} + (\gamma - \delta)\Sigma^{-1}]^{-1} \quad (9)$$

The parameter $\alpha < 1$ models the observed recency phenomena, or exponential discounting of old data, where smaller α implies more underweighing of the older information by the DM. The parameter β is used to model the undervaluing of the other team member's information quality, or perception of the partner's information, as compared to the normative model. When $\beta < 1$, the decision maker is weighing the partner's communication less than optimally. The parameter $\gamma \geq 0$ is used to model the anchoring bias. The parameter δ models the removal of common prior knowledge when updating $\hat{a}$ using communicated data.

By allowing δ to be greater than or equal to zero, we are able to model the degree to which the common prior information is discounted by the decision maker. Note that the normative model uses $(\alpha, \beta, \gamma, \delta) = (1, 1, 0, 1)$. Thus, with the descriptive parameter set $(\alpha, \beta, \gamma, \delta)$, we are able to quantify the four cognitive biases that were identified in the information assessment process.

The descriptive parameter values were adjusted by trial and error to produce the best possible prediction of the information combining process for all cases considered. An example of the results is shown in Figure 8.3a and 8.3b for the MPC condition with differential expertise. It is evident from these figures that the normative-descriptive model predicts the weights of Eq. (5) for each update step far more accurately than does the normative model. Similar results were obtained for all other conditions using a reasonably consistent parameter set $(\alpha, \beta, \gamma, \delta) \approx (0.91, 0.75, 0.13, 0.0)$. Only the value of β showed some variation over the six different experimental conditions with a standard deviation 0.26. This variability in β can be explained by a phenomenon that we call a "polarization of perception" of the partner's expertise. While quite interesting, a discussion of this phenomenon is beyond the scope of this presentation. A detailed discussion can be found in Bushnell (1987).

Summary. A major objective of this modeling effort was to show that the normative-descriptive modeling approach is a valid and powerful method for quantifying information-processing activities of a *team* of decision makers. These activities include the combination and integration of various internal and external sources of information. Optimal estimation theory served as the basis for the normative model. By inspecting the differences between experimental and normative model results, we were able to identify four *cognitive biases* in the team information fusion process. These biases were then quantified and integrated in a normative-descriptive model that predicted the actual experimental data far better than the normative model did. The first bias was that the subjects consistently overweighed the most recent information. Such actions are interpreted as strong *recency* effects. Another behavior pattern was that the subjects continually placed some weight on the prior knowledge, even though such weightings were not predicted by the normative model. This bias can be interpreted as *anchoring* to prior knowledge. A third observation was that the subjects were *not discounting the common prior knowledge* on the communication exchange update step. A fourth pattern was that the subjects systematically *undervalued the information received from their partners,* independently of the quality, as compared to the normative model predictions. These last two observed patterns are team characteristics and demonstrate the inability of team members to integrate correctly information sent by other DMs. One can postulate that the appropriate amount of training should reduce these biases by correctly focusing on the quality and reliability of the subject's information sources, including the other team members.

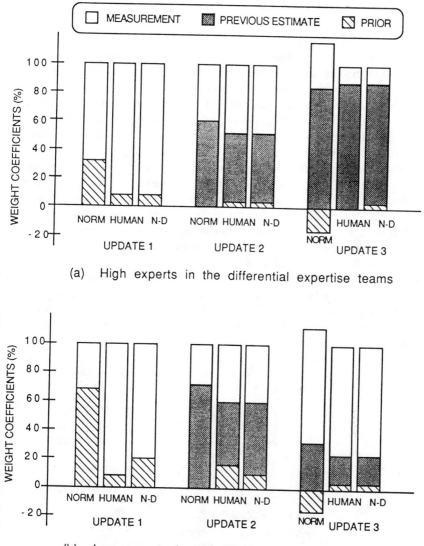

(a)   High experts in the differential expertise teams

(b)   Low experts in the differential expertise teams

Figure 8.3.   Information Weight Comparisons in the Differential Expertise Teams, MPC order (N = 1280). From Bushnell, Serfaty, and Kleinman (1988)

The Hierarchical Information-Processing (HIP) Model

The successful application of the normative-descriptive theory approach in the DIP study, combined with past research on the issues of ambiguity and uncertainty in probabilistic inference and belief updating (Einhorn & Hogarth, 1985), motivated us to investigate how a leader in a three-person hierarchical team combines the opinions and confidences of his or her two subordinates to solve an event identification (or hypothesis-testing) problem. The details on the resulting hierarchical information-processing (HIP) model may be found in Mallubhatla (1990) and Mallubhatla et al. (1991).

Problem description. The team structure and its information flow are shown in Figure 8.4. The team is hierarchical, with a leader (DM0) and two subordinates (DM1 and DM2). Given ambiguous attribute information on a target, the objective of the team is to correctly decide the target type: a neutral (H_0) or a threat (H_1). The team has access to conditionally independent attribute measurements y_i from sensors s_i, (i = 0, 1, 2). The measurement, y_0, from sensor s_0 is global and is available to all three DMs, while the measurement y_i from the local sensor s_i is accessible only to DMi (i = 1, 2). Each of the measurements y_i is a noisy version of a two dimensional vector of target attributes, a. In addition to being noisy, the data obtained by the subordinates is ambiguous; that is, at certain times (when the sensor breaks down) the measurements provide absolutely no information on the target attributes.

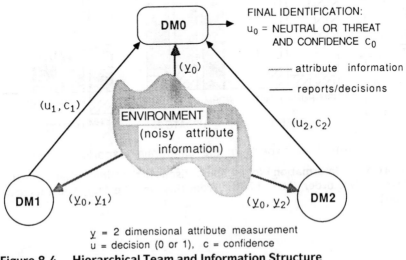

y = 2 dimensional attribute measurement
u = decision (0 or 1), c = confidence

Figure 8.4.   Hierarchical Team and Information Structure

The two subordinates have differential expertise: DM1 is an expert in detecting threats (event H_1), while DM2 is an expert in detecting neutrals (event H_0). The expertise is manipulated via adjustment of the measurement noise covariances of y_1 and y_2. The subordinates (DM1 and DM2) report their opinions (u_1, u_2) and their associated confidences (c_1, c_2) in their decision. The leader (DM0) makes the final event decision u_0 (H_0 or H_1) based on the team's common measurement data, y_0, and the opinions and confidences of the subordinates (u_1, c_1, u_2, c_2).

Normative model formulation. The normative model for the team is comprised of (a) a model for each subordinate (DM1 and DM2), and (b) a model for the leader (DM0). A subordinate DMi ($i = 1, 2$) bases his or her decision u_i and the confidence estimate c_i on his or her own private data set y_i and the global measurement y_0. When the prior probabilities of H_0 and H_1 are equal, and the costs of misclassification are equal, the normative decision strategy used for DMi ($i = 1, 2$) is a likelihood ratio test given by:

$$L(y_0,y_i) = \frac{p(y_0,y_i|H_1)}{p(y_0,y_i|H_0)} = \frac{p(y_0|H_1)p(y_i|H_1)}{p(y_0|H_0)p(y_i|H_0)} = L(y_0)L(y_i) \underset{\underset{u_i = 0}{<}}{\overset{\overset{u_i = 1}{>}}{1}} 1 \qquad (10)$$

where $u_i = 0[1]$ implies that DMi's decision is $H_0[H_1]$, and $L(y_i)$, $i = 0, 1, 2$ are the likelihood ratios.

The confidence is defined as the probability that the decision made is correct given the measurement data. The confidence c_i that DMi attaches to his decision u_i is given by:

$$c_i = p(H = u_i \mid y_0, y_i); \, i = 1, 2 \qquad (11)$$

Since there are only two possible decisions, the confidence c_i can be rewritten in terms of c_{i1}, the confidence of DMi conditioned on the fact that the decision is a threat, as:

$$c_i = [u_i c_{i1} + (1 - u_i)(1 - c_{i1})]; \, 1 = 1, 2 \qquad (12)$$

Using Bayes's rule, c_{i1} can be expressed in terms of the likelihood ratios as:

$$c_{i1} = L(y_0)L(y_i)[1 + L(y_0)L(y_i)]^{-1}; \, i = 1, 2 \qquad (13)$$

Note that the confidence c_{i1} is a monotonic function of each likelihood ratio. The leader's decision, which is also the team's final decision, is based on the reports of the subordinates and the global data. The optimal decision rule for DM0 is also a likelihood ratio test:

$$\frac{p(y_0,u_1,c_1,u_2,c_2|H_1)}{p(y_0,u_1,c_1,u_2,c_2|H_0)} \begin{array}{c} u_0 = 1 \\ > \\ < \\ u_0 = 0 \end{array} 1 \tag{14}$$

where u_0 is the final decision made by DM0. It can be shown (Mallubhatla, 1990) that the likelihood ratio of Eq. (14) can be conveniently written in terms of the individual likelihood ratios as:

$$\frac{p(y_0,u_1,c_1,u_2,c_2|H_1)}{p(y_0,u_1,c_1,u_2,c_2|H_0)} = L(y_0)L(y_1)L(y_2) \tag{15}$$

The above relation implies that DM0's decision rule is precisely what would result if DM0 had access to a centralized database containing all three measurements $\{y_0, y_1, y_2\}$; that is, the likelihood ratios are sufficient statistics for the decision problem. The likelihood ratios $L(y_i)$ can be obtained from Eqs. (12)–(13), given c_i, u_i, and $L(y_0)$.

Experimental design and procedure. Experiments were conducted using the DDD paradigm on a network of three SUN workstations. The teams had to identify a series of static targets appearing on their screens as threats or neutrals from (noisy) measurements of the task's attributes. In truth, a threat had $a_1 = a_2 = 5.6 = m_t$ for both attributes, while those for a neutral were $a_1 = a_2 = 4.4 = m_n$. The prior probabilities of threats and neutrals were both equal to 0.5. The cost of making a correct decision was zero, while the cost of making an incorrect decision was unity. For a detailed description of the experiments, see Koenig et al. (1988).

The standard deviation of the measurement noise for a DM was related to the expertise level of that DM. For example, if the target was a threat, the measurement noise for DM1 (who was expert at detecting threats) had a standard deviation $\sigma_{1t} = 0.8$. But if the target was a neutral, the measurement noise had $\sigma_{1n} = 2.0$. A similar condition held for DM2. The measurement noise variances were chosen such that an expert would make errors 10% of the time, while a nonexpert would make errors 30% of the time on a particular target type when the measurements were nonambiguous. The global data had $\sigma_0 = 2.0$ for all DMs.

Two levels of ambiguity were considered in the experiments, one in which there was no ambiguity and the other in which the measurements were ambiguous 20% of the time. When a measurement was nonambiguous, it was drawn from a normal distribution $N(m, \sigma^2)$ with a different mean, m, for threat and neutral targets. The ambiguous measurements were drawn from a uniform distribution over [0, 10], U(0, 10). Thus, the probability density function for DMi's measurement of attribute y_j, $p(y_{ji})$, $j = 1, 2$; $i = 1, 2$ is:

$$p(y_{ji}) = 0.5[(1 - \rho)N(m_t, \sigma_{it}^2) + \rho U(0, 10)] + 0.5[(1 - \rho)N(m_n, \sigma_{in}^2) + \rho U(0, 10)] \tag{16}$$

where ρ is the fraction of time (or probability that) the measurements were ambiguous.

Each of six teams was asked to identify 60 different targets spread over four experimental sessions. The decision-making process was done in two stages. In stage 1, the subordinates made their decisions, along with confidence levels, based on their own private data and the global data. In addition, DM0 made a decision based on the global data alone and attached a confidence level to his or her decision. The subordinates then transmitted their opinions and confidences to the leader. In stage 2, DM0 made the final team decision, along with a confidence report, based on the global data and the reports from the subordinates.

Comparisons between model predictions and experimental results. The normative model was implemented for each of the 60 targets presented to the subject teams for both ambiguous data and nonambiguous data conditions. Although the model and the subjects performed the task with approximately the same overall probability of error, the comparisons on a target-by-target basis were in disagreement for some 20%–25% of the cases, most of which were borderline cases, with likelihood ratios ≈ 1.0. The confidences are best compared assuming that the DM makes a decision that the target is a threat. For example, when DMi decides that the target is a threat with a confidence of c_{i1}, we take it as is. However, when he or she makes a decision that the target is a neutral with a confidence of c_{i0}, we use $c_{i1} = 1 - c_{i0}$ in the model–data comparison. For each of the 60 targets, the confidence data for each DM was averaged over the six experimental teams to obtain the average confidence estimates for each DM, and these results were plotted versus the corresponding log-likelihood function, $L(y_0, y_i)$. To smooth the graphs, we divided the abscissa into 20 regions, and the set of points lying within each region was replaced by a single point having the same root mean square value. The plots generated by this method show more clearly the general trend of the confidences versus L.

The confidence results corresponding to the ambiguous data conditions are compared in Figure 8.5. In Figure 8.5a the normative model predictions for the subordinate DM2 is compared with the smoothed experimental results. (The results for subordinate DM1 are similar, and hence, not shown.) Figure 8.5b shows the comparison for DM0. It can be seen from these figures that the subordinates and the leader in stage 2 are conservative in their confidence estimates, as compared to the normative model predictions. In the previous DIP effort, it was found that humans exhibit sequential recency effects (they over-

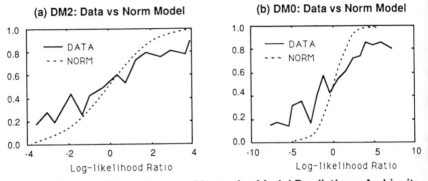

Figure 8.5.   Confidence Data vs. Normative Model Predictions, Ambiguity Conditions

weigh the more recent data) when estimating target attributes. Also, a human (in this case DM0) tends to undervalue the communication/opinion received from other team members. Furthermore, it is known that subjects tend to misperceive base-rate statistics, so that an incorrect weighting given to the ambiguous data—wherein subjects assume that ambiguous data occurs a fraction of time which is not equal to the prescribed 0.2—is quite likely. We next develop a normative-descriptive model that takes into account the above mentioned cognitive biases.

Normative-descriptive model formulation. Our initial hypothesis is that the conservative behavior of the DMs is a consequence of sequential ordering effects, and misperception of the underlying probability distributions and other team members' expertise. As in the DIP model, recursive least squares theory is used to develop normative-descriptive models that take into account these cognitive limitations of the human subjects.

Normative-Descriptive Models for the Subordinates. The normative-descriptive model has two steps. In the first step, the model recursively estimates the target attributes from the measurements y_0 and y_i. In step 2 it uses these estimates in a likelihood ratio test to obtain the decisions and the confidences of the DMs. Since the two attribute measurements in $y = [y_1, y_2]$ are conditionally independent, the update equations can be written for a scalar y_k and then applied to the two attributes separately.

The actual measurement y_{ji}, $j = 1, 2$, made by DMi comes from either the threat distribution, or the neutral distribution, or the uniform distribution—a mixture of Gaussian and uniform densities as in Eq. (16). Our modeling approach approximates the actual Gaussian and uniform mixture by a *single* (normal) distribution having the same first and second moments. A Gaussian mixture $w_1 N(m_1, p_1) + w_2 N(m_2, p_2)$, where w_1 and w_2 are weights that add to unity, is first approximated by a single normal density $N(\mathbf{m}, \mathbf{p})$, with $\mathbf{m}$ and $\mathbf{p}$ given by:

$$\mathbf{m} = w_1 m_1 + w_2 m_2 \tag{17}$$

$$\mathbf{p} = w_1 p_1 + w_2 p_2 + (w_1 m_1^2 + w_2 m_2^2 - \mathbf{m}^2) \tag{18}$$

Note that the approximation is better when m_1 and m_2 are close. The process is then repeated to combine this normal density with the uniform density (Mallubhatla, 1990). To account for the subordinates' misperception of the underlying probability of ambiguous data, a descriptive factor ρ' (generally $\neq \rho$) is used in the model in lieu of the actual probability factor ρ in Eq. (16).

The attribute estimate $\hat{a}$ is initialized with $\hat{a}_0 = \mathbf{m}$, and a variance $P_0 = \mathbf{p}$ from Eqs. (17)–(18). Following the DIP model, the update of the target attribute estimate (decoupled for each attribute) is given by:

$$\hat{a}_k = [\alpha P_{k-1}^{-1} + V_k^{-1}]^{-1} \times [\alpha P_{k-1}^{-1} \hat{a}_{k-1} + V_k^{-1} z_k] \tag{19}$$

$$P_k = [\alpha P_{k-1}^{-1} + V_k^{-1}]^{-1} \tag{20}$$

where z_k is the current measurement upon which the update is based and V_k is the corresponding measurement noise covariance. The above equations are applied sequentially first to y_0, and then to y_i for each DMi. The parameter $\alpha < 1$ is a descriptive factor that is used to account for the sequential recency effects shown by the human subjects. When $\alpha < 1$, the model gives more weight to the current measurement (i.e., less weight to older information) than does the normative model.

At the end of estimation process we obtain $\hat{a}_f$, a 2-dimensional vector of the estimate of the target attributes, and its error covariance matrix P_f. The estimate $\hat{a}_f$ serves as an "effective" measurement for the decision process (subsuming y_0 and y_i), so that:

$$p(y_0, y_i \mid H_1) = p(\hat{a}_f \mid H_1) \sim N(m_t, P_f) \tag{21}$$

$$p(y_0, y_i \mid H_0) = p(\hat{a}_f \mid H_0) \sim N(m_n, P_f) \tag{22}$$

Note that the above is a standard binary hypothesis testing problem with different means and the same noise covariance under the two hypotheses. Thus, a likelihood ratio test (Eq. 10) using the "effective" measurement yields the decision of each DMi; the confidence c_i can be calculated from Eqs. (12)–(13).

Normative-Descriptive Model for the Leader. Our normative-descriptive model for DM0 in stage 2 assumes that DM0 sequentially combines the confidence reports of the subordinates with his confidence from stage 1 to arrive at his or her final confidence estimate. We further assume that he or she processes the reports of DM1 before those of DM2. This assumption is consistent with the experimental set up, where the reports from DM1 appeared first in the list of reports.

We use a single update equation in the estimation of DM0's confidence in stage 2. The confidence update equations, treating the confidence report from the subordinate DMi as a "measurement" are:

$$c^{(k)} = [C_{k-1}^{-1} + \beta V_k^{-1}]^{-1} \times [C_{k-1}^{-1} c^{(k-1)} + \beta V_k^{-1} z_k]; \; k = 1, 2 \qquad (23)$$

$$C_k = [C_{k-1}^{-1} + \beta V_k^{-1}]^{-1} \qquad (24)$$

A descriptive factor, β, is used in the update equations to represent the bias that DM0 will tend to undervalue the confidence reports from the subordinates. When $\beta < 1$, the model gives lower weight to the report than does an optimal data fusion model. Assuming that DM0's decision at the end of stage 1 is $u_0 = 1$ with confidence $c_{01}^{(1)}$, the update process starts with $c^{(0)} = c_{01}^{(1)}$ as its initial state with an initial covariance C_0. It then uses the reports c_{11} and c_{21}, in that order, as a "measurement" z_k with associated covariance V_k, $k = 1, 2$, and updates the confidence estimate. All the confidences are assumed to be normally distributed for the estimation process. The covariances C_0 and V_k can be calculated from the definition of confidence given by Eq. (11). After each update the leader's decision u_0 is taken to be either H_0 or H_1, depending on whether $c_{01}^{(k)}$ is $<$ or > 0.5. The final update, $c_{01}^{(2)}$, is the confidence estimate of the leader at the end of stage 2.

The normative-descriptive models for DM0, DM1, and DM2 were implemented for the 60 experimental targets. The values of the descriptive parameters α, β and ρ' were chosen by trial and error to minimize the mean square error (calculated as the mean of sum of squares of differences) between the experimental confidence data and the normative-descriptive model predictions. The obtained values were $(\alpha, \beta, \rho') \approx (0.91, 0.92, 0.3)$.

Table 8.2 compares the performance of the normative and normative-descriptive models in predicting the data. Mean squared deviations are significantly lower for the normative-descriptive model. Also, this model is more consistent with the humans' actual decisions, with far fewer deviations between the model and data. Figures 8.6a and 8.6b show the normative-descriptive model confi-

Table 8.2.   Performance of the Two Models in Predicting Human Data

	NORMATIVE MODEL		NORM.-DESC. MODEL	
	MSE	#Deviations	MSE	#Deviations
DM1	0.0314	15/60	0.01	8/60
DM2	0.0352	14/60	0.011	9/60
DM0	0.0545	8/60	0.0049	3/60

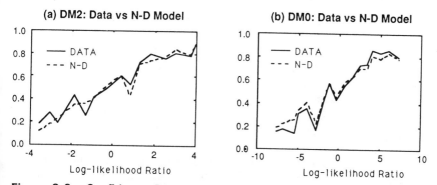

Figure 8.6. Confidence Data vs. Normative-Descriptive Model Predictions, Ambiguity Conditions

dence predictions versus the experimental data for DM2 and DM0, respectively. Clearly, the normative-descriptive models predict the human data far better than did the purely normative models.

Summary. The major emphasis of the HIP study was to demonstrate and validate the normative-descriptive approach for modeling a *hierarchical* team of human decision makers solving a binary hypothesis-testing problem. The normative models, which were based solely on likelihood ratio tests, failed to predict the subjects' decisions in 20%–25% of the cases presented. Upon comparing the confidence predictions, it was seen that subjects generally followed the normative model but with biases away from the confidence extremes. The descriptive features that were added to the model were the same as those observed in the DIP effort, namely *recency* in the process of sequential estimation of target attributes, and *undervaluation of other team members' information reports*. The resulting normative-descriptive model is in significantly better agreement with the subjects' decisions, and can also replicate accurately the variations in the subjects' confidence estimates.

The HIP study provides added validity to the DIP results in that similar team performance biases and characteristics, such as recency and misperception of other team members' information value, are observed and measured in different task environments and team structures. While the DIP teams are dyads operating in a continuous information environment, the HIP teams are hierarchical triads, whose information messages consisted of discrete judgments and confidences. Implications for training to enhance team information-processing performance are threefold: (a) improvements in the way uncertain information, especially in probabilistic form, is presented, consumed, and exchanged; (b) better assessments of team members' expertise and resulting judgment value; and (c) increased sensitivity to the age and order of incoming information in the team.

RESOURCE ALLOCATION MODELS

Unlike the static information-processing problems discussed in the previous section, the resource allocation problems that we have analyzed using the normative-descriptive approach consider a *dynamic* environment where task deadlines and processing-time requirements are salient features of the team decision problem. In keeping with our separation of information-processing and resource allocation functions, the team has no uncertainty with respect to *existing* task resource requirements; the only uncertainty being in the random arrival of *future* tasks and the decisions of the other decision makers. Thus, the problem is to determine how a team of geographically separated humans allocate and exchange their limited resources to process a mix of randomly arriving tasks with *known* resource requirements in a dynamic environment.

The Distributed Resource Allocation and Management (DREAM) Model

This first study of dynamic resource allocation in a team (Miao et al., 1988; Kohn et al., 1987; Kohn, 1988), developed a normative-descriptive model that could predict individual DM's actions on a time-by-time basis. The mathematical approach is to represent the time evolution of task appearance and movement, as well as resource flow, within a dynamic programming framework and then obtain a suboptimal solution to the formulated optimization problem.

Problem description. The DREAM study considered a two-person team that is required to process multiple types of randomly arriving tasks with a set of shareable resources. Tasks have different rewards/values, processing resources required, time required, and arrival statistics. After arriving, a task remains within an opportunity window for a certain time within which it can be processed. The team members have different but overlapping task processing responsibilities. Thus, each DM could only process those tasks preassigned to him or her, or tasks from a common pool—that is, those of shared responsibility. All active (existing but yet unprocessed) tasks could be seen by both DMs via a centralized information display.

The team owns a limited amount of sharable resources, which DMs use to process their tasks. The resources have multiple capabilities to support the needs of more than one DM and can be exchanged between DMs subject to a time delay. Since each DM has tasks of various rewards and resource requirements at any particular time, team coordination is required to assign common tasks (those of joint responsibility) to individual DMs, and to effect the exchange of resources. The objective of the team is to maximize the total reward, or equivalently, to minimize the amount of loss.

Normative model formulation. The normative model for team decision making is formulated in a discrete-time framework, assuming a centralized information structure and perfect team coordination. The model solves a centralized team problem with the solution then being implemented in a decentralized manner.

In the model a type i task, $1 \leq i \leq I$, is characterized by: $r(i)$, the amount of resources required to process the task; $T_r(i)$, the time required to process the task; $T_{ao}(i)$, the initial time available for task processing (a random variable); and $V(i)$, the value of the task. Each task is uniquely preassigned to either DM1 or to DM2, or to the set of common responsibility, denoted by DMc.

At the current time n, the amount of time remaining for a task to reach its deadline is called the task's "time available," which decreases monotonously from $T_{ao}(i)$ to zero as time elapses. Since a task is uniquely determined by its type (static feature), time available (dynamic feature), and responsibility set, we use a triple (i, j, p) to denote a type i task with j units of time available at time n, in the responsibility set of DMp, $p = 1, 2$, or c. At time n, the *Active Task Set* $S^p(n)$ is DMp's set of yet-unprocessed tasks. During the time interval from n to n + 1, some new tasks, $a^p(n + 1)$, may arrive into set $S^p(n)$. Also, let $u^1(n)$ and $u^2(n)$ denote the set of tasks selected for processing by DM1 and DM2, respectively, at time step n.

At the next time step n + 1 an active task set will consist of the current task set, plus newly arrived tasks, minus the tasks selected for processing, with corresponding changes in time available for all tasks. Mathematically, the task set dynamics can be written as:

$$S^p(n + 1) = \{(i, j, p) \mid (i, j + 1, p) \in S^p(n) \cup a^p(n + 1), j > 0, \text{ but } (i, j, p) \notin u(n)\}, \; p = 1, 2, c \tag{25}$$

where $u(n) = u^1(n) \cup u^2(n)$ and $u^1(n) \cap u^2(n) = 0$.

If, say, DM1 selects a task (i, j, p) in either $S^1(n)$ of $S^c(n)$, he or she will allocate some $r^1(n; i, j, p)$ units of resource to this task at time n. These resources will be tied up for $T_r(i)$ units of time before they return to DM1. Also, when the other DM (DM2) transfers $v^1(n)$ units of resources to DM1 at time n, these resources will reach DM1 after a τ unit time delay. Since the resource dynamics can be likened to a flow in a pipeline involving time delay, a state model can be developed to describe the flow by ordinary difference equations. Let the "state" $x^d(n + k)$ denote the amount of resources that will be available to DMd at time step n + k (so that $x^d(n)$ is the amount of resources available for DMd to use at the present time n). If $v^d(n)$ is the total amount of resources transferred *to* DMd at time step n, then

$$x^d(n + \tau + 1) = x^d(n + \tau) + v^d(n) \tag{26}$$

Also, if $\{r^d(n; i, j, p) \mid T_r(i) = m\}$ denotes the amount of resources allocated at time n to tasks requiring $T_r = m > 1$ units of time, then

$$x^d(n + m + 1) = x^d(n + m) + \{r^d(n; i, j, p) \mid T_r(i) = m\} \text{ for } m = 1, 2, \ldots, \max T_r \tag{27}$$

Finally, if $r^d(n)$ is the total amount of DMd's task-allocated resources, and $v^q(n)$ is the total amount of resources he or she transfers to DMq at time step n, then

$$x^d(n + 1) = x^d(n) - r^d(n) - v^q(n) \qquad (28)$$

that is, the next resource state equals the current state minus the current resource allocation and transfers.

The team tries to maximize its total reward/value in task processing subject to timeliness of processing and accuracy of resource allocation. The reward earned for processing task (i, j, p) is given by:

$$V(i)g_1[(i, j, p)]g_2[r(i, j, p)] \qquad (29)$$

where $g_1[(i, j, p)]$ is the timeliness score which is equal to 1 if $j \geq T_r(i)$, but < 1 if $j \leq T_r(i)$. The quantity $g_2[r(i, j, p)]$ is the accuracy score defined by:

$$g_2[r(i,j,p)] = \frac{r(i,j,p)}{r(i)} \qquad (30)$$

The multistage distributed team resource allocation problem is then formulated as:

$$\max E \left\{ \sum_{k=n}^{N-1} \sum_{u(k),r(k),v(k)} V(i)\, g_1\, [i,j,p]\, g_2\, [r(i,j,p)] \right\} \qquad (31)$$

where the maximization is over who should process which task at time step k ($u^d(k)$), with how many units of resource ($r^d(k; i, j, p)$), and how many units of resource should be transferred, ($v^d(k)$), subject to the task flow equation, Eq. (25), and the resource flow equations, Eqs. (26)–(28).

Normative-descriptive model phase 1 (ND-P1). The optimal resource allocation problem formulated above can be solved, at least in principle, by stochastic dynamic programming (Luh, Miao, Chang, & Castañon, 1989). But, as is often the case in this class of problems, computation of the optimal (normative) solution is intractable due to the computational complexity that results from: (a) the need to know the probability distribution of future task arrivals, (b) the need to plan far into the future,[1] and (c) the need to consider simultaneous resource coordination and task coordination (for those tasks in $S^c(n)$).

In these situations where optimal models may not be feasible, suboptimal models that include salient human limitations (descriptive factors) may provide a

---

[1] A decision at step n will affect the resource states for times k $>$ n, and all future decisions.

judicious starting point by making the problem tractable. Moreover, if certain descriptive factors are well known a priori, why not include them in the model at an early stage? With respect to the stochastic nature of the problem and the concomitant need to know future probability distributions in the normative model, Simon (1982) has noted that *people* do not seem to use probability distributions of future events, but instead content themselves with point predictions (expectations) in making decisions. Thus, our preliminary normative-descriptive model (ND-P1) assumes that the *future tasks will arrive according to their expected times* (the "certainty-equivalence" principle). This assumption is equivalent to setting the standard deviation of the task arrival process to zero, thereby reducing a stochastic problem to a deterministic one.

The purely normative approach makes its *current* decisions only after all *future* possibilities are evaluated. It is well accepted (Simon, 1982) that a human is either unwilling or incapable of projecting the effects of a potential decision far into the future. This can be interpreted either as a myopic behavior, (wherein options are evaluated based on only a short planning horizon), or the consequence of limited short-term memory, in which only a small group of facts can be utilized to make a decision. To capture this limitation ND-P1 looks ahead only a few (M) steps at each time n (i.e., the upper limit in the summation in Eq. (13) is set to $n + M$). The number of tasks considered in making a decision can also be limited (e.g., DM1 considers only a subset of $S^1(n) \cup S^c(n)$ in selecting his or her tasks $u^1(n)$). This short horizon problem is easily solved, but only the *current* decisions at step n are implemented. The decisions at the next step $n + 1$ will be generated at that time, taking into account any new information on tasks and/or resources. From previous experience (Pattipati et al., 1983), we have chosen a planning horizon corresponding to two attacks—the current processing decision and one more.

Finally, it is known that DMs are more inclined to keep resources rather than to transfer them to other DMs (Roby, 1968). We incorporate this bias into the ND-P1 model by assuming that a DM considers the transfer of some of his or her resources only if he or she has extra resources after processing his or her tasks. This is a crude, but effective, representation for resource coordination.

The purely normative approach requires the *simultaneous* solution of task coordination and resource coordination. It is unlikely that a human can deal with both jobs at the same time if they each require a lot of information-processing capacity. Consequently, it is assumed that a team first considers task coordination under a given distribution of resources (i.e., resource state). Resource coordination is considered as the last means to improve performance. This assumption places a structure on the decision making process, and leads to a three level procedure to solve the ND-P1 problem, as shown in Figure 8.7. At the lowest level is the single decision maker resource allocation (SIDRA) algorithm, which solves the single person task scheduling problem for a given resource and task state using forward dynamic programming (DP) over the time interval [n, n +

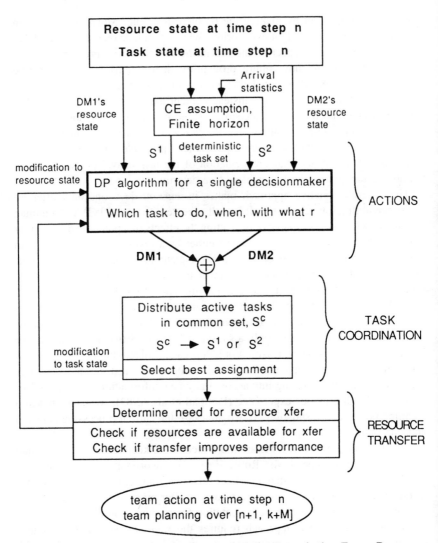

Figure 8.7. Solution Process for Normative-Descriptive Team Resource Allocation Model

M]. With SIDRA as the core, task coordination to allocate tasks in $S^c(n)$ to either $S^1(n)$ or $S^2(n)$ is done by evaluating the different possibilities for common task assignment under the fixed current resource state, and taking the best assignment. The resource coordination problem is solved next to determine whether resource transfer (subject to the DM bias described above) can improve the team's performance. Only the decisions for time step n are implemented, and the entire algorithm is repeated at the next step n + 1. Details of the solution process are found in Miao et al. (1988).

Experimental design. A distributed decision-making experiment was designed to help develop and validate the model. The experiment is based on the DDD paradigm with two separated workstations, one for each subject. The workstation display, which was identical for each DM, showed each task with its identification number, responsibility set, resources required, time required, time available, and reward. The subjects interacted with the workstations to implement their decisions: process tasks, transfer resources, and communicate using formatted messages. When a task was completed, or when an unprocessed task left its opportunity window, the resulting loss was subtracted from the team's strength. The goal of the team was to maximize its final strength.

The experiment was designed across three levels of task arrival rates (low, medium, and high) and two levels of resource transfer delays (instantaneous and delayed). A detailed description of the experiment can be found in Kohn (1988). The major dependent variables included final team strength, percentage of tasks processed, average accuracy score, average timeliness score, percentage of common tasks processed by each DM, and resource transfers per task.

Comparison between model predictions and experimental results. Over all experimental conditions, the ND-P1 model predictions of averaged team performance were obtained with the *same* set of parameters. This is an important feature of predictive models that employ a goal-oriented construct—*model parameters do not have to be retuned for each change in an independent variable.* Figure 8.8 compares model and experimental results for the condition of instantaneous resource transfers over three levels of tempo. Generally speaking, the model gives good predictions of the final team strength, with most model predictions falling within the ±2 standard error (SE) regions of the experimental results. However, a notable pattern of differences in percentage of processed tasks, average accuracy score, and average timeliness score is seen across all three levels of arrival rate. The model is processing *all* tasks (with better timeliness), but achieving a lower accuracy score. The humans opt for processing fewer tasks, but with better accuracy. This suggests that additional descriptive factors that could explain these biased timeliness/accuracy tradeoffs need to be identified and included in the model.

Normative-descriptive model phase 2 (ND-P2). The above results indicate that, as the task arrival rate increases, subjects fail to process some tasks, whereas the model still processes them with fewer resources. We conclude that subjects have a tendency to ignore a task if they cannot allocate sufficient resource for processing that task. This can be interpreted as a filtration strategy (eliminating actions on some tasks or Elimination by Aspects), as suggested by Tversky (1972). To incorporate this human bias into the model, we assume that a DM ignores a task unless he or she can achieve at least a 60% accuracy score on that task. Adding this feature into the model gives the ND-P2 results in Figure 8.8 for

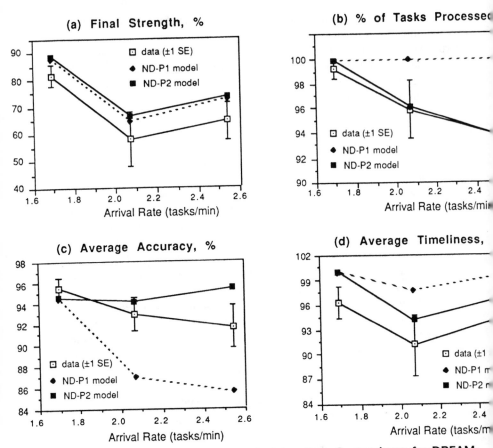

Figure 8.8.   ND-P1 and ND-P2 Model vs Data Comparisons for DREAM:
Instantaneous Resource Transfer Conditions

the case of instantaneous resource transfer. Note that model and experimental results now match well, both in range and in pattern.

Summary. A normative-descriptive model was developed, based on a three-level constrained optimization framework, that provides time-by-time predictions of individual DMs' actions in team resource allocation. The model captures the key ingredients of team resource coordination, task coordination, stochastic task arrivals, finite time available, task and resource dynamics, and so on. Observing how a normative formulation is altered to capture human behavior yields insights to the human decision-making process. By modeling human perceptual and cognitive processes, we can begin to better understand the effects of various biases, heuristics, and other inherent limitations of human DMs on team performance. The model can suggest ways to improve human performance through alleviating these limitations and biases. For example, when we relax the constraints on the number of tasks a DM can consider at one time, increase the planning horizon, or make resource coordination strategy less self-centered and less myopic, the model is able to achieve a higher overall performance in almost all cases. This suggests that team performance could be further improved through decision aiding and/or adequate training. It should be emphasized that the above insights into the complex cognitive mechanisms affecting team performance are obtained through an analysis of the DREAM normative-descriptive models and would be more difficult to observe through a purely empirical approach.

The Team Distributed Scheduling (TDS) Model

A major goal of the TDS study is to identify and model the strategies used by a team of *three* DMs facing a distributed dynamic scheduling problem. In contrast to the DREAM effort, our emphasis here is to examine how team decision-making and coordination strategies adapt to increased task load and resource scarcity under different responsibility structures. A description of this work may be found in Sullivan and Kleinman (1988, 1989).

Problem definition. Consider a team of three DMs confronted with randomly arriving tasks that require processing by one of the team members before the task deadline. The team has a fixed number of resources that can be used to process tasks, and each DM can only process one task at a time so that tasks (and resources) must be "shared" by team members to achieve optimal results. Resources can be transferred among DMs, but a significant delay occurs before the resources actually arrive at their destination. The tasks are classified into one of three types (A, B, C) and have the following attributes: (a) the number of resources required to process the task; (b) the time required to process the task, T_r, (c) slack time, or the amount of time remaining before the tasks' deadline; and (d) penalty or loss—the amount subtracted from the team strength should this task not be processed with the right amount of resources and within a given window of opportunity. The job of the DMs is to assign resources to incoming tasks, and to share the limited number of resources in order to maximize the team's final strength.

Experimental design and procedure. The experimental task environment developed for the TDS study was based on the DDD paradigm. Each of the three DMs sat at a workstation that was networked to the other DMs. A centralized information structure was used, so that all DMs saw the same information on all active tasks in the opportunity window. For simplicity in the subsequent modeling, all tasks had a processing time $T_r = 30s$ and resource transfer time was 15s. To allow coordination in resource sharing and task processing, the DMs were provided with a formatted communication capability as in the DDD.

Several independent variables were chosen to be manipulated in the experiments, based on their ability to affect team performance and strategy. These included functional overlap, resource scarcity, and tempo or arrival rate of tasks.

Table 8.3. Experimental Design for Overlap of Responsibility

	NO OVERLAP(NO)			PARTIAL OVERLAP(PO)			FULL OVERLAP(FO)		
	Task Type			Task Type			Task Type		
DM	A	B	C	A	B	C	A	B	C
1	×	−	−	×	×	−	×	×	×
2	−	×	−	−	×	×	×	×	×
3	−	−	×	×	−	×	×	×	×

Functional overlap, in this context, is defined as the number of DMs capable of processing/attacking a single task type. This variable was investigated by Boettcher and Levis (1982) and by Serfaty (1990), and their work indicates that the effectiveness of a team depends on the type and degree of functional allocation. In the TDS effort the degree of functional overlap was operationalized at three levels: (a) No overlap—sole responsibility by a single DM for a task type, (b) Partial overlap—shared responsibility between pairs of DMs for a single task type, and (c) Full overlap—shared responsibility among three DMs for a single task type. Table 8.3 shows how overlap of responsibility was implemented.

The second independent variable was the number of resources owned by the team, which was selected to be either five or seven. The third independent variable was the load on the team as a whole, implemented as the task tempo or task arrival rate. The findings of Payne, Bettman, and Johnson (1988), wherein humans adapt their strategy via a process of acceleration and filtration, were expected to be replicated over the three levels of increasing load but not necessarily equally among all the DMs.

The dependent variables collected fall into the four categories of team performance, strategy, coordination, and workload, although only the first two were of concern for the normative-descriptive modeling effort. The performance variables included the team's final strength and the average slack time at the time of attack. This latter variable provides an indication of how quickly teams were able to perform the required scheduling. The strategy variables indicate how teams adapt to the experimental conditions in their attempts to achieve optimal results, and are the best indicators for determining human cognitive limitations and biases. The strategy measures included: (a) team resource transfers, (b) the number of tasks processed by each decision maker,[2] (c) the number of each task type (A, B, C) processed, and (d) the number of tasks processed requiring one,

---

[2] This quantity was computed without regard for the actual DM that performed the processing but rather according to the busiest, second busiest, and least busy DM. Therefore, we were interested in the actual load balance rather than the number of tasks processed by DM1.

two, or three resources. A subclass of (c), *the percentage of tasks processed that were secondary,* was computed to investigate the degree to which teams were biased toward their primary responsibility. *Primary* task type is defined as the type that is processed by a DM in the "no overlap" condition. In the "partial" and "full" overlap conditions DMs were allowed to process other task types, which are denoted as *secondary.*

Normative model formulation. The normative approach that we used was to transform the scheduling program into a weighted assignment problem and then solve the optimal assignment problem using any one of a number of conventional algorithms. A simple example demonstrates the transformation from a scheduling problem to a weighted bipartite matching problem. Assume there is only one DM who owns two resources and is presently idle. At an instant in time, we take a snapshot of the dynamic scenario and attempt to schedule the tasks in the picture (see Figure 8.9). Since the processing time associated with each task is a constant $T_r = 30s$, the tasks are grouped conveniently into the following three sets:

$$SET\ 1 = \{Tasks\ with\ \ 0 < slack\ time < 30\}$$
$$SET\ 2 = \{Tasks\ with\ 30 < slack\ time < 60\}$$
$$SET\ 3 = \{Tasks\ with\ 60 < slack\ time < 90\}$$

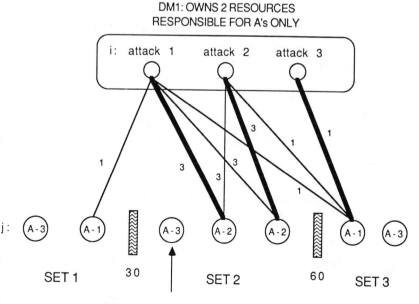

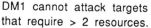

DM1 cannot attack targets
that require > 2 resources.

Figure 8.9.   Example of a Weighted Bipartite Matching Graph

The scheduling solution is constrained by the fact that a DM can only be processing one task at a time. Thus, the DM can select at most one task from SET 1 because, when the attack is completed, 30 seconds would have elapsed and the slack time of tasks in SET 1 will be negative. Similarly, the DM can select at most two tasks from SET 2 and three tasks from SET 3.

To implement the scheduling, we assume a DM will attack three tasks in the next 90 seconds (1 task every T_r sec). For the DM's first attack, any of the tasks in SETs 1, 2, 3 can be selected. Planning ahead to the next attack, the DM can only choose tasks from SETs 2 and 3. Finally, he can only select tasks in SET 3 for the third attack. Figure 8.9 shows the available matchings as mentioned above. The numbers displayed along the arcs represent the reward gained upon processing the associated task. Also, the task type and resources required are shown within the circles that represent tasks. It should be noted that by maximizing the reward gained in attacking, the penalty associated with not processing tasks is minimized. The bold arcs show the optimal matching for this example.

When there is more than one DM a matching graph similar to that of Figure 9 can be constructed with arcs from each DM to a common pool of tasks, being careful to place the tasks in sets according to each DM's availability, responsibility, and amount of resource ownership. The details may be found in Sullivan and Kleinman (1988). This mapping of the scheduling problem to a weighted matching problem can be completed for three DMs in any resource state $\mathbf{R} = (R_{DM1}, R_{DM2}, R_{DM3})$, and any overlap condition.

We now present the solution approach to the Weighted Matching problem. A matching in a graph is defined as a set of edges where no two edges share a common node. Bipartite means that the nodes belong to two distinct sets (e.g., in the TDS problem, DM processing intervals and tasks to be processed). In the weighted bipartite matching problem weights are assigned to the edges of the graph and the challenge is to find the matching that has the largest total weight. If we order the tasks using index $j = 1, 2, \ldots$, and let $i = 3(k - 1) + n \in \{1, 2, \ldots, 9\}$ denote the attack by DMk in the nth time interval, $n = 1, 2, 3$, then by defining:

w_{ij} = reward gained if attack i successfully processes task j

x_{ij} = 1 if attack i is matched to task j, and 0 otherwise,

the objective of the algorithm can be defined mathematically as finding the x_{ij} to maximize:

$$j(x_{ij}) = \sum_{i,j} w_{ij} x_{ij} \qquad (32)$$

The following three constraints assure that no two edges in the matching share a common node, i.e., that each task is attacked by at most one DM and each DM attacks at most one task in a time interval:

$$\sum_j x_{ij} \leq 1, \ \sum_i x_{ij} \leq 1, \quad x_{ij} \geq 0 \tag{33}$$

Thus, the problem is reformulated as a linear programming problem and can be solved by an algorithm such as the Hungarian Algorithm (Papadimitriou & Steiglitz, 1982). This is a primal-dual method that finds a solution in $O(mn^2)$ steps, where m and n are the number of arcs and nodes in the graph. Throughout the scenario the scheduling problem is re-solved each time a DM becomes idle and tasks are available. The problem is re-solved for *all* the resource states. (There is only a finite number of available resource states when the team owns either five or seven resources.) When forming the matching graphs for resource states other than the present state, the time to effect the necessary resource transfers must be included. This delay time for DMk consists of the time until a DMj has free resources to transfer to DMk, plus the actual resource transfer delay, plus any remaining processing time on the task DMk is attacking once the resources arrive. Therefore, the slack times are largest when solving for the present resource state (no transfer delay). A transfer to another resource state diminishes the time available for all viewable tasks.

Normative descriptive model development. As in the previous DREAM model, our phase 1 normative-descriptive model emulates the limited short-term memory/planning horizon of humans by reducing the number of steps that the model looks into the future from three to two. Therefore, instead of computing the next *three* attacks for all three DMs, the normative-descriptive model only computes the next *two* attacks for each DM. This means that the tasks are grouped into two sets rather than three. The results of this phase 1 model (ND-P1) are shown in Figures 8.10a–f.

The ND-P1 results show final strength and slack time performance variables at levels similar to those of the human teams. However, the strategy measures show several significant differences. One such difference is seen in Figure 8.10f, which indicates that teams adopted a nearly normative strategy under low and medium tempos, but began to ignore tasks that required one resource (reward = 1) in the high tempo case. This is analogous to an "elimination by aspects" strategy (Tversky, 1972) in which DMs determine the most important attribute of a task and establish that attribute's cutoff value. Next, all alternatives with ratings below the cutoff value for that attribute are eliminated from the DM's decision space. To implement an elimination by aspects strategy, the model was altered to reflect the devaluing of tasks that required only one resource by assigning reward of 0.5 for these tasks. (Note that tasks requiring one resource actually received 1 unit of reward.)

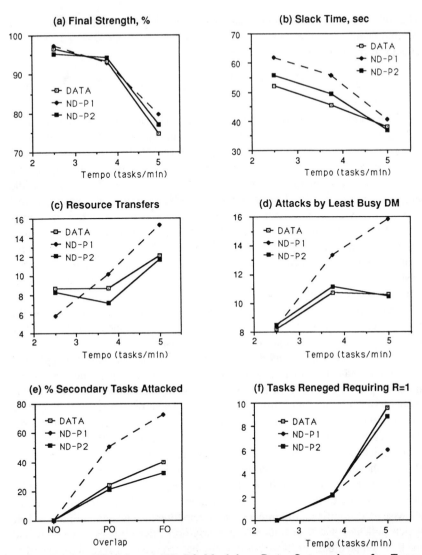

Figure 8.10.   ND-P1 and ND-P2 Model vs Data Comparisons for Team Distributed Scheduling

The last descriptive factor added to the model captures the phenomena of "evenly distributing load" among team members. In general, the ND-P1 model would eliminate an individual from the three person team, thereby reducing the number of resource transfers required and increasing the resource utilization. However, subjects did not show this behavior, especially in noncritical situations. In low and medium tempos, teams would try to equalize the load among the members despite an increase in the number resource transfers required. The method of operationalizing this descriptive factor was derived from a posteriori sessions with the subjects and from watching the experimental sessions. By increasing the reward received for tasks of primary responsibility by 10%, the model was capable of duplicating a heuristic the human teams employed. Under these conditions, the model chooses a scheduling strategy that optimizes *perceived* team reward and so shows a tendency to distribute the tasks among DMs. This descriptive factor was included in the model for low- and medium-tempo scenarios, and is only appropriate in partial overlap and full overlap conditions. This descriptive factor was not included in the high-tempo scenarios.

The second phase model, ND-P2, which incorporates the "elimination by aspects" and the "evenly distributed load" phenomena, schedules tasks in a manner similar to the human DMs. The resulting normative-descriptive model (ND-P2) has been shown to successfully replicate human behavior in the TDS experiment for *all* the important dependent variables, as shown in Figure 8.10.

Summary. The normative-descriptive model developed for the TDS study predicts team performance and strategy for a task scheduling problem and provides insights to team decision-making behavior. A normative suboptimal (matching graph) model produced a very good starting point for the normative-descriptive modeling process. The normative modeling algorithm used to solve the TDS problem was selected because of its intuitive appeal and ease of accepting descriptive factors, rather than for its ability to achieve optimal results. Therefore, in further normative-descriptive modeling efforts, where optimal models may not be possible, suboptimal models may be a judicious starting point.

The salient human biases that were found to affect team performance for this problem include: (a) myopia or human reluctance to project the effects of a decision far into the future, (b) the workload-adaptive elimination by aspects strategy through reduction of decision alternatives, and (c) the team phenomenon of load balancing in low-workload conditions. The last factor perhaps implies that the humans have a secondary subjective goal as well as a performance goal. The ND-P1 model solved the scheduling problem according to the single objective of maximizing performance, whereas the humans added an additional objective of keeping all team members involved in the decision process. If teams were taught to recognize the biases, through team training and/or the use of decision aids in critical situations, performance might improve. For example:

1. Teams need to be instructed not to eliminate choices that result in small rewards or small penalties. In certain situations, it is advantageous to select tasks with small rewards rather than concentrating on large rewards.
2. Teams must be careful that the performance objective is met when considering a secondary goal such as load balancing among team members. Teams must have the ability to recognize when a problem becomes too difficult to accomplish a secondary objective.

CONCLUSIONS

The model-vs.-data results obtained in the two team information-processing and the two team resource allocation studies described above show the power of the normative-descriptive approach for modeling team decision-making performance. There is a significant amount of knowledge one gains, simply in the process of developing these types of models. Observing how a normative formulation must be altered to capture human behavior yields insight into the human decision-making process—insights that are not necessarily obvious from a purely experimental approach. For example, by combining the findings of these four modeling efforts, several conclusions can be drawn:

- The dynamic decision strategies used by DMs in a team have a very limited planning horizon, rarely exceeding two or three future look-ahead stages. This decision myopia becomes more critical with increased workload.
- In a team environment, individuals tend to overvalue their own information and responsibilities and undervalue those of their teammates.
- Team members may be biased or have individual motivations for over-requesting team resources and holding them in their possession. This self-centeredness is detrimental to the team performance, especially in scarce resource environments.
- In sequential information processing tasks, DMs do not seem to discount for the common redundant prior information within the team.
- Team members adapt their decision strategies to variations in external conditions (e.g., workload, resource scarcity, etc.) largely through a process of elimination by aspects.
- Partial overlap of responsibility among team members leads to the best performance/workload trade-offs. A centralized information structure is needed to support functional overlaps under high workload.
- Well-trained teams are able to coordinate reasonably well their actions and resources under low and moderate workload conditions.
- Team coordination may break down under high workload conditions. Task load is not equally distributed and the team tends to break apart into a collection of individuals when the workload goes beyond a certain threshold. In other words, under these conditions, DMs have a tendency to focus on taskwork rather than on teamwork.

The above are fundamental cognitive characteristics, limitations and biases, indigenous to human decision makers. The likelihood that, under high workload, a human will: (a) show an increasing tendency to hold resources for his or her own tasks, as the perceived value of other team members' tasks are reduced; and (b) eliminate from consideration tasks of low value, provide the impetus to diminish team effectiveness. Indeed, the job at hand for the human engineering and training community is to determine how to ameliorate these effects through different team training, displays that enhance flexible coordination, decision aids, online feedback, different organizational designs (e.g., the use of a leader), etc. We believe that a normative-descriptive modeling approach, coupled with a strong model-based empirical component, provides a framework within which to proceed.

Future Research Directions in Team Coordination

The normative-descriptive models have shown an excellent ability to match human and team data across a range of independent variables. Model predictions have included various dependent measures associated with team performance and team strategy. However the set of models described in this chapter do not *directly* produce predictions of team *coordination*. The reason is that these models were developed under the assumption of a perfectly coordinated team—that is, the models have been built to *solve* a centralized problem, with the solution then being *implemented* in a decentralized manner. The development of truly distributed normative-descriptive mathematical models is a major requirement for current and future research that aims to explore issues in team coordination.

In general, teams must learn to coordinate their information, their resources, and their actions to maximize performance. We believe that future research should, and will, focus on relevant issues in team coordination, especially in hierarchical teams with a leader. We have evidence from our empirical research and modeling efforts that DMs within a team adapt both their individual decision strategies and coordination strategies to variations in the imposed workload. Increasing task demands tends to polarize (break apart) the team into individual entities (Kohn et al., 1987; Sullivan & Kleinman, 1988) as the DMs trade off coordinating activities with pursuing their own self-interests. Thus, research work is needed to: (a) define the various forms of coordination available to a team of decision makers, (b) determine those exogenous and endogenous factors that most strongly affect coordination, and (c) understand and model the mechanisms by which adaptation/change occurs in coordination strategy.

REFERENCES

Boettcher, K. L., & Levis, A. H. (1982). Modeling the interacting decision-maker with bounded rationality. *IEEE Transactions on Systems, Man and Cybernetics, 12*(3), 334–344.

Bushnell, L. G. (1987). *Team information processing.* Unpublished master's thesis, Department of Electrical and Systems Engineering, University of Connecticut, Storrs, CT.

Bushnell, L. G., Serfaty, D., & Kleinman, D. L. (1988). Team information processing: A normative-descriptive approach. In S. E. Johnson & A. H. Levis (Eds.), *Science of command and control: Coping with uncertainty* (pp. 62–72). London: AFCEA International Press.

Einhorn, H. J., & Hogarth, R. (1985). Ambiguity and uncertainty in probabilistic inference. *Psychological Review, 92*(4), 433–461.

Gelb, A. (1968). *Applied optimal estimation.* Cambridge, MA: M.I.T. Press.

Kleinman, D. L., Baron, S., & Levison, W. H. (1971). A control-theoretic approach to manned-vehicle systems analysis. *IEEE Transactions on Automatic Control, 16*(6), 824–832.

Kleinman, D. L., & Serfaty, D. (1989). Team performance assessment in distributed decisionmaking. *Proceedings of the Symposium on Interactive Networked Simulation for Training* (pp. 22–27). Orlando, FL.

Kleinman, D. L., Serfaty, D., & Luh, P. B. (1984). A research paradigm for multi-human decision-making. *Proceedings of the 1984 American Control Conference* (pp. 6–11). New York, NY: Institute for Electrical and Electronics Engineers.

Koenig, D., Burton, G., & Kleinman, D. L. (1988). *Hierarchical information processing: The effects of information feedback on team performance* (Tech. Rep. No. TR-88-9). Storrs, CT: Department of electrical and Systems Engineering, University of Connecticut.

Kohn, C. (1988). *Team distributed resource allocation and management* (Tech. Rep. No. TR-88-4). Storrs, CT: Department of Electrical and Systems Engineering, University of Connecticut.

Kohn, C., Kleinman, D. L., & Serfaty, D. (1987). Distributed resource allocation in a team. *Proceedings of the 1987 Command and Control Research Symposium* (pp. 221–234). McLean, VA: Science Applications International Corporation.

Luh, P. B., Miao, X. Y., Chang, S. C., & Castañon, D. A. (1989). Stochastic task selection and renewable resource allocation. *IEEE Transactions on Automatic Control, 34*(3), 335–339.

Mallubhatla, R. (1990). *Team information processing under ambiguity.* Unpublished master's thesis, Department of Electrical and Systems Engineering, University of Connecticut.

Mallubhatla, R., Pattipati, K. R., Kleinman, D. L. & Tang, Z-B. (1991). A normative-descriptive model for a team in a distributed detection environment. *IEEE Transactions on Systems, Man and Cybernetics, 21*(4), 713–725.

Miao, X. Y., Luh, P. B., Kleinman, D. L., & Castañon, D. A. (1988). Distributed stochastic resource allocation in teams. *Proceedings of the 1988 IEEE International Conference on Systems, Man, and Cybernetics* (pp. 445–448). New York, NY: Pergamon Press.

Papadimitriou, C. H., & Steiglitz, K. (1982). *Combinatorial optimization: Algorithms and complexity.* Englewood Cliffs, NJ: Prentice-Hall.

Pattipati, K. R., & Kleinman, D. L. (1979). *A survey of the theories of individual choice behavior* (Tech. Rep. No. TR-79-12). Storrs, CT: Department of Electrical and Systems Engineering, University of Connecticut.

Pattipati, K. R., Entin, E. E., Kleinman, D. L., & Gully, S. G. (1982). A normative-descriptive model of a power system dispatcher in emergency situations. *Proceedings of the 1982 American Control Conference* (pp. 283–291). New York, NY: Institute for Electrical and Electronics Engineers.

Pattipati, K. R., Kleinman, D. L., & Ephrath, A. R. (1983). A dynamic decision model of human task selection performance. *IEEE Transactions on Systems, Man, and Cybernetics, 13*(2), 145–166.

Payne, J. W., Bettman, J. R., & Johnson, E. J. (1988). Adaptive strategy selection in decision-making. *J. Experimental Psychology: Language, Memory, and Cognition, 14*(3), 534–552.

Rapoport, A. (1975). Research paradigms for studying dynamic decision behavior. In D. Wendt & C. Vlek (Eds.), *Utility, probability and human decisionmaking* (pp. 349–369). Dorleecht, Holland: Reidel.

Reid, G. B., Shingledecker, C. A., Nygren, T. E., & Eggemeier, F. T. (1981). Development of multidimensional subjective measures of workload. *Proceedings of the 1981 IEEE International Conference on Cybernetics and Society* (pp. 403–406). New York, NY: Institute for Electrical and Electronics Engineers.

Roby, T. B. (1968). *Small group performance.* Chicago: Rand McNally and Co.

Serfaty, D. (1990). *Distributed dynamic decisionmaking in teams.* Unpublished doctoral thesis, Department of Electrical and Systems Engineering, University of Connecticut.

Serfaty, D., & Kleinman, D. L. (1985). An experimental plan for distributed tactical decision-making. *Proceedings of the 8th MIT-ONR Workshop on C³ Systems* (pp. 65–68). Cambridge, MA: Massachusetts Institute of Technology.

Simon, H. A. (1969). *The sciences of the artificial.* Cambridge, MA: The MIT press.

Simon, H. A. (1982). *Models of bounded rationality: Behavioral economics and business organization.* Cambridge, MA: The MIT press.

Slovic, P., Fischoff, B., & Lichtenstein, S. (1977). Behavioral decision theory. *Annual Review of Psychology, 28,* 1–39.

Sullivan, D. R., & Kleinman, D. L. (1988). *Team distributed scheduling: A normative descriptive approach* (Tech. Rep. No. TR-88-6). Storrs, CT: University of Connecticut, Department of Electrical and Systems Engineering.

Sullivan, D. R., & Kleinman, D. L. (1989). A normative descriptive approach to team distributed scheduling. *Proceedings of the 1989 IEEE International Conference on Systems, Man, and Cybernetics* (pp. 466–473). New York, NY: Institute for Electrical and Electronics Engineers.

Tversky, A. (1972). Elimination by aspects: A theory of choice. *Psychological Review, 79*(4), 281–299.

Willsky, A. S., Bello, M. D., Castañon, D. A., Levy, B. C., & Verghese, G. C. (1982). Combining and updating of local estimates and regional maps along sets of one-dimensional tracks. *IEEE Transactions on Automatic Control, 27*(4), 799–813.

Wohl, J. G., Serfaty, D., Entin, E. E., Deckert, J. C., & James, R. M. (1988). Human cognitive performance in anti-submarine warfare: Situation assessment and data fusion. *IEEE Transactions on Systems, Man, and Cybernetics, 19*(5), 777–786.

Guidelines for Use in Team-Training Development*

Robert W. Swezey and Eduardo Salas

Although considerable literature addresses the topic of team training, recent reviews have noted the scarcity of behavioral guidance that may be used to develop and model team-training programs and devices in applied situations (Denson, 1981; Dyer, 1984; Salas, 1987). This situation is cause for concern, particularly in today's environments, where many tasks require application of coordinated teamwork for successful completion. Of note, however, is that few of these tasks are actually practiced in team situations or supported by training programs specifically designed to accommodate integrated team performance characteristics. One reason for this situation may be that prescriptive design guidance in terms of specifications and/or guidelines for team training or for devices which support team training are typically lacking in the literature (Laughery, 1984).

Over a decade ago, Hall and Rizzo (1975) characterized the art of team training in the Navy as follows:

> Naval training personnel, for the most part, apparently do not possess a clear understanding of what specific objectives should be accomplished by team training.

* The views expressed herein are those of the authors and do not reflect the official position of their organizations. The authors wish to express their appreciation to several individuals who have contributed substantially to various aspects of this effort. These include Dennis Faust, Robert Llaneras, Jineen Reed, Janis A. Cannon-Bowers, and Randy Hollister.

Training objectives are stated in loose, general ways not optimally conducive to the development of well-ordered training programs. Most of the training programs examined failed to reflect the application of the systematic procedures of current educational technology for training program development. Training is conducted largely through the medium of practice with nonstandard but structured exercises. (p. 43)

And according to Modrick (1986), not much was changed in the subsequent 10 years:

The state-of-the art in team training is inadequate. Deficiencies exist in taxonomy for team activities and phenomena, task analysis methods, training methods and strategies, quantitative performance standards, and methods for feedback to teams and individuals. (p. 160)

Further, a recent metaanalysis of the literature has suggested that there have been few empirical studies of team training since the early 1960s (Salas, Dickinson, Tannenbaum, & Converse, in press).

Nevertheless, some general guidance relevant to team training and performance does exist in the team process and small group literatures; however, concrete statements or guidelines which provide prescriptive applications for use in designing team training programs continues to be virtually nonexistent.

Yet, according to Gurette, Miller, Glickman, Morgan, and Salas (1987), "The most effective and efficient means of improving the instructional processes in future team training systems may be to adopt empirically-based team training design and development guidelines built upon job analyses and learning principles that embrace teamwork as well as individual technical task learning requirements" (p. 27). Gurette et al. have suggested that such guidelines be developed and integrated with current instructional system development (ISD) procedures, or even that they be provided separately to training developers. They suggested several aspects of training that such guidelines should cover, and emphasized the need for guidelines covering *team* task analysis. Typical existing procedures are oriented toward identifying *individual* tasks and teamwork skills involving interactions among individuals. In order for teamwork skills to be improved during training, identifications, organizations, and precise specifications of such skills is necessary.

Kessler, Macpherson, and Mirabella (1988) have recently compiled a series of "lessons learned" information from the Army Maintenance Training and Evaluation Simulation System (AMTESS) studies, for use by military training developers; and have confirmed that much of the existing training information appears to suffer from at least two types of problems. First, it is not sufficiently prescriptive for actual use by training designers. The information is often written in the language of psychology and/or education, and does not provide direct "what to do and how to do it" statements. Second, inadequate information exists on the direct application of instructional principles to the design of training programs or devices. This second point is particularly acute with the proliferation of computer-based training devices, including videodisc, expert system, CAI, intelligent CBI, and other technologies. A glaring shortfall is the almost total lack of existence of prescriptive design guidance on the so-called "courseware" aspects of computer-based training (Criswell & Swezey, 1984).

Accordingly, this chapter identifies and presents in guideline form, a variety of team-oriented processes and characteristics which may be employed in the design and development of team training programs. Such characteristics may, in turn, be used to generate hypotheses for subsequent team training research and/or for the design of team training tools and procedures.

Classification System Development

Elsewhere Swezey and Salas (1987) have discussed developing a system for classifying team-training guidelines and characteristics. We have argued that a need exists to create a classification system for team-training (and team-training device) design categories and issues; and to identify and classify within the system actual team-training guidelines for use by training development and engineering personnel.

The establishment of a classification system that is sufficiently generic yet comprehensive enough to support the plethora of available training and instructional guidelines is itself a considerable task. To the extent that such a system might be empirically based, the task becomes even more substantial. An effort by Swezey, Streufert, and Mietus (1983) has resulted in development of an empirical taxonomy applied to the domains of organizational and systems theories. Similarly, a number of sophisticated team-oriented taxonomies have been developed by Fleischman and his co-workers (see Fleischman & Zaccaro, this volume, for a discussion of this issue).

Without belaboring the point therefore, Table 9.1 shows a simple classification system used to organize team-oriented guidelines. The categories in Table 9.1 comprise merely one small component of the more comprehensive classification system discussed in our previous articles, and literally hundreds of additional guidelines have been extracted from the literature and included within the other categories; but are not included here for reasons involving space limitations.

In Table 9.1, we have included 12 categories which address team process principles. These categories expand upon a previous classification system as reported by Franz, Prince, and Salas (1990). That system consisted of seven primary (or, as termed by the authors, *generic*) categories as follows: communication, leadership, mission analysis, decision making, assertiveness, adaptability, and situational awareness. It, in turn, was based upon the previous work of Morgan, Glickman, Woodard, Blaiwes, and Salas (1986), who categorized 90 team-oriented behaviors into seven very similar dimensions, which were able to

Table 9.1.   Classification System for Team Process Guidelines

I.   Team Mission and Goals
II.   Environment and Operating Situation
III.   Organization, Size, and Interaction
IV.   Motivation, Attitudes, and Cohesion
V.   Leadership
VI.   Communication: General, Conveying Information, Feedback
VII.   Adaptability
VIII.   Knowledge and Skill Development
IX.   Coordination and Cooperation
X.   Evaluation
XI.   Team-Training Situation: General, Role of the Instructor, Training Methods
XII.   Assessment of Team-Training Programs: Pretraining Assessment, Overall Assessment

discriminate between effective and ineffective crews. In that research, effective crews exhibited higher numbers of critical team behaviors in each of the seven dimensions than did ineffective crews.

Essentially, the domain of teamwork deals with *process* issues (i.e., the techniques or means applied to achieve an anticipated outcome). We therefore view a logical way to organize teamwork guidelines as proceeding from those external aspects of a situation that serve to influence team performance (such as Category I: Mission and Goals; and Category II: Environment); through process issues per se (Categories III: Organization, Size, and Interaction; IV: Motivation, Attitudes, and Cohesion; V: Leadership; VI: Communication; VII: Adaptability; VIII: Knowledge and Skill Development; IX: Coordination and Cooperation); to X: Evaluation (which deals primarily in team *formative* evaluation issues). Additionally, we have added categories which deal specifically with training issues facing teams (XI: Team Training Situational Issues), and overall *summative* evaluation issues on team training program success (XII: Assessment of Training Programs). This, in our view, is consistent with the work of previous authors who have commented on teamwork organization issues (see, for example, Boguslaw & Porter, 1962; Davis, Gaddy, & Turney, 1985; Dyer, 1984; Glanzer, 1965; Hritz, Lewis, & Roth, 1983; Knerr, Nadler, & Berger, 1980; Morgan et al., 1986; Salas, 1987; Turney & Cohen, 1981).

Guidelines Identification and Development

In preparation for the identification of learning and instructional guidelines for use in the development of team-training programs and devices, approximately 2,000 documents were acquired.

All documents were scanned to determine the existence of so-called *guidelines* and *principles* that conformed to our requirements and could be classified within the categories of interest. In this context, a *Guideline* was defined as: "A brief statement that describes or suggests action(s) or condition(s) that, if correctly and appropriately applied, could be used to improve or facilitate either instructional or training device, design and development activity." To the extent possible, a guideline should address team-training or training device design and development; however, statements relevant to team contexts which also applied to individual situations were not excluded.

Applying this criterion, approximately 150 articles (from the 2,000 document database) were initially identified as having such guidelines (although large numbers of cross-references existed among the articles) and, accordingly, a total of over 1,200 guidelines were identified and extracted for classification.

Two primary problem areas were uncovered during this process. These were: (a) redundancy of stated guideline information, and (b) lack of adequate prescription. As guidelines were identified and extracted from the literature, many were considered redundant in that they essentially addressed the same (or very similar) issue(s) and/or provided the same (or similar) guidance. When this occurred, the guidelines were combined and referenced to primary references. Additionally, many guidelines were identified that, in the opinion of the authors, were sufficiently vague that they were inappropriate to justify inclusion in the database. That is, in our opinion, the information presented was inadequate to suggest training-development activity. Although potentially helpful theoretically, if the information presented by such a guideline was considered inadequate for actual use, the guideline was deleted from the database.

This winnowing processing resulted in a reduction of the number of guidelines from the original list of approximately 1,200, to approximately 500. While by no means final (and/or complete, as discussed above), this does provide an approximation to the more thorough and easily accessible database which is under development.

As all guidelines were extracted from one or more source documents, each was necessarily removed from the context of the document(s) in which it was found. In virtually all cases, therefore, it was necessary to exercise some amount of editorial license in reporting the guideline. Care was taken not to manipulate the meaning and/or intent of the guideline as offered by the original author(s), yet virtually all guidelines were edited in order to enter them into the database. Additionally, since the guidelines generally suffered from a lack of prescription vis-à-vis *training* orientations, separate *comments* have been included. This approach, which had been successfully utilized in other previous work (cf. Swezey & Davis, 1983), was intended to provide additional clarity and/or prescription to the information. It should be pointed out however, that these comments are strictly *our* opinions, as derived from the guideline information, and are therefore in no way the responsibility of the cited guideline author(s).

Since redundancy of the guideline information was a major consideration, and many authors have essentially stated that same (or similar) issues in their work, only one (or in some cases, a few) primary references are cited for each guideline. Many of the citations are, themselves, from review articles. This was done in order to minimize unnecessary clutter in the guideline database. Although it is not possible to include all guidelines generated for the database in this chapter, we provide in the following pages 146 selected guidelines which address team process characteristics and teamwork *only*. Learning and instructional-oriented guidelines are provided primarily in other sections at the database. Additional development of the guidelines database continues, and guidelines in all categories of the taxonomy continue to be developed.

No claim is made as to the comprehensiveness of the resulting list of guidelines. Without doubt, many additional documents could be identified and reviewed, and numerous additional guidelines could be developed. The guidelines identified and classified here represent a point of departure against which the use of guidelines in team-training development may be validated. Many additional guidelines are readily available and identifiable. This area is a fertile ground for additional research and development.

Summary

Although the literature on teamwork is sparse, recent efforts by Morgan, Salas, and associates (Cannon-Bowers, Prince, Salas, Owens, Morgan, & Gonos, 1989; Glickman, Zimmer, Montero, Gurette, Campbell, Morgan, & Salas, 1987; Gurette et al., 1987; Ilgen, Shapiro, Salas, & Weiss, 1987; Morgan et al., 1986; McIntyre, Morgan, Salas, & Glickman, 1988; Mullen, Symons, Hu, & Salas, 1989; Oser, McCallum, Salas, & Morgan, 1989) have enhanced the knowledge base in team process development. Nevertheless, the area remains an underinvestigated one and a fertile field for additional research. To our knowledge, this chapter is the first effort to extract and codify guideline-oriented information on teamwork and team process activities. It is our hope that this information may be used by several categories of investigators and/or developers. Researchers may find this information helpful to generate hypotheses and to suggest areas for further research. Trainers and training developers may also find it useful in the design of training-program activities on these topics. Engineers and designers may find it useful for the design and development of training equipment and simulators. Finally, such diverse occupations as educators, coaches, teachers, and managers may find it useful to enhance teamwork in the various contexts in which they function.

That this is an important topic is evidenced by recent teamwork failures in such industries as power generation, process control, and aircraft operation, to name merely a few. In this chapter, codified into guideline format, lies much of the important known information on teamwork and team process characteristics. It is our hope that it will be both useful and thought provoking.

TEAM PROCESS GUIDELINES

Team Mission and Goals: Guidelines

- Every team member should be able to state the title and purpose of the team mission. (Lewis et al., 1983)
- Every team member should be able to describe how his or her own special (or subsidiary) team(s) will satisfy its task(s) in the execution of the team mission. (Lewis et al., 1983)
- Every team member should be able to describe the general approach the team will employ to accomplish mission objectives. (Lewis et al., 1983)
- Team goals should be clearly and objectively stated. (Dyer, 1984; Hall & Rizzo, 1975)
- Individuals should be provided with specific goals relative to their understanding and knowledge of details, tasks, and facts of team training. (McIntyre et al., 1988)
- Individual and group goals need to be consistent. When individual goals are consistent with group goals, individuals feel motivated to achieve the goal. (Ilgen et al., 1987)
- Goal specificity will enhance the feedback process. (Ilgen et al., 1987)
- Commitment to goals makes them more attainable. (Ilgen et al., 1987)
- Teams should be provided with direct indications of goal and subgoal achievement. (Glickman et al., 1987)
- Job aids such as "user-friendly" manuals, individual training materials, and field guides should be developed to present clear goals. (McIntyre et al., 1988)
- Clear specification of, and orientation toward goals fosters improved crew coordination. (Helmreich, 1982)

Mission and goals: comments. Thorough understanding of, and belief in, a team's mission and goals are central to its performance. Outstanding material resources and highly developed skills are not enough to ensure a team's success. A clearly defined mission and set of concomitant goals focuses potentially divisive energy in a common direction.

The above guidelines spell out the need for knowledge of team mission and goals. Training should employ methods that frequently remind team members of the mission and goals. For example, requiring articulation of concrete goals by all team members periodically during training will serve to reinforce their importance.

Mission and goal conceptualization can be used to focus all team tasks. Each task has a set of goals, the open articulation of which: (a) ensures that they are understood, (b) establishes the relation between the part and whole (completing the interim goals of any project brings the team one step closer to realization of its overall mission), and (c) reinforces commitment to the mission and goals, and thereby increases the likelihood that both will be achieved. *Use* concrete mission statements to direct teamwork training applications by prescribing interim objectives specifically designed to achieve project goals.

Environment and Operating Situation: Guidelines

- It is easier for teams to adapt to simple conditions than to complex, demanding conditions. (Dyer, 1984)
- Every team member should be able to describe environmental constraints which affect completion of the team mission. (Lewis et al., 1983)
- Teams should be trained under conditions that approximate the operational environment. (Dyer, 1984; Gaddy, 1987)
- To the extent possible, training environments should include important constraints which actually operate in the operational setting. (McIntyre et al., 1988)

Environment: comments. The key consideration here is that the training environment should accurately simulate appropriate aspects of the operational setting and conditions. Training should adjust the extent to which it simulates actual conditions and environments in a way designed to facilitate learning. For example, high-fidelity representations of team situations may be appropriate for use in training specific job tasks which deal with complex environments; however, for more abstract tasks, lower fidelity simulations may be equally appropriate.

Organization, Size, and Interaction: Guidelines

- The optimum size of a team depends on its task. The optimum size for most problem-solving discussions seems to be reached with five or six members, but for many production tasks, the optimum size may be two. (Bass, 1982)
- In order to improve team performance, it is important for all team members to understand how team interactions affect that performance. (NATO, 1980)
- Members should learn aspects of team-oriented tasks that demand adaptive, interdependent actions. (NATO, 1980)
- Teams should be trained on the following specific details of team tasks: how individual member roles interrelate, how the performance of the team depends upon the specific performances of the individuals, and what makes the

team task different from the sum total of the individual tasks. (McIntyre et al., 1988)

- The extent of the interpersonal interaction requirements of a task may be used to determine the need for team training. (Gaddy, 1987)
- Interdependencies among team members should be clarified. (Dyer, 1984)
- Team behavior and process patterns change over time. (NATO, 1980)
- In general, team members benefit from getting to know each other's interaction styles. (Gaddy, 1987)
- Team training has been found to especially improve performance on tasks that rely heavily on intermember interaction. (Gaddy, 1987)
- Every team member should be able to recognize and smoothly execute expected transitions among team activities. (Lewis et al., 1983)
- To satisfy the need for affiliation, establish trust and provide opportunities for no-risk, cooperative interaction. (Keller, 1987)

Organization, size, and interaction: comments. How a team is organized and interacts is directly related to its performance. Teams that are well organized and interact fluently generally will perform well. The above guidelines provide specific suggestions for team organization, size, and interaction.

- The nature of tasks influence the appropriate number of team members in any activity. Have no more than six members in a group when performing problem-solving or decision-making tasks.
- Make use of graphed representations of timeline and critical paths to demonstrate interdependence.
- Divide teams into groups of observers and participants for various time periods during training. Observers can then watch and take notes on interaction patterns of team members as the latter perform a task. Then observers should inform the team of their interaction patterns as observed, and specify improved interaction patterns.
- All task responsibilities for team members should be specific and free from ambiguity. Tasks that require interdependent actions should be specified during training.
- Instructors and course developers should specify the extent of team member interaction requirements as a foundation for training team tasks.
- Team training should identify the causes of change in team behavior and process, so that teams can be informed of those dynamics.
- Team members having responsibilities for different task areas may wish to interview each other to promote group interaction and better understanding of the tasks, responsibilities, and difficulties of fellow teammates.
- Organize training program activities, that involve especially challenging teamwork-oriented tasks, to promote personal interaction and trust.

Motivation, Attitudes, and Cohesion: Guidelines

Motivation and attitudes.

- Motivated teams will "stretch" themselves to achieve beyond what individuals, thinking about the capability of the team, might deem possible. (Ilgen et al., 1987)
- Team members who do not feel central to the team's successes will not feel as satisfied as members who feel central to those successes. (Ilgen et al., 1987)
- Provide motivational guidance to individual team members and identify common factors that inhibit team member motivation. (McIntyre et al., 1988)
- Enthusiasm and the "right" attitude are often viewed by instructors as the most important difference between good and poor teams. (NATO, 1980)
- Like-minded individual team members can often work together more easily, but are likely to be less creative. Members with diverse attitudes will generate more conflict, but will also more often hammer out more creative solutions. (Bass, 1982)
- Team members should be encouraged to show verbal and physical (i.e., verbal compliments and "pats on the back") signs of support for other members and the team as a whole. (Morgan et al., 1986; Oser et al., 1989)
- Members of successful teams praise the accomplishments of fellow teammates. (Morgan et al., 1986)
- Team members should be supportive of teammates when the latter make mistakes. (Morgan et al., 1986)
- Effective team members make positive statements to motivate the team. (Oser et al., 1989)

Cohesion.

- Foster group cohesion; team success is dependent upon cohesion with respect to group goals. (NATO, 1980)
- In order to improve team performance, it is important to recognize the differences in individual and group goals, foster cohesion and commitment to the group, and acknowledge individual contributions as integral and essential parts of total team performance. (NATO, 1980)
- Teams should progress through a series of levels of understanding of "teamness" through practice, feedback, and coaching. In this fashion, they become progressively more conscious of the effects of communication, shared attitudes, values, leadership, authority, and work standards on team effectiveness. (McIntyre et al., 1988)
- Courseware should be designed to increase the level of team cohesion. (Marcus, 1987)
- Every team member should be able to recognize and list all members of the team by position. (Lewis et al., 1983)

- The importance of one's position in a team effort is likely to be strongly linked to an individual's performance as a team member. (Bass, 1982)
- Individuals performing as part of a team often demonstrate different kinds of behaviors than they would if they were alone, even if assigned the same task as individuals. (Bass, 1982)
- Every team member should be able to describe the consequences of team dependency failure(s). (Lewis et al., 1983)
- Development of accurate expectations on the part of team members implies a need for familiarization with the operational requirements of other team members. (Branson, Rayner, Cox, & Hannum, 1975; Cream, 1978; Dyer, 1984; Lewis et al., 1983)
- Accurate expectations of the contributions of other team members to overall team performance should be developed, both for the overall team and for special or subsidiary teams. (Cream, 1978; Lewis et al., 1983)
- Discord among team members with respect to production of errors is related to later deficiencies in team coordination. (Foushee, 1984)
- Every team member should be able to identify the event(s) which cause the special (or subsidiary) team(s), of which he or she is a member, to form and to disband. (Lewis et al., 1983)
- Team members become more similar in their perceptions of team behavior as training progresses. (NATO, 1980)
- Team skills proceed through the following stages of evolution and maturation. (Glickman et al., 1987)

For *operational* team skills training:

- Development of task assignments
- Orientation to task
- Emotional response to task demands
- Open exchange of relevant interpretations
- Emergence of solutions
- Adjustment of framework
- Drive to completion
- Delivery and completion of task
- Withdrawal from task
- Review of accomplishments

For *generic* team skills training:

- Investigation of group
- Testing of dependence
- Intragroup conflict
- Development of group cohesion
- Development of role relatedness

- Refinement of roles
- Fulfillment of roles
- Adjustment to environmental demands
- Exiting from group
- Remembering group

Motivation, attitudes, and cohesion: comments. Motivation and attitudes play important roles in determining team performance. Here are some concrete suggestions which follow from the above:

- Provide opportunities for each team member to take major responsibility for designing and directing a major task-related activity that affects the entire team. Each team member should experience the challenge and anxiety that stems from such an endeavor.
- Employ positive reinforcement techniques throughout training and promote their proliferation beyond training to the work environment. Develop a system of rewards for those who exhibit supportive behavior towards teammates.
- Establish homogenous groupings of team members for some teamwork activities and heterogenous groupings for other activities during training. The combination gives members a chance to work with individuals of similar and differing capabilities and backgrounds.

It is also clear that cohesion is important to the performance of the team. Team training should specifically address the issue of cohesion among team members. Following are some suggestions:

- Team training should employ methods that foster deeper understanding and ways of bringing about greater team cohesion. This can be achieved by recognizing the stages in teamwork development as postulated by Glickman et al. (1987) and training team members specifically in this area.
- Instruction should stress the importance of various team members' positions relative to the overall performance of the team; and, team members should be aware that they share, not only in the teams' successes, but in its less successful moments as well.
- Specific methods should be developed to address the issues of practice, feedback, and coaching in team training.

Leadership: Guidelines

- Every team member should be able to recognize when he or she is the Team Leader or is expected to assume the Team Leader's position. (Lewis et al., 1983)

- Every team member should be able to recognize when the Team Leader is unable to lead the team. (Lewis et al., 1983)
- Team leaders should be trained to acquaint them with the details of the team's operation, as well as with the individual tasks required of each team member. (McIntyre et al., 1988)
- Every team member should recognize the authority of the team leader, both for the entire team and for all relevant subsidiary or special teams. (Lewis et al., 1983)
- Team leaders should keep the team focused on the task at hand. (Franz et al., 1990)
- Team leaders should ask for input and discuss potential problems. (Franz et al., 1990)
- Team leaders should *verbalize* their plans for achieving the team goal. (Helmreich, 1982)
- Team leaders should be good communicators; they must keep the team informed about matters that affect team performance. (Franz et al., 1990)
- Leaders who engage in leadership behavior provide an important need for subordinates. (Mullen et al., 1989)
- Team leaders an be expected to engage in more initiating structure behavior as team size increases. (Mullen et al., 1989)
- All people in leadership positions should recognize that team skills are at least as important as task skills. This can be demonstrated via specifically articulated media such as videotapes of teams performing in actual environments. (McIntyre et al., 1988)
- Team leaders should be provided with supplemental training (beyond that provided to other team members) in team performance concepts. (Glickman et al., 1987)
- Reluctance by team members to assume control when leaders are unable to do so, can lead to overall failure of the team's mission. (Foushee, 1984)

Leadership: comments. Leadership serves a critical function in the operation of teams and is closely related to all team processes, both directly and indirectly. In our view, all team training programs should address the issue of leadership and the many practices which enhance leadership and the performance of the team:

- Leadership training in the context of team training should be skill based. That is, it should reflect those critical skills and behaviors appropriate for the team's task requirements. For example, leaders should be trained to handle information overload when team members are performing under stressful conditions.
- Team training should include discussions about what teams should expect from the leader and what the leader should expect from team members. This should include establishing criteria by which team members can determine

whether or not the team leader is effective and can take control of a situation when necessary.

- Team training should address specific means through which both the leader and the team can monitor and enhance communication. Videotaped scenarios may be useful for this purpose in some situations.
- Team training programs should specify behaviors the leader should exhibit to cultivate team members' confidence in the leader. These include assertiveness when necessary, initiation of structure with respect to team tasks, and consideration of others' viewpoints.
- Team training should specify the measures the leader should take in familiarizing himself or herself with the tasks and responsibilities of all team members. Basically, the leader should be competent in all team member functions to the extent practicable.

Communication: Guidelines

General.

- Effective communication is central to interactive team performance. (Davis et al., 1985)
- Team performance results depend heavily upon communication among team members. (Davis et al., 1985)
- Team training should seek, not only to improve specific task performance, but also to enhance the team's ability to communicate, relate, and interact among themselves. (NATO, 1980)
- Tasks that involve requirements for frequent communication should be given priority in team training. (Gaddy, 1987)
- It is important that individual contributions be acknowledge as essential parts of total team performance. (NATO, 1980)
- Task sequences, methods of communication, and potential barriers to communication should be identified and included when planning for team coordination training. (Cream, 1978)
- Casual communication among team members during periods of low workload can improve overall team performance. (Helmreich, 1984)

Conveying information.

- Training should remind team members of the importance of good communication relative to the performance of the team. (Morgan et al., 1986)
- Team members need to communicate information to team members in proper sequence. (Morgan et al., 1986)

- Proper information exchange facilitates the development or coordination of teamwork strategies by assuring that all team members have access to relevant information. (Foushee, 1984)
- Team members should use proper terminology when communicating information to other team members. (Morgan et al., 1986)
- Team members should be encouraged to ask for clarification of information that is unclear. (Morgan et al., 1986; Oser et al., 1989)
- Effective team members thank other team members for catching mistakes. (Oser et al., 1989)
- Unnecessary interruptions of individual team member tasks by other team members can lead to overall team performance failures. (Foushee, 1984)

Feedback.

- Provide teams with specific feedback mechanisms to clearly communicate how their team tasks are being performed. (McIntyre et al., 1988)
- Feedback of performance information among team members is especially important in task conditions that are changing rapidly and where direct equipment or instrument feedback is unavailable. (Davis et al., 1985)
- Team training should include techniques for training individuals to analyze their own errors, to sense when the team or individual team members are overloaded, and to adjust their behavior when overloads occur. (Dyer, 1984)
- In operational situations where it is not possible for one team member to compensate for the deficiencies of another, the use of direct feedback to individual team members is desirable. (Dyer, 1984; Hall & Rizzo, 1975)
- Checklists and benchmarks aid in evaluating team performance and minimizing subjectivity. (Gaddy, 1987)
- Feedback should be provided on all important aspects of team functioning, since individuals tend to maximize performance on aspects about which they received positive feedback. (Dyer, 1984)
- Peer critique can be used to develop a team member's ability to provide accurate feedback. (Gaddy, 1987)
- Training should provide reminders to team members to double check each other's performance and to provide feedback. (Gaddy, 1987)
- Trainees are usually eager to offer feedback to the team and to each other, provided the atmosphere is nonthreatening. (Gaddy, 1987)
- Team members need to be adept at giving feedback in appropriate, nonthreatening ways. (Morgan et al., 1986)
- Team members need to be prepared to accept constructive feedback in appropriate ways. (Morgan et al., 1986)
- Training should encourage team members to point out mistakes made by a team member without being negative. (Morgan et al., 1986)

- Team members should discuss mistakes made by a team member privately rather than announcing the mistake to the group. (Morgan et al., 1986)
- Praising and other team members making positive statements are correlated with successful team performance. (Oser et al., 1989)
- Asking for help when in need of assistance is positively related to successful team performance. (McCallum, Oser, Morgan, & Salas, 1989)

Communication: comments.

As can be seen from the above principles, communication among team members is important to successful team performance. In many situations, however, team-training programs do not address this issue specifically. In our opinion, *any* training program which purports to address the issue of teamwork or team performance must *specifically* address the issue of communication among team members. A number of ways in which the above issues might be addressed for a given training program include:

- When conducting the task/skill analysis, identify the unique *communication requirements* among team members for *each* specific team task.
- Develop a preferred *format* (i.e., verbal? written?) for all identified communication requirements.
- Specify the *direction* of all communications (i.e., from whom, to whom).
- Ensure that the language (or nonverbal cues) used in all communications are thoroughly understood by team members.
- Specify the *frequency* of all communications (i.e., the times when communications should be delivered).
- Specify the *conditions* under which each specific communication should be delivered.
- Specify the *length* of each identified communication (i.e., what is too much?, what is too little?).
- Communications that involve criticism should be constructive and should be offered in a manner that is nonthreatening.
- Use of real, life-based scenarios which incorporate the above techniques may be one way to enhance training in communication skills.

Adaptability: Guidelines

- Team members should be able to adapt relevant information to the task at hand. (Morgan et al., 1986)
- Adaptable team members should be able to provide information on ways of locating and correcting errors. (Morgan et al., 1986)
- Adaptable team members are able to change the way they perform a task when necessary or when asked to do so. (Morgan et al., 1986)

- Team skill training should focus on "emergent" tasks since these tasks involve unpredictable events that cannot be fully specified in advance. (Gaddy, 1987)
- Every team member should be able to list the most likely contingency situations which might occur during a mission. (Lewis et al., 1983)
- Every team member should be able to recognize unexpected events and to describe actions which he or she would expect to take when an unexpected event interferes with, or changes, the team's purpose, structure, or dependency situation. (Lewis et al., 1983)

Adaptability: comments. The above principles on adaptability suggest some concrete activities for use in team-training situations:

- Use video presentations of contrived or real situations in which the use of available relevant information could have made a positive difference in the execution of a task.
- Use video presentations of scenarios in which errors prevented the accomplishment of a task that is of the type that the team in training would encounter. Require that the team complete the task by locating the error(s) and move ahead.
- Design tasks that have several specific and sensible avenues for solution. Require that team members demonstrate the ability to perform the task through several different approaches.
- Construct activities which are designed to "go wrong" at specific points. Team members must confront and resolve the anomaly by using rational and available means. (Note: for progression in training, begin with challenges in which the team members know that something is going to go wrong. At the next stage of difficulty, do not forewarn team members that something will go wrong.)

Knowledge and Skills Development: Guidelines

- Before team members can focus on developing effective teamwork skills, they must reach some threshold level of competence in their individual knowledge and skills. (Guerette et al., 1987)
- Individual skills are important components of team performance, and training should be designed to develop both individual and team skills. (Davis et al., 1985; Dyer, 1984; Hall & Rizzo, 1975; NATO, 1980)
- Established tasks involve predictable sequences that can be specified in advance. In such situations, less variation in performance due to team member interactions may be expected. (Gaddy, 1987)

- Differences in team performance can often be directly related to the proficiency of individual team member(s) during pretraining. (Collins, 1977)
- Cross-train students so that they may perform other activities and thus act as replacements for other team members. (Branson et al., 1975; Cream, 1978; Dyer, 1984; Lewis et al., 1983)
- The development of norms, and the identification of specific changes in behavior from these norms, may be used as benchmarks of the stages of development of teamwork skills. (Glickman et al., 1987)
- Untrained team members tend to acquire individual performance skills at the same rate, independent of the team-training load. (Morgan, Coates, Kirby, & Aluisi, 1984)
- The performance of teams may be more or less than the sum of the technical knowledge, skills, and abilities of individual team members. (NATO, 1980)
- Individuals should be periodically tested for mastery of details, tasks, and facts of team performance. (McIntyre et al., 1988)
- Trainees should be aware of the relationships between individual preparation and team performance, and of the relationship of team performance to individual development and achievement. (McIntyre et al., 1988)

Knowledge and skills: comments. Training in the domains of knowledge and skilled performance include techniques to enhance retention of trained material.

- Training programs should use resource individuals, who possess expertise in specific skills and knowledges that need to be developed in trainees.
- The skill levels of trainees should be assessed at an early stage of training.
- Develop assessment instruments to accurately evaluate trainees' mastery of skills, both before and after training. The use of criterion-based job performance tests, and/or rating scales, which assess mastery of skill or knowledge components of tasks are especially encouraged.

Coordination and Cooperation: Guidelines

- Well-coordinated teams are often successful. Members of well-coordinated teams move easily from the completion of one task to the beginning of another. (Morgan et al., 1986)
- Members of well-coordinated teams are able to obtain information about their tasks from other team members when necessary for the completion of a task. (Morgan et al., 1986)
- Cooperative team members will consult with other teammates when uncertain about what to do next at any given time. (Morgan et al., 1986)

- Members of well-coordinated teams are often able to anticipate when team-mates are going to need specific information for the completion of a task. They also provide such information. (Morgan et al., 1986)
- Effective team members typically help other team members who are having difficulty with a task. (Oser et al., 1989)
- Effective team members coordinate information gathering activities in a structured fashion. (Oser et al., 1989)
- Teams which lack effective interpersonal orientations show increased break-downs in group process activities such as effective information exchange. (Foushee, 1984)
- When members of well-coordinated teams are not busy with their own tasks, they seek to learn about (and assist with) the tasks other members are working on. (Morgan et al., 1986)
- Cooperative teammates will assist other team members when the latter are having difficulty. (Morgan et al., 1986)
- Members of cooperative teams will help teammates perform tasks, even when such tasks are not part of the helper's normal responsibility. (Morgan et al., 1986)
- Training in team coordination should proceed after individual members have mastered their own duties. (Collins, 1977; Glickman et al., 1987; Robinson & Knirk, 1984)

Coordination and cooperation: comments. Like other teamwork skills, coordination and cooperation are important for optimum team performance. The following are specific suggestions for developing coordination and cooperation in teams:

- Develop major tasks that require sophisticated, well-orchestrated teamwork. Multiphase efforts in which the execution of each subsequent phase depends on the completion of the previous phase are especially effective for this purpose.
- In a later phase of team-training activity, have members rotate to different phases, in which they are "practical" novices in the subject domain. Teammates from one phase may be used to explain the process of that phase of work to the (now) novice, and vice-versa, before it will be possible to execute the task.
- Divide teams into groups and assign different tasks to different groups. One way to encourage cooperation across groups might be to have members of each group interview members of the other groups about each other's tasks.
- Establish activities that require individuals from one group (or phase of a project) to work *actively* with members of another group (or phase of a project).

Evaluation: Guidelines

- Team leaders should be evaluated with respect to their understanding of team performance, including both general and specific tasks of each member of the team. (McIntyre et al., 1988)
- Team performance criteria should take into account dynamics brought about by factors such as turnover, change in status, and change in assignments. (NATO, 1980)
- Team performance measurement should consider the level of team development, the quality of team performance, and the effectiveness of person-to-person interaction within the team. (NATO, 1980)

Evaluation: comments. Critical to the functioning of any team is evaluation of its leadership and overall performance. A few specific suggestions are:

- Training programs should expose team members to instruments that are used in evaluating the performance of the leader and of the team.
- Specify precise criteria for evaluating the leader's knowledge of team performance.
- Develop instruments that assess the leader's understanding of the responsibilities of team members.
- Quantify behavioral aspects such as team development, the quality of team performance, and the effectiveness of person-to-person interaction within the team, for use in team evaluations.
- Quantify dynamic forces such as turnover, change of assignment, and change in status which affect the performance of the team.

Team Training Situation: Guidelines

General.

- Team training should include systematic procedures for providing feedback information to the trainee(s) while they are learning team skills. (Hall & Rizzo, 1975)
- Training should seek to provide feedback to the team members on their performance, and help establish and reinforce a positive set of team norms. (Marcus, 1987)
- Teams should be trained as entire units. (Davis et al., 1985; Dyer, 1984)
- Team training should be sequenced according to increasing task complexity, as well as by the degree of teamwork required. (Davis et al., 1985; Dyer, 1984)

- The performance effectiveness of a team is degraded in proportion to the team-training load, that is, to the percentage of untrained members assigned to the team. (Morgan et al., 1984)
- The design of self-paced training and testing should pay very careful attention to not making it a punishing experience. To the extent possible, training should be enjoyable. (McIntyre et al., 1988)
- Team members entering training often do not have realistic expectations of their *individual* performance skills (they think they are better than they are), nor do they have an accurate picture of the team's performance ability. (NATO, 1980)

General team training principles: comments. A few concrete suggestions emanate from these general principles.

- Where appropriate and useful, divide team members according to tasks and train members individually in their specific task domains.
- In any training domain, curriculum material should be presented beginning with the simple and moving to the complex.
- Specify skill levels of all team members at the beginning of training. For maximum efficiency and effectiveness, team training should take into consideration the skill level of trainees. Having all team members trained together may be productive for some endeavors (such as simple and/or preliminary tasks); however, for more complex areas it may be useful to train variously proficient team members separately.

Role of the instructor.

- Instructors should be able to identify: (a) the critical behaviors that comprise team effectiveness, and (b) examples of these behaviors in real life scenarios. (McIntyre et al., 1988)
- Team instructors should be capable of providing specific examples to individuals on effective or ineffective aspects of team performance in their specific situation. (McIntyre et al., 1988)
- The instructor may play different roles in training better and poorer teams; his or her judgement, and the nature of his intervention, are crucial to the development of a team. (NATO, 1980)
- Instructors function as an important team member, particularly in poorer teams, and their behaviors change as training progresses. (Morgan et al., 1986)
- In addition to real-time verification of the effectiveness of team member actions, instructors should provide feedback via constructive critiques after training sessions. (Dyer, 1984; Gaddy, 1987)

- The training staff should monitor how individuals are faring in self-paced training. Monitoring should involve audit of the circumstances under which individuals are taking the training, as well as whether competent resource people exist to help individual team members. (McIntyre et al., 1988)
- Instructor guides and exercises provide increased structure and consistency in team task training. (Gaddy, 1987)

Role of the instructor: (comments). The above guidelines are relatively clear, and suggest a number of areas about which instructors need be cognizant. Above all, instructors should be knowledgeable and experienced in the functions, tasks, and processes of all phases of teamwork. In addition, instructors need to know each team being trained intimately. Such knowledge includes being alert to the level of competence of teams and their members, and the plethora of tasks and functions in which the team is engaged.

Training methods.

- Team training should be structured to allow for roleplaying exercises and to provide for constructive feedback. (Davis et al., 1985)
- Illustrations should be presented to show the consequences of errors to a team's performance. (Dyer, 1984)
- The use of modeled vignettes in specific situations are helpful in providing examples of good team skills for team members to model. (Davis et al., 1985)
- Team training should be repeated periodically to increase long-term retention of skills. (Dyer, 1984)
- To optimize team performance, opportunities to experience mistakes that involve interpersonal dependencies should be provided. (Bass, 1982)
- Development of scenarios for team training should provide for adequate levels of realism and use instructor guides. (Gaddy, 1987)

Training methods: comments. The above guidelines are specific and, for the most part, self-explanatory. A few things to consider in preparation for and during training include the following:

- All team members should, to the extent possible, be involved in all phases of training.
- Activities and scenarios should be designed with the intent to re-create necessary teamwork skills required by the actual operational environment. This pertains to interpersonal behavior and roleplaying skills.
- Making constructive use of errors for educational purposes is not a new idea. Doing it systematically and well, however, is difficult. Exploit in positive ways the concept of using mistakes for educational purposes in team training.
- Videotaping is an extremely useful heuristic. It should be used whenever appropriate in various phases and domains of training.

- An important method in training involves the simple but instructive use of periodic testing to determine the extent to which training either is or is not being successful. Employ periodic testing throughout training.

Assessment of Team Training Programs: Guidelines

Pretraining assessment.

- Pretraining assessments should be based on the program's training objectives and resemble the format of posttraining measures. (Cannon-Bowers et al., 1989)
- Pretraining evaluation seeks to provide some preliminary information regarding the teams' attitudes towards their tasks, objectives, mission, work environment, etc. (Cannon-Bowers et al., 1989)
- Develop and implement pretraining capabilities diagnostic test. (Guerette et al., 1987)
- Pretraining assessment should probe teams' expectations for the training program. (Cannon-Bowers et al., 1989)
- Pretraining assessment should investigate teams' beliefs about how training in their domain can improve their level of performance. (Cannon-Bowers et al., 1989)

Pretraining assessment: comments. These principals are sufficiently detailed. Pretraining assessment is as important as the training program itself. Criterion-based instruments the provide the information outlined by the above guidelines should be developed and employed prior to training.

Overall Assessment:

- An effective means of evaluation involves formalization and standardization of task-related and team-related feedback throughout training. (Guerette et al., 1987)
- Assessment methods should determine whether the program objectives were met. (Cannon-Bowers et al., 1989)
- A main objective of evaluation is to assess team needs and performance, and make the appropriate adjustment, throughout training. (Guerette et al., 1987)
- Evaluation instruments should be used to assess the validity of the training program content. (Cannon-Bowers et al., 1989)
- The assessment process should help determine the impact of the training program on individual trainees in terms of knowledge, skills, performance, and attitudes. Such an evaluation should investigate the extent to which

training affects performance in the operational environment. (Cannon-Bowers et al., 1989)
- Assessment instruments should assess the impact of the training program on the overall mission effectiveness. (Cannon-Bowers et al., 1989)
- Final assessment should provide feedback to improve the training program. (Cannon-Bowers et al., 1989)

Overall assessment: comments. Training programs are designed to help trainees better perform tasks in the operational setting. The focus on training per se should not distract the program from constructing and implementing an evaluation that serves, not only the trainees, but the training program and instructor as well. In order to ensure that training programs are effective, an overall assessment of the instructor, the training curriculum, and its methods (including methods of instruction and evaluation) is required. Such an evaluation can provide invaluable feedback about the strengths and limitations of training programs.

Training programs should employ assessment instruments that evaluate the programs across a range of issues, including the use of instruments that solicit substantive feedback on the program from the trainees. Consideration should be devoted to the unit(s) of analysis in training program evaluation. That is, both broad, substantive criteria (such as perceived program effectiveness); and specific task-oriented content criteria (such as criterion-referenced individual task performance measures) should be employed in evaluation programs.

REFERENCES

Bass, B. (1982). Individual capability, team performance, and team productivity. In M. Dunnette & E. Fleischman (Eds.), *Human performance and productivity: Human capability assessment.* Hillsdale, NJ: Erlbaum.

Boguslaw, R., & Porter, E. (1962). Team functions and training. In R. Gagne (Ed.), *Psychological principles in system development* (pp. 387–416). New York: Holt, Rinehart, and Winston.

Branson, R., Rayner, G., Cox, J., & Hannum, W. (1975). *Interservice procedures for instructional systems development.* Ft. Benning, GA: U.S. Army Combat Arms Training Board.

Cannon-Bowers, J., Prince, C., Salas, E., Owens, J., Morgan, B., & Gonos, G. (1989). *Determining aircrew coordination training alternatives.* Paper presented at the 11th Interservice/Industry Training Systems Conference, Ft. Worth, TX.

Collins, J. (1977). *A study of potential contributions of small group behavior research to team training technology development.* Alexandria, VA: Essex Corporation.

Cream, B. W. (1978). A strategy for the development of training devices. *Human Factors, 20*(2), 145–148.

Criswell, E., & Swezey, R. W. (1984, November). Behavioral learning theory-based computer courseware evaluation. *Educational Technology,* pp. 43–46.

Davis, L. T., Gaddy, C. D., & Turney, J. R. (1985). *An approach to team skills training of nuclear power plant control room crews* (NUREG/CR-4255GP-R-123022). Columbia, MD: General Physics Corp.

Denson, R. W. (1981). *Team training: Literature review and annotated bibliography* (AFHRL-TR-80-40). Wright Patterson AFB, OH: U.S. Air Force Human Resources Laboratory.

Dyer, J. (1984). Team research and team training: A state-of-the-art review. In F. Muckler (Ed.), *Human factors review* (pp. 285–323). Santa Monica, CA: Human Factors Society.

Foushee, C. (1984). Dyads and triads at 35,000 feet: Factors affecting group process and aircrew performance. *American Psychologist, 39*(8), 885–893.

Franz, T. M., Prince, C., & Salas, E. (1990). *Identification of aircrew coordination skills.* Paper presented at the 12th Annual Department of Defense Symposium, Colorado Springs, CO.

Gaddy, C. (1987). *A practitioner's perspective on team skill training in industry.* Paper presented at the meeting of the American Psychological Association, New York.

Glanzer, M. A. (1965). Experimental study of team training and team functioning. In R. Glaser (Ed.), *Training research and education* (pp. 379–408). New York: Wiley.

Glickman, A., Zimmer, S., Montero, R., Guerette, P., Campbell, W., Morgan, B., & Salas, E. (1987). *The evaluation of teamwork skills: An empirical assessment with implications for training* (Tech. Rep. No. 87-016). Orlando, FL: U.S. Naval Training Systems Center.

Guerette, P., Miller, D., Glickman, A., Morgan, B., & Salas, E. (1987). *Instructional processes and strategies in team training* (Tech. Rep. No 87-017). Orlando, FL: U.S. Naval Training Systems Center.

Hall, E., & Rizzo, W. (1975). *An assessment of U.S. Navy tactical team training* (TAEG Report No. 18). Orlando, FL: Training Analysis and Evaluation Group.

Helmreich, R. L. (1982, August). *Pilot selection and training.* Paper presented at the meeting of the American Psychological Association, Washington, DC.

Helmreich, R. L. (1984). Cockpit management factors. *Human Factors, 26*(5), 583–589.

Hritz, R., Lewis, C., & Roth, J. (1983). *Understanding and improving teamwork: Three levels at team training* (Report No. 5). Valencia, PA: Applied Science Associates.

Ilgen, D., Shapiro, J., Salas, E., & Weiss, H. (1989). *Functions of group goals: Possible generalizations from individuals to groups* (Tech. Rep. No. 87-022). Orlando, FL: Naval Training Systems Center.

Keller, J. M. (1987). Development and use of the ARCS model of instructional design, *Journal of Instructional Development, 10*(3), 2–10.

Kessler, J., Macpherson, D., & Mirabella, A. (1988). *Army maintenance training and evaluation simulation systems (AMTESS): Lessons learned* (Army Research Institute Research Report No. 1471). Alexandria, VA: U.S. Army Research Institute.

Knerr, C., Nadler, L., & Berger, D. (1980). *Toward a naval taxonomy* (Contract No. N00014-80-C-0781). Arlington, VA: Litton Mellonics.

Laughery, K. R. (1984). *A select review of the recent (1979–1983) behavioral research literature on training simulators.* Boulder, CO: MicroAnalysis and Design.

Lewis, C. M., Hritz, R. J., & Roth, J. T. (1983). *Understanding and improving teamwork: identifying training requirements* (Report 4). Valencia, PA: Applied Science Associates, Inc.

Marcus, A. M. (1987). *Correlates of sports team success.* Unpublished masters thesis, College Park, MD: University of Maryland.

McCallum, G. E., Oser, R., Morgan, B., & Salas, E. (1989). *An investigation of the behavioral components of teamwork.* Paper presented at the American Psychological Association Convention, New Orleans, LA.

McIntyre, R. M., Morgan, B., Salas, E., & Glickman, A. (1988). *Teamwork from team training: New evidence for the development of teamwork skills during operational training.* Paper presented at the Interservice/Industry Training Systems Conference, Orlando, FL.

Modrick, J. (1986). Team performance and training. In J. Zeidner (Ed.), *Human productivity enhancement* (Vol. 1, pp. 130–166). New York: Praeger.

Morgan, B., Jr., Coates, G. D., Kirby, H., & Aluisi, E. A. (1984). Individual and group performances as functions of the team-training load. *Human Factors, 26*(2), 127–142.

Morgan, B. B., Glickman, A. S., Woodard, E. A., Blaiwes, A. S., & Salas, E. (1986). *Measurement of team behaviors in a Navy environment* (NTSC-TR-86-014). Orlando, FL: Naval Training Systems Center.

Mullen, B., Symons, C., Hu, L., & Salas, E. (1989). Group size, leadership behavior, and subordinate satisfaction. *The Journal of General Psychology, 116*(2), 155–169.

NATO (1980). Oosterveld, W. J. (Chairman) Working Group 10, Advisory Group for Aerospace Research and Development, AGARD-AR-159 report, Neuilly sur Seine, France.

Oser, R., McCallum, G., Salas, E., & Morgan, B. (1989). *Toward a definition of teamwork: An analysis of critical team behaviors* (Tech. Rep. No. 89-004). Orlando, FL: Naval Training Systems Center.

Robinson, E. R., & Knirk, G. (1984). Interfacing learning strategies and instructional strategies in computer training programs. In F. Muckler (Ed.), *Human factors review* (pp. 209–238). Santa Monica, CA: Human Factors Society.

Salas, E. (1986). Examination of the empirical evidence in team performance. In A. F. Smode (Ed.), *Independent research and Independent exploratory development (IR/IED) programs; Annual report FY86* (NAVTRASYSCEN TR87-004). Orlando, FL: Naval Training Systems Center.

Salas, E. (1987). *Examination of the empirical evidence in team performance.* Orlando, FL: U.S. Naval Training Systems Center.

Salas, E., Dickinson, T., Tannenbaum, S., & Converse, S. (in press). *A meta-analytic review of the team training and performance literature* (Tech. Rep. No. TR-87-036). Orlando, FL: Naval Training Systems Center.

Swezey, R. W. (1981). *Individual performance assessment: An approach to criterion-referenced test development.* New York: New Prentice-Hall.

Swezey, R. W., & Davis, E. G. (1983, November). A case study of human factors guidelines in computer graphics. *IEEE Computer Graphics and Application,* pp. 21–30.

Swezey, R. W., Llaneras, R., & Salas, E. (1989). *User format preferences for team training guidelines.* McLean, VA: Science Applications International Corp.

Swezey, R. W., & Salas, E. (1987). Development of instructional design guidelines for team training devices. *Proceedings of the Human Factors Society 31st Annual Meeting.* Santa Monica, CA: Human Factors Society.

Swezey, R. W., Streufert, S., & Mietus, J. (1983). Development of an empirically derived taxonomy of organizational systems. *Journal of the Washington Academy of Sciences, 73*(1), 27–42.

Turney, J., & Cohen, S. (1981). *Defining the nature of team skills in Navy team training and performance* (Contract No. N0014-80-C-0811; NR 170-919). Arlington, VA: Office of Naval Research.

10

Team Decision Making and Performance: A Review and Proposed Modeling Approach Employing Petri Nets *

Michael D. Coovert
Kathleen McNelis

Approaches to studying decision making by teams have been guided to two different philosophical perspectives. One perspective states that team decision making should be unstructured, and that this will lead to superior decisions. Under the unstructured perspective are such techniques as traditional interacting groups, consensus approaches, assessment centers, and quality circles. The second perspective argues that superior team decisions will result from orderly and systematic strategies of decision making. The nominal group, Delphi, and functional techniques typify this perspective.

This chapter has two main purposes or goals. The first is to review the major philosophical perspectives of team decision making, highlighting techniques from each. Our focus is only on understanding the decision-making processes

* We thank Sandra Sibson and Pradnya Takalkar for their assistance with the literature review. Correspondence regarding this chapter should be addressed to: Michael D. Coovert, Department of Psychology, University of South Florida, Tampa, FL 33620-8200.

utilized by teams required to perform judgmental tasks. We will not transgress to situations such as labor negotiations (team of management versus team of union representatives) or parliamentary procedures. The second purpose is to introduce the reader to a modeling tool called Petri nets. We believe Petri nets provide the capability for modeling and understanding team decision making from various perspectives and at multiple levels of abstraction, thus enhancing our understanding of the variables and processes important under various conditions of team decision making.

BACKGROUND

Important judgmental decisions are required in situations where: (a) the potential benefits are substantial, the costs of error are high, and it is difficult to reverse or salvage a poor decision after action has begun; (b) information is incomplete or uncertain; (c) there are many feasible alternatives, but only a few are known; (d) it is difficult to identify an optimal solution; and (e) feedback about results is not available until long after the decision has been rendered (Zand, 1974, 1978). Decision makers are generally advised to consult or work with planning committees, task forces, or teams of subordinates, colleagues, or experts prior to rendering a decision (Maier, 1963; Tannenbaum & Schmidt, 1958; Vroom & Yetton, 1973).

Team decisions can impact the individual, group, and organization level of analysis. Understanding the process and means by which teams arrive at decisions require going beyond a simple extension of individual decision-making practices. The phenomenon of team decision making involves the analysis and consideration of a plethora of factors unique to this process, such as group dynamics, interpersonal and communication skills, conflict, competition, and hidden agendas. For example, in Hill's (1982) summary of the literature comparing individual and group productivity, he reports that the functional size of a group is smaller than its actual size (Bray, Kerr, & Atkin, 1978; Steiner & Rajaratnam, 1961), and that team members who cannot solve the problem continue to consume their share of the group time (Equalitarion Model—Davis, 1969; Restle & Davis, 1962).

The two traditional and diametric philosophical camps providing the groundwork for research in this area maintain that (a) orderly and systematic approaches enhance the quality of group decision making (McBurney & Hance, 1950; Tinbergen, 1956; March & Simon, 1958; Barnlund & Haiman, 1960; Maier, 1963; Delbecq, Van de Ven & Gustafson, 1975; Kepner & Tregoe, 1968; Katz & Kahn, 1978; Phillips, Pedersen, & Wood, 1978; Scheidel & Crowell, 1979); and (b) unstructured task approaches enhance the quality of group decision making (Lindblom, 1959; Pfiffner, 1960; Gordon, 1961; Braybrooke & Lindblom, 1963; Diesing, 1967; Prince, 1970; Rickards, 1974; Mintzberg, Raisinghani, & Theoret, 1976). Both camps challenge proponents of the functional perspective of group decision making that an overreliance on the discussion format per se by which team members arrive at decisions (structured versus unstructured) has dominated this research. The primary determinant of quality decisions rests on whether the group's procedures allow it to satisfy certain critical decision-making functions (Fisher, 1974; Janis & Mann, 1977; Hirokawa, 1982; Gouran & Hirokawa, 1983; Poole, 1983).

UNSTRUCTURED PROCESSES

Interacting Groups

Interacting groups reflect the traditional unstructured team decision making process. It is the conventional group discussion format where the role of the team leader typically is limited to the introduction of prepared agenda items. Teams not specifically instructed in a particular decision making process will typically default to the use of majority votes, averaged rankings, trading, political powering, and other "legitimized" strategies to do so (Nemiroff, Pasmore, & Ford, 1976).

Process characteristics associated with interacting groups tend to inhibit decision-making performance. This list is quite extensive and includes: the high variability in member and leader behavior that occurs across groups; a tendency for discussion to fall into a rut with members focusing on a single train of thought for extended periods; the absence of an opportunity to think through independent ideas that results in a tendency for ideas to be expressed as generalizations; search behavior that becomes reactive and characterized by short periods of focus on the problem; a tendency for task avoidance; tangential discussions; high efforts in establishing social relationship and generating social knowledge; and high status, expressive, or strong personality-type individuals that tend to dominate in search, evaluation, and choice of group product. The negative results of these process characteristics are that meetings tend to conclude with a high perceived lack of closure, low felt accomplishment, and low interest in future phases of problem solving (Delbecq et al., 1975).

Many of the problems victimizing conventionally interacting teams can be explained by what Janis (1972) has termed *groupthink*. It is defined as a mode of group decision making marked by "deterioration of mental efficiency, reality testing, and moral judgment that results from in-group pressures" (Janis, 1972, p. 7). It is this type of blind conformance that can explain why covert judgments are made by group members even though they might not be expressed as overt criticisms in the meeting (Collaros & Anderson, 1969), the inevitable presence of status incongruities in most groups, wherein low-status members may be inhibited and "go along with" opinions expressed by high-status members (Torrance,

1957), and the implied threat of sanctions from the more knowledgeable group members (Hoffman, 1965). Groupthink operates to facilitate a mindset striving to maintain harmonious relations among group members and to obtain group consensus on critical issues. Janis links several United States foreign policy fiascoes to the groupthink phenomenon: the failure to anticipate the Japanese attack on Pearl Harbor in 1941, the escalation of the Vietnam War in the 1960s, and the Bay of Pigs disaster in 1961.

Delbecq et al. maintain that the conventional interacting group does realize some benefits in terms of increasing group motivation and cohesion, increasing a sense of group consensus, and increasing the belief that each alternative solution has been carefully reviewed.

Consensus Approach

The consensus approach adds a critical ingredient to the decision-making process within the interacting groups described above. In the group consensus approach, members are encouraged to first address their assumptions and recommendations, to openly discuss them with the group, and then render a final consensus decision. This approach is a commonly used method among management to arrive at a solution that everyone can "live with." The consensus approach does appear to produce higher quality decision than those of the conventional interacting groups (Nemiroff et al., 1976).

The synergistic decision-making approach, made popular by the Moon Survival exercise, stems from this basic framework. The critical thesis behind this approach is that many organizations fail to plan beyond the requisite task skills, knowledge, and resources necessary for team decision making. Ignoring the team member interactions during the assumption challenging phase of the process can be quite detrimental to the quality of the team's final product.

Efforts to facilitate the development of alternative sets and assumptions within these discussion formats have relied on the use of constructive programmed group conflict, specifically investigating the roles of devil's advocacy and dialectical inquiry in this process (Cosier, 1978, 1980; Cosier & Aplin, 1980; Cosier, Ruble, & Aplin, 1978; Lourenco & Glidewell, 1974; Mitroff, Barabba, & Kilmann, 1977; Schwenk, 1982, 1984; Schwenk & Cosier, 1980; Schweiger, Sandberg, & Ragan, 1986). Dialectical inquiry uses debates between diametric sets of recommendations and assumptions, whereas devil's advocacy relies on critiques of single sets of recommendations and assumptions. By definition, conflict management becomes an integral component in this process. Both strategies appear to produce higher overall quality assumptions and recommendations when compared with conventional and consensus groups. More research is warranted concerning the application of these techniques to specific types of problems and situations (Schweiger et al., 1986).

APPLICATIONS OF CONSENSUS DECISION-MAKING APPROACHES

Two specific organizational applications of consensus decision making will be explored: the assessment center and quality circles. Research concerning the process by which teams render decisions is then summarized.

Assessment Center

As originally conceived, assessment centers were intended to allow for the assessment of traits and qualities that would be used to predict future success on the job (Guion, 1987). The assessment center staff is composed of a team of decision makers who must arrive at consensus evaluation of candidates based on a series of exercises designed to tap critical performance dimensions. Resultant decisions can be utilized for a variety of personnel decisions, including selection, promotability, and performance appraisals.

Although the application of assessment center methodology in organizations has become more widespread, our understanding of why they work has not been as prolific. For example, Klimoski and Strickland (1977) speak to the issue of whether assessment centers are valid or merely mirror existing promotional practices within the organization. The concern is that assessment center evaluation teams may be influenced by their intuitive sense of what is and what is not considered promotable to decision makers within the organization. Subsequently formalized by Klimoski and Brickner (1987) as the subtle criterion contamination hypothesis, assessment centers serve only as a substitute for existing organizational promotional policies and are more apt to be considered as policy capturing. The factors needed to get ahead in the organization are being assessed instead of the traits and qualities the center is designed to measure.

Examples and summaries of the effects of consensus rating processes in the assessment environment can be found in McNelis and Coovert (1988), Sackett and Wilson (1982), and Herriot, Chalmers, and Wingrove (1985).

Quality Circles

The quality circle concept was brought to the forefront of our attention by the successes it evidenced in Japanese businesses. The basic tenet of a quality circle is to generate high quality solutions to work-related problems and to improve channels of communication, both hierarchically and laterally (Thompson, 1982; see also Cannon-Bowers et al., this volume). Small teams of people who perform similar types of work meet regularly on a voluntary basis to discuss, analyze, and propose solutions to work-related problems involving quality (e.g., safety, efficiency, effectiveness, working conditions, cost savings). A facilitator is typically present.

The opportunity to participate in the management presentation further reinforces the commitment of management that the employees are the most valuable resource in the organization, and the corporate climate encourages active employee participation in the circle process (London & Moulton, 1986). It is an ill-conceived notion, however, for organizations to assume that encouragement and support of team decision making alone will lead to quality.

Greenbaum, Kaplan, and Metlay (1988) formulated a systems model for improving the performance of problem-solving teams. The four system elements are inputs (prevailing conditions), processes (interaction processes), outputs (results of team activities), and feedback (information to the group about its performance). The subcategories within each system element address factors relating to the task, the individual, the group, and the organization.

The systems model was used to analyze the 16 evaluation studies of quality circle programs reported from 1981 and 1986 (Greenbaum et al., 1988). Of the eight studies addressing at least one subcategory of the process component, only two specifically looked at the task problem-solving procedures employed. The need to advance our understanding of how team decisions are actually made within the circle environment remains a salient research demand.

STRUCTURED FORMATS

Recognizing that two distinctive phases exist in the decision-making process, each warranting unique strategies to accomplish these ends (Simon & Newell, 1958), several structured group decision-making formats have been developed. They are designed to improve the opportunity for the generation and evaluation of quality solutions by combating some of the inherent limitations of the interacting group decision-making process.

Nominal Group Technique

Delbecq and Van de Ven (1975) authored the nominal group technique (NGT). The premise underlying the NGT is the elimination of group member interaction during the idea generation and the idea voting phases of the process. Member interaction is carefully structured during the idea clarification and idea evaluation phases. Procedurally, a NGT session commences with independent, silent generation of ideas from group members in writing, followed by a round-robin style listing from group members. Each idea is recorded in flip chart format before the group to facilitate discussion of each idea for clarification and evaluation. Independent, silent voting in writing is then required on the priority ideas. The group decision is then mathematically derived through rank ordering, rating, or other statistical aggregate process.

Some of the process characteristics that enhance decision-making performance include: consistency in decision making due to the low variability in member and leader behavior, a balanced concern for social-emotional group maintenance roles and performance of task-instrumental role, high quality of generated ideas resulting from silent generation and active listening, proactive search behaviors stemming from the clarification phase and the task-oriented nature of the group, equality of participation in the idea generation phase, and a perception of closure, accomplishment, and interest in future phases of problem solving at the conclusion of the session (Delbecq et al., 1975, pp. 33–34). The NGT format seems best suited for single topic meetings, as it requires significant preparation time to conduct and the process must be adhered to by all participating group members.

Delphi Technique

The Delphi technique, also a derivative of the premise that group member interaction is detrimental to overall quality, is a "method for the systematic solicitation and collation of judgments on a particular topic though a set of carefully designed sequential questionnaires interspersed with summarized information and feedback of opinions derived from earlier responses" (Delbecq et al., 1975, p. 10). Since member interaction is perceived as a deterrent to effective decision making, group members do not interact in traditional face-to-face meetings. Iterative survey techniques administered by a third party allow anonymous statistical summaries of the opinions of group members (Dalkey & Helmer, 1963).

In step with this philosophy, Turoff (1970) recommends that at least three different groups of individuals perform the three different roles implicit in this process: one group of individuals to utilize the output of the process; one group responsible for designing, administering, and summarizing the questionnaires; and one group whose judgments are being solicited.

The process characteristics of the Delphi technique contributing to effective decision-making performance include the isolated generation of ideas in writing, forcing respondents to think through the complexity of the problem prior to submitting specific ideas, proactive rather than reactive search behavior, decreased member conformity pressures, equality of participation through simple pooling of independent ideas and judgments and moderate perceptions of closure are attained at the conclusion of the process (Delbecq et al., 1975, pp. 34–35). The technique is valuable for obtaining judgments when physical proximity imposes constraints on group members.

The Delphi technique, however, does have certain drawbacks. For example, it can: (a) contribute to feelings of isolation and detachment from the decision-making process, (b) foster communication and interpretation difficulties among team members (i.e., if members experience writing skill deficits), and (c) encourage a lack of conflict resolution due to the absence of group interaction. In addition, the significant time investment inherent in this approach does not make it conducive to problems requiring solutions "yesterday."

Functional Perspective

As mentioned earlier, advocates of the functional perspective of group decision making maintain that an overreliance on the discussion format per se by which team members arrive at decisions (structured versus unstructured) has undeservingly dominated much of the research. Their posture is that the primary determinant of quality decisions rests on whether the group's procedures allow it to satisfy certain critical decision-making functions.

The general decision-making functions common to most group decision-making tasks as espoused by Janis and Mann (1977), Hirokawa (1982), and Gouran and Hirokawa (1983) are that the group: (a) needs to understand thoroughly and accurately the problem presented to it, (b) must marshal a range of realistic and acceptable alternatives, (c) must assess thoroughly and accurately the positive consequences associated with each alternative choice, and (d) must assess thoroughly and accurately the negative consequences associated with each alternative choice. These "requisite functions" persist independent of the situational variants of the decisions making task (Gouran & Hirokawa, 1983).

To investigate the proposition that group accomplishment of important task-achievement functions is a better predictor of decision-making success than the discussion format used, Hirokawa (1985) compared four discussion formats of comparable diversity (reflective-thinking, ideal-solution, single-question, free discussion) to identify appropriate disciplinary action for students caught plagiarizing. Groups were evaluated on the quality of the final decision and the four requisite conditions for group effectiveness.

No differences were found in the quality of group decisions across discussion formats. Groups that satisfied two or more requisite conditions produced higher quality decision than groups satisfying less than two. Further conclusions suggest differential weighting of requisite conditions in terms of importance. The group's ability to "understand the choice-making situation" and to "assess the negative qualities or consequences associated with alternative choices" may prove to be the integral components in identifying quality decisions.

Designing Decision-Making Groups

Fundamental to a discussion of how teams make effective decisions is the designing of groups for judgmental decisions. Stumpf, Zand, and Freedman (1979) outline a model which incorporates both type of membership and method of functioning as operational parameters to consider in this process, see Figure 10.1. Membership categories include experts, representatives, and co-workers; methods of functioning include interacting, nominal, or Delphi groups.

Decision criteria are then introduced into a system of propositions to ascertain the judgmental decision-making group to increase decision effectiveness. The decision criteria are quality, acceptance, span of control, originality, expertise, and conflict. Figure 10.2 presents the propositions underlying JDM group design, and Figure 10.3 poses the challenge in flowchart format. In all, 15 unique paths are defined and may serve as a springboard for future research in this arena.

SUMMARY

The first portion of this chapter examined various strategies for understanding and applying team decision making. Historically, team decision making was recommended to occur in either a highly structured or unstructured manner. Despite these efforts, a theoretical framework for representing this process remains elusive. We feel that this has been due, at least in part, to a lack of appropriate methodological tools. The second section of this chapter introduces a methodology that we feel is useful for modeling and analyzing the decision-making process of teams. The approach is a very general one and is appropriate for modeling and analyzing teams at various levels of abstraction.

The modeling technique described here is an instance of graph theory called *Petri nets.*[1] Developments in Petri nets are based on the dissertation of C. A. Petri (1962), whose purpose was to develop a representation applicable to all systems with well-defined activities. Indeed, Petri nets have proven useful for modeling and analysis in such diverse areas as parallel computer systems (Andrè, Diaz, Girault, & Sifakis, 1979;), mathematical knowledge (Jantzen, 1980), satellite protocols (Estraillier, Girault, & Ilie, 1985), computer-integrated manufacturing systems (Oh, Favrel, Campagne, Doumeingts, & Cartor, 1984), chemical reactions (Agerwala, 1979), and legal systems (Meldman & Holt, 1971). As a representational tool Petri nets are obviously very general and can be very useful.

OVERVIEW OF PETRI NETS

Generally, Petri nets specify the relationship between two types of entities, places (or states) and transitions (or events). Places and transitions are represented as circles and rectangles, respectively, and are typically connected by

---

[1] For an overview of graph theory, see Gould (1988), and of Petri nets, Peterson (1981) and Reisig (1985).

Types of Judgmental Decision-Making Groups

Method of Functioning

	Interacting (group interacts throughout JDM process)	Nominal (direct interaction only during evaluation phase)	Delphi (no face-to-face meetings occur)
Expert (members selected from relevant internal & external organizational areas)	E/I	E/N	E/D
Representative (members selected from relevant interest groups)	R/I	R/N	R/D
Co-worker (members selected by manager)	CW/I	CW/N	CD/D

Figure 10.1. Types of Judgmental Decision-Making Groups. From Stumpf,

Propositions Underlying JDM Group Design

P1. Quality and Acceptance Needed.
 $A \cap B$ --> Elimate Delphi Method

P2. Quality but Not Acceptance Needed.
 $A \cap \bar{B}$ --> Eliminate Representative Groups

P3. Acceptance but Not Quality Relevant.
 $B \cap \bar{A}$ --> Eliminate Expert Groups

P4. Quality and Originality Needed.
 $A \cap D$ --> Eliminate Interacting Method

P5. Quality, Acceptance, and Broad Span.
 $A \cap B \cap C$ --> Eliminate Co-worker Groups

P6. Quality, Acceptance, and Narrow Span.
 $A \cap B \cap \bar{D}$ --> Eliminate Expert Groups

P7. Quality but No Internal Expertise.
 $A \cap \bar{E}$ --> Eliminate Co-worker Groups

P8. Quality, Acceptance, No Orginality, but Conflict.
 $A \cap B \cap \bar{D} \cap F$ --> Eliminate Nominal and Delphi

---

[a]Legend A = Quality, B = Acceptance, C = Decision Span, D = Originality, E = Expertise, F = Conflict. The inverted U is set theory notation for "intersection" meaning both conditions apply simultaneously. A bar over a letter signifies "no" or elimination.

Figure 10.2. Propositions Underlying Judgmental Decision-Making Group Design. From Stumpf, Zand, and Freedman (1979)

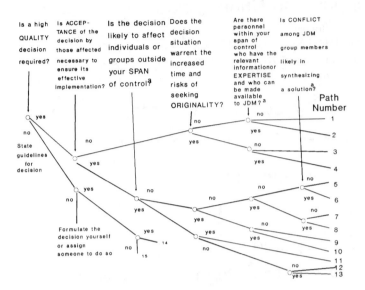

Path Number	Preferred Set[b]	Path Number	Preferred Set[b]	Path Number	Preferred Set[b]
1	E/I, E/N, E/D	6	R/I	10	R/N, CW/N
2	E/I, E/N, E/D CW/I, CW/N	7 & 15	R/I, R/N, CW/I CW/N	11	E/N, R/N
		8	R/I, CW/I	12	E/I, E/N, R/I, R/N
3	E/N, E/D	9	R/N	13	E/I, R/I
4	E/N, E/D, CW/N				
5 & 14	R/I, R/N				

[a] The absence of a node means that the parameter is not relevant to that path

[b] See definitions of group type in Figure 1

Figure 10.3.   Flowchart for Designing a Judgment Decision-Making Group. From Stumpf, Zand, and Freedman (1979)

directed arcs (also called edges or arrows). Directed arcs serve to connect places to transitions and transitions to places. Two places would never be connected by an arc without an intervening transition, and likewise, two transitions would never be connected by an edge except through an intervening place. Only rarely would undirected arcs connect places and transitions. Figure 4a illustrates two places and one transition connected by two directed edges.

Formally, the structure of a Petri net is a bipartite directed graph, $G = [P, T,$

A] where $P = \{p_1, p_2, \ldots, p_n\}$ is a set of finite places, $T = \{t_1, t_2, \ldots, t_m\}$ is a finite set of transitions, $A = \{P \times T\} \cup \{T \times P\}$ is a set of directed arcs. The set of input places of a transition (t) is given by $I(t) = \{p|(p,t)\epsilon A\}$, and the set of output places of transition (t) is given by $O(t) = \{p|(t,p)\epsilon A\}$. Sometimes the net will be defined as a function of the four entities: places (P), transitions (T), input functions (I), and output functions (O), so $N = [P, T, I, O]$. The two representations are equivalent.

MARKED PETRI NET

Information, data, or conditions are represented as tokens in a Petri net. Tokens reside in places and move from one place to another through the firing of the transitions which connect the places. Figure 10.4b represents a marked Petri net with a token in p_1 and p_2 is called an "empty place." Figure 10.4c represents the state of the net after t_1 fires. Conceptually this simple net might represent a piece of information passing between two individuals.

The marking of a Petri net is the assignment of tokens to places in the net, $M: P \rightarrow I$, where I is an integer vector representing the number of tokens (M)

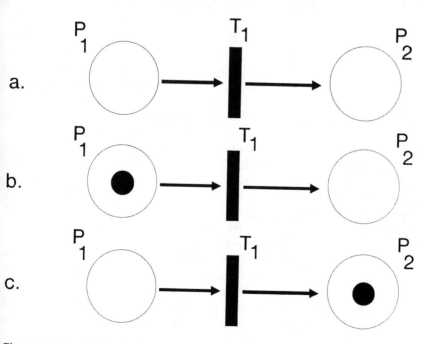

Figure 10.4.   A Simple Petri Net

assigned to each place (p_i). A marked Petri net, then, is identified as: N = (T, P, A, M). A transition becomes enabled in a marked Petri net for all p∈I(t), and enabled transitions fire by removing a token from the input place(s) and placing it in the output place(s).

The marking of a Petri net is important, because it controls the firing of the transitions in the net. Thus, the execution of the net is determined (within certain constraints) by the marking of the graph. Asynchronous behavior is typical of Petri nets. It should be apparent that, once a transition fires, the net has a new marking. Consider again our simple example of Figure 10.4. The marking of Figure 10.4a, b, and c, are, respectively, $M_a[0,0]$, $M_b[1,0]$, and $M_c[0,1]$. As mentioned above, there often are certain constraints on the firing order of transitions (Hura, 1987). For example, if a transition is not enabled, it cannot fire (this could occur either if the place contains an insufficient number of tokens or if other firing conditions of the transitions are not satisfied). A second constraint is that a transition cannot fire and remove a token which is not present. A third constraint is the firing of a transition will always result in the places of a Petri net containing a number of tokens greater than or equal to zero.

THE MEANING OF A PETRI NET

A Petri net is merely an abstract model, and as such, is not very useful until meaning is attached to its places, transitions, and tokens. Consider the net in Figure 10.5. As it stands, the net could represent any cyclic process. In one example, the places p_1–p_4 might be labeled spring, summer, fall, and winter, respectively, while transitions would represent climatic conditions which cause the change in one season to another (e.g., t_1 represents those conditions which lead from spring to summer). The net would represent the yearly cycle of the seasons. A second example would have the net representing a (not very useful) arithmetic logic unit of a computer. Transitions t_1 and t_3 represent multipliers, taking the tokens at their inputs (p_1 and p_3, respectively) and doubling the number of those tokens. Transitions t_2 and t_4 might represent dividers, taking the number of tokens at their inputs (p_2 and p_4, respectively), halving them and placing the remaining tokens in their outputs (p_3 and p_1, respectively). If p_1 contains one token, as it does in the figure, when t_1 fires, p_2 contains two tokens and p_1 is empty. Transition t_2 is now enabled and fires with p_3 receiving one token and p_2 is empty. Transition t_3 then fires placing two tokens in p_4. Finally, t_4 fires placing one token in p_1, and the cycle begins all over again. A third example would have the nets representing a four member team. Places p_1–p_4 would represent the four individuals of the team, the arcs represent a channel of communication between members, a token a piece of information, and a transition, the act of communication (including possible modification to the message) between team members.

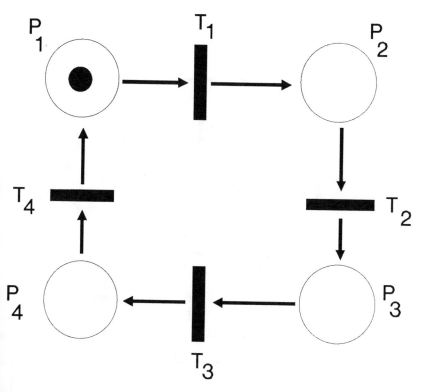

Figure 10.5. A Cyclic Petri Net

DESIRABLE PROPERTIES OF PETRI NETS

As a modeling tool for teams, Petri nets have three properties that make them very attractive. The first property is their ability to model two critical aspects of teams: conflict and concurrency. Consider the net in Figure 10.6a. When t_1 fires, p_1 is empty and p_2 and p_3 each contain a token, as illustrated in Figure 10.6b. Once that occurs, t_2 and t_3 are enabled and fire in parallel (concurrently), with the result depicted in Figure 10.6c. Transitions t_4 and t_5 are now each enabled, but this state is one of conflict as either t_4 can fire (resulting in Figure 10.6d) or t_5 fires (resulting in Figure 10.6a). This state is one of conflict as the firing of either t_4 or t_5 disables the other. If t_4 fires, a token is placed in p_3, but t_5 is now disabled since only one of its input places contains a token. The result of t_4 firing is depicted in Figure 10.6d. If on the other hand t_5 had fired, the net would be as depicted in Figure 10.6a.

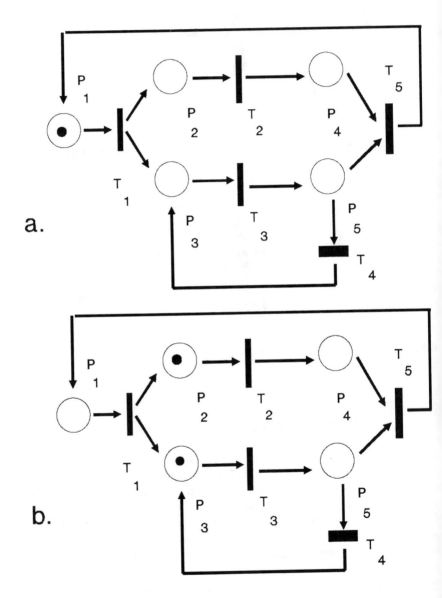

a.

b.

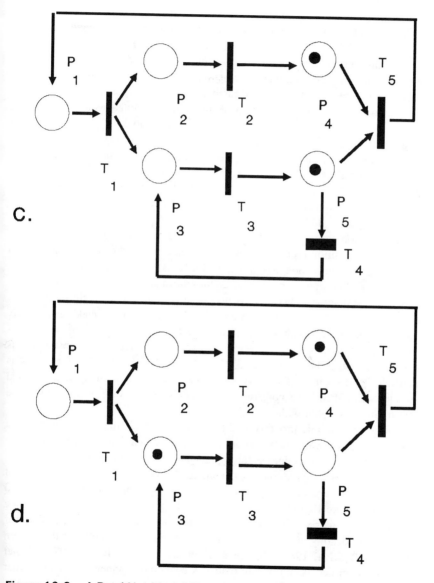

Figure 10.6.   A Petri Net Model Illustrating Concurrency and Conflict

The second desirable property is that Petri nets are useful for modeling at various levels of abstraction. If one were interested, for example, in modeling communication patterns, an approach might be to begin with a single individual and construct a net to represent information sensing, processing, and output for a single individual. A second net would be added to represent a second individual, a third to represent a third individual, and so on until the desired number of individuals were represented. The nets could be connected to represent interacting subteams and teams until an entire department or organization is represented. Furthermore, the connections could easily represent serial and/or parallel interactions among members, subteams, or teams. Once the linkages are established, one can examine the influence of constraints at various levels of abstraction (e.g., individual, subteam, team, department, organization). Figure 10.7 presents a model of a hierarchical decision-making team composed of eight individuals connected by directed edges into four two-member subteams, three four-member subteams, and one team. In the figure, individuals are represented as the first two places connected by a transition on the left side of the figure. Conceptually, for each individual, the first place represents information sensing/recognition (e.g., recognition of stimulus information present on a radar scope), the transition represents cognitive operations on the sensed information (e.g., target identification and anticipated actions), and the second place represents information output (e.g., making the information available for the level-1 subteam coordinator). This process occurs in parallel for the eight individuals, but the passing of information up each level of the decision-making hierarchy occurs sequentially. Conditions regarding the firing of the transitions are embedded in the transitions at each level of the hierarchy. Each level of abstraction is enclosed by either a broken or solid rectangle. Analysis could occur for the net as a whole or at each level of abstraction. Of course, alternative organizational structures could also be constructed and analyzed, as well as modifying the constraints associated with transitions.

The third desirable property is that Petri net models may be analyzed in a variety of ways to validate the model and to gain insight into the behavior of the system. One way this is done is through the construction of an incidence matrix. An incidence matrix represents the net where $C = [C_{ij}]$ n by m where $C_{ij} = -1$ if p_i is an input place of t_j, $C_{ij} = 1$ if p_i is an output of place t_j, and $C_{ij} = 0$ otherwise. Figure 10.8a is the incidence matrix for the net of Figure 10.6a. Once the incidence matrix (C) is constructed, net invariants can be identified for purposes of locating modeling errors and verifying the properties of the system (Martinez & Silva, 1982; Memmi & Roucairol, 1980; Murata, 1977). A net invariant is defined as an n-vector matrix $\mathbf{X}$ containing nonnegative integers that satisfy the condition of $\mathbf{X}^T C = 0$. The set of places corresponding to the elements of X which are strictly positive is the support of X, denoted as $\|\mathbf{X}\|$.

Invariants are useful because $\mathbf{X}$ is an invariant if and only if, for any initial marking M^0 and any reachable marking M, $X^T M = x^T M^0$. What this means is

Subteam level 1   level 2   level 3

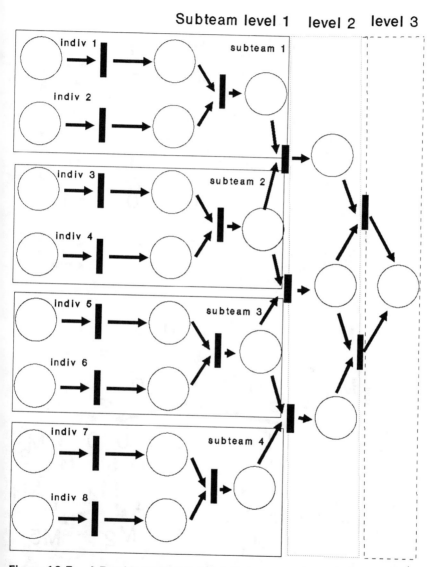

Figure 10.7.   A Petri Net Model of Eight Individuals, Four 2-Member Subteams (Level 1), Three Four-Member Subteams (Level 2), and One Team (Level 3)

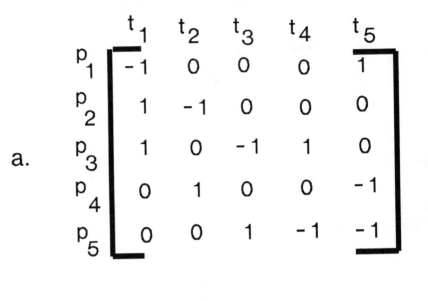

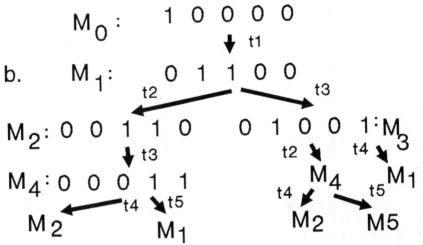

Figure 10.8.   Petri Net: a. Incidence Matrix, and b. Reachability Tree

266

that the total number of tokens in the set of places $\|X\|$ is invariant for any transition firing. Thus, the accuracy of the net may be verified through invariants analysis. For example, if the net represents a team of individuals on an assembly line, a set of mutually exclusive places can be identified where a part has the status of "being modified" or "finished" but not both.

Reachability trees are a second major analysis technique for Petri nets. This approach is useful for identifying conflicts and blockages in the net. Specifically, one analyzes the tree to ensure all branches of the tree reach a desired state (Lein, 1976).

The tree is constructed by beginning with the initial markings of the net (M_0) and generating all reachable states ($M_{1,2,\ldots,n}$) from the firing of the transitions. If a new marking is identical to an old marking, mark it according to the old marking. Figure 10.8b represents the reachability tree for the net of Figure 10.6a.

EXTENSIONS OF PETRI NETS

Several extensions have been made to general Petri net theory. These have proved very useful for certain modeling problems and have made other classes of problems addressable by the methodology. Some of the more useful extensions are briefly described here, and further discussion can be found in Peterson (1982), Reisig (1985), and the yearly Petri net conference proceedings, as well as the references listed in this chapter.

Timed Petri Nets

The notion of adding timed firing delays associated with transitions is the focus of timed Petri nets (Coulahan & Roussopoulos, 1985; Menache, 1985; Smigelski, Murata, & Sowa, 1985). A *timed Petri net* is defined as a marked Petri net with vector $\Theta = (\Theta_1, \Theta_2, \ldots, \Theta_3)$ of delays associated with transitions. Formally, a timed Petri net is: $TPN = (P, T, A, M_o, \Theta)$.

Stochastic Petri Nets

Stochastic Petri nets (Lin & Marinescu, 1987; Lu, Zhang, & Murata, 1987; Molloy, 1982, 1985, 1987) expand the notion of time by allowing enabled transitions to fire after a random exponentially distributed enabling time (which can be marking dependent). The model is: $SPN = (P, T, I, O, M_o, L)$ where $L = (l_1, l_2, \ldots, l_m)$ is a vector of firing rates associated with timed transitions. Molloy (1981) demonstrated that stochastic Petri nets are isomorphic to continuous-time Marcov chains. Marcov chains have often proven useful for modeling aspects of human behavior such as learning (Wickens, 1982).

Generalized Stochastic Petri Nets

Petri nets that combine the transition time firings of both timed and stochastic Petri nets are called *generalized stochastic Petri nets* (Marsan, Balbo, Chiola, & Conte, 1986). These nets contain some transitions that fire immediately and others that fire after a random exponentially distributed enabling time. Related nets contain transitions with both deterministic and exponential firing. The deterministic transitions are of two types, those that fire immediately and those that fire after a constant enabling time. Thus, generalized Petri nets contain three types of transitions.

Extended Stochastic Petri Nets

Some modeling situations are more probabilistic in nature as opposed to time dependent. In these instances, extended stochastic Petri nets can prove useful. A simple example is transition with two output arcs, one connected to P_1 and the second connected to P_2. When the transition fires, there is a probability of τ that a token is deposited in P_1, and a probability of $1-\tau$ that a token will be placed in P_2.

Colored Petri Nets

These nets have the potential for greatly decreasing the overall size of the net. The general strategy is to use color to represent different (yet similar) entities. For example, one could use four different colored tokens to represent different types of information which would be passed to team members. Transitions contain constraints allowing only certain colored tokens to pass at specified times when fired. Of course, the use of colors, although simplifying the net, does induce certain additional complexities.

Abstract Petri Nets

This very powerful class of Petri net has recently been proposed by Guha (1988; see also Etessami, 1988). They include the capability of representing different token types and can also represent the assignment of differential properties with the places as well as the transitions, thus incorporating all Petri net extensions to date into one Petri net model.

APPLICATIONS OF PETRI NET MODELING TO TEAMS

Over the past few years Levis along with his colleagues (cf. Boettcher & Levis, 1982, 1983; Levis, 1989; Remy, Levis, & Jin, 1988; Tabak & Levis, 1985; Weingaertner & Levis, 1989) have employed Petri nets to study the organizational structure of decision making. An individual is considered a two-stage model consisting of situation assessment and response selection. Constraints placed on the net model follow the performance of an individual decision maker with bounded rationality. Individuals are linked together into a team, and various constraints are placed on the nets to model alternative decision strategies, work load, and organizational structures. Their approach has been successfully employed to model submarine emergency decision making.

Our approach is somewhat different from that of Levis and his colleagues. We employ Petri nets in a sequential manner to answer a variety of questions about team performance. For example, we have constructed a Petri net representation of the Replenishment at Sea task. The task is a three-member team task designed to simulate the naval task of transferring supplies from a supply ship to a receiving ship while at sea. In this case, the task level net consists of 76 places and 91 transitions. Figure 10.9 is the Petri net representation of the task, and Figure 10.10 contains descriptions of the associated places and transitions. Once the task-level (functional) Petri net is constructed, other nets representing such things as communication patterns, individual decision making, and so on, can be "layered" on top of the functional net. Furthermore, the functional net can be studied to observe how it changes as a function of such variables as team member experience and stress.

Because Petri nets are a graphical representational tool, one's theory about team decision making can be easily expressed, analyzed, and communicated. We have found, for example, that successful teams tend to spend more time in certain subnets than do less successful teams. Additionally, as teams members spend more time together, the evolution of their performance is easily modeled by the net. We see, for example, the probabilities associated with transitions firing being very different for mature teams versus immature teams.

In conclusion, theories of team decision making can be explicitly tested and evaluated through the application of Petri net modeling. Petri net models can further serve theory development and testing through enabling the generation and assessment of alternative hypotheses regarding team decision-making strategies.

GENERAL SUMMARY

This chapter reviewed traditional approaches for understanding team decision making. We saw that decision making has typically been studied as a function of

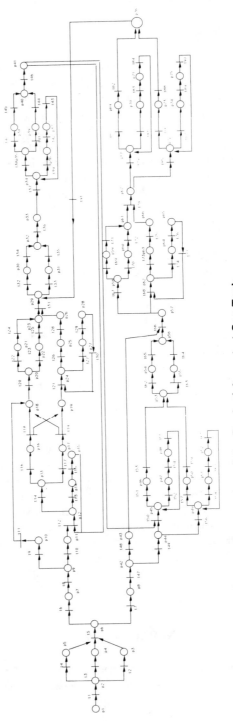

Figure 10.9. Petri Net Representation of the Replenishment at Sea Task

PLACES	Description
p1	Task initiated
p2	Decision to use a piece of equipment
p3	Use the net
p4	Use the orange platform
p5	Use the black platform
p6	Choice of whether to use the crane or pulley is reached
p7	Use of crane
p8	Use of pulley
p9	Information gathering: Knowledge of whether the crane is on the supply ship
p10	Awareness that the crane is on the supply ship
p11	Awareness that the crane is not on the supply ship
p12	Information gathered: Knowledge of whether or not the crane is on the supply ship
p13	Awareness that the crane operator is free
p14	Awareness that the crane operator is not free
p15	Wait for the crane operator to be free
p16	Crane operator told to move the crane
p17	Crane operator perceives the need to move the crane
p18	Perception that the crane is on the supply ship
p19	Wait for the crane to move to the supply ship
p20	Information gathering: Knowledge of whether there is previous equipment attached to the crane
p21	Awareness that there is previous equipment attached to the crane
p22	Awareness that there is no previous equipment attached to the crane
p23	Perception that the crane is free (to transfer additional cargo)
p24	Information gathered: Knowledge of whether the required equipment is on board
p25	Awareness that the required equipment is on board
p26	Cargo loaded
p27	Awareness that the required equipment is not on board
p28	Waiting for the required equipment
p29	Equipment is ready for transfer
p30	Personnel on receiving ship informed that the crane (pulley) is ready for movement
p31	Personnel on receiving ship have perceived that the crane (pulley) is ready for movement
p32	Awareness that equipment is ready for cargo transfer
p33	Cargo is on the receiving ship
p34	Information gathered: Knowledge of whether teammate is free
p35	Awareness that teammate is free
p36	Awareness that teammate is not free
p37	Waiting for teammate to be free
p38	Teammate instructed to assist in unloading cargo
p39	Teammate has perceived that cargo needs to be unloaded
p40	Awareness that cargo is ready for unloading
p41	Equipment is free; operator is free
p42	Information gathered: Knowledge of whether pulley is or is not on supply ship
p43	Awareness that pulley is on supply ship
p44	Awareness that pulley is not on supply ship
p45	Information gathered: Knowledge of whether pulley operator on receiving ship is free
p46	Awareness that pulley operator on receiving ship is free
p47	Awareness that pulley operator on receiving ship is not free
p48	Wait for pulley operator on receiving ship to become free

(continued)

Figure 10.10. Descriptions of the Places and Transitions for Figure 10.9

Figure 10.10. *(Continued)*

p49   Information gathered: Knowledge of whether pulley operator on supply ship is free

p50   Awareness that pulley operator on supply ship is free

p51   Awareness that pulley operator on supply ship is not free

p52   Wait for the pulley operator on the supply ship to become free

p53   Information gathered: Knowledge that pulley operator teammate is free

p54   Pulley operator teammate instructed to move the pulley

p55   Pulley operator teammates have perceived the need to operate the pulley

p56   Readiness to move the pulley

p57   Pulley on the supply ship

p58   Information gathered: Knowledge that there is previous equipment on the pulley

p59   Awareness that there is previous equipment on the pulley

p60   Awareness that there is no previous equipment on the pulley

p61   Information gathered: Knowledge that the pulley is ready to take new cargo

p62   Information gathered: Knowledge of whether the required equipment is on board

p63   Awareness that the required equipment is on board

p64   Awareness that the required equipment is not on board

p65   Wait for the required equipment

p66   cargo loaded

p67   Pulley loaded with cargo and ready for movement

p68   Information gathered: Knowledge ofwhether the pulley operator on the receiving ship is free

p69   Awareness that the pulley operator on the receiving ship is free

p70   Awareness that the pulley operator on the receiving ship is not free

p71   Wait for the pulley operator on the receiving ship to become free

p72   Information gathered: Knowledge of whether the pulley operator on the supply ship is free

p73   Awareness that the pulley operator on the supply ship is free

p74   Awareness that the pulley operator on the supply ship is not free

p75   Wait for the pulley operator on the supply ship to become free

p76   Information gathered: Knowledge that fellow pulley operator is free

TRANSITIONS Description

t1   Information gathering: Observe the net, black and orange platforms

t2   Direct (self) to use the net

t3   Direct (self) to use the orange platform

t4   Direct (self) to use the black platform

t5   Information gathering: Choice between the pulley and the crane

t6   Information evaluation: Decide to use the crane

t7   Information evaluation: Decide to use the pulley

t8   Information gathering: Is the crane on the supply ship

t9   Information evaluation: Awareness/realization that the crane is on the supply ship

t10   Information evaluation: Awareness/realization that the crane is not on the supply ship

t11   Perceiving that the crane is on the supply ship

Figure 10.10. *(Continued)*

t12 Information gathering: Determine if the crane is on the supply ship
t13 Information evaluation: Becoming aware/realizing that the crane operator is not free
t14 Information evaluation: Becoming aware/realizing that the crane operator is free
t15 Information evaluation: Becoming aware/realizing that the need to wait
t16 Instruct the crane operator to operate the crane
t17 Crane operator perceives the need to operate the crane
t18 Crane operator manipulating the crane -- crane swinging across
t19 Crane operator manipulating the crane -- crane swinging across
t20 Information gathering: Is there previously used equipment attached to the crane
t21 Information gathering: Is the required equipment on board
t22 Information evaluation: Awareness/realization that there is previously used equipment attached to the crane
t23 Information evaluation: Awareness/realization that there is no previously used equipment attached to the crane
t24 Unhook the equipment from the crane
t25 Perceiving that the crane is free
t26 Information evaluation: Awareness/realization that the required equipment is on board
t27 Information evaluation: Awareness/realization that the required equipment is not on board
t28 Load the cargo
t29 Information evaluation: Awareness/realization of the need to wait
t30 Waiting
t31 Hook cargo to the crane
t32 Instructing receiving ship personnel that the crane (pulley) is ready for transportation
t33 Personnel on the receiving ship perceives that the crane (pulley) is ready for transportation
t34 Information evaluation: Awareness/realization that the equipment is ready for cargo transfer
t35 Information evaluation: Awareness/realization that the equipment is ready for cargo transfer
t36 Operating the equipment
t37 Information gathering: Is teammate free
t38 Information evaluation: Awareness/realization that teammate is free
t39 Information evaluation: Awareness/realization that teammate is not free
t40 Instructing teammate to help unload
t41 Teammate perceives the need to unload
t42 Information evaluation: Awareness/realization of the need to wait
t43 Waiting
t44 Information evaluation: Awareness/realization that the equipment is ready for unloading
t45 Information evaluation: Awareness/realization that the equipment is ready for unloading
t46 Unloading
t47 Information gathering: Is the pulley on the supply ship
t48 Information evaluation: Awareness/realization that the pulley is on the supply ship
t49 Information evaluation: Awareness/realization that the pulley is not on the supply ship

(continued)

Figure 10.10. (*Continued*)

t50	Information gathering: Is the pulley operator on the receiving ship free
t51	Information evaluation: Awareness/realization that the pulley operator on the receiving ship is free
t52	Information evaluation: Awareness/realization that the pulley operator on the receiving ship is not free
t53	Perceiving that the pulley operator on the receiving ship is free
t54	Information evaluation: Awareness/realization of the need to wait
t55	Waiting
t56	Information gathering: Is the pulley operator on the supply ship free
t57	Information evaluation: Awareness/realization that the pulley operator on the supply ship is free
t58	Information evaluation: Awareness/realization that the pulley operator on the supply ship is not free
t59	Perceiving that the pulley operator on the supply ship is free
t60	Information evaluation: Awareness/realization of the need to wait
t61	Waiting
t62	Instruct the other pulley operator to operate the pulley
t63	The pulley operators perceive the need to operate the pulley
t64	Information evaluation: Awareness/realization that the pulley needs to be operated
t65	Information evaluation: Awareness/realization that the pulley needs to be operated
t66	Operate the pulley
t67	Information gathering: Is there previously utilized equipment still attached to the pulley
t68	Information gathering: Is the required equipment on board
t69	Information evaluation: Awareness/realization that there is previously utilized equipment attached to the pulley
t70	Information evaluation: Awareness/realization that there is no previously utilized equipment attached to the pulley
t71	Unhook the equipment
t72	Perceiving that the pulley is free
t73	Information evaluation: Awareness/realization that the required equipment is on board
t74	Information evaluation: Awareness/realization that the required equipment is not on board
t75	Load the cargo
t76	Information evaluation: Awareness/realization of the need to wait
t77	Waiting
t78	Hook the cargo to the pulley
t79	Information gathering: Is the pulley operator on the receiving ship free
t80	Information evaluation: Awareness/realization that the pulley operator on the receiving ship is free
t81	Information evaluation: Awareness/realization that the pulley operator on the receiving ship is not free
t82	Perceiving that the pulley operator on the receiving ship is free
t83	Information evaluation: Awareness/realization of the need to wait
t84	Waiting
t85	Information gathering: Is the pulley operator on the supply ship free

(*continued*)

Figure 10.10.   (*Continued*)

t86	Information evaluation: Awareness/realization that the pulley operator on the supply ship is free
t87	Information evaluation: Awareness/realization that the pulley operator on the supply ship is not free
t88	Perceiving that the pulley operator on the supply ship is free
t89	Information evaluation: Awareness/realization of the need to wait
t90	Waiting
t91	Perceiving that the equipment is ready for transfer

either highly structured or unstructured teams. The concept of Petri nets as an approach for modeling and understanding team decision-making behavior was then introduced. Because Petri nets are a graphical representational tool, one's theory about team decision making can be easily expressed and communicated. In addition, Petri nets are very powerful in that they can represent many different phenomena characteristic of team decision making (e.g., conflict, concurrency, asynchronous behavior, hierarchical behavior). Theories of team decision making can be evaluated through the application of Petri net modeling, and these models can further serve by enabling the generation of alternative hypotheses about decision making strategies.

Petri net models, however, are not an immediate panacea for understanding team decision making. Considerable care must be exercised in the identification of places, transitions, and tokens, and the constraints placed on them. Additionally, one must be careful in constructing the models so they are a valid representation either of one's theory of decision-making behavior, or of a descriptive representation of observed team decision-making behavior. We invite researchers and practitioners alike to apply Petri nets as a tool to aid in understanding team decision making.

REFERENCES

Agerwala, T. (1979). Putting Petri nets to work. *Computer, 12*, 85–94.

Andrè, C., Diaz, M., Girault, C, & Sifakis, J. (1980). Survey of French research and applications based on Petri nets. In W. Brauer (Ed.), *Net theory and applications* (pp. 321–346). New York: Springer-Verlag.

Barnlund, D. C., & Haiman, F. S. (1960). *The dynamics of discussion.* Boston: Houghton Mifflin.

Boettcher, K. L., & Levis, A. H. (1982). Modeling the interacting decisionmaker with bounded rationality. *IEEE Transactions on Systems, Man, and Cybernetics, SMC-12*, 334–344.

Boettcher, K. L., & Levis, A. H. (1983). Modeling and analysis of teams of interacting decisionmakers with bounded rationality. *Automatica, 19*, 703–709.

Bray, R., Kerr, N., & Atkin, R. (1978r). Effects of group size, problem difficulty, and sex on group performance and member reactions. *Journal of Personality and Social Psychology, 36,* 1224–1240.

Braybrooke, D., & Lindblom, C. E. (1963). *A strategy of decision.* New York: Free Press.

Collaros, P. A., & Anderson, L. R. (1969). Effect of perceived expertness upon creativity of members of brainstorming groups. *Journal of Applied Psychology, 53,* 159–163.

Cosier, R. A. (1978). The effects of three potential aids for making strategic decisions on prediction accuracy. *Organizational Behavior and Human Performance, 22,* 295–306.

Cosier, R. A. (1980). Inquiry method, goal difficulty, and context effects on performance. *Decision Sciences, 11,* 1–16.

Cosier, R. A., & Aplin, J. C. (1980). A critical view of dialectical inquiry as a tool in strategic planning. *Strategic Management Journal, 1,* 343–356.

Cosier, R. A., Ruble, T. A., & Aplin, J. C. (1978). An evaluation of the effectiveness of dialectical inquiry systems. *Management Science, 24,* 1483–1490.

Coulahan, J. E., & Roussopoulos, N. (1985). A timed Petri net methodology for specifying real-time system timing requirements. *International Workshop on Timed Petri Nets* (pp. 24–31). Torino, Italy: IEEE Press.

Dalkey, N. C., & Helmer, O. (1963). An experimental application of the Delphi method to the use of experts. *Management Science, 9,* 458–467.

Davis, J. H. (1969). Individual-group problem solving, subject preference, and problem type. *Journal of Personality and Social Psychology, 13,* 362–374.

Delbecq, A. L., Van de Ven, A. H., & Gustafson, D. H. (1975). *Group techniques for program planning: A guide to nominal group and Delphi processes.* Glenview, IL: Scott Foresman.

Diesing, P. (1967). Noneconomic decision-making. In M. Alexis & C. Z. Wilson (Eds.), *Organizational decisionmaking.* Englewood Cliffs, NJ: Prentice-Hall.

Estraillier, P., Girault, C., & Ilie, J. M. (1985). Satellite protocol modeling by synchronous predicate transition nets. *International Workshop on Timed Petri Nets* (pp. 280–287). Torino, Italy: IEEE Press.

Etessami, F. S. (1988). *Abstract Petri nets: A generalization of Petri nets.* Unpublished master's thesis, University of Central Florida, Orlando.

Fisher, B. A. (1974). *Small group decision-making.* New York: McGraw-Hill.

Gordon, W. J. J. (1961). *Synectics: The development of creative capacity.* New York: Harper & Row.

Gould, R. (1988). *Graph theory.* Menlo Park, CA: The Benjamin/Cumming Publishing Company, Inc.

Gouran, D. S., & Hirokawa, R. Y. (1983). The role of communication in group decision-making: A functional perspective. In M. S. Mander (Ed.), *Communications in transition.* New York: Praeger.

Greenbaum, H. H., Kaplan, I. T., & Metlay, W. (1988). Evaluation of problem-solving groups: The case of quality circle programs. *Group & Organization Studies, 13,* 133–147.

Guha, R. K. (1988). *Abstract Petri nets with an application to software design* (Tech. Rep. No. CS-TR-88-25). Orlando: University of Central Florida, Computer Science Department.

Guion, R. M. (1987). Changing views for personnel selection research. *Personnel Psychology, 40,* 199–213.

Herriot, P., Chalmers, C., & Wingrove, J. (1985). Group decision making in an assessment center. *Journal of Occupational Psychology, 58,* 309–312.

Hill, G. W. (1982). Group versus individual performance: Are N + 1 Heads better than one? *Psychological Bulletin, 91,* 517–539.

Hirokawa, R. Y. (1982). Group communication and problem-solving effectiveness: A critical review of inconsistent findings. *Communication Quarterly, 30,* 134–141.

Hirokawa, R. Y. (1985). Discussion procedures and decision-making performance: A test of a functional perspective. *Human Communication Research, 12,* 203–224.

Hoffman, L. R. (1965). Group problem solving. In L. Berlowitz (Ed.), *Advances in experimental social psychology* (Vol. 2). New York: Academic Press.

Hura, G. (1987, October). Petri nets. *IEEE Potentials,* pp. 18–20.

Janis, I. L. (1972). *Victims of groupthink: A psychological study of foreign policy decisions and fiascoes.* Boston: Houghton Mifflin.

Janis, I. L., & Mann, L. (1977). *Decision making.* New York: Free Press.

Jantzen, M. (1980). Structured representation of knowledge by Petri nets as an aid for teaching and research. In W. Brauer (Ed.), *Net theory and applications* (pp. 507–518). New York: Springer-Verlag.

Katz, D., & Kahn, R. L. (1978). *The social psychology of organizations* (2nd ed.). New York: John Wiley.

Kepner, C. H., & Tregoe, B. B. (1968). *The rational manager: A systematic approach to problem solving and decision making.* New York: McGraw-Hill.

Klimoski, R. J., & Brickner, M. (1987). Why do assessment centers work? The puzzle of assessment center validity. *Personnel Psychology, 40,* 243–260.

Klimoski, R. J., & Strickland, W. J. (1977). Assessment centers: Valid or merely prescient. *Personnel Psychology, 30,* 353–361.

Lein, Y. E. (1976). Termination properties of generalized Petri nets. *SIAM Journal of Computing, 5,* 251–265. .

Levis, A. H. (1989). Generation of architectures for distributed intelligence systems. *Proceedings of the 1989 IEEE International Conference on Control and Applications (ICCON '89).* Jerusalem, Israel: IEEE Press.

Lin, C., & Marinescu, D. C. (1987). On stochastic high-level Petri nets. *International Workshop on Petri Nets and Performance Models* (Vol. 65, pp. 34–43). New York, NY: IEEE Press.

Lindblom, C. E. (1959). The science of "muddling-through." *Public Administrative Review, 19,* 79–88.

London, D. N., & Moulton, S. (1986). Quality circles: What's on them for employees? *Personnel Journal,* pp. 23–26.

Lourenco, S. V., & Glidewell, J. C. (1974). A dialectical analysis of organizational conflict. *Administrative Science Quarterly, 20,* 489–508.

Lu, M., Zhang, D., & Murata, T. (1987). Stochastic Petri net model for self-stability measures of fault tolerant clock synchronization. *International Workshop on Petri Nets and Performance Models* (pp. 104–110). New York: IEEE Press.

Maier, N. R. F. (1963). *Problem-solving discussions and conferences: Leadership methods and skills.* New York: McGraw-Hill.

March, J. G., & Simon, H. A. (1958). *Organizations.* New York: John Wiley.

Marsan, M. A., Balbo, G., Chiola, G., & Conte, G. (1987). *International Workshop on Petri Nets and Performance Models* (pp. 44–53). New York: IEEE Press.

Martinez, J., & Silva, M. (1982). A simple and fast algorithm to obtain all invariants of a generalized Petri net. *Lecture notes in computer science.* Berlin, FRG: Springer-Verlag.

McBurney, J. H., & Hance, K. G. (1950). *Discussion in human affairs.* New York: Harper & Row.

McNelis, K., & Coovert, M. D. (1988, April). *The role of criterion contamination and experience in assessment centers.* Paper presented at the 3rd Annual Conference of the Society for Industrial and Organizational Psychology. Dallas, TX.

Meldman, J. A., & Holt, A. W. (1971). Petri nets and legal systems. *Jurimetrics, 12,* 65–75.

Memmi, G., & Roucairol, G. (1980). Linear algebra in net theory. In G. Goos & J. Hartmanis (Eds.), *Lecture notes in computer science, 84,* 213–223.

Menache, M. (1985). Parade: An automated tool for the analysis of timed Petri nets. *International Workshop on Timed Petri Nets* (pp. 162–169). Torino, Italy: IEEE Press.

Mintzberg, H., Raisinghani, D., & Theoret, A. (1976). The structure of "unstructured" decision processes. *Administrative Science Quarterly, 21,* 246–275.

Mitroff, I. I., Barabba, V. P., & Kilmann, R. H. (1977). The application of behavioral and philosophical technologies to strategic planning: A case study of a large federal agency. *Management Science, 22,* 44–58.

Molloy, M. K. (1981). *On the integration of delay and throughput measures in distributed systems.* Unpublished doctoral dissertation, UCLA.

Molloy, M. K. (1982, September). Performance analysis using stochastic Petri nets. *IEEE Transactions on Computers,* pp. 913–917.

Molloy, M. K. (1985). Discrete time stochastic Petri nets. *IEEE Transactions on Software Engineering, SE-11,* 417–423.

Molloy, M. K. (1987). Structurally bounded stochastic Petri nets. *International Workshop on Petri Nets and Performance Models* (pp. 156–163). New York: IEEE Press.

Murata, T. (1977). State equations, controllability, and maximum matchings of Petri nets. *IEEE Transactions on Automatic Control, 22,* 412–416.

Nemiroff, P. M., Pasmore, W. A., & Ford, D. L. (1976). The effects of two normative structural interventions on established and ad hoc groups: Implications for improving decision making effectiveness. *Decision Sciences, 7,* 841–855.

Oh, G. R., Favrel, J., Campagne, J., Doumeingts, G., & Carter, W. A. (1984). Graphic modeling by Petri nets for production planning. *Advances in production management systems.* Amsterdam, Netherlands: North-Holland.

Peterson, J. L. (1981). *Petri net theory and the modeling of systems.* New York: Prentice-Hall.

Petri, C. A. (1962). *Kommunikation mit Automaten.* Bonn: Institut für Instrumentelle Mathematik, Schriften des IIM Nr 2.

Pfiffner, J. M. (1960). Administrative rationality. *Public Administrative Review, 20,* 125–275.

Phillips, G. M., Pedersen, D. J., & Wood, J. T. (1978). *Group discussion: A practical guide to participation and leadership.* Boston: Houghton Mifflin.

Poole, M. S. (1983). Decision development in small groups III: A multiple sequence model of group decision development. *Communication Monographs, 50,* 321–341.

Prince, G. M. (1970). *The practice of creativity: A manual for dynamic group problem solving.* New York: Harper & Row.

Rickards, T. (1974). *Problem-solving through creative analysis.* New York: John Wiley.

Reisig, W. (1985). *Petri nets.* New York: Springer-Verlag.

Remy, P. A., Levis, A. H., & Jin, V. (1988). On the design of distributed organizational structures. *Automatica, 24,* 81–86.

Restle, F., & Davis, J. H. (1962). Success and speed of problem solving by individuals and groups. *Psychological Review, 69,* 520–536.

Sackett, P. B., & Wilson, M. A. (1982). Factors affecting the consensus judgment process in managerial assessment centers. *Journal of Applied Psychology, 67,* 10–17.

Scheidel, T. M., & Crowell, L. (1979). *Discussing and deciding.* New York: Macmillan.

Schweiger, D. M., Sandberg, W. R., & Ragan, J. W. (1986). Group approaches for improving strategic decision making: A comparative analysis of dialectical inquiry, devil's advocacy, and consensus. *Academy of Management Journal, 20,* 51–71.

Schwenk, C. R. (1982). Effects of inquiry methods and ambiguity tolerance on prediction performance. *Decision Sciences, 13,* 207–221.

Schwenk, C. R. (1984). Effects of planning aids and presentation media on performance and affective responses in strategic decision making. *Management Science, 30,* 263–272.

Schwenk, C. R., & Cosier, R. A. (1980). Effects of the expert, devil's advocate, and dialectical inquiry methods on prediction performance. *Organizational Behavior and Human Performance, 26,* 409–424.

Simon, H. A., & Newell, A. (1958). Heuristic problem solving: The next advance in operations research. *Operations Research, 6,* 1–10.

Smigelski, T., Murata, T., & Sowa, M. (1985). A timed Petri net model and the simulation of a data flow computer. *International Workshop on Timed Petri Nets* (pp. 56–63). Torino, Italy: IEEE Press.

Steiner, I. D., & Rajaratnam, N. (1961). A model for the comparison of individual and group performance scores. *Behavioral Science, 6,* 142–147.

Stumpf, S. A., Zand, D. E., & Freedman, R. D. (1979). Designing groups for judgmental decisions. *Academy of Management Review, 4,* 589–600.

Tabak, D., & Levis, A. H. (1985). Petri net representation of decision models. *IEEE Transactions on Systems, Man, and Cybernetics, SMC-15,* 812–818.

Tannenbaum, R., & Schmidt, W. (1958). How to choose a leadership pattern. *Harvard Business Review, 36,* 95–101.

Thompson, P. C. (1982). *Quality circles: How to make them work in America.* New York: AMACOM.

Tinbergen, J. (1956). *Economic policy: Principles and design.* Amsterdam: North-Holland Publishing.

Torrance, E. P. (1957). Group decision making and disagreement. *Social Forces, 35,* 314–318.

Turoff, M. (1970). The design of a policy Delphi. *Technological Forecasting and Social Change, 2,* 50–71.

Vroom, V. H., & Yetton, P. W. (1973). *Leadership and decision-making.* Pittsburgh: University of Pittsburgh Press.

Weingaertner, S. T., & Levis, A. H. (1989). Analysis of decision aiding in submarine emergency decisionmaking. *Automatica, 25,* 349–358.

Wickens, T. D. (1982). *Models for behavior.* San Francisco, CA: W. H. Freeman.

Zand, D. E. (1974). Collateral organization: A new change strategy. *Journal of Applied Behavioral Science, 10,* 63–89.

Zand, D. E. (1978). Management in Israel. *Business Horizons, 21,* 36–46.

Part III
APPLICATIONS OF TEAMWORK SKILLS

11

Training Technologies Applied to Team Training: Military Examples *

Dee H. Andrews
Wayne L. Waag
Herbert H. Bell

INTRODUCTION

Teams are found in virtually every setting where work is performed. Experience has shown that training teams to perform well, especially teams which perform technical tasks, often requires the use of highly sophisticated training technologies. The purpose of this chapter is to describe training technologies that have been successfully applied to military team training. We first begin with some definitions of team training and training technology. A model is then presented that broadly categorizes training technology into two major functions—training development and training delivery. We then discuss some of the R&D that has been done to date in support of these functions. Requirements for military team training are described, and reasons discussed why the military has been so interested in training-technology developments. Specific examples of training

---

* Opinions or conclusions contained in this chapter are those of the authors and do not necessarily reflect the view or endorsement of the Department of Defense.

technology applied to teams in the Air Force, Army, and Navy are then presented. The final section of the chapter examines future trends and presents conclusions.

Definitions of Training Technology and Team Training

Training refers to a structured process through which skills or knowledge are acquired or refined. *Training technology* is defined as *systematic* methods, techniques, tools, and devices that aid in defining, analyzing, developing, delivering, and evaluating training. *Team training* focuses on the acquisition or refinement of skills and knowledge that are specific to the collective or group environment that characterizes a team.

In discussing team training, it should be made clear that it is the individuals and not the "team" that learns. Although individual and team skills may differ, the fundamental learning processes (e.g., cognitive processes such as pattern recognition, short and long term memory, and response selection) are the same for individual and team skills. From a training perspective, what distinguishes individual from team skills? The essence of "teamness" is that skilled performance is interdependent; each individual's behavior is interdependent in that it occurs in response to other team members' behaviors or cues (Dyer, 1984). Communication and coordination of action *cannot* be done individually. The shortstop and the second baseman cannot learn to turn the double play without each other, yet fielding and throwing the ball are individual actions—its the sequential flow, the timing of action, that separates an individual from a team task. We feel that we cannot look for "teamness" unless we focus on the interrelated patterns of behavior, the flow of information (verbal and nonverbal), the patterning of responses based on the information already given, and the expectations based on the team's history together.

From this discussion, it should be clear that, although the focus of this chapter is team training, there is considerable overlap with individual training. In turn there is much commonality among the training technologies that support individual and team training. In preparation of this chapter, we found that there are actually few training technologies that have application solely to the training of teams. In fact most of the technologies described in our examples might be considered an outgrowth or expansion of individual training technologies. So, as we discuss training technologies in this chapter, the reader should not be surprised to find that they have application to the training of both individuals and teams.

A Training Technology Model

Producers and deliverers of training often become so enmeshed in the design and development of expensive computer-based training and training devices that they

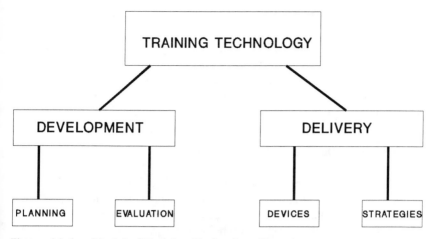

Figure 11.1.   Model of Training Technology Functions

lose sight of the fact that the training hardware and software are only part of the training technology. Although we devote the lion's share of the discussion to training hardware and software systems in this chapter (because that is where most of the work has occurred), we want to stress that training technology also includes methods for planning, analyzing, designing, and assessing team-training requirements and solutions.

Figure 11.1 presents a very simplified model of the various functions that are included under the general rubric of training technology. As shown, there are two major categories, development and training delivery. The training development function includes all those aspects of the process including analysis, planning, design, and evaluation. The training delivery function includes both the devices (hardware and software) and the strategies that concern their use within the training environment.

To this point the military training community has generally put greater emphasis on the training delivery technologies (i.e., training hardware and software) than the training development technologies required to define, design and evaluate team training. One reason for this emphasis on training delivery is the tendency for military planners and trainers to often think first about hardware solutions to most military problems. It is often the nature of military solutions to be technology driven. The results of this emphasis can be training-technology applications which sometimes do not meet the real training need.

A second problem is the lack of training-development tools, especially for team applications. Since we don't have many good tools for defining team-training needs we often try to replicate the cues from the actual equipment and hope that the "training delivery" technologies will carry the day (Andrews, 1988). Unfortunately, this approach is often ineffective since the cues which trainees need for optimizing learning may be somewhat different than those which they will use when they actually operate the equipment. Cues may need to be made larger, smaller, slower, or faster than in the actual equipment in order for trainees to learn. For example, the symbology which appears on a radar screen used by different members of an air traffic control team may have to be simplified and enlarged for a radar novice. Then, as the trainee develops proper radar interpretation skills, the symbology cues can be made to resemble more accurately the cues the trainee will find in the "real world."

Team-Training Development Technologies

Why do we need different and/or additional training planning and development technologies for team training? The nature of team skills is probably different from that of individual skills (Briggs & Naylor, 1965; Denson, 1981; Morgan, Coates, Kirby, & Alluisi, 1984). Therefore our normal methods of doing task analysis (Jonassen & Hannum, 1986) do not allow us to capture and examine the requisite cues, conditions, and standards for team skills. We can use those methods to make rough approximations of team task analyses, but ultimately we find they are not totally satisfactory. The same can be said about our normal set of tools for specifying instructional objectives, defining team media, measuring team performance, and so on.

For example, one of the team training devices described later in this chapter is Device 14A12. This is a Navy training device which accommodates over 20 trainees from an antisubmarine warfare team. Using traditional task analysis techniques from the military's Instructional Systems Development (ISD) model, the training analysts were easily able to define and analyze the individual tasks of the 20-plus trainees. However, these techniques proved to be inadequate when it came time to specify team skills and tasks such as communication, coordination (sequencing), and team decision making. Because team skill and task analysis techniques were not available, the analysts were forced to adapt task analysis for individuals from the ISD model.

Performance measurement requirements also differ between teams and individuals. We are just beginning to understand team performance measurement requirements for technical and decision-making training. We currently do not have technologies sufficient for defining performance measurement requirements for teams. We do not have adequate training planning and development tools that then allow us to adequately measure teams against an overall standard.

Despite what we perceive as the current paucity of quality technologies for the planning/development of team training, we feel the situation can be improved. Perhaps the training community needs to cast beyond the traditional disciplines normally associated with training in order to find useful planning/development tools for team training. For example, social scientists have spent years diagramming interactions between people. Biologists and ethologists can describe complex ecological chains. Computer systems run multiple subprograms that pass information between different parts of the system. Perhaps what we really lack is the necessary knowledge of potential technologies outside our normal area of consideration, and the discipline to develop new methods for using those technologies for team training.

A Team-Training Development Technology Example

One example of a "training planning and development" tool which has potential for helping team-training instructors in diagnosing teams and providing sound pedagogical guidance is the "Instructor's Diagnostic Aid for Feedback in Training (IDAFT)" developed by Andrews and Uliano (1988). IDAFT is a team instructor's job aid. It was evaluated with the instructors of a large antisubmarine warfare team training device (Device 14A2), but the concept should be applicable in any team-training setting. This aid is programmed to question an instructor about individual and team behaviors and errors that have been observed (e.g., a sonar team passes incorrect information to a commander, or a commander interprets incoming information from the team incorrectly). The instructional concepts are built into the IDAFT. Some of these important instructional concepts are (a) error analysis, (b) events of instruction (Gagne & Briggs, 1979), and (c) domains of learning (Gagne & Briggs, 1979).

Based upon the cause of the error, IDAFT recommends remedial instructional prescriptions to the instructor. These prescriptions are based upon events of instruction (e.g., present instructional objective to the learner, provide learning guidance). Carey and Briggs (1977) matched instructional events to domains of learning (intellectual skills, verbal information, motor skills, attitudes, and cognitive strategies). The resulting matrix contains 99 event statements that can be called instructional prescriptions. For example, the instructional event of providing learning guidance for problem solving has the following prescription: "Provide a minimum amount of indirect verbal cues for selection of previously learned rules to achieve a novel combination." This prescription is different from the learning guidance prescription for any other domain.

The IDAFT program automatically presents the instructional events to an instructor in question form. For example, the instructional event presented in the previous paragraph would be given to the instructor in the form of a question. The purpose of all of the previous steps is to get an instructor to this point. Instructors can now make decisions about which instructional events were performed adequately during previous team instruction. Each event is phrased in question form, so that a "yes" answer moves the program to the next event. The assumption is that the event had been adequately addressed. If, however, an instructor answers "no," the program reveals the specific prescription. This questioning process continues through all nine events of instruction.

IDAFT aids the instruction of teams because it requires team instructors, most of whom have not had formal training in educational techniques, to consider pedagogical concepts and requirements. Normally these concepts and requirements would not be considered by military team instructors. This type of aid can be especially important in a team training setting because of the rapidity and complexity of team interactions. An instructor who is not trained or aided to look for pedagogical deficiencies may be overwhelmed in a team-training setting.

Training-Delivery Technologies—Team-Training Devices

The primary requirement for any team-training system is that it provides the opportunity to learn and practice within an environment in which all of the relevant attributes are found for achieving the training objective. Generally speaking, there are three major approaches to team training that have been employed within the military. The first is to conduct training within a realistic physical environment using actual equipment to whatever degree possible. By far this is generally considered the most desirable, since it is usually the most realistic, especially in terms of the equipment that is being used. However, there are certain limitations, including the cost of such training, the fact that certain "key" attributes are generally missing (e.g., realistic enemy forces and threats), and restrictions on the use of live munitions. The second alternative is to conduct training within a synthetic environment, using simulation as a means of modeling the relevant attributes. While such synthetic training systems may ensure that all the relevant attributes are indeed modeled, there may exist limitations in the realism of the individual components, thereby reducing the effectiveness of the training. Despite some compromises to realism, the decided advantages in terms of cost and safety have resulted in decisions to invest quite heavily in such synthetic systems. The third approach is actually a hybrid of the first two, in which some type of simulation capability is embedded within the actual equipment. In such cases onboard systems (usually sensors and communications) are "stimulated" in order to provide a simulation of the external environment. To date, most examples of this approach have been found in the Navy.

Perhaps the most important decision in the design of team-training systems is to identify precisely the training requirements that are to be addressed. Such decisions are important in that they will determine to a large degree the types of technologies that are necessary. For example, within tactical aviation the basic fighting element is the two-ship. While learning and practicing basic two-ship tactics in a high-threat environment may be considered an example of "team training," it is considered but a basic building block of much larger and perhaps more realistic training scenarios involving scores of aircraft. The training of battle management decision-making skills in terms of how to employ or control air assets is also an example of "team training." However, the required technologies to support such training are quite different. The requirement in both instances is to model all of the relevant attributes of the environment. However, the method by which this is accomplished, and the degree of accuracy with which each attribute is modeled, will greatly depend upon the focus of the "team-training" system.

The modeling of the same attributes within the environment is likely to be quite different for training two-ship skills as opposed to battle management skills. For example, in our two-ship tactics trainer, the air weapons control function would likely be a man-in-the-loop simulation. Air tasking orders would simply be part of the scripted scenario. Threat aircraft would probably be digital simulations, although for some scenarios man-in-the-loop simulations might be desirable. Weapons and threat modeling would be as accurate as possible, since the learning of reactions to such threats may be possible only within the simulation environment. On the other hand, the battle management trainer would most likely have no man-in-the-loop simulations of the various aircraft that are being controlled. Each aircraft would probably be represented by a fairly simplistic digital simulation model that could be controlled to some limited degree by an operator. Weapons and threat modeling would also be fairly simplistic, with no requirement for accurate fly-outs.

Thus far we have discussed the "simulation" component of a training delivery system. Without the capability to simulate the physical and functional fidelity of the real world to some degree, it would be impossible to train adequately many team skills in the military. For example, imagine trying to train a pilot and co-pilot to communicate and make team decisions if the aircraft environment could not be at least partially simulated. Simulation is, of course, used for many purposes in today's world (science, engineering, economics, business, etc.). However, when it is produced primarily for training purposes, we have chosen to call it a form of training technology.

There are two additional categories of training-technology functions incorporated within training-delivery systems that aid the training of military teams. There are those technologies which are of direct aid to the instructor and trainees in providing instruction and feedback that will increase the probability that the trainee will learn the desired skills and knowledge (Instructional technologies). IDAFT is an example. There are also those technologies which support the instructor in designing and managing the training environment (Training Management technologies). These three technology categories, Simulation, Instructional, and Training Management, will later be used in the examples section as a means of describing the capabilities of the various team training systems.

Training-Delivery Technologies—Training Strategies

There are many examples of training technologies applied to team training (i.e., team-training devices) that are more oriented toward practice or evaluation of team skills already possessed by the trainees than the development of new team skills (Andrews, 1988). New team skills are frequently not taught systematically because the technologies for teaching new skills are not well understood or developed. Sometimes, there is an implicit assumption that, if we take skilled individuals and put them in a team performance environment, training (learning of new team skills) will automatically occur. Unfortunately, this approach may not produce the desired results.

The "unstructured" approach of putting trainees into a team performance environment, and then expecting them to automatically learn new skills, is not efficient. Work teams seldom have the luxury of taking enough time away from their operational settings to practice enough to gain team skills by discovery alone. The skills should be clearly identified, and then systematic training should be developed and applied. Structured guidance from the instructors to the trainees is required. The team-training technologies described later in the chapter often do not satisfactorily help the instructors in providing that structured guidance. (The SMARTT technology, also described below, is an exception to that statement.)

An example of the inefficiencies, and sometimes ineffectiveness, of the often unstructured approach to team training may be helpful. Aircrew coordination skills are important to aircrews. These are the communication and joint decision-making skills that are vital to teams that pilot and navigate airliners and warplanes. There are many examples of fatal and near-fatal airplane accidents that occurred because aircrews did not possess coordination skills in sufficient numbers or kinds (Foushee & Helmreich, 1988). "An L-1011 went down at night in the Florida Everglades in 1972 killing 99 passengers and crew members. The accident sequence was initiated by a burned-out light bulb in the system indicating that the landing gear was down and locked; a problem which occupied all three crew members' attention to the extent that no one noticed that the autopilot had become disengaged" (p. 194). When these incidents occur, it is usually found that the team members each possessed the necessary skills and knowledge to perform their individual jobs. It is also usually the case that the team members had a large number of hours in flight simulators. Why, then, were the crews found to be lacking the necessary coordination skills?

The crews had simply been placed in the flight simulator with little or no systematic training in how to communicate or make joint decisions. It was assumed that, if they were placed in simulated emergencies enough times and allowed to practice together, they would automatically "discover" the right coordination skills. After all, the assumption went, these were professional pilots. Naturally, some crew members did discover some of the skills. However, the airlines and military have determined that, despite the fact that the members of aircrews are intelligent, motivated, and dedicated to their jobs, they still often are not able to "absorb" the requisite team skills through exposure alone. A systematic program is required.

Most airlines and military services now have established systematic aircrew coordination training. It often goes by the name of *cockpit resource management* (CRM) training. The Federal Aviation Administration and the military currently have ongoing research programs to determine how best to train CRM skills and knowledge in a systematic fashion.

The Requirement for Team Training in the Military

Instead of a group of executives meeting to determine how to implement a new sales campaign for next year's product line, military teams are concerned with the successful completion of combat missions. However, just like the sales team, each member of a military team has a unique set of tasks that must be performed in cooperation with other individuals. These tasks are directed toward a common objective and interrelated. For example, infantrymen must close with and destroy the enemy at the time and location selected by their commander, the staff officers must insure that information is correctly analyzed and relayed to the appropriate individuals and that supplies are sent to the correct locations, and the commanders must coordinate the activities of their staffs and subordinate units to insure the mission is accomplished.

To give the reader a feel for the ways that team-training technology is used in the military, we will present several examples of how teams are composed and interact in the world of tactical aviation combat. The tactical aviation community has a considerable requirement for team training at a number of different levels. Of aircraft within the current inventory, many have multiple crew members. The training of individual members to function as an integrated crew represents a sizable challenge. Of particular importance to the effective functioning of a multicrew aircraft are the training of higher-order team skills such as crew coordination, cockpit resource management, and captaincy. Considerable effort is expended toward the training of such skills, since it is the interaction among such crew members that will largely determine the effectiveness of the flight or mission. While the effective functioning of the individual aircraft or weapons system is important, the fact is that they rarely function in isolation.

As previously discussed, the basic element for tactical flight (i.e., fighter/attack aircraft) is a two-ship. While each aircraft may be "single-seat," they will fly and fight as a team; hence, the requirement for learning team tactics. Even such basic flight elements are usually part of a larger "team." Depending upon the type of mission, there are likely to be multiple numbers of basic "elements." For example, a composite force "strike package" may consist of four attack aircraft flying at low altitudes plus four additional fighters at high altitude who are providing protection to the strikers from enemy fighters. In addition to these aircraft and their crews, there are also ground elements which play a critical role. For most missions, there is likely to be radar coverage, both ground and airborne, that provides information to the "strike package" concerning the location of other air vehicles. Thus, the tactical air controller becomes an integral part of the "team" and must be considered in the development of an overall team-training strategy. Other aircraft may also play a crucial role, depending upon the particular mission. Because of mission duration, there may be a requirement for aerial refueling. Aircraft with sophisticated jamming equipment may be used for "defense suppression" of enemy radars. To effectively function as an integrated team places a tremendous demand upon training and the technology required for its support.

While training the basic mission is of critical importance, it is but part of the larger picture. Training for battle management is an essential part of combat preparation. It is necessary that battlefield commanders have training and practice at exercising their battle staff functions in a way similar to what would be experienced under actual combat operations. To practice such functions short of actual combat requires that all reports, message traffic, telephone communications, and computer links be simulated to function as they would in the real world. It is necessary that commanders and their staffs be trained at giving direction to lower echelons and having those orders carried out as they would be in the real world. In summary, the military has the requirement for training team skills at varying levels of complexity ranging from the operation of individual multicrew aircraft to the management of large-scale wartime operations.

Reasons for Military Investment in Training Technology Which Can Be Applied to Team Training

Despite the problems mentioned above about the military's approach to designing and delivering team training, we still consider the advancements made by the military in applying training technology to team training to be significant. From the perspective of this chapter, the strongest reason for applying training technology to team training revolves around the added combat effectiveness and safety such technology can provide. There are many combat skills that cannot be adequately trained in the actual weapon system for security reasons. Much of the future battle will be fought with electronic signals (radar and voice/data communications and their attendant jamming). It is not now possible to allow weapons platforms to turn on all of their emitters and jammers in a realistic fashion, because a potential enemy may be listening. Simulation can provide a secure environment for such training.

Considerable resources are expended by the military in developing and applying training technology to individual and team training. The reasons are many. When actual equipment (ships, planes, etc.) is used for training, the cost of fuel and ordinance alone is prohibitive. For example, it now costs approximately $5,000 an hour to fly the F-15 aircraft. Any bombs, bullets, or missiles expended for training purposes are extra; some modern missiles cost over a half-million dollars apiece.

Operators and maintainers are always concerned about the wear and tear on the weapon system when it is used for training. They know that same weapon system may someday be used in war, and every hour spent for training means one less hour that the weapon system will be available for combat before it needs maintenance. Environmental concerns are now making simulation a necessity when teams are trained. Both noise and chemical pollution from weapon systems have made it necessary to seek simulation alternatives. For example, teams that are trained to fight fires on ships and aircraft used to light huge open fires with various types of fuel. The Environmental Protection Agency has severely restricted such activity, and large fire fighter simulators are now used that burn propane gas.

Examples from the Three Military Services

Described below are a number of training technologies that have been successfully applied to team training in the military. These examples are representative of a host of specific instances found in the training of military teams. While most of these examples of training technology are discussed in terms of their training-delivery function, we do point out areas where training-development technologies and concepts have been used. To aid the reader in determining what type of training technology is being utilized in the examples, we will provide the following designations after a training technology has been described: (INSTRUCTIONAL TECHNOLOGY), (TRAINING MANAGEMENT TECHNOLOGY), (TRAINING SIMULATION TECHNOLOGY).

EXAMPLES OF TRAINING TECHNOLOGY APPLIED TO AIR FORCE TEAM TRAINING

The Air Force, like the other services, makes use of two primary classes of training equipment—the actual aircraft itself, and a variety of synthetic ground-based training systems. The following examples of technologies that support team-training requirements address the use of both types of equipment. They include: (a) *air combat maneuvering instrumentation* (ACMI), a system designed for tracking aircraft during flight; (b) the air combat maneuvering performance measurement system, a research tool that was designed to develop and test measures of team performance during air combat; (c) a multiship air combat simulation facility that enables the training and practice of wartime mission scenarios; and (d) the Warrior Preparation Center, a system that enables the training and practice of battle management skills. The following sections will provide a brief description of each of these systems and provide information on how they are currently being used in support of training.

Air Combat Maneuvering Instrumentation (ACMI)

For the Air Force, the majority of training and practice still occurs using the actual aircraft itself. An essential requirement for the use of actual equipment for training is that there must exist adequate feedback or knowledge of results to support efficient learning. In an analysis of performance measurement requirements to support tactical flying, Waag, Pierce, and Fessler (1987) identified aircrew performance monitoring as an area wherein current capabilities were considered inadequate fully to support training. This is especially true of team training, where it is the interaction among aircraft that is of prime concern. Today the primary onboard capabilities that provide performance feedback for debriefing are audio and video recordings. However, such information by itself is of limited value for team training, since it does not present the "big picture." While useful for the terminal phases of an air engagement, for example, it provides little information on the maneuvering phases of the mission. Thus the important element for team training, namely the interaction among the flight lead and his wingman, is missing.

A solution to the problem of poor mission feedback has been solved to some degree with the development of instrumented ranges which are capable of tracking aircraft while in flight. Both the US Navy and Air Force have developed ranges that provide such a tracking capability in support of their flight training programs. The Air Force refers to the system as *Air Combat Maneuvering Instrumentation* (ACMI) while the Navy calls it the *Tactical Air Combat Training System* (TACTS). Although their names are different, their capabilities are essentially the same. The TACTS/ACMI ranges enable the real-time monitoring of air combat engagements and a graphic reconstruction of the mission for use as a debriefing aid. The essential requirements for providing such a capability are the determination of exact aircraft position in space plus the capture of critical onboard events such as missile firings. The ACMI display unit is shown in Figure 11.2.

The ACMI consists of four major subsystems: the *airborne instrumentation system* (AIS); the *tracking instrumentation subsystem* (TIS); the *control and computation subsystem* (CCS); and the *display and debriefing subsystem* (DDS). The AIS can be either a cylindrical pod or internal unit that is carried onboard the aircraft. It contains an inertial unit for generating aircraft attitude information, and transponders for telemetering such information to ground-based tracking stations. For some systems, it can access data directly from the internal bus of the aircraft. (The AIS is a TRAINING MANAGEMENT TECHNOLOGY.) The TIS is a network of tracking stations that receive data from the AIS and determine the position of each aircraft through triangulation procedures. (The TIS is a TRAINING MANAGEMENT TECHNOLOGY.) These data are then relayed to the CCS, using a microwave link where a track file is established for each aircraft. It computes the state vector for each aircraft, as well as their relative positions. The CCS is also responsible for weapons simulation computations and preparation of the data

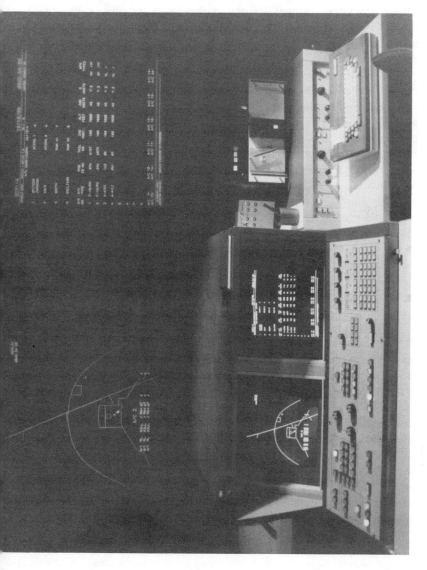

Figure 11.2. Air Combat Maneuvering Instrumentation Display Unit

that is sent to the DDS for display. (The CCS is a TRAINING MANAGEMENT TECHNOLOGY and a TRAINING SIMULATION TECHNOLOGY.) The DDS, which is the primary interface with the crews, consists of a graphics processor, training delivery copy unit, display consoles, a range operator console, and two large screen displays. It is the DDS that provides the graphic reconstruction of the mission to the crews for mission feedback. (The DDS is an INSTRUCTIONAL TECHNOLOGY.)

The ACMI can support training in a variety of modes. In mode 1, a tone is presented when the aircraft is within a rule-of-thumb weapons envelope. Mode 2 is the same, except that it provides such an indication only at the time of trigger squeeze. In mode 3, more representative missile envelopes based on fighter-target geometry are calculated. These are displayed continuously at the DDS as being IN or OUT of envelope condition. Mode 4 is the same, except that it provides such information only at the time of trigger squeeze. Mode 5 incorporates real-time missile fly-out models. The results are based only on the missile's dynamic ability to reach the target. Mode 6 also incorporates additional missile probability factors such as inflight reliability. Mode 1 is intended to train new pilots in weapons envelop recognition, while mode 2 allows a test of their proficiency. Modes 3 and 4 were designed to train recognition of fighter-target geometries associated with missile employment, while mode 5 increases the crew's familiarity with the actual performance of a specific weapon. Mode 6 adds uncertainty that is associated with weapons reliability and the target's attempt to defeat the weapon between the time of launch and target-weapon intercept.

Of primary value are the displays that depict progress of the air engagements. These displays are available in real-time or may be replayed for debriefing purposes. Computer graphics are used to reconstruct the dynamics of the engagement and provide the student and instructor the ability to perform a detailed evaluation of the crew's maneuvering performance, weapon employment effectiveness, and tactical decision making. Display options include a "God's-eye," rotatable 3D view with different range scales and centering on selected aircraft; paired interaircraft data such as range, closing velocity, and so on; safety data such as G, angle of attack; an out-of-the-cockpit view from any aircraft; energy management data; and summary data of critical engagement events such as weapons firing, kills, misses, and so on. As mentioned, these displays are available real-time during the course of an engagement. This enables the range training officer to identify kills and thus direct the "destroyed" aircraft to leave the engagement. Overall, the TACTS/ACMI provides the most comprehensive replay, engagement reconstruction, and data display capability of any tactical training system today.

Air Combat Maneuvering Performance Measuring System (ACM PMS)

The ACM PMS is a research tool that was designed to provide a means of developing and validating measures of team performance during air combat. The purpose of the program was to provide measures of combat performance applicable to both the flight simulator and the ACMI. Although much work had been done in the area of air combat performance measurement at the time this program was initiated, the results had not produced any systems capable of providing the desired capabilities. Models had been developed, although they were in need of refinement. Work supported by the U.S. Navy had produced an all-aspect maneuvering index (AAMI) model which held promise. The model evaluated performance in terms of relative position of the opposing aircraft and incorporated weapons range models which determined location within the weapon envelope. Although the model appeared useful, refinements seemed necessary and validation data needed to be collected. Aside from the models themselves, there was no means of implementing them so that measures could be routinely generated. It was also desirable that equivalent measures be computed which could describe performance in both the simulation and airborne environments.

The goal of this program became the development of a system which generated measures of air combat performance using data obtained from either the Simulator-for-Air-to-Air Combat (SAAC) or the Air Combat Maneuvering Instrumentation (ACMI). The SAAC is the only simulator within the US Air Force that was used for close air-to-air combat training. The ACMI, on the other hand, enabled the monitoring of airborne engagements. The functional capabilities of the system and its intended use are the major focus of the following discussion.

Functional capabilities. The ACM PMS was designed to provide the following functional capabilities:

- Data Acquisition. The ACM PMS acquires sampled performance data in digital and audio form from both the SAAC and the ACMI. These data may be used for research purposes and/or for the conduct of training. A dedicated operator is required for control and monitoring of data acquisition for research purposes. Data acquisition from the SAAC exclusively for training purposes requires no operator attention except to make inputs at the start of a simulator period with a student. (Data acquisition is a TRAINING MANAGEMENT TECHNOLOGY.)

- Real-Time Assessment. The ACM PMS provides a real-time assessment of the performance of aircrews during an air combat engagement. Two forms of real-time assessment are provided. One is an index of maneuvering based on spatial and orientation factors of the aircraft involved, and the characteristics of the weapons carried (*All Aspect Maneuvering Index*—AAMI). The other is an index of energy usage based on considerations of thrust and aerodynamic considerations at the existing altitude (*energy maneuverability*). Both have been shown to have value in training. However, these also provide a capability for initial testing and, by establishing a capacity, or a basis for modification, to serve the purposes of future research. In particular, the maneuvering index includes provisions for future expansion and modification. (Real-time assessment is a TRAINING MANAGEMENT TECHNOLOGY.)

- Real-Time Displays. The ACM PMS presents real-time displays of ACM performance which permit (a) the data collection operator to monitor ACM events and control the ACM PMS; (b) instructor personnel to access information which can enhance the training in progress; and (c) research personnel, together with subject-matter experts, to review selected engagements in order to improve performance measurement and training feedback techniques. The users have controls to select the type of information desired for a particular engagement. (Real-Time Display is a TRAINING MANAGEMENT TECHNOLOGY and an INSTRUCTIONAL TECHNOLOGY.)
- Debriefing Display (Figure 11.3). The ACM PMS presents information after a training session, which can be used for debriefing by the instructor and student. This information is in the form of engagement outcome displays, training delivery/copy, briefing report, and offline replay of real-time displays. The design of debriefing displays was based upon the requirements of SAAC training. The displays also facilitate the review of ACM performance data by the research scientist and subject-matter experts. (Debriefing display is an INSTRUCTIONAL TECHNOLOGY.)
- Research Analysis. The ACM PMS permits storage of ACM performance data for research analysis. The ACM PMS facilitates retrieval and processing of acquired data to produce data bases suitable for analysis and the statistical analysis of the data to derive research conclusions.

Multiship Air Combat Research and Development

While the majority of Air Force training is still accomplished using the aircraft, there is a trend toward increased usage of ground simulation as a means of developing and maintaining the team skills needed for air combat. An example of such an air combat simulation capability is the facility of the McDonnell Douglas Company at St Louis, Missouri. What is to be described in the following paragraphs is the configuration that is being used by the US Air Force in support of their F15 training program. The system presents a combat environment including both computer-controlled and manned adversaries, electronic combat, communications jamming, surface threats, and manned air tactical control. Weapons effects are based on missile fly-out models and permitted real-time kill removal. The out-the-window visual imagery for the F-15 simulators supports low-altitude tactics, visual lookout, and weather penetration. Training is further served with audio and video recordings of each engagement for debriefing and a "War Room" with cockpit video displays and audio for observing engagements. Each component of the simulator system is described in further detail below.

- Manned Air Combat Simulators (MACS). Two full-mission F-15C simulators are being used in support of the training program. Both MACS are equipped

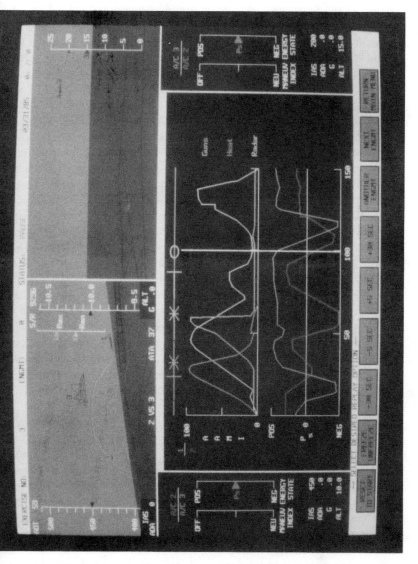

Figure 11.3. Air Combat Maneuvering Performance Measurement System Sample Display

299

with active flight controls (i.e., control stick, throttle, rudder pedals, etc.), instruments, and flight dynamics (i.e., rate of climb, roll rate, etc.) representative of the F-15C. Each cockpit also presents appropriate audio cues such as engine RPM, threat warnings, infrared missile tones, and missile launch. Specific F-15C systems and weapons simulated in each cockpit include the air-to-air radar, head-up display (HUD), and the other electronic systems that would be used during combat operations. (MACS is a TRAINING SIMULATION TECHNOLOGY.)

Each cockpit is located in a 40-foot-diameter dome. Out-the-window visual imagery representing the earth and sky for the forward hemisphere is produced by using two channels of a General Electric Compu-Scene IV computer image generator. One channel of this projected imagery is a narrow field-of-view patch of high-resolution graphics boresighted on the nose of the aircraft. The other channel provides a lower resolution background for the rest of the forward hemisphere. The earth and sky for the rear hemisphere is produced by a gimballed point-light projector. Aircraft and missile images are produced through laser and video target projectors. An example of imagery produced by this system is shown in Figure 11.4.

- Manned Interactive Control Station (MICS). The MICS is a desk-top flight station designed to provide a manned adversary. As many as four MICS are used in some of the training scenarios to help create the uncertainty associated with manned combat. The MICS provide the pilot with stick, throttle, and primary flight and weapon instruments based on the F-15. Out-the-window and cockpit instrument displays are presented on a CRT. Air-to-air radar displays are always presented, along with generic HUD symbology and alphanumeric displays of basic flight information (e.g., airspeed, altitude, heading, angle of attack, fuel). Geometric shapes are used to represent friendly, unfriendly, and unidentified aircraft. (MICS is a TRAINING SIMULATION TECHNOLOGY.)

- Computer-Controlled Threats and Strikers. Some of the adversary fighters and strikers are controlled by computer and fly predetermined routes and rely upon programmed tactical maneuvers. These maneuvers are typically initiated based upon range to the F-15s, and adversary fighters react to subsequent F-15 maneuvers. To prevent predictability, the maneuvers of these computer-controlled adversaries are periodically modified from the test director's console, and initial altitude and formation of adversaries are varied. The flight characteristics and weapon system capabilities of these adversaries model a number of threat aircraft. In addition, adversary electronic countermeasures (ECM), communications jamming, and surface-to-air missiles (SAMs) are provided through computer control. (Computer controlled threats and strikers is a TRAINING SIMULATION TECHNOLOGY.)

- Air Weapons Control Stations. Two air weapons control stations are provided: one for the F-15s, and one for the adversaries whenever the engagements

Figure 11.4.   F-15 Manned Air Combat Simulator

include the manned MICS. These stations are composed of a video monitor, trackball, and headphones. The display provided by the stations is based on a generic design and does not represent operational equipment used by Air Force air weapons controllers. A plan view of the engagement is presented, with 12-second updates of position and velocity for all aircraft. Symbols are used to indicate friendly, foe, or neutral aircraft. Ground references are also represented and include the location of airbases, targets, enemy territorial boundaries, and close control limit times. (Air weapons control station is a TRAINING SIMULATION TECHNOLOGY.)

- War Room. Observation of the pilots' performance is possible through the displays and audio provided in the War Room. This room is equipped with displays showing the HUD, radar, and threat warning systems from both F-15 cockpits and a large-screen "God's-eye" display showing the entire engagement. Audio of the communications between the F-15 pilots and air weapons controller is also provided. The War Room is furnished with seating for 15 people, permitting the opportunity for pilots and controllers to observe their counterparts in action and discuss their tactics and employment. During each mission, videotape recordings are used of the "God's eye" view of the entire engagement, the F-15 radar and threat warning displays from each cockpit, and audio of friendly force communications. These tapes are furnished for debriefing immediately after each team's simulator session. (The war room is an INSTRUCTIONAL TECHNOLOGY.)

Warrior Preparation Center

While the trained aircrew is considered to be the central component of military airpower, it is the management of such resources that, to a large degree, will determine their successful employment. Battle management is concerned with the employment of force. Elements of the process include planning, tasking, deploying, directing, and controlling such military resources. The *Warrior Preparation Center* (WPC) is a joint Air Force and Army training facility located in Europe. Its purpose is to provide senior commanders the opportunity to exercise their battle staff functions as if they were directing actual combat. The goal is to enable these staff functions to control and direct simulated combat operations with as few restrictions and artificialities as possible.

The training audience for the WPC include elements of the Army Corps and Air Force's Air Tactical Operations Center (ATOC). A block diagram of the major elements are shown in Figure 11.5. Staff members representing these elements have no direct interface to computer simulations but rather communicate over voice and data links to the command and response cell players. For reporting to higher headquarters, a small cell representing the Army Group and Allied Tactical Air Force receives reports from the Corps and ATOC sections and

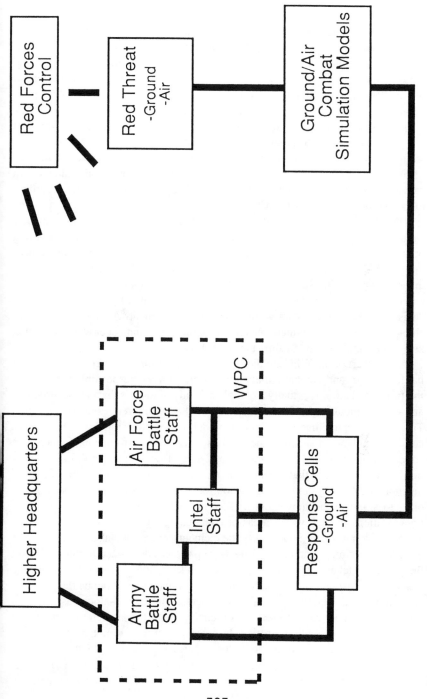

Figure 11.5.   Joint Warrior Concept for the Warrior Preparation Center.

subsequently provides command guidance on the conduct of the war and allocation of resources and assets. At the other end are the response cells that carry out
the direction, orders, and taskings from the Corps and ATOC. These members sit
in front of computer terminals and fight the war using computer models. Such
inputs given to the computer models include orders to units on the battlefield to
fire artillery, attack, defend, fly various types air missions, movement of supplies
and materials, and so on. The response cell members also receive reports back
from the simulated units and, in turn, report such information to the Corps and
ATOC staffs through communication links. In addition to the response cell directing the friendly or BLUE forces, there is also an exercise response cell that are
commanding the RED or attacking forces. The RED cell commander attempts to
provide as much realism to the battle as possible by directing his forces according
to known threat tactics and doctrine.

The WPC uses a combination of both human role players and computer
simulations in order to create the conditions of combat as they would appear to a
battle staff in a war headquarters. Such things as reports, telephone communications, message traffic, and computer links are simulated as they would exist in
the real world. The focus of the WPC is not on simulation of the physical
environment, but rather the information environment that forms the basis of the
decision making that occurs within such an environment. As mentioned, a key
element is the use of a human role model for the RED commander who uses actual
RED forces and doctrine against the NATO players.

At the heart of the WPC are the simulation models for the various elements of
battle. The ground combat simulation model, which is responsible for fighting
the front line battle, is actually a complete family of models that can be turned on
and off in a modular fashion to support a variety of different exercise scenarios.
There is also an intelligence collection model working in parallel with the ground
combat simulation that tasks the various sensors to perform intelligence data
collection missions and report back the results. There is also an offensive electronic warfare model that performs jamming missions against enemy communication and radar systems. A follow-on force attack model has also been developed to simulate the movement of second echelon forces as they move from
home stations to deployment areas near the battle area.

In addition to these models of battle elements, there have also been a number
of different training planning and software packages developed to interface with
the ground database and display the status and location of forces on a real-time
basis. These displays provide automated operational maps of the battle area. The
simulation model family can either be operated in a stand-alone fashion with
limited air play or can be used in conjunction with the air defense simulation
models for high resolution air play. In essence each of the models can be activated independently in order to tailor a particular exercise to the particular
training audience. For each player, the result is an experience in battle management that can be achieved in no other way short of war. (The Warrior Preparation
Center is a TRAINING SIMULATION TECHNOLOGY.)

EXAMPLES OF TRAINING TECHNOLOGY APPLIED TO ARMY TEAM TRAINING

In order to accomplish its mission, the Army faces a wide variety of team-training requirements. At one extreme this training is directed primarily at hands-on type skills. Examples of this type of team training include training devoted to building team proficiency in using crew-served weapons or practicing infantry squad tactics. At the other extreme is team training that focuses on command and staff training. An example of this type of training is the command and control training conducted during a battalion command post exercise. The entire spectrum of team training may be combined in field training exercises where hands-on skills are practiced based on actual command decisions. This section will describe a training device for tank gunnery team training, a simulated system for force-on-force team training, the National Training Center, and Command and Control Training.

M-1 Tank Conduct of Fire Trainer

One example of team training for a crew-served weapon system involves tank gunnery. Although the M-1 tank is crewed by four men (tank commander, gunner, driver, and loader), tank gunnery is primarily conducted by the tank commander and the gunner. Training tank gunnery used to involve having the entire crew practice on tank gunnery ranges. Unfortunately, there are a number of factors that limit the effectiveness of such live-fire training, including limited operating budget and maneuvering space, lack of frequent practice in the rapid engagement of multiple enemy targets, lack of a replay opportunity, and lack of a full range of realistic environmental conditions.

To overcome these training limitations, the Army developed the *Conduct Of Fire Trainer* (COFT). The COFT system was developed in the early 1980s to meet the Army's need to train tank commanders and gunners to engage enemy targets at realistic ranges, under a variety of environmental conditions. The purpose of the COFT system is to train tank commanders and gunners to successfully engage enemy combat vehicles. The successful engagement of these enemy vehicles depends on the ability of the tank commander and the gunner to: (a) Detect and acquire enemy vehicles, (b) select and initialize the appropriate weapon, and (c) aim and fire the weapon.

To accomplish this training requirement, the COFT system combines simulated operator stations for the tank commander and gunner, a computer image generator, a host computer with vehicle dynamics and gunnery simulations, a computer-based training management system with adaptive training, and an instructor/operator station.

Both the tank commander and gunner stations include the appropriate operating controls, displays, and weapon sights. Sighting characteristics such as diopter adjustment, field of view, and optical/thermal sights are realistically simulated. In addition, realistic vehicle dynamics allow the tank to maneuver as it would on the actual battlefield. The Crew COFT device, which provides simulated crew positions for the M-1 commander, gunner, and driver and is used for continuation training of combat ready crews, is shown in Figure 11.6. The Institutional COFT used at the Army Armor School for training novice M-1 crews is depicted in Figure 11.7. (The COFT trainee positions are examples of TRAINING SIMULATION TECHNOLOGY.)

The COFT system uses computer-generated images to represent the battlefield viewed by the crewmembers. The computer image generator provides full color daylight, nighttime, and infrared images to depict the terrain, targets, and cultural features that define the battlefield. The computer image generator can also simulate the presence of fog and smoke on the battlefield. The host computer system is a general purpose 32-bit machine that interfaces with the crew compartment, instructor/operator station, computer image generator, and digital database that describes the battlefield. This general purpose computer carries out a number of functions including:

- Controlling moving models (TRAINING SIMULATION TECHNOLOGY)
- Providing computer-aided diagnostics (TRAINING MANAGEMENT TECHNOLOGY and INSTRUCTIONAL TECHNOLOGY)
- Calculating ballistic equations for both trainee and enemy weapons (TRAINING SIMULATION TECHNOLOGY)
- Calculating aimpoint errors (TRAINING SIMULATION TECHNOLOGY)
- Monitoring crew responses (TRAINING MANAGEMENT TECHNOLOGY)
- Performing training management and instructional support functions (TRAINING MANAGEMENT TECHNOLOGY and INSTRUCTIONAL TECHNOLOGY)

The training management functions performed by the COFT host computer include recommending the training exercise sequence, preparing end-of-session training summaries, and maintaining a performance history on each crew. The training sequence is adaptive in that training scenarios are recommended to the instructor based on previous crew performance. The instructor, however, retains the option of overriding the computer recommended selection (TRAINING MANAGEMENT TECHNOLOGY).

An instructor/operator station (IOS) allows the instructor to control and evaluate crew performance. The IOS includes full color displays that allow the instructor to view the same scenes being presented to the tank commander and gunner. The IOS also contains an intercom that allows the instructor to communicate with the tank crew and simulate radio transmissions. A full range of functions is available at the IOS. These functions include freeze, record/playback, malfunction control and selection of problem difficulty (TRAINING MANAGEMENT TECHNOLOGY and INSTRUCTIONAL TECHNOLOGY).

Figure 11.6. Crew Conduct of Fire Trainer

307

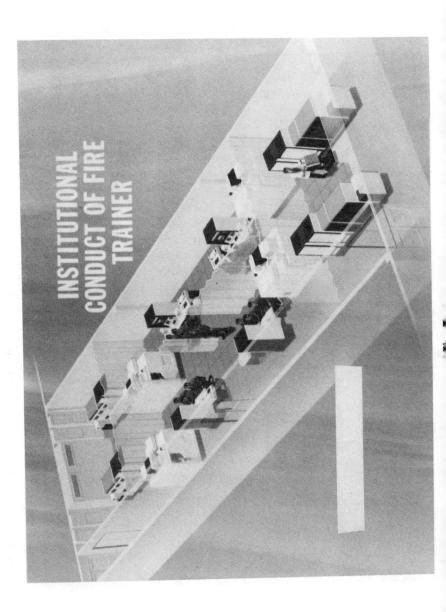

INSTITUTIONAL
CONDUCT OF FIRE
TRAINER

Simulated, Large-Scale, Force-on-Force Team Training

The Army has traditionally used field-training exercises to train its personnel to operate as part of the large extended teams that characterize battalion-level combat. The purpose of these field-training exercises is to allow the participants an opportunity to work as part of a coordinated combat element. In addition to allowing the personnel to practice their individual skills, such training exercises also allow participants the opportunity to practice mutual support, command and control, and team work. Unfortunately, field-training exercises are expensive, logistical, complex events that do not occur frequently enough to maintain optimal levels of combat effectiveness.

In an attempt to overcome the limited opportunities for field training exercises, the Defense Advanced Research Projects Agency and the Army have developed a prototype large-scale simulator network system that provides extended practice in force-on-force warfighting skills.

This force-on-force simulation system, known as SIMNET, consists of a large number of armor and aircraft simulators, workstations to support command and logistical functions, and extensive local area and long haul communication networks. Whereas the COFT system was developed to meet individual crew-training needs involving gunnery skills and crew coordination one crew at a time, the purpose of SIMNET is to allow multiple participants to practice war-fighting skills as part of a battalion task force.

SIMNET assumes that the participants have the basic procedural skills needed to operate their individual equipment. Instead of developing a training system that addresses individual or single crew skills, SIMNET focuses on coordinated activities of various combat elements by providing a functional (versus high physical fidelity) representation of what the trainees would see and hear in actual combat (TRAINING SIMULATION TECHNOLOGY).

To achieve its goal of simulating a realistic combat environment for task-force level training, SIMNET has relied on commercially available microprocessors, developed an open, nonproprietary network architecture, and emphasized using minimal levels of fidelity that are just good enough for effective training. The prototype SIMNET system is located at Fort Knox, KY, with additional elements located at several other locations within the United States and Germany. Each location has several simulators that are interconnected by means of a local area network. These local area networks can then be integrated using long haul network technology to increase the number of participants. Each simulator and its crew participates in the simulated battle just as they would in the actual battle. This means that each participant is part of a combined arms team that is practicing warfighting in a complex battlefield. Information flows up and down through the chain of command, command decisions are made, and the consequences of those decisions, as well as the team's ability to execute those decisions, are played out in real-time man-in-the-loop simulation. The SIMNET architecture is shown in Figure 11.8.

Technical progress and user acceptance have been extremely high. Platoons pretrained in SIMNET have been shown to perform better in both competitions and field training tests than nontrained platoons (Kraemer & Bessemer, 1987; Gound & Schwab, 1988). Based on such positive evaluations, the Army is currently developing an acquisition plan that will expand the current SIMNET prototype into the *Combined Arms Tactical Trainer* (CATT) system by the mid-1990s. The CATT system will combine armor, aviation, and command and control elements through simulation. This increased use of simulation will allow the Army to increase the frequency of combat-oriented training without the expense of field-training exercises. Indeed, the Army's current acquisition plan assumes that CATT will be funded by reducing the number of days spent in current command post and field-training exercises.

While both COFT and SIMNET have addressed team-training needs by simulating both the battlefield and the equipment needed to fight that battle, hands-on-training using actual equipment under battlefield conditions is still a necessary part of Army training. Although the Army plans to reduce field-training days to help pay for systems such as CATT, such systems are still seen as complements to field training. The hope is that such computer-based simulations can keep troops at higher levels of combat proficiency and increase the value of actual field-training exercises.

National Training Center

The most sophisticated of these field training exercises occur at the Army's National Training Center at Fort Irwin, CA. The NTC is a heavily instrumented range that can track and record the instantaneous position of friendly and enemy vehicles as they maneuver across the range. Thousands of soldiers each year practice battalion tactics against a resident opposing force. Each battalion fights this highly trained enemy using actual equipment and operating under actual field conditions. Brigade commanders and staffs plan and initiate tactical operations that are executed by the battalions. Infantry, armor, artillery, and aviation units are realistically employed. These combat units are supported by electronic-warfare, medical, engineering, and supply units.

During a typical unit's visit to the NTC, it will fight six battles against the opposing force. Some of these battles will last several days. During this entire period, the troops will suffer the hardships associated with field combat. For example, if the main supply route is captured or a logistical error occurs, food and fuel will not reach the troops.

The NTC represents the marriage of old-fashioned Army field training with high-technology laser simulation. Instead of firing live ammunition, which

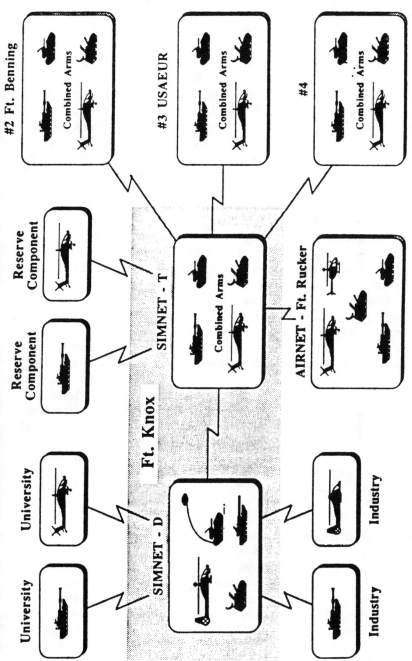

Figure 11.8. SIMNET Architecture.

311

would obviously impose a number of unrealistic safety constraints on the training, each weapon is equipped with a gallium arsenide laser that fires an eye-safe pulse. These lasers are boresighted to the weapons and effectively simulate the actual weapon's range and coverage. Each soldier and vehicle is also equipped with a laser-sensitive receiver. If a laser shot comes close enough to count as a kill its total energy is detected by the receiver.

This laser-based engagement system is known as the *Multiple Integrated Laser Engagement System* (MILES). It provides an effective means of scoring combat at NTC. If a laser "kills" a soldier, an alarm attached to the soldier's helmet is set off. To shut off the alarm, the soldier must use a key lodged in his weapon. Removing the key from the weapon automatically shuts off the weapon's laser capability, thereby removing that soldier from effective combat. When a vehicle such as a tank is hit by a laser, its onboard sensors read the laser pulse frequency to determine what type of weapon fired the shot. If shot would not normally be a threat to the vehicle, the laser hit is ignored. If the shot would have destroyed the vehicle, a large strobe light is turned on to signify a "kill" and the vehicle's weapons are automatically shut off. Over 50 different types of vehicles, weapons, and munitions are modeled in MILES (TRAINING SIMULATION TECHNOLOGY).

During the battles, transponders send information back to headquarters that represent the location and status of individual soldiers and vehicles. This information is computer processed and can be viewed by senior commanders during the battle. In addition, these computer battle records are saved and used to debrief the commanders and the soldiers following the battle. These computer records are supplemented with videotapes recordings of actual engagements (TRAINING MANAGEMENT TECHNOLOGY and INSTRUCTIONAL TECHNOLOGY).

The NTC, like any other peacetime training environment, has its limitations. For example, laser "bullets" are deflected more easily than real bullets, and the psychological stress of actual combat is missing. Still, the NTC allows entire battalions to train as combat elements under warlike conditions that include coordinating the activities of thousands of men and exercising the chain of command in a dynamic field environment.

Command and Control Training

Each of the team-training technologies described above includes hands-on combat skills. This is by no means the only type of team training conducted by the Army. Command and control training has traditionally been a major focus of the Army's team-training efforts. Command and control training systems have been the responsibility of the Combined Arms Center at Fort Leavenworth, KS. These command and control training systems have evolved from command post exercises and board games to microcomputer-based training systems.

Recent microcomputer-based systems developed for the Army include the *Combined Arms Tactical Training System* (CATTS), the *Army Training Battle Simulation System* (ARTBASS), and the *Battalion Battle Game Simulation System* (BABAS). Although the specific implementation of each system varies slightly, they share a common structure. Each system is designed to train battalion-level commanders and their staffs to command and control combined arms operations. Each system relies on computers to simulate the action of units in combat. These computers move the elements around the battlefield based on orders issued by the battalion commander and calculate engagement outcomes. These engagement outcomes are based on such variables as personnel and equipment status, line of sight, soil type, use of suppressive fires, and weather. (These Command and Control training systems all use TRAINING SIMULATION TECHNOLOGY.)

These command and control training systems involve not only the personnel being trained but also a number of supporting controllers who play the roles of other units, react to the trainees' actions, and mediate between the trainees and the computer. The emphasis in these training systems is on the proper routing of information, evaluating and reacting to that information, and decision making. The typical organization for such systems is illustrated in Figure 11.9.

Realism is enhanced through the use of radio and telephones to communicate with other units and staff officers (e.g., S1 and S4) who are not normally in the tactic operations center with the command group. The battalion radio nets, including brigade command, brigade intelligence, brigade administration/ logistics, battalion command, battalion administration/logistics, and air support, are typically represented. In addition, normal field telephone and message service is provided.

Each training session begins with an overview of the situation that includes the status of their troops, the status of other simulated units, logistical and manpower considerations, a description of the enemy force, and so forth. Missions, warning orders, or operations orders are then issued from higher headquarters, and the battalion commander and his staff begin to execute their duties. The orders and requests for information generated by the battalion are received by the controllers. The controllers either respond as appropriate role players in other units or enter the appropriate commands into the computer battle simulation. Either way the events unfold based on the actions of the battalion commanders and their staffs. The consequences of those actions are reported back through the appropriate communication channels and the battalion commanders and their staffs must continually evaluate their progress and decide whether or not to modify their plan of operations.

At the completion of each training session, feedback is provided to the trainees through a combination of media. After-action reports allow trainees and the controllers to describe their perception of battle and the reasoning behind their course of action. Significant portions of the engagement can be recalled from the computer and played on video monitors to show the actual position and strength

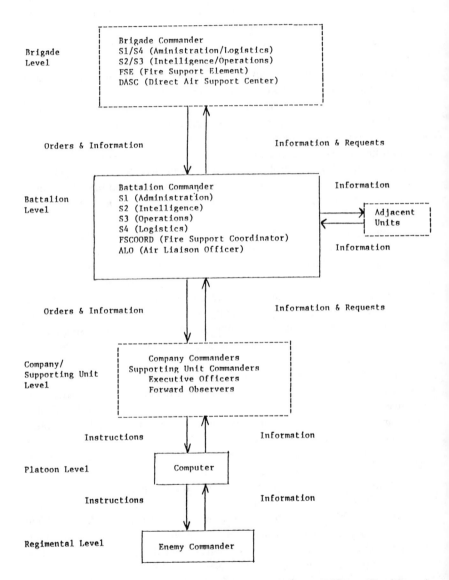

Figure 11.9. Communication between Controller and Player Positions in CATTS. Controller Positions are Inclosed by Broken Lines.

of friendly and enemy forces. Engagement outcomes can be numerically scored and presented to the battalion commanders and their staff. Finally, feedback conferences allow the participants to identify problem areas and develop solutions for those problems (INSTRUCTIONAL TECHNOLOGY).

EXAMPLES OF TRAINING TECHNOLOGY APPLIED TO NAVY TEAM TRAINING

Certainly, the Navy faces many of the same team-training challenges described for the other services. The major difference is the length of time which Navy teams must usually spend away from training devices like those described below. For example, 6-month sea deployments are not uncommon. While this allows much interaction among the team members, the opportunity for actually training systematically in a realistic combat situation are normally limited. For this reason, the Navy has invested heavily in training technology which can be used in team training. The investment until now has been primarily in shore-based facilities. However, new technologies (i.e., embedded training and networking) are now making it more possible to conduct extremely realistic team training on the actual weapons system while it is deployed.

This section describes a sample of recent applications of training technology to team training. Device 14A12 represents a team trainer for the crew members of a single surface ship. Device 20A66 allows commanders from different ships to train together. Device 21A43 provides opportunity for submarine crews to train on tactical problems. The *Submarine Advanced Reactive Tactical Training System* (SMARTTS) is an example of a team-training technology that provides instructional features to a training device that did not previously have that capability. Finally, the 20B5 Pierside trainer is a device that allows teams to train on their own shipboard equipment rather than having to go to a shorebased training facility.

Device 14A12, *Surface Anti-Submarine Warfare* (ASW) Tactical Team Trainer for Single Ships *and* Device 20A66, *Anti-Submarine Warfare* (ASW) Team Trainer for Multiple Ships

The purpose or primary mission of Device 14A12 is to provide antisubmarine warfare (ASW) team procedural and team tactical training to a team of over 20 sailors and officers. The training is done in a multithreat environment for a variety of ship classes. The emphasis of the device is on team training rather than individual operator training. The different sensor (sonar) and weapon equipment configurations for each of the ship classes are simulated by general purpose consoles (GPCs). The GPCs can be configured under training planning and software control to provide the functionality of a particular trainee station without physically duplicating the sensor or weapon system.

Device 14A12 is based on a distributed processing approach, consisting of self-contained physical areas of mockups for the ship's Combat Information Center, sonar, bridge, own ship aircraft (i.e., helicopters), exercise control and debrief, and exercise development, which are interfaced with local area networks (LANs). Control over an individual trainee console is primarily by means of touch screens, a numeric keypad, and a trackball.

The purpose or mission of Device 20A66 is to provide multiplatform coordinated ASW team procedural and tactical training and evaluation for ASW ships, aircraft carriers, ASW aircraft, and submarines within a multithreat environment. The primary emphasis of training is in the areas of tactics, procedures, and decision making for selected personnel from the level of sensor/weapon supervisor through the Battle Group Commander. The device trains department supervisors through battle group commanders. At any one time, dozens of senior level personnel may take part in a team-training scenario.

All functions of the actual sensor systems are computer simulated; no sensor operators are physically present in the trainer, and no "raw" sensor data is presented to the trainee. The device is intended to provide simulation characteristics of actual platform dynamics, sensor system performance, weapon system performance, and communication system performance. A depiction of the 20A66 is shown at Figure 11.10.

For both Device 14A12 and 20A66 simulation control of friendly platforms is provided from mockups, from Exercise Control/Exercise Support (EC/ES) consoles, or from programmed commands. Seven unique types of trainee mockups comprise Device 20A66: Tactical Flag Command Center, Aircraft Carrier Combat Information Center, Aircraft Carrier Combat Information Center ASW Module, Warfare Commander, AEGIS class guided missile cruiser Combat Information Center, Surface/Subsurface Combat Information Center, and Aircraft. Since total simulation of all pertinent operational equipment is not required, the student mockups utilize General Purpose Consoles, which are configurable under training planning and software control, to represent a variety of operational equipment. Other equipment in the mockups include status boards, automated status boards, plot tables, helm units, large screen displays, chart tables, and miscellaneous terminals (TRAINING SIMULATION TECHNOLOGY).

Both Device 14A12 and Device 20A66 have detailed simulation programs to accurately represent real-world events and phenomena. There are simulation programs to reproduce platform motion characteristics (i.e., ship, submarines, and aircraft); weapon system simulation (missiles, torpedoes, guns, bombs); damage assessment; environmental factors (weather, sea state, currents, sonar conditions); and sensor detection simulation (radar, sonar, Forward Looking Infra-Red, Magnetic Anomaly Detection, Identification Friend or Foe) (TRAINING SIMULATION TECHNOLOGY).

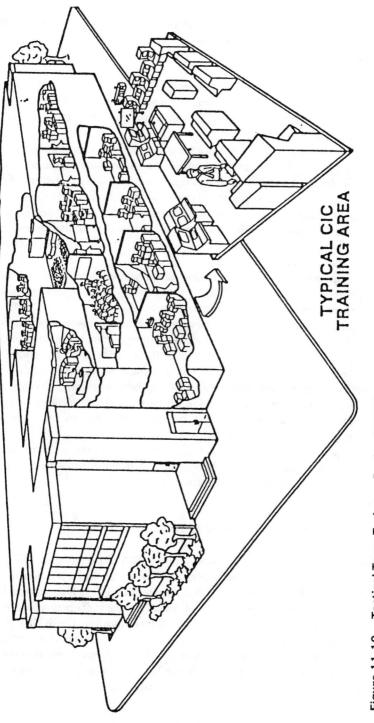

TYPICAL CIC
TRAINING AREA

Figure 11.10.   Tactical Team Trainer – Device 20A66.

317

Both devices have a sophisticated array of instructional features that aid the instructors in setting up, running, evaluating exercises and in providing feedback to the trainees. These include:

Exercise definition library—a database of existing weapons, environmental and weapons platform parameters which can be called up for any new exercise scenario development. (TRAINING MANAGEMENT TECHNOLOGY.)

System initialization—provides a means for the device operators to bring up the complete system quickly and in a known state from a power-off condition. An objective of this function is to make the start-up of the system as simple as possible. (TRAINING MANAGEMENT TECHNOLOGY.)

Exercise initialization—a user-friendly method for placing platforms at specific positions within the exercise boundaries with their own headings and speeds ready for exercise start. (TRAINING MANAGEMENT TECHNOLOGY.)

Exercise brief—capability to inform the trainees of the exercise and show demonstrations of "right" and "wrong" ways to handle different situations. (INSTRUCTIONAL TECHNOLOGY.)

Exercise conduct—various features available to the instructors that help them run the exercise. These include prompts about upcoming exercise events and freeze capability to stop the exercise at certain points for instructional purposes. (TRAINING MANAGEMENT TECHNOLOGY.)

Performance measurement—automatic capability to record individual and team performance parameters (e.g., time to arrive at tactically optimal location, time to acquire target, time to launch weapons, etc.). (TRAINING MANAGEMENT TECHNOLOGY.)

Post exercise debrief—various technological aids to the instructor in informing teams how they have done and in remediating team performance. (INSTRUCTIONAL TECHNOLOGY.)

Device 21A43—Submarine Combat Systems Team Trainer

The *Submarine Combat Systems Team Trainer* (SCSTT), Device 21A43, provides the capability to train Navy personnel in the tactical operation of the *Combat Control System MK1* (CCS MK1). The SCSTT include tactical Fire Control and Over-the-Horizon equipment and allows the trainees to gain experience in equipment operation, tactics, and team co-ordination. The SCSTT simulates Combat System functions external to the Attack Center and simulates appropriate tactical system interfaces to allow Attack Center Team Training on CCS MK1. (See Figure 11.11.) This device has only limited instructional features. The Submarine Advanced Reactive Tactical Training System described

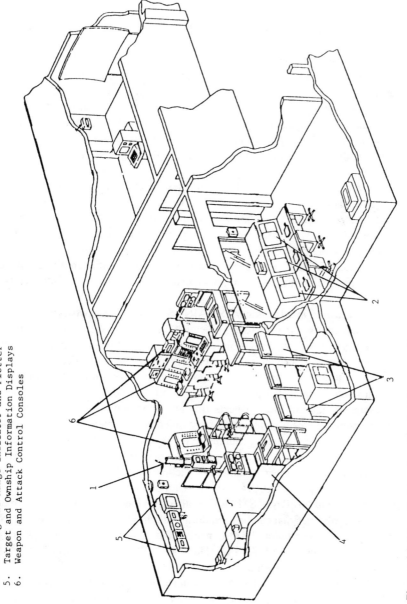

3. Status Boards
4. Bearing and Range Indicator and Plotter
5. Target and Ownship Information Displays
6. Weapon and Attack Control Consoles

Figure 11.11. Submarine Combat Systems Team Trainer – Device 21A43.

319

below added a very sophisticated instructional capability (TRAINING SIMULATION TECHNOLOGY).

Submarine Advanced Reactive Tactical Training System (SMARTTS)

SMARTTS was designed to be the "training subsystem" of the Submarine Combat System Trainer, which is the US Navy's principle training device for teaching submarine tactics (Hammell & Crosby, 1980) (see the description above). It is a stand-alone device using its own computational system and peripherals. It was installed on an operational trainer (Device 21A43) at the Fleet ASW Training Center located at Norfolk, VA. It was designed to support instruction in both the classroom and the host trainer, the 21A Series Submarine Combat Systems Trainers.

Exercise generation. SMARTTS enables the creation of a library of tactical exercises which may be automatically loaded into the trainer. These exercises contain all parameters and initial conditions pertinent to a particular training mission. Contents of each exercise may be previewed by the instructor and modified as desired. Such "modified" scenarios may then be added to the existing library. Thus, new scenarios can be created in either an off-line mode or immediately before the beginning of an exercise (TRAINING MANAGEMENT TECHNOLOGY).

Performance measurement. SMARTTS provides for two types of performance indicators. First, there are objective measures produced by the computer, and second, there is the provision for the manual input of subjective assessments by the instructor. The objective measures make use of tactical data that are generated throughout the mission and may be displayed in real-time throughout the mission or presented graphically upon mission completion. The subjective assessments address those aspects that are important for mission success but which cannot be readily calculated from objective parameters. Included are such things as periscope search technique, plot coordinator effectiveness, recognition of target maneuvers, etc. In addition to these performance indicators, SMARTTS also computes a number of objective tactical variables that are necessary for proper debriefing (INSTRUCTIONAL TECHNOLOGY).

Information displays. SMARTTS also provides a number of information display capabilities that can be used during all phases of a training exercise. Such displays have been tailored to the needs of both the instructor and the trainee. The major features of SMARTTS (Hammell, 1983) are shown in Figure 11.12 (INSTRUCTIONAL TECHNOLOGY).

Brief/debrief. SMARTTS has an exercise preview capability that can be used by the instructor for briefing purposes. It enables the running of an exercise in the classroom or attack center without using the main simulation. In this manner the instructor can demonstrate problems as well as acceptable and unacceptable sets

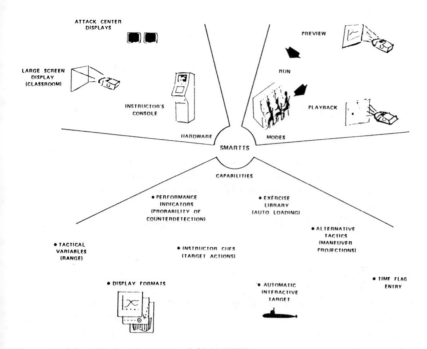

Figure 11.12. Major Aspects of SMARTTS

of tactical actions to the student. The system also enables the insertion of time flags by either student or instructor to facilitate location of points in the mission that are to be discussed. During replay, all real-time displays are available. The exercise may be run at ether real-time or fast-time (16 times normal speed) (INSTRUCTIONAL TECHNOLOGY).

Controller models. SMARTTS has a computer-controlled target model designed to alleviate instructor workload and increase the simulation quality of enemy targets. The *Automatic Interactive Target* (AIT) has an internal decision structure based on available intelligence information. It acts as an intelligent adversary by reacting to ownship actions as well as information from the environment and intelligence sources. During operation, SMARTTS alerts the instructor to impending AIT actions and he may choose to override its decisions if desired (TRAINING MANAGEMENT TECHNOLOGY).

Alternative tactics. SMARTTS also provides the capability to explore alternative tactics during both the brief and debrief. In a sense, it provides a "what-if" capability. For example, during the brief the instructor can illustrate the effects of different tactics throughout the exercise by demonstrating the effects of choosing various alternatives. In other words, what happens if I choose this tactic as opposed to choosing another? During the debrief the instructor can stop the replay at any point and illustrate the effects of tactics other than those used by the student. SMARTTS will display these alternative tactics in addition to those employed by the student, thus graphically depicting the differences. Effects of alternative tactics may be displayed in a fast-time mode thus speeding the operation (INSTRUCTIONAL TECHNOLOGY and TRAINING SIMULATION TECHNOLOGY).

Perry Class Frigate Pierside Combat System Team Trainer (Device 20B5)

This training device is designed to provide continuation and refresher training to skilled team members who have already completed their formal school training in their individual skill areas. Since Navy crews are so often deployed away from shore-based facilities, it is vital that the time they do get in port be put to the best training use.

Feiock (1988) states that Device 20B5 (see Figure 11.13) provides realistic training on board the Frigate's Combat Information Center (CIC) and the Sonar room. Device 20B5 uses front-end stimulation of all the ship's sensors, fire control systems, navigation and communications equipment. A stimulation sends realistic signals directly to an operational piece of equipment. A simulation provides simulated signals to a piece of equipment that is not intended for operational use. "Simulation is used to artificially create the environment external to the ship (threats, media, etc.). Stimulation is used to place the ship's systems inside this artificially created environment" (Feiock, 1988, p. 586) (TRAINING SIMULATION TECHNOLOGY).

The 20B5 is mounted in a van that is driven to the pier at which the frigate is docked. On the van is a computer system that maintains the training environment and provides modeling of the combat environment. There are five instructor consoles that allow members of the training unit to control the training problem and to role-play friendly and hostile platforms. There are 14 units that are carried onto the ship and connected to the ship's equipment to provide the front-end stimulation. Fiber optic cables connect the van to the ship.

The pierside trainer concept has been successful. The crews and instructors like the idea of training with the actual equipment they would use in combat. In the conclusion section we will discuss briefly the concept of embedded training that is used onboard ship while it is underway. While such an approach has many advantages, it lacks one feature which the pierside trainer has, dedicated instructors. The instructors on the pierside trainer have instruction as virtually their only duty. That advantage can really only be obtained in a training setting on shore. It would be very difficult logistically to have such dedicated instructors onboard deployed ships.

Future navy initiatives. In closing we would like to briefly note two training technology application areas that are of particular interest to the Navy currently. The first is an exploration of how best to take advantage of recent advances in networking technology. Clearly the Navy could take great advantage of linking

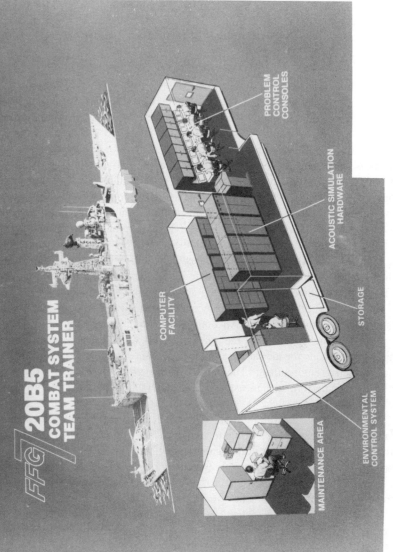

Figure 11.13. Combat System Team Trainer for the FFG7-Device 20B5

ships and shore-based training centers to allow large numbers of crews to "play" in tactical scenarios.

The Navy has also expressed interest in placing *Weapon Systems Trainers* (WST) for aircraft on aircraft carriers. Once these WSTs are networked, a number of aircrews could fly simulated tactical-training missions while they are on a sea deployment.

CONCLUSIONS AND FUTURE TRENDS

We have presented in this chapter a number of definitions and examples of training technologies applied to team training. Despite the fact that the "training planning and development" technologies we spoke of earlier have not yet emerged that will fully optimize team training, there have been some impressive advances, especially in the training hardware and software area. What team-training technology might we expect to see in the future? Certainly we would hope and expect that "training planning and development" technologies will advance. The systems approaches to instructional analysis and design which have proven to be fairly successful for individual training (Branson et al., 1975) will have to be modified or replaced with models and approaches more tailored to team skills. The work of Morgan, Salas and their colleagues (described elsewhere in this volume) over the last few years has shown some promise in defining new techniques for analyzing and designing team training.

We also expect the team performance measurement technologies to improve. As described in the section on Air Force team-training technology, the Aircrew Training Research Division of the Air Force Armstrong Laboratory is presently exploring methods for measuring fighter pilot teams in a highly threat-intensive and interactive environment. The work is hampered by the lack of a full set of valid, proven performance measures at the individual pilot level, but progress is being made.

On the training hardware/software side we can expect to see improvements in a number of areas. Networking technology will improve. SIMNET-like approaches to networking for both local and long haul simulation exercises will be expanded. A standard protocol will eventually be settled on and all new training devices will have a requirement to be "networkable." For example, the Army has already issued that requirement.

It is not certain that the capability to use satellites to link multiple user sites together for internetted exercises will be viable. As more high-fidelity simulators are added to the multiuser network, the time delay problem of sending signals to satellites and back down to other simulators will be problematic. However, this problem can probably eventually be solved technically. The larger problem may be of an economic nature. It simply may be too expensive to use satellite resources to relay the large amounts of data that will be required for simulator networks.

While we have not talked about artificial intelligence and neural networks in this chapter, we would certainly expect these technologies to play a much larger role in team training in the future. Possible uses would be to help structure team performance models (how do good teams operate?), permit performance measurement for complex team interactions, help instructors in remediating teams with performance problems, be of assistance to instructors in developing scenarios that are appropriate for teams of different skill levels, and provide realistic adversaries.

We expect the military to become more and more adept in understanding the need for, and limitations of, team-training technology. The military has so far spent billions of dollars in developing and using team-training technologies. As one might expect with such a vast undertaking, mistakes have been made. Too often, training devices have been procured and delivered to a training site with little thought given to how the device would fit into the total training system. When that happens, it is no surprise that the device is far less effective than it could be. We have seen encouraging signs that the military is beginning to understand this problem and make efforts to correct it.

Embedded training is a concept that is becoming more accepted in the technical training world, especially the military. *Embedded training* is defined as a capability resident within the operational equipment that allows trainees to use the operational equipment to receive training and practice skills (Andrews, 1991). The embedded capability may be an inherent part of the operational equipment (i.e., part of the equipment's resident computer capacity may be devoted to training functions) or the capability may be "strapped on" the operational equipment. That is, an additional computer capability may be connected to the operational equipment. The Navy has a number of embedded training examples presently being used onboard submarines and surface ships.

Thus far, embedded training has proven useful in the training and retention of some skills used by individual operators. There is no reason to believe that embedded training won't be useful for certain types of team skills. The pierside trainer discussed above has shown that trainees can learn team skills while at their operational equipment.

We believe that the technologies discussed in this chapter have application to most team-training settings, be they military or not. The technologies we have described for analyzing team skills, developing and delivering team instruction, describing and measuring team performance, aiding instructors in briefing and debriefing trainees, and helping instructors in remediating teams should apply in many different team settings for technical and decision-making training.

Much remains to be done to develop and improve team training technology. We have touched on a number of concepts and approaches which still need considerable research and development. We are at a crucial stage in the development of this technology. Future developments in the "training delivery" technologies will undoubtedly continue at a very rapid rate. Unless the "training planning and development" technologies are developed and refined that can help us understand how and when to best use the "training delivery" technologies, we feel that the teams who use the technologies for training will receive considerably less benefit than they might.

REFERENCES

Andrews, D. H. (1991). Embedded training and embedded practice. *Educational Technology, 21* (10), 41–44.

Andrews, D. H. (1988). The relationship among training devices, simulators and learning: A behavioral view. *Educational Technology, 18*(1), 48–54.

Andrews, D. H., & Uliano, K. C. (1988). An instructor's diagnostic aid for feedback in training. *Journal of Industrial Teacher Education, 25*(4), 49–60.

Branson, R. K., Raynor, G. T., Cox, J. L. Furman, J. P., King, F. J., & Hannum, W. H. (1975). *Interservice procedures for instructional systems development* (5 Vols.) (TRADOC Pam 350-30 & NAVEDTRA 106A). Fort Monroe, VA: U.S. Army Training and Doctrine Command. (NTIS N. AD A019 486 through AD A019 490).

Briggs, G. E., & Naylor, J. C. (1965). Team versus individual training, training task fidelity and task organization effects on transfer performed by three-man teams. *Journal of Applied Psychology, 49,* 387–392.

Carey, J. & Briggs, L. J. (1977). Teams as designers. In L. J. Briggs (Ed.), *Instructional design* (pp. 261–311). Englewood Cliffs, NJ: Educational Technology Publications.

Denson, R. W. (1981). *Team training: Literature review and annotated bibliography* (Report No. AFHRL-TR-80-40 AD A099 994). Wright-Patterson Air Force Base, OH: Logistics and Technical Training Division.

Dyer, J. L. (1984). Team research and team training: A state of the art review. In F. A. Muckler (Ed.), *Human factors review* (pp. 285–324). Santa Monica, CA: Human Factors Society.

Feiock, D. H. (1988). Integration of a shipboard sensor trainer into a combat system team trainer. *Proceedings of the 10th Interservice/Industry Training Systems Conference* (pp. 583–591). Orlando, FL: National Security Industrial Association.

Foushee, C. F., & Helmreich, R. L. (1988). Group interaction and flight crew performance. In E. L. Wiener & D. C. Nagel (Eds.), *Human factors in aviation.* San Diego: Academic Press.

Gagne, R. M., & Briggs, L. J. (1979). *Principles of instructional design* (2nd ed.). New York: Holt, Rinehart and Winston.

Gound, D., & Schwab, J. R. (1988). *Concept evaluation program of simulation networking (SIMNET)* (TRADOCTRMS No. 86-CEP-0345, TRADOC ACN 86299). Ft Knox, KY: US Army Armor and Engineering Board.

Hammell, T. J., & Crosby, T. (1980). Development of SMARTTS Training Technology *Proceedings of the 2nd Interservice/Industry Training Equipment Conference* (pp 269–276). Salt Lake City, UT: National Security Industrial Association.

Hammell, T. J. (1983). Training assistance technology. *Proceedings of the 5th Interservice/Industry Training Equipment Conference* (pp. 181–193). Washington, DC American Defense Preparedness Association.

Jonassen, D. H., & Hannum W. H. (1986). Analysis of task analysis procedures. *Journal of Instructional Development, 9*(2), 2–12.

Kraemer, R. E., & Bessemer, D. W. (1987). *U.S. tank platoon training for the 1987 Canadian Army Trophy (CAT) competition using a simulation networking (SIM-NET) system* (Research Rep. 1457). Fort Knox, KY: US Army Research Institute for the Behavioral and Social Sciences, ARI Field Unit.

McGuinness, J., Forbes, J. M., & Rhoads, J. E. (1984). *Air combat maneuvering performance measurement system design* (AFHRL-TP-83-56, AD B081 060L). Williams AFB, AZ: Operations Training Division, Air Force Human Resources Laboratory.

Morgan, B. B., Jr., Coates, G. D., Kirby, R. H., & Alluisi, E. A. (1984). Individual and group performances as functions of the team-training load. *Human Factors, 26*(2), 127–142.

Waag, W. L., Pierce, B. J., & Fessler, S. (1987). *Performance measurement requirements for tactical aircrew training* (AFHRL-TR-86-62, AD A183 814). Williams AFB, AZ: Operations Training Division, Air Force Human Resources Laboratory.

12

Aircrew Coordination – Achieving Teamwork In the Cockpit*

Carolyn Prince
Thomas R. Chidester
Clint Bowers
Janis Cannon-Bowers

Serious thought about the possibility of flight was recorded as early as the 13th century; fables of manned flight exist from a still earlier time, with stories of emperors soaring in winged chariots. In the 17th century, John Wilkins presented four possible ways that humankind might be able to fly (*The New Encyclopedia Britannica*, 1984). His first suggestion, "with the spirits of angels," captures some of the yearnings that man has long held for movement through the fluid of air.

A collection of synonyms listed under *spirit* includes togetherness, communality, unity, oneness, attitude, reason, and motivating force (Rodale, 1978), but these words were rarely used in the ensuing developments of manned flight. The focus was on updating the equipment of flight, the fabled "winged chariot." From Leonardo da Vinci's aircraft sketches to the present day, aircraft design has evolved, taking full advantage of the laws of physics and of technological ad-

---

* The opinions, views, and/or findings contained in this chapter are the authors' and should not be construed as an official position policy or decision of the organizations with which they are affiliated, unless so designated by other official documentation.

vances. Such attention to improvement has not characterized the study of the human element in flight, however.

BACKGROUND

The only real goal of early pilots was aircraft control. As flight became more reliable, accomplishing other objectives was added to the pilots' concerns. Transport of passengers increased safety considerations, and made back-ups to the pilot commonplace (Foushee & Helmreich, 1988). More complex equipment increased workload beyond one person's capabilities, and emerging military requirements called for additional people in the aircrew. In such ways, the cockpit crew came into being.

The cockpit crew is a work group whose environment can be unforgiving of mistakes, with results costly in the extreme. Crew members must fly with experienced instructors until they reach a certain level of expertise, and training emphasizes the acquisition of individual technical skills. As a result, the habit of concentrating on one's own performance is developed early.

Lacking the specific training needed for effective coordination, flight crews developed spontaneous, idiosyncratic practices in order to cope with the interactive demands of their tasks. In the 1970s, the insufficiency of these spontaneous practices was brought to the aviation community's attention with information from three independent sources, aircraft accident data, research, and pilot opinions (Lauber, 1987).

As the overall numbers of flights and passengers per plane increased, and the recording and reporting of accidents improved, the impact of each aviation accident was magnified. An analysis of accidents for the years 1968 to 1976 revealed an alarming number in which the causes could be ascribed to human errors in decision making, leadership, judgment, and communications (Cooper, White, & Lauber, 1979). Christian and Morgan (1987) provided added detail. Basing their report on a review of accidents and of National Aeronautics and Space Administration (NASA) studies, they found multiple instances of inadequate leadership and monitoring, preoccupation with minor mechanical irregularities, and failures in the delegation of tasks, assignment of responsibilities, setting of priorities, utilization of available data, and communication of intents and plans.

Adding to the accident data was research reported by Ruffell Smith (1979). While studying crews for the effects of workload on performance, he noted and documented wide variations in crew performance. Ruffell Smith reported that the behaviors that differentiated crew effectiveness lay in the areas of leadership, decision making, and resource management.

The third source of information about the existence of a serious problem in the cockpit was a series of interviews conducted with line pilots (Lauber, 1987). A deficiency in aviator training was uncovered when pilots expressed a need for more than technical training and revealed a dissatisfaction with their preparation in the skills necessary for human work interaction in the cockpit. This convergence of evidence from accident data, research, and pilot experience helped to generate a variety of attempts to deal with the human resource problem in the cockpit.

With increasing acceptance of aviation as a routine part of modern life, the numbers of accidents caused by human error has captured worldwide attention (Orlady & Foushee, 1987). Technically qualified aircrews, and well-designed aircraft, have not been sufficient to assure safety of flight. Research has identified some of the specific failures in cockpit teamwork; now aviation interests are seeking remedies. In this chapter, the approaches to improving crew coordination, their present status, and unresolved issues, are first presented. This is followed by a description of the specific behavior approach to aircrew coordination training as a promising method to augment other training currently in use. The chapter closes with a discussion of the requirements and difficulties of evaluating coordination training.

APPROACHES TO CREW COORDINATION

There are at least three countermeasures to the problems of coordination in the cockpit; they are selection, task redesign, and training. All three of these remedies include qualifications: (a) if stable individual characteristics associated with superior abilities in crew coordination can be identified, steps to select the right people can be made; (b) if characteristics of the flying task can be found to facilitate or inhibit coordination, tasks can be redesigned; and (c) if the knowledge, skills, and strategies used to facilitate coordination can be identified, crews can then be trained. An ideal plan to ensure effective crew performance within an organization would select the right people, provide them with a task designed for superior performance, and train them in coordination skills.

Each part of this strategy is conditional upon research to identify both optimal individual characteristics for selection and optimal task characteristics for design, and the critical knowledge, skills, and strategies for training. This section reviews basic research and applications bearing on each of these approaches. Clearly, this is an area of an evolving technology. As more programs are implemented, and as evaluation and developmental research continue, there are certain to be new insights and new issues.

By far, intervention programs in both civilian and military aviation have focused on training rather than selection or task design (cf. Orlady & Foushee, 1987). Given the rapidity with which the issue of crew coordination emerged (Cooper et al., 1979), and the cost and time interval with which each strategy has an impact, this was the most reasonable focus. Selection changes an existing population very slowly. As pilots retire, optimal selection ensures they are replaced with the best possible candidates. More extreme selection approaches (such as reselecting among current pilots), could be unfair, expensive, and wasteful of valuable operating experience. Likewise, *task design* (defined in terms of the physical interface between crews and their aircraft) slowly changes as older planes are replaced or as new designs are retrofitted to existing cockpits. Wholesale replacement is impossible, given the demands for air transportation, the production capacity, and equipment costs.

Training is the preferred approach; it is far less expensive than the other two measures, and far more practical. Within limits, training can have an impact on an entire population in a relatively short time. Selection and task design move to center stage after training, when they have been associated with factors limiting the training's impact. As will be seen later, research is beginning to identify such limits.

Selection

Selection becomes important in areas where training is unlikely to have an effect. Within the crew coordination sphere, Helmreich (1984) has suggested that attitude and personality domains may have an impact on all components of crew performance. A distinction can be drawn between the amenability of these two domains to selection and training. *Attitudes* are defined as learned patterns of responding which are more or less modifiable through training. Hence attitudes have been used as a training criterion. *Personality traits* are defined as stable, deep-seated predispositions to respond in particular ways; because of this stability, personality traits may be resistant to change through training and, therefore, become an issue for selection.

Two instruments have been developed for the measurement of personality traits and attitudes for the pilot population, and have been proven useful for research. For personality measurement, the *Personal Characteristics Inventory* (PCI), composed of the *Extended Personal Attributes Questionnaire* (EPAQ; Spence, Helmreich, & Holman, 1979), *Work and Family Orientation Questionnaire* (WOFO; Spence & Helmreich, 1978), and *Achievement Striving and Impatience/Irritability* scales (AS, I/I; Pred, Spence, & Helmreich, 1986) derived from the Jenkins Activity Survey (Jenkins, Zyzanski, & Rosenman, 1971), has been used. The PCI reveals two trait dimensions, *instrumentality* (defined as independence and goal level) and *expressivity* (defined as interpersonal warmth or sensitivity), each with positive and negative components (Chidester & Foushee, 1989). Crew attitudes are assessed by the *Cockpit Management Attitudes Questionnaire* (CMAQ; Helmreich, 1984; Helmreich, Wilhelm, & Gregorich, 1988). The CMAQ has three primary dimensions which have been shown to sample the curriculum of aircrew coordination training (Helmreich, Foushee,

Benson, & Russini, 1987). These dimensions form the subscales of Coordination and Communication, Recognition of Stressor Effects, and Command Responsibility.

Three recent studies have suggested ways in which personality as measured by the PCI may serve as a limit on training effectiveness. The first of these was conducted by Chidester, Helmreich, Gregorich, and Geis (1991) to assess whether the pilot population could be classified in meaningful personality-based subgroups, or clusters, and if these groups offered any performance consequences. Two samples of military pilots were given the PCI. Cluster analyses were conducted to assess the generality or replicability of personality profiles associated with each cluster, and personality profile consequences were assessed by examining differences in rate of promotion and impact of aircrew coordination training as a function of cluster membership. These analyses were accomplished by the use of a statistical technique for combining subjects into groups based upon each subject's similarity to other subjects along any specified set of dimensions. The identified subgroups then represent meaningful constellations of traits as they are distributed across individuals (Anderberg, 1973). Results identified three subgroupings that were equivalent across the two samples: (a) a Positive Instrumental/Interpersonal cluster, with elevated levels of both instrumental and expressive traits; (b) a Negative Instrumental cluster characterized by elevated levels of positive and negative (impatience, irritability, hostility) instrumental traits combined with low levels of positive expressive traits; and (c) a Low-Motivation cluster, with below average scores on positive instrumental and expressive traits.

Based on previous research (e.g., Spence & Helmreich, 1983; Helmreich, 1986, 1987), Chidester et al. (1991) predicted that these traits might set limits on the effectiveness of training to improve interpersonal relations and coordination in the cockpit, and that superior performance within the organization might be associated with higher levels of both instrumental and expressive traits. Results of the research indicate that personality clusters indeed appeared to set limits on attitude change (as measured by the CMAQ) in some curriculum areas. Pilots fitting the positive Instrumental/Expressive profile (a) showed more positive attitudes about Communication and Coordination, both before and after training, than did Negative Instrumental or Low-Motivation pilots; (b) appeared to gain greater Recognition of Stressor Effects with flight experience than Negative Instrumental or Low-Motivation pilots; and (c) responded more positively to training along the Command Responsibility dimension than did Low-Motivation pilots. Negative Instrumental pilots had more favorable Communication and Coordination attitudes, and responded more favorably to training on Command Responsibility, than did Low-Motivation pilots. With regard to performance as measured by promotion, Positive Instrumental/Expressive pilots did gain promotion at a significantly faster rate than did Negative Instrumental or Low-Motivation pilots.

A second experiment (Chidester, Kanki, Foushee, Dickinson, & Bowles, 1990) found additional performance consequences by applying cluster membership to crew performance in a full-mission simulation study. Chidester et al. contrasted crews led by captains fitting each of the three profiles. Crews completed a simulation of a 1½-day trip consisting of five flight segments, two of which included aircraft failures requiring a coordinated response by crewmembers. Each crew's effectiveness was based on the judgment of a recently retired, experienced airline captain, and on the number and severity of errors made by the crew. Those crews led by a Positive Instrumental/Expressive captain were rated as consistently effective and made fewest errors during the abnormal flight segments. Crews led by Low-Motivation captains were rated as less effective and made significantly more errors during the abnormal segments. Crews led by Negative Instrumental captains appeared to vary in performance over the 2 days. The observer rated these crews as relatively ineffective on the first day, but equal to the best on the second day. Further research exploring crew communication processes in these crews (using techniques developed by Kanki, Lozito, & Foushee, 1988) is now in progress.

Finally, Helmreich and Wilhelm (1989) have begun to look carefully at pilots who reject training. Rejection of the concepts in a coordination training program is considered problematic, because positive attitudes are considered necessary for effective crew performance. Using a conservative criterion based upon CMAQ attitude change opposite to that advocated by aircrew coordination training, they found that 5%–15% of pilots show clear rejection of the concepts. Helmreich and Wilhelm have found also that these pilots are significantly likely to fit the Low-Motivation profile identified by Chidester et al. (1991).

A consistent profile begins to emerge of pilots who may be predisposed toward developing effective crew coordination skills and those likely to respond negatively to training, suggesting that personality may serve to limit training effects. If there is further evidence of validity of these concepts, organizations may need to give motivational and other personal attributes the kind of consideration in selection accorded measures of aptitude. Personality appears to set some limits, is stable over time, and is resistant to change; it therefore meets the same criteria that make aptitude subject to selection techniques.

Task Design

Though the bulk of human factors research tends to focus on task design issues, there is little research on their consequences for crew coordination. Wiener (1988), in studying the impact of automated systems on crew performance, has observed that automation may change the type and timing of errors rather than preventing them, and may result in an unevenness in workload savings. As an example of the unevenness of workload, an automated aircraft can be programmed to fly with little input from the crew, until flight plan changes are required, and the system must be reprogrammed to fit the new instructions. Such changes are most likely to occur immediately following departure or in preparation for landing, adding a task to the crew's work at their busiest times.

If automation as implemented provides new problems for crew coordination, solutions should be considered. Redesign of automated systems is slow and potentially costly. Changing the airspace system (since it is often the limits of the system and not of the aircraft that lead immediately to flight plan changes) would be extremely expensive, requiring modification and replacement of equipment at literally hundreds of facilities. As in response to crew coordination issues in general, the first response to task design problems is likely to be training, in the form of an aircrew coordination training module seeking to optimize the crew's use of automated systems.

In a larger sense, the task design issue can be extended to include checklists, abnormal procedures, and even organizational policies and governmental regulations. Hackman (1988) has initiated an observational study of day-to-day flight operations to capture ways in which crews across organizations interact with their flight environment. If reliable and meaningful differences among organizations can be identified at the crew level, it may provide the first real information to be used as guidance for the most effective leadership behaviors, role structure within crews, and interfaces between crews that interact with each other.

In summary, the impact of task design factors on crew coordination is a relatively unexplored area. Research is underway to understand the effect of automation, crew structure, and organizational and regulatory practices. As problems are identified, training is likely to be the initial response to task design problems; as research continues, new aircraft systems may come to reflect sound crew factors principles.

Training Approaches

In response to the recognition of the human element role in accidents and incidents, training programs addressing this problem began to develop. In the late seventies, both KLM (Royal Dutch Airlines) and United Airlines independently established such programs. In the decade to follow, many more programs came into being (Orlady & Foushee, 1987).

Aircrew coordination training (ACT) programs are often referred to as *cockpit resource management* (CRM) training. The term *CRM* is used to emphasize the need to integrate and utilize all the resources available to the cockpit, human resources as well as hardware and software (Lauber, 1987). In practice, ACT and CRM programs are virtually indistinguishable, and the two terms will be used interchangeably throughout this chapter. By either designation, the increase in the use of these programs has been remarkable. A survey by the International Air

Transport Association (White, 1987) was able to confirm only 14 carriers that had a program designed to teach aircrew coordination (10% of the worldwide membership of IATA). An informal survey taken 4 years later revealed an increase so significant that a second full survey by IATA was undertaken (L. White, personal communication, November 1989).

The training programs have been implemented in a variety of forms, but a consensus now appears to be emerging on both form and content of training (Orlady & Foushee, 1987). In an advisory circular soon to be released, the Federal Aviation Administration (FAA) recommends that training programs be broken into three phases: (a) an awareness phase, in which crewmembers complete seminar instruction and group exercises to learn the basic concepts of CRM; (b) a practice and feedback phase, in which crews fly a realistic scenario in a simulator and receive feedback on their performance; and (c) a reinforcement phase, in which the concepts become part of the organization's overall training and operation practices.

Awareness phase seminars focus on such topics as communication, decision making, stress or workload management, leader and subordinate responsibilities, and management styles. Some organizations have implemented this awareness phase but have gone no further in terms of feedback and reinforcement.

Practice and feedback most often are provided in the form of *line-oriented flight training* (LOFT; Lauber & Foushee, 1981), completed during the organization's mandated recurrent training cycle. LOFT is a technique wherein a high-fidelity aircraft simulator is flown with a complete crew performing as if on an actual line flight. Preparations, paperwork, communications, and all routine procedures required for a normal flight are part of the simulation. Usually, each LOFT session includes an aircraft system failure or weather-related problem for the crew to solve while completing normal duties. Crew performances are videotaped for review by the instructor and the trainees. Ideally, LOFT would occur immediately after awareness training, but the realities of simulation scheduling often result in some delay.

Reinforcement requires integration of crew coordination into the recurrent training cycle and performance evaluation cycle. Typically, LOFT becomes a permanent fixture in recurrent training. Often a brief live or videotaped presentation focusing on one CRM curriculum area is made to each crew. In this way, some crewmembers receive a short refresher every 6 months. Perhaps the most critical part of the reinforcement phase is ensuring that supervisory pilots (training or line check airmen) highlight crew coordination issues during evaluation of simulator-based proficiency checks or line checks. Helmreich and Wilhelm (1986) have argued that reinforcement by supervisors when it counts—when one must demonstrate competency to maintain one's rating—will quickly determine whether coordination skills are embraced and applied by crewmembers.

In summary, training approaches to crew coordination have been widely implemented. Although the FAA advocates that an awareness-feedback-reinforcement model be followed, general guidelines and recommendations for CRM training do not assure uniformity in the resulting programs. There is some variety in the application of the recommendations, and there is no assurance of organizational reinforcement of the training.

CURRENT PRACTICES AND PROBLEMS IN AWARENESS PHASE SEMINARS

The Ruffell Smith (1979) research suggested the possibility of applying business management concepts to aircrew coordination (Lauber, 1987). Perhaps because of this common base and similar goals, a sampling of the CRM programs reveals a number of congruities in stated objectives, training methods, and even specific program activities.

The stated objectives of CRM invariably include safety. Often the shocking scenes from an aircraft accident caused by human error are used to introduce the trainees to the program. The accident issue may be raised again through a discussion of coordination related accidents, or the reading of accident transcripts.

Course length ranges from half-day courses to those of several days. Although the length of the course dictates to some extent the training techniques used, most courses include lecture, videotape presentations, role-play, discussion, and group exercises. Group exercises and role-plays are generally selected with two objectives: to be interesting, and to illustrate information from a lecture. Some materials borrowed from management training or other fields appear to satisfy the first of the two objectives but are unrelated to aviation and do not readily bridge the gap between the lecture and the individual trainee's experience. In addition, they provide no skill practice for the operational environment. Others appear more relevant, and not only illustrate a point, but provide practice that can transfer to the cockpit. However, when behavioral practice and feedback are used (typically in role plays), only a few volunteers or selected class members are able to directly benefit.

Trainees are expected to learn from each other and often discuss experiences that are related to the courses' learning points. This sharing of experience is intended to give trainees some workable solutions to real problems and may help them to be more aware of others as a potential source of information.

Although specific course content is not generally available for review, there is enough information about courses that strongly suggests similarities in their contents. The use of the Blake-Mouton Managerial Grid (Blake & Mouton, 1978) in CRM training began with United Airlines in 1979 (Orlady & Foushee, 1987), and since then, very simplified quad charts based on the Grid concepts have been incorporated in other programs, including Continental Airlines and Northwest Airlines (Jensen, 1989). United Airlines, Continental Airlines, and the 1550th Combat Crew all include the teaching of "inquiry and advocacy" (Orlady & Foushee, 1987). United Airlines and the 349th Military Air Wing both use a "synergy formula" in their training (Orlady & Foushee, 1987). These examples suggest that, while each program may be different in sum from all the others, the difference may be more in the combinations of program elements than in the elements themselves.

Coordination Skills

Even though there is some commonality in methodology, the lack of standardized definitions for the skill dimensions being addressed in the various CRM programs causes confusion when attempting to review and compare programs. One behavior may be classified under a number of skill dimension areas. Planning behaviors, for example, are classified under skill dimensions labeled "strategy development," "leadership," "delegation and assignment," and "plan development" (Orlady & Foushee, 1987). On the other hand, skill dimension names, from program to program, stand for combinations of different behaviors. The communication dimension for Trans-Australia Airlines (Davidson, 1987) includes training in how to be more assertive, training in the technical aspects of communication (summarizing, reflecting, directing, proposing), and problem-solving activities such as diagnosing and problem-and-solution inquiry. Krey and Rodgers (1987), who have provided ACT to a number of different operators, are proponents of a view that communications be taught with a model that covers interaction, information processing, and the making of decisions. Continental Air Lines approaches the training of communication by helping trainees understand the way they relate and communicate with others (Christian & Morgan, 1987). The CRM Curriculum Development Working Groups at a CRM conference in 1986 (Orlady & Foushee, 1987) recommended that communication include the subtopics of cultural influence, barriers, assertiveness, participation, listening, feedback, and legitimate avenue of dissent.

Variability of concepts across training programs likely reflects organizational and cultural differences among carriers. This represents a legitimate and perhaps optimal customizing of concepts to unique characteristics of the organization and its niche (Helmreich, Chidester, Foushee, Gregorich, & Wilhelm, 1989). From a research and evaluation perspective, however, a lack of agreement on the skill dimensions that are critical to crew coordination, and on the behaviors that comprise each skill dimension, presents real problems. Meaningful comparisons of concepts between programs are difficult and sometimes impossible to make. From this perspective the FAA Advisory Circular on CRM training may represent a first step towards a consensus of skills essential to crew coordination by suggesting that programs include such skills as communication, situation awareness, decision making, team management, stress management, team review (mission analysis), and interpersonal skills.

Cockpit coordination and resource management programs have borrowed heavily from management development programs; there is still more of value that can be applied to the cockpit. Prince and Salas (1989) reviewed CRM program materials for the skill dimensions and interactive behaviors considered necessary for training. These skill dimensions and behaviors were classified on a common basis with skill dimensions that were found to be associated with effective team performance (Morgan, Glickman, Woodward, Blaiwes, & Salas, 1986). The common basis used was a list of skills and their behavioral definitions that are routinely used in managerial assessment (Maher, 1983). This skill integration effort demonstrated a strong relationship between the CRM skills, team skills, and skills that have already been applied to the task of coordination in other work environments.

There are three advantages to establishing this commonality among the skill dimensions and adopting the existing behavioral definitions when appropriate: (a) a common understanding among programs can be established to aid communication and comparison; (b) the research results from the observation and training of these skills in management can be utilized; and (c) valuable team training research results can be applied to aircrew training. In a recent review (Franz, Prince, Cannon-Bowers, & Salas, 1990), these data were considered and combined with a needs analysis conducted with military helicopter pilots. The reviewers determined that the following seven skill dimensions should be included in an aircrew coordination training program for rotary wing pilots: communication, situational awareness, decision making, mission analysis, leadership, adaptation, and assertiveness. While differences in equipment and operations for other air communities require some variation in the skill dimensions required for effective coordination, there is sufficient similarity in team coordination requirements that these skill dimensions have relevance for other aircrews. The evidence of their potential application can be seen by comparing these skills to those identified in the FAA Advisory Circular. The skill dimensions for rotary wing pilots (Franz et al., 1990) were developed independently of the FAA Advisory Circular and provide more complete behavioral information for skill definitions, yet a remarkable similarity with the FAA suggested skills can be seen.

The seven skill dimensions can be classified into two major categories: taskwork skills and teamwork skills. Although all of the skills can be defined for an individual, the emphasis in crew coordination is on the group aspects of the skill dimensions.

The skill dimensions that refer primarily to taskwork are situational awareness, mission analysis, and decision making. These dimensions are closely related and are hypothesized to have the most immediate impact on crews' operational performance. Situational awareness is related to the managerial skill dimension of perception. It comprises, not only the crew member's knowledge of his or her current position in three-dimensional space, but the ability to accurately project this information into the future. This skill is dependent upon the perception of the individual, but the sharing of that information is crucial to the team. Mission analysis requires crew members to plan a sequence of subtasks for each mission and to monitor progress towards mission completion during the flight. Decision making encompasses the collection, integration, and implementation of data into the most effective strategy for successful task performance.

The teamwork skills of leadership and communication require at least two people for performance. In aircrew coordination, communication effectiveness depends primarily on the clarity and timeliness of the information presented. Several investigators have indicated that quality of communications is related to performance of air crews as well (Foushee & Manos, 1981; Ruffell-Smith, 1979). Leadership skills as applied to aircrew coordination include delegating tasks, providing feedback, promoting crew motivation, and creating a cockpit in which crew members can express alternatives without fear of criticism. Even though leadership is a clearly assigned position in the cockpit, leadership behaviors may be demonstrated by any crew member (Ginnett, 1986). Adaptability and assertiveness are closer to personal characteristics than are the other identified skills. Adaptation emphasizes the ability to change behaviors in order to meet changing demands during a flight, and is important, not only in reacting to the requirements of the flight, but also in reacting to other crew members. Because individuals often may feel intimidated by their colleagues' position or experience, they may be unwilling to present ideas. Assertiveness assures that the special knowledge of any individual crew member becomes general information for the entire crew.

Practice and Feedback

Program developers see LOFT as the opportunity for the practice of aircrew coordination, and trainee reactions invariably give high marks to the LOFT session, (Helmreich, Kello, Chidester, Wilhelm, & Gregorich, 1989). An informal survey of crews taking part in a LOFT-type scenario for research purposes found crews report learning from the experience even when there was no training given (Lauber & Foushee, 1981).

It is the combination of a highly realistic recreation of a work environment, coupled with the opportunity for self-confrontation, that are considered to be the strengths of LOFT. There is evidence of acceptance on the part of the trainees that the LOFT scenarios do elicit real behavior patterns. This can be seen in agreements for maintaining strict confidentiality of the crew's performance in the scenarios, and for the immediate erasure of the tapes after feedback.

There are no conclusive data on the effectiveness of LOFT for changing aircrew behavior, but there is an indication that it is a training technique that is accepted by crewmembers. Wilhelm, Helmreich, and Gregorich (1989) have looked at participant reactions to LOFT and found results that support LOFT training from the participant's viewpoint. Crewmembers value, not only the opportunity to practice dealing with critical situations in a realistic manner, but also the technical training of well-designed scenarios.

There are some practical questions about LOFT that have not yet been answered. Helmreich et al. (1989a) raised some important concerns, including how representative a scenario should be of an actual full line operation. They have noted that the use of simulation that most closely resembles operations puts a constraint on feedback being provided close to an action or event, and there is no evidence to determine whether timely feedback or realism are more valuable for training. Another training concern involves the effect of prior knowledge of a scenario's events on performance. With a limited number of scenarios, crewmembers may know what is required before their session in the simulator, but there is no information on how this knowledge affects performance.

Wilhelm et al. (1989) have identified a problem in the implementation of LOFT. They have found variability in the flight realism simulated by instructors, in the faithfulness of instructors to the LOFT scenario syllabus, and in the utilization of videotapes for feedback. This probably does not indicate active rejection of LOFT by instructors as much as a lack of training in its use and a genuine discomfort with how to conduct a debriefing. Instructors may not be sure of the specific behavior to look for and reinforce.

In awareness phase training, most instructors are typically line crewmembers who have expressed an interest in working with this type of training. Rarely have they worked with team training in other settings. As such, their role is viewed more as that of a facilitator than an instructor. Implementing training in this fashion represents a tradeoff between high credibility with the audience and in-depth knowledge of the psychology of group dynamics. Credibility is critical; nonpilot instructors are given little weight by pilots who may view the instructor as "knowing less about the job than I do." But at the same time, a credible facilitator may often encounter difficult questions. It is customary for the facilitator to turn the question back to the trainees to answer, rather than providing the "right" answer. While this technique may be effective for the awareness phase of training, it will likely be inadequate for the practice and feedback during LOFT. Those who evaluate crew performance in LOFT or on the line need to be familiar with the desired behaviors and specifically trained in observing behavior and providing feedback (Helmreich & Wilhelm, 1986).

A vital issue for optimal utilization of LOFT is the way trainees perceive the self-performance information the videotapes provide. *Self-awareness*, "the degree to which individuals understand their own strengths and weaknesses" (Wohlers & London, 1989, p. 236), has been identified as an important contributor to individual development (Holland, 1973). Duval and Wicklund (1972) had suggested that self-evaluation can occur when the self becomes an object of conscious awareness. They found that self-focus could be increased by allowing subjects to see themselves while performing a task.

Videotape offers the opportunity for an individual to be placed in the position of observer of his or her own behavior. It has been assumed that, with this self-focus, individuals would become aware of their own strengths and weaknesses in the task performed. Salomon and McDonald (1970), however, had found that, unless individuals know what the desired behaviors are, they are unable to accurately rate their own behaviors. Prince (1984) confirmed this finding with managerial candidates who watched their videotaped performance in simulated managerial scenarios. She found that, despite the trainees' confrontation with their own performance, self-ratings were no more accurate than those made by other subjects who had not been exposed to their own videotaped performance. It appeared that, without the knowledge of the behaviors that defined the skill categories to be rated, or the training in how these behaviors should be rated, self-confrontation was not sufficient to increase an individual's ability to judge his or her own performance. This research is particularly relevant to ACT, because the skill dimensions used are similar (e.g., leadership, communication, decision making). This suggests the importance of training instructors in the observation of necessary skill behaviors so that they may guide the videotape viewing session with the crew and provide the information on the desired behaviors (Helmreich et al., 1989a).

Instructors may also be helped by a relatively straightforward change in how LOFT scenarios are designed and scripted. Often LOFT scenarios are designed to fit time constraints or simulator limitations. Helmreich et al. (1989b) have suggested that LOFT design begin with a set of objectives that include a desired training outcome. If the objectives are well written and sufficiently specific, they can guide scenario design, communicate the designer's goals to the instructor, and in turn, guide the instructor's observation, evaluation, and debriefing. Both training for instructors and careful LOFT construction could lead to its more uniform and effective implementation.

In the decade of rapidly developing crew-coordination-training programs, the awareness phase of training has been most used. This has a basis in an assumption that awareness will change attitudes, and attitudes will change behavior. The link between attitude and behavior is not direct, however, and is affected by a number of other variables (Fishbein & Ajzen, 1975). Even when training includes an opportunity to practice new behaviors in the simulator, there has been no systematic attempt to teach the behaviors that need practice. There is clearly a gap between making trainees aware of the need for coordination, and having them practice coordination in a simulator. That gap may be filled by behavioral training in the specific skill dimensions that make up aircrew coordination.

THE SPECIFIC-BEHAVIOR APPROACH TO TRAINING

This section describes one general approach to training aircrew coordination that may be a valuable addition to training programs designed to accomplish attitude change: the specific-behavior approach. Specific-behavior training goes beyond the delineation of skill areas that must be trained to enhance aircrew coordination; it seeks to identify particular behaviors within skill dimensions that result in effective aircrew performance and, thus, require training. This is in contrast to programs which purport to be skill-based but do not specify skill areas at the behavioral level. In order to train and evaluate crew coordination, the construct of coordination is distilled into knowledge, skills, and abilities and expressed as a set of specific targeted behaviors. In other words, the specific behavioral complex that comprises aircrew coordination is systematically identified. This is akin to defining the concept of teamwork as it applies to cockpit operations.

Several areas of research converge to suggest that the training of specific behaviors may be an effective way to improve aircrew coordination. For example, various investigators have concluded that teamwork skills develop most efficiently when they are appropriately trained (e.g., Nieva, Fleishman, & Reick, 1978; Dyer, 1984). Further, Dyer (1984) has suggested that team training will be most effective when the skills (i.e., behaviors) to be trained are chosen using the following criteria: (a) skills that have been empirically demonstrated to have an effect on team success, (b) team skills that are difficult to learn, (c) skills that require more than simple repetition for development, (d) skills that require practice to prevent their loss, and (e) skills that may be infrequently required but are essential for survival. In addition, skills that are not included in higher level training programs should be chosen for training. The work of Glickman, Zimmer, Montero, Guerette, Campbell, Morgan, and Salas (1987), Morgan et al. (1986), and Oser, McCallum, and Salas (1989) have also added to our understanding of the behavioral basis of teamwork.

Training Interventions for a Behavior-Based ACT Program

Various methods have been used for skill dimension instruction in the existing CRM programs. It is likely that the interventions used are differentially effective in creating both long-term change in crew members and in improving effectiveness for the critical skill dimensions. Since relatively little research has been generated in training that is specific to aircrew coordination, there are little data to recommend the training interventions that will best train aircrew coordination skills. There is research in progress in the air transport community, but it has not yet yielded specific recommendations for training methodology (Helmreich & Wilhelm, 1986).

A review of the general training literature suggests a number of candidate training strategies for CRM. Two appear to be particularly well suited to behavior-based training, although there is no explicit information about their value for training. One of these is behavioral modeling. This intervention is based on the observation that people learn by imitating the behaviors of others when those behaviors result in positive outcomes. The second intervention is active practice with feedback, which is being provided on a limited basis through LOFT.

Because operational flight trainers are not available for repeated use throughout a training program, the potential for providing active practice with LOFT has been limited. It may be possible to develop low-fidelity simulation that will provide realistic coordination practice that can be used to augment LOFT sessions. Low-fidelity simulation typically includes presentation of either the entire task, or specific parts of the task, via computer. This type of simulation is a novel approach, but it appears to provide enough salient cues to elicit coordination behaviors (Stout, Cannon-Bowers, Salas, & Morgan, 1990).

Refresher Training for ACT

A final consideration with respect to training is that aircrew coordination skills may degrade with time. It is important to measure long-term changes in crew coordination behavior so that appropriate practice or refresher training can be developed. As mentioned above, some organizations do include ACT in their recurrent training. Without evidence of the duration of the effects of the initial training, the course content can only be based on opinions of course developers as to what should be included. Important organizational decisions about training cannot be based on complete information, only on the information we have to date.

EVALUATING ACT EFFECTIVENESS

While the need for aircrew coordination training has been well established, relatively few attempts to evaluate ACT effectiveness have been reported. An ACT evaluation project undertaken by NASA-Ames and the University of Texas (Helmreich & Wilhelm, 1986) is the only large scale attempt at evaluation and is still in progress. In this project, the CMAQ is being given to trainees before and after training, with the expectation that, as a result of the training, responses on the CMAQ will move in the direction of those associated with effective crew coordination. Reaction measures are being collected from trainees, and simulator performance of a limited number of crews is being rated. Early results from this study indicate there is a change in attitude as measured by the CMAQ, and that the reactions of trainees to CRM training are generally positive. Performance measurement does indicate that crews containing at least one member who has undergone some type of air crew coordination training perform better than those crews in which no member has had such training (Helmreich, Chidester, Foushee, Gregorich, & Wilhelm, 1989a, 1989b).

   Evaluating ACT effectiveness is critical for a number of reasons (Helmreich et al., 1989a; Cannon-Bowers, Prince, Salas, Owens, Morgan, & Gonos, 1989). According to Cannon-Bowers et al. (1989), aircrew coordination evaluation data can be used to provide feedback to both trainees and instructors, and to indicate: (a) if objectives are being met, (b) the appropriateness of the training content and methods, (c) how to maximize transfer of training, (d) suggestions for program improvement, and (e) the efficiency of training (i.e., time and resource expenditure in relation to program goals).

In order to achieve such diverse purposes, several researchers in the general training area (e.g., Benson, Riddlebarger, Hornsby, & Salas, 1988; Goldstein, 1986; Kirkpatrick, 1976) and aircrew coordination area (e.g., Orlady & Foushee, 1987; Chidester, 1987; Lauber & Foushee, 1981; Helmreich & Wilhelm, 1987, 1990; Jensen, 1987; Cannon-Bowers et al., 1989) have recommended a multivariable, multicomponent approach as a means to assess training effectiveness. The logic behind such an approach is that diverse types of information are needed to fulfill the evaluation purposes outlined above. This information is also required to provide confidence in evaluation results in the absence of a single, well defined, measurable "ultimate" criterion.

Framework for Evaluating ACT Effectiveness

Helmreich et al. (1989a, 1989b) propose two types of ACT effectiveness measures: outcome and process. *Outcome measures* include aircraft incidents, crew member attitudes, ratings of crew performance, and indirect measures (such as organizational climate). *Process measures* involve crew interaction and behavior as measured by expert raters and communication analyses.

Cannon-Bowers et al. (1989) have presented a comprehensive framework for ACT evaluation, based on the work of Kirkpatrick (1976). This framework includes several "levels" of evaluation variables, conceptualized as comprising an evaluation hierarchy. They include reactions to training, extent of learning, extent of performance change, and the impact of training on organizational effectiveness. In addition to the levels of evaluation proposed by Kirkpatrick, Cannon-Bowers et al. have added content validity and pre-training assessment. This approach to ACT evaluation casts the possible effectiveness measures into an organized framework for systematic study. The following describes each of these components.

Content Validity

Content validity refers to the extent to which a training program covers fully the universe of behaviors that comprise effective performance. Content validity is enhanced when training objectives are based on empirically determined knowledge, skills, and abilities.

Pretraining Assessment

The purposes of pretraining assessment are to establish a baseline with which posttraining measures can be compared (Goldstein, 1986), and to indicate "readiness" for training, or trainability. Trainability factors such as attitudes, self-confidence, expectations, and involvement in job and career have been shown to affect training motivation and outcomes (Goldstein, 1986). Assessment of trainability factors is critical for indicating whether unsuccessful outcomes are attributed to the program or to motivational problems, and to suggest interventions that may be needed to augment the program.

Reaction

Measuring reactions involves a posttraining assessment of trainee opinions about the training. According to Helmreich and Wilhelm (1987), enthusiastic endorsement of a program does not ensure desired behavioral change, but a failure to endorse can help indicate when a program is without value. These self-reported evaluations can provide important guidance for program modification.

Learning

This level of evaluation measures the learning of concepts, principles and information necessary for successful performance. Such information indicates how successfully the training program imparted targeted knowledge. Jensen (1987), in a review of ACT programs, reported that a variety of techniques have been used to assess learning, including paper-and-pencil questionnaires, interactive lectures, and small group discussions. Many researchers also employ posttraining attitude measures as an index of success.

Performance

Evaluating posttraining performance provides information regarding the extent to which trainees learned how, and when, to perform necessary skills and behaviors. While measures of performance change are desirable as indices of training effectiveness, they are often difficult to design and collect. Objective measures of performance (e.g., instrument readings, or time on task) are not typically sensitive enough to detect changes in behavior. Subjective measures (i.e., instructor ratings) can be more sensitive but are subject to error and bias and can be difficult to develop. In aircrew coordination training, Benson et al. (1988) and others (e.g., Orlady & Foushee, 1987) recommend use of flight simulators to provide necessary performance information. Helmreich and associates (e.g., Helmreich & Wilhelm, 1986, 1987) successfully trained expert observers in aircrew coordination and then had them observe and rate crews during a LOFT session and during operational flight. This process is facilitated by the development of behavioral definitions of the required coordination skills.

Another type of performance data that seems to be useful for ACT evaluation is communication patterns. Foushee and Manos (1981) found that these were significantly related to crew member errors in a large simulation study. These results were more recently replicated by Kanki et al. (1987).

Mission Effectiveness

The final level of Kirkpatrick's evaluation hierarchy is the extent to which a training program has an impact on overall organizational performance or mission effectiveness. This measurement is most difficult to accomplish, since a host of extraneous factors influence mission performance and confound assessments of performance.

None of these possible evaluations is easily completed or without potential problems. Helmreich and Wilhelm (1986) described barriers to achieving optimal evaluation. These included organizational differences in trainee characteristics, climate, and practices, as well as the political and ethical constraints within an organization against collecting data. Although it is the training program that is to be evaluated, trainees may perceive the evaluation to be personally threatening, and may be reluctant to submit to an evaluation process. This reluctance adds to the difficulties of collecting evaluation data in an area of complex, interrelated behaviors. Helmreich and Wilhelm (1986) addressed these constraints by designing an evaluation plan that includes the collection of levels of evaluation data but represents a necessary compromise between the optimum in evaluation and what could be realistically accomplished within organizational limitations.

The obstacles to evaluation have served to retard its progress. Aviation interests have the difficult but critical task to continue working toward the development of evaluation measures that approach the optimal, represent the levels of evaluation outlined above, and can be practically implemented.

Evaluation Summary

Each evaluation component with the kind of evaluation information it will yield is summarized in Table 12.1. Inspection of Table 12.1 reveals that the evaluation components are both complementary and interrelated. In isolation, each component provides specific data in support of a subset of evaluation questions. Together they can provide a comprehensive assessment of aircrew coordination training effectiveness.

SUMMARY

Almost 90 years after the Wright brothers, working together as a team, achieved the first recorded flight, the concept of teamwork has become an important element for the cockpit. Tremendous advances have occurred in the years follow-

Table 12.1.   Proposed Components of Evaluation and Resulting Data for Air Crew Training Effectiveness Evaluation

Purpose/Use of Data	Evaluation Component				
	1	2	3	4	5
Assess whether program objectives are met	X	X	X	X	X
Assess validity of program content		X	X	X	X
Assess training methods		X	X	X	
Assess trainee readiness for training	X				
Assess impact on individual trainees	X	X	X	X	
Assess impact on overall mission effectiveness				X	
Provide feedback to make program improvements	X	X	X	X	X

Component 1 = Pretraining Assessment
Component 2 = Trainee Reactions to Training
Component 3 = Learning Assessment
Component 4 = Performance Assessment
Component 5 = Mission Effectiveness Assessment

ing that first flight, with increases in the capabilities of aircraft, and in the size and tasks of the crews. Technical skill training has kept pace with the technological advances, but until recently, little attention has been paid to the training of the skills necessary for effective interaction with other crew members. The cost of this neglect has been high, with more than half of all aircraft incidents and accidents attributed to human error.

A review of the air crew coordination literature yields three critical points. The first is the recognition of the seriousness and importance of the behaviors in the cockpit. Training programs have been instituted to address this problem and are being widely implemented in both civil aviation and in the military (Orlady & Foushee, 1987; L. White, personal communication, November, 1989).

Thanks primarily to the research conducted under the auspices of NASA, there is some information available about the conduct of ACT programs, and trainee reactions to them (Helmreich et al., 1989a, 1989b), but evidence of the most effective methods for training CRM has not been presented. Individual differences are rarely addressed in the training, despite evidence that, not only can individual differences be discerned, but they have a relationship to aircrew performance (Ginnett, 1986; Chidester, 1987). With courses ranging in duration, in content, and in methods, no one training program has been established as superior, nor has any aspect of a program been proven effective for changing cockpit behavior. This second point to be made from a review of the aircrew coordination domain is the lack of a variety of evaluation information on the existing training programs.

The training of aircrews has been the focus of attention, with less concern demonstrated for the training of instructors. The third point is the critical need for the development of instructor training to provide the training skills and the confidence in those skills that are required for effective instruction (Wilhelm et al., 1989).

Fourth, due in part to the economic constraints of research, there has been far greater progress in the active development of programs than in investigation of critical elements of coordinated behavior in the cockpit. NASA-Ames has a well-established research program in cockpit resource management and has been responsible for much of the existing research knowledge. They have provided important information about communication, personality, and attitudes (Foushee & Helmreich, 1988). The magnitude of the investigation that is still required, however, suggests the need for the commitment of more resources and the involvement of additional research communities to expand the work that is being done. Air crew coordination is a complex area encompassing such issues as personality, behavior, attitude, communication, equipment design, and team training. Each of these issues presents numerous challenges for research and requires investigation from a variety of perspectives. Relatively recently, the military services have begun research into coordination and resource management requirements for their aviation communities. A coordinated effort among the various research interests could maximize their individual efforts and assure a more rapid response to the issues raised.

Observing a well-trained crew handle the technical aspects of aviation tasks can be impressive. This is what they were trained to do. The aviation community will truly benefit when the same level of expertise and facility in team function are routine in all phases of flight. More than 300 years after Wilkins used the word *spirits* as a means to flight, its meaning in the form of togetherness and communality—coordinated, concerted action—will finally be implemented in flight.

REFERENCES

Anderberg, M. R. (1973). *Cluster analysis for applications.* New York: Academic Press.
Benson, P. G., Riddlebarger, S., Hornsby, J. S., & Salas, E. (1988). *Assessment of team performance measurement techniques for training systems* (Tech. Rep. No. DAALo3-86-d-0001). Orlando, FL: Naval Training Systems Center.
Blake, P. R., & Mouton, J. S. (1978). *The new managerial grid.* Houston, TX: Gulf.
Cannon-Bowers, J. A., Prince, C. W., Salas, E., Owens, J. M., Morgan, B. B., & Gonos, G. H. (1989). Determining aircrew coordination training effectiveness. *Proceedings of the Eleventh Interservice/Industry Training Systems Conference.* Fort Worth, TX: National Security Industrial Association.
Chidester, T. R. (1987). Use of full-mission simulation to identify variables influencing

crew effectiveness. *Proceedings of the Commission of European Communities Workshop on Simulation in Traffic Systems.* Bremen, West Germany.

Chidester, T. R., & Foushee, H. C. (1989). Leader personality and crew effectiveness: A full-mission simulation experiment. In R. S. Jensen (Ed), *Proceedings of the Fifth International Symposium on Aviation Psychology.* Columbus, OH: Ohio State University.

Chidester, T. R., Helmreich, R. L., Gregorich, S., & Geis, C. E. (1991). Isolating subgroups of pilots on personality dimensions: Implications of cluster analyses for training and selection. *International Journal of Aviation Psychology, 1,* 29–42.

Chidester, T. R., Kanki, B. G., Foushee, H. C., Dickinson, C. L., & Bowles, S. V. (1990). *Personality factors in flight operations: I. Leader characteristics and crew performance in full-million air transport simulation* (NASA Technical Memorandum 102259). Moffett Field, CA: NASA-Ames Research Center.

Christian, D., & Morgan, A. (1987). Crew coordination concepts: Continental airlines CRM training. In H. W. Orlady & H. C. Foushee (Eds.), *Cockpit resource management training* (Tech. Rep. No. NASA CP-2455). Moffett Field, CA: NASA Ames Research Center.

Cooper, G. E., White, M. D., & Lauber, J. K. (Eds.). (1979). *Resource management on the flight deck* (NASA Conference Publication 2120). Moffett Field, CA: NASA-Ames Research Center.

Davidson, J. (1987). Introduction to Trans Australia Airlines CRM training. In H. W. Orlady & H. C. Foushee (Eds.), *Cockpit resource management training* (Tech. Rep. No. NASA CP-2455). Moffett Field, CA: NASA Ames Research Center.

Duval, S., & Wicklund, R. A. (1972). *A theory of objective self-awareness.* New York: Academic Press.

Dyer, J. (1984). Team research and team training: A state-of-the-art review. In F. Muckler (Ed.), *Human factors review* (pp. 285–323). Santa Monica, CA: Human Factors Society.

Fishbein, M., & Ajzen, I. (1975). *Belief, attitude, intention and behavior: An introduction to theory and research.* Reading, MA: Addison-Wesley Publishing Company.

Foushee, H. C., & Helmreich, R. L. (1988). Group interaction and flight crew performance. In E. L. Wiener & D. C. Nagel (Eds.), *Human factors in aviation.* San Diego, CA: Academic Press, Inc.

Foushee, H. C., & Manos, K. L. (1981). Information transfer within the cockpit: Problems in intracockpit communication. In C. E. Billings & E. S. Cheaney (Eds.), *Information transfer problems in aviation systems* (TP-1875). Moffitt Field, CA, NASA-Ames Research Center.

Franz, T. M., Prince, C., Cannon-Bowers, J. A., & Salas, E. (1990, April). *The identification of aircrew coordination skills.* Paper presented at the 12th Annual Department of Defense Symposium, U.S. Air Force Academy, Colorado Springs, CO.

Ginnett, R. C. (1986). *First encounters of the close kind: The first meetings of airline flight crews.* Unpublished doctoral dissertation, Yale University, New Haven, CT.

Glickman, A., Zimmer, S., Montero, R., Guerette, P., Campbell, W., Morgan, B., & Salas, E. (1987). *The evaluation of teamwork skills: An empirical assessment with implications for training* (Tech. Rep. No. 87-016). Orlando, FL: U.S. Naval Training Systems Center.

Goldstein, I. L. (1986). *Training in organizations: Needs assessment, development and evaluation.* Monterey, CA: Brooks/Cole Publishing Company.

Hackman, J. R. (1988). *Resource management training and cockpit crew coordination.* Invited address to the General Flight Crew Training Meeting, International Air Transport Association, New Orleans, LA.

Helmreich, R. L. (1984). Cockpit management attitudes. *Human Factors, 26,* 583–589.

Helmreich, R. L. (1986). *Studying flight crew behavior: A social psychologist encounters the real world.* Invited address to the annual meeting of the American Psychological Association, Washington, DC.

Helmreich, R. L. (1987). Exploring flightcrew behavior. *Social Behavior, 2,* 63–72.

Helmreich, R. L., Chidester, T. R., Foushee, H. C., Gregorich, S., & Wilhelm, J. A. (1989a). *How effective is Cockpit Resource Management Training: Issues in evaluating the impact of programs to enhance crew coordination* (NASA/UT Tech. Rep. No. 89-2. Draft 6.0). Moffett Field, CA: NASA Ames Research Center.

Helmreich, R. L., Chidester, T. R., Foushee, H. C., Gregorich, S., & Wilhelm, J. A. (1989b). *Critical issues in implementing and reinforcing Cockpit Resource Management Training* (NASA/UT Tech. Rep. No. 89-5). Moffett Field, CA: NASA Ames Research Center.

Helmreich, R. L., Foushee, H. C., Benson, R., & Russini, W. (1987). Cockpit management attitudes: Exploring the attitude behavior linkage. *Aviation, Space, and Environmental Medicine, 57,* 1198–1200.

Helmreich, R. L., Kello, J. E., Chidester, T. R., Wilhelm, J. A., & Gregorich, S. E. (1989). *Maximizing the operational impact of Line Oriented Flight Training: Lessons from initial observations* (NASA/UT Tech. Rep. No. 89-6). Moffett Field, CA: NASA Ames Research Center.

Helmreich, R. L., & Wilhelm, J. A. (1986). *Evaluating CRM training: I. Measures and methodology* (NASA/UT Tech. Rep. No. 86-8). Moffett Field, CA: NASA Ames Research Center.

Helmreich, R. L., & Wilhelm, J. A. (1987). Evaluating Cockpit Resource Management Training. In R. S. Jensen (Ed), *Proceedings of the Fourth International Symposium on Aviation Psychology* (pp. 440–446). Columbus, OH: Ohio State University.

Helmreich, R. L., & Wilhelm, J. A. (1989). When training boomerangs: Negative outcomes associated with Cockpit Resource Management programs. In R. S. Jensen (Ed), *Proceedings of the Fifth International Symposium on Aviation Psychology* (pp. 16–21). Columbus, OH: Ohio State University.

Helmreich, R. L., & Wilhelm, J. A. (1990) *Reinforcing and measuring flight crew resource management: Training captain/check airman/instructor reference manual* (NASA/UT Tech. Manual No. 90-2). Moffett Field, CA: NASA Ames Research Center.

Helmreich, R. L., Wilhelm, J. A., & Gregorich, S. (1988). *Revised versions of the cockpit management attitudes questionnaire (CMAQ) and CRM evaluation form* (NASA/UT Tech. Rep. No. 88-3). Moffett Field, CA: NASA Ames Research Center.

Helmreich, R. L., Wilhelm, J. A., & Gregorich, S. (1988). Notes on the concept of LOFT: An agenda for research. In T. R. Chidester (Ed.), *Emerging issues for the second decade of line oriented flight training* (NASA/UT Tech. Rep. No. 88-1). Moffett Field, CA: NASA Ames Research Center.

Helmreich, R. L., Wilhelm, J. A., Gregorich, S., & Chidester, T. R. (1990). Preliminary results from the evaluation of cockpit resource management training: Performance ratings of flightcrews. *Aviation, Space, and Environmental Medicine, 61*, 576–579.

Holland, J. L. (1973). *Making vocational choices: A theory of carriers.* Englewood Cliffs, NJ: Prentice-Hall.

Jenkins, C. D., Zyzanski, S. J., & Rosenman, R. H. (1971). Progress toward validation of a computer scored test for the Type A coronary prone behavior pattern. *Psychometric Medicine, 33*, 193–202.

Jensen, R. S. (1987). *Cockpit resource management training* (Final Report, Contract No. DTFA01-80-C-10080). Arlington, VA: Systems Control Technology, Inc.

Jensen, R. S. (Ed). (1989). *Proceedings of the Fourth International Symposium on Aviation Psychology.* Columbus, OH: Ohio State University

Kanki, B. G., Lozito, S. C., & Foushee, H. C. (1988). Communication indexes of crew coordination. *Aviation, Space, and Environmental Medicine, 60*, 56–60.

Kirkpatrick, D. L. (1976). Evaluation of training. In R. L. Craig (Ed.), *Training and development handbook: A guide to human resource development.* New York: McGraw Hill.

Krey, N. C., & Rodgers, D. (1987). CRM training for Parts 91 and 135 operations (SimuFlite). In H. W. Orlady & H. C. Foushee (Eds.), *Cockpit resource management training* (Tech. Rep. No. NASA CP-2455). Moffett Field, CA: NASA Ames Research Center.

Lauber, J. K. (1987). Cockpit resource management: Background studies and rationale. In H. W. Orlady & H. C. Foushee (Eds.), *Cockpit resource management training* (Tech. Rep. No. NASA CP-2455). Moffett Field, CA: NASA Ames Research Center.

Lauber, J. K., & Foushee, H. C. (1981). *Guidelines for line oriented flight training* (Tech. Rep. No. NASA CP-2184). Moffett Field, CA: NASA Ames Research Center.

Maher, P. (1983). An analysis of common assessment center dimensions. *Journal of Assessment Center Technology, 6*(3), 1–8.

Morgan, B. B., Glickman, A. S., Woodard, E. A., Blaiwes, A. S., & Salas, E. (1986). *Measurement of team behaviors in a Navy environment* (Tech. Rep. No. NTSC TR-86-014). Orlando, FL: Naval Training Systems Center.

Nieva, V. F., Fleishman, E. A., & Rieck, A. M. (1978). *Team dimensions: Their identity, their measurement, and their relationships.* Washington, DC: ARRO.

Orlady, H. W., & Foushee, H. C. (1987). *Cockpit resource management training* (Tech. Rep. No. NASA CP-2455). Moffett Field, CA: NASA Ames Research Center.

Oser, R., McCallum, G. A., & Salas, E. (1989). *Toward a definition of teamwork: An analysis of critical team behaviors* (Tech. Rep. No. NTSC TR-86-014). Orlando, FL: Naval Training Systems Center.

Pred, R. S., Spence, J. T., & Helmreich, R. L. (1986). The development of new scales for the Jenkins Activity Survey measure of the Type A construct. *Social and Behavioral Science Documents, 16*, 51–52 (Ms. No. 2769).

Prince, C. W. (1984). *The effect of self observation by videotape on self assessment of managerial skills in an assessment center.* Unpublished doctoral dissertation, Department of Psychology, University of South Florida, Tampa, FL.

Prince, C. W., & Salas, E. (1989). Aircrew performance coordination and skill development. In D. E. Daniels, E. Salas, & D. M Kotick (Eds.), *Independent research and independent exploratory development (IR/IED) programs: Annual report FY88* (Tech. Rep. No. NTSC 89-009). Orlando, FL: Naval Training Systems Center.

Rodale, J. I. (1978). *The synonym finder*. New York: Warner Books.

Ruffell-Smith, H. P. (1979). *A simulator study of the interaction of pilot workload with errors, vigilance, and decisions* (NASA TM-78482). Moffett Field, CA: NASA-Ames Research Center.

Salomon, G., & McDonald, F. J. (1970). Pretest and posttest reactions to self-viewing one's teaching performance on video tape. *Journal of Educational Psychology, 61*(4), 581–596.

Spence, J. T., & Helmreich, R. L. (1978). *Masculinity and feminity: Their psychological dimensions, correlates, and antecedents*. Austin, TX: University of Texas Press.

Spence, J. T., & Helmreich, R. L. (1983). Achievement-related motives and behavior. In J. T. Spence (Ed.), *Achievement and achievement motives: Psychological and sociological approaches*. New York: W. H. Freeman & Co.

Spence, J. T., Helmreich, R. L., & Holman, C. K. (1979). Negative and positive components of psychological masculinity and feminity and their relationships to self-reports of neurotic and acting out behaviors. *Journal of Personality and Social Psychology, 37*, 1673–1682.

Stout, R., Cannon-Bowers, J., Salas, E., & Morgan, B. B. (1990). Does crew coordination behavior impact performance? *Proceedings of the Human Factors Society 34th Annual Meeting*. Santa Monica, CA: Human Factors Society.

The New Encyclopedia Brittanica, 7, 380. (1984). Chicago, IL: Encyclopedia Britannica, Inc.

White, L. (1987). Cockpit resource management training (an international survey). In H. W. Orlady & H. C. Foushee (Eds.), *Cockpit resource management training* (Tech. Rep. No. NASA CP-2455). Moffett Field, CA: NASA Ames Research Center.

Wiener, E. L. (1988). Cockpit automation. In E. L. Wiener & D. C. Nagel (Eds.), *Human factors in aviation*. San Diego, CA: Academic Press, Inc.

Wilhelm, J. A., Helmreich, R. L., & Gregorich, S. E. (1989). *LOFT from the airman's perspective* (NASA/UT Tech. Rep. No. 89-3). Moffett Field, CA: NASA Ames Research Center.

Wohlers, A. J., & London, M. (1989). Ratings of managerial characteristics: Evaluation difficulty, co-worker agreement, and self-awareness. *Personnel Psychology, 42*, 235–262.

13

Work Teams in Industry: A Selected Review and Proposed Framework

Janis A. Cannon-Bowers
Randall Oser
Deborah L. Flanagan

INTRODUCTION AND OVERVIEW

There is clearly a consensus among those who study industrial and organizational behavior that work groups are the cornerstone of modern American industry (Hackman & Morris, 1975; Cummings, 1981; Shea & Guzzo, 1987; Sundstrom, De Meuse, & Futrell, 1990). According to Hackman and Morris (1975), for example, "genuinely important tasks" are typically assigned to groups for solution (p. 1). Cummings (1981) describes work groups as the "basic components comprising organizations and the contexts within which workers work" (p. 250). Given these sentiments regarding the importance of work groups in industry, it is not surprising that they have been the topic of countless theories and studies over the past century. Unfortunately, due to the complexities inherent in studying work groups in organizations, the literature tends to be fragmented, incomplete, and sometimes contradictory. Despite this contention, it is nonetheless important to glean from past work those lessons that are potentially beneficial to work group design and function. The purpose of this chapter is to first review the types of work groups that are popular in industry and the kinds of functions they perform; and then to present a summary of empirical literature regarding several types of work groups common in industry. Finally, a proposed framework to guide researchers and practitioners interested in work team design and performance will be presented.

STUDYING WORK GROUP EFFECTIVENESS IN INDUSTRY

Determining the ideal structure, organization, and functioning of work groups in industry has been the subject of countless investigations reported in the literature. Despite this volume of work, however, it is difficult to draw definitive conclusions regarding work group effectiveness or optimal work group design. This is due, in part, to the fact that many different types of work groups are employed in industry, each with its own task, structure, and goals. Table 13.1, which lists several common types of work teams, indicates that there is wide diversity in the kinds of teams employed in industry, and in what they are expected to accomplish (Guest, 1986).

Inspection of Table 13.1 also raises an important question regarding *why* work groups are such a popular form of organization in industry. The answer to this question appears to be multifaceted. First, some tasks simply cannot be accomplished by a single individual working alone. For example, tasks that require simultaneous processing, particularly high workload, or a variety of expertise demand the pooled effort of several individuals for completion. Examples of

Table 13.1.   Common Types of Work Teams Employed in Industry

Task Force Teams
Problem-Solving Teams
Quality Circles
Productivity Action Teams
Multidisciplinary Teams
Multiskilled Teams
Semiautonomous Work Groups
Management Teams
Committees
Employee Involvement Groups
Production Teams
Maintenance and Repair Crews
Research & Development Teams
Product Development Groups
Planning Commissions
Negotiating Teams
Medical/surgery Teams
Cockpit Crews
Instructor Teams
Delivery Crews
Athletic Teams

teams in this category include air crews, research and development teams, surgical teams, and sports teams.

The second reason why industry may employ teams is the notion that teams perform better than individuals working independently (Hackman & Morris, 1975). This belief stems from the "two heads are better than one" adage, but is not necessarily supported by research into small group behavior (e.g., Kidd, 1961; Steiner, 1972). Groups formed for this reason include problem-solving groups, management teams, and various types of committees. Related to this, particularly dangerous or critical tasks (e.g., nuclear power operations) are seen to benefit from the redundancy that teams can offer.

A final reason that group-centered structure has become popular in industry has grown out of the humanistic movement in management theory. Specifically, participative management (Likert, 1967), job design (Hackman & Oldham, 1980), and sociotechnical systems theory (Davis & Trist, 1979) all have in common the notion that workers must be involved meaningfully in, and share responsibility for, the organization's functioning. Further, these perspectives hold that workers must have opportunities for self-expression, self-development, and involvement in order to achieve desired organizational outcomes. Work groups are seen as a means to achieve these objectives. In keeping with this view, Cummings (1981) maintained that work groups are expected to achieve technological, political, and human outcomes simultaneously. Examples of groups in industry formed for these reasons include semiautonomous work groups, multiskilled teams, and quality circles.

Because work teams are formed to accomplish a variety of purposes, research investigating work team effectiveness is inherently complex. To complicate matters further, such groups must function in a larger organizational context. By adopting a systems approach to the study of work groups in industry, it becomes apparent that several classes of variables must be considered at the input, process, and output levels when studying work group effectiveness. These include organization-level variables (e.g., technology, structure, nature of supervision), individual member variables (e.g., skills, expectations), group-level variables (e.g., strategy, norms, communication patterns), various outcome measures (e.g., productivity, member satisfaction), and task requirements and characteristics.

SELECTED REVIEW OF WORK GROUP
EFFECTIVENESS LITERATURE

The review of the literature that follows is limited to three types of work groups employed in industry: quality circles, semiautonomous work groups, and research and development teams. These types of work groups were selected for review for several reasons. First, they are popular manifestations of the work

group in industry; second, they vary considerably in mission and function, allowing for a broad exposure to literature; and third, they have all been subject to a
fair amount of empirical study.

Quality Circles

Quality circles (QCs) originated in Japanese industry in the late 1950s as a means
to improve quality standards and productivity (Ferris & Wagner, 1985; Steele &
Shane, 1986). Influenced by Americans Edward Deming and J. M. Duran, QCs
seek to gather worker-level consultation in identifying and resolving work-related problems (Steele & Shane, 1986). QCs typically consist of between 3 to 15
members and employ a variety of problem-solving techniques (Ferris & Wagner,
1985).

Quality circles in the U.S. have changed in focus somewhat from Japanese
predecessors (Steele & Shane, 1986). According to Barrick and Alexander
(1987), Japanese QCs have maintained an emphasis on quality and productivity
issues, with attitudinal changes seen as a by-product of the process. On the other
hand, American QCs seem to focus primarily on human process (i.e., attitudinal)
variables. In fact, QCs are often included as part of larger *quality of worklife*
(QWL) interventions that are aimed at improving employee well-being and morale (Ferris & Wagner, 1985; Mohrman & Lawler, 1984; Zahra, 1984; Drago,
1988).

The issue raised above regarding what QCs can be expected to accomplish
(i.e., quality or attitudinal improvement) is, in large part, an empirical one.
Unfortunately, however, reviewers of the QC literature uniformly agree that the
caliber of empirical research in this area is seriously low (Griffin, 1988; Steele &
Shane, 1986; Barrick & Alexander, 1987; Ferris & Wagner, 1985). Specifically,
the literature on QC effectiveness is characterized by anecdotal case studies,
testimonials, and other nonscientific methods (Barrick & Alexander, 1987;
Marks, Mirvis, Hackett, & Grady, 1986; Ferris & Wagner, 1985). In addition,
many programs are not evaluated at all (Greenbaum, Kaplan, & Metlay, 1988).
Consequently, it is impossible to draw definitive conclusions regarding the impact of QCs on organizational outcomes, or factors that contribute to QC effectiveness.

Despite methodological shortcomings, investigations into QC effectiveness
are deserving of review, since they can provide some insight into optimal team
design and effectiveness. The following section is not meant to represent a
comprehensive review of all QC literature; rather, it will survey recent studies in
this area. To this end, research will be organized into two sections: the effects of
QCs on various outcome measures, and input/process factors that contribute to
QC effectiveness.

Impact of QCs on Individual and Organizational Outcomes

Recently, Barrick and Alexander (1987) reviewed 33 studies of QC effectiveness conducted in the 1980s. These authors were particularly interested in determining whether a positive reporting bias existed in QC efficacy research (i.e., a tendency for only positive results to be reported). The studies reviewed included a variety of outcome measures at the individual and organizational levels. Results of this descriptive review did not confirm a positive reporting bias. Of the 33 studies, 16 reported positive findings, 9 reported mixed or nonsignificant findings, and 8 reported uniformly negative findings (Barrick & Alexander, 1987). The authors noted further that, of the 8 negative studies, 5 were conducted in Department of Defense organizations, indicating that something in these settings may inhibit QC success.

In other recent work, a longitudinal study by Marks et al. (1986) comparing 46 QC participants to a group of control employees in a manufacturing setting found significant differences in QWL attitudes in areas proximal to the QC. These included: perceived involvement, participation and communication, and perceived opportunity for accomplishment and self-development. No differences were found in perceived job characteristics. Marks et al. pointed out, however, that these postintervention differences were not due to improvement of QC participants in these areas, but to significant declines in the control group over the 24-month experimental period. The authors concluded that QCs appeared to have buffered participants from negative organizational factors. Finally, Marks et al. (1986) did find significant improvements in productivity and declines in absenteeism in the QC groups.

In a second longitudinal study that included a control group design, Griffin (1988) found significant changes in job satisfaction, organizational commitment, performance (rated by supervisors), intention to quit (negative), and managerial assessment of QC effectiveness 18 months after QCs were introduced into a manufacturing plant. Measures of these variables then declined, however, eventually reaching their original levels. Given these results, Griffin (1988) suggested that the Lawler and Mohrman (1987) notion of a "honeymoon effect" may have been a viable explanation of effects. According to Lawler and Mohrman (1987), the initial period when QCs are introduced is when gains can be expected. These authors concluded that QCs may best be viewed as a transitional technique useful for moving an organization toward more participative management practices.

Two recent studies regarding the impact of QCs on supervisor/subordinate relationships also obtained some positive results. First, Zahra (1984) reported survey results indicating that a majority of supervisors who participated in QCs with their subordinates reported that relationships with staff were improved as a result of QC participation. A majority also reported that QC leadership helped them to perform their jobs better, and that, overall, QCs had a positive impact on the organization.

In a second study, Berman and Hellweg (1989) investigated supervisor/subordinate relations as a function of QC participation in a large defense contracting organization. Results indicated that, compared with control subjects, subordinates who participated in QCs with their supervisors reported high satisfaction with supervisors and perceived them to have higher competence in communication. The authors concluded that QCs provide opportunities for supervisors and subordinates to increase the quality of communication via joint participation in decision making (Berman & Hellweg, 1989).

Henry and Malmstrom (1985) recently investigated a different outcome factor: the problem-solving skills of QC participants. Results of this study did not support hypotheses that problem-solving skills would be better in QC participants than in nonparticipants. Namely, control group subjects were more flexible in their problem-solving approach, more prone to recognize problems, and more willing to accept and delegate authority than QC participants. The authors speculated that the organizational setting (i.e., that it was a government rather than private facility) may have contributed to negative results (Henry & Malmstrom, 1985).

In another recent investigation, Krigsman and O'Brien (1987) compared the impact of QCs to a self-monitoring instructions intervention on absenteeism, lost time, and clip losses (i.e., a waste measure). Results indicated that the self-monitoring instructions were initially as effective as QCs in decreasing waste, but not as enduring. Clip losses in self-monitoring groups returned to baseline after the instructions had been withdrawn. In addition, QC groups showed significantly less absenteeism and lost time compared to controls; self-monitoring groups showed no such changes.

As is evident to this point, a number of studies to date have reported that QCs produce positive changes in organizations. This conclusion is sufficient to warrant future attention of QCs as a viable organizational tool. Caution must be advised, however, since mixed and negative results were also commonly found.

Input/Process Factors in QC Effectiveness

A second group of studies in the literature has been concerned with the input and process factors that affect QC functioning. Nagamachi, Nakai, Hatamoto, and Matsushima (1989) recently reported, for example, that 23 QCs rated "best" could be distinguished from 23 rated "worst" on the basis of questionnaire responses concerning management policy, organizational culture, involvement, and knowledge of QC problem-solving techniques. From this analysis, the authors concluded that "soft" (i.e., participative) management "supports the work of QC activity" (p. 844).

Wayne, Griffin, and Bateman (1986) also attempted to distinguish more effective from less effective QCs. In this case QC ratings were based on three criteria: number of improvements suggested by the group, number of suggestions adopted by management, and member satisfaction. A median split of ratings was employed, yielding 22 QCs that were classified as "more effective," and 23 that were classified as "less effective." Results revealed no significant differences between more and less effective QCs in member age, age range, tenure, satisfaction with leader, or extrinsic satisfaction. Significant differences between groups were found, however, in cohesion, performance norms, job satisfaction, self-esteem, and perceived organizational commitment to QCs, with effective QCs being higher on all variables. Wayne et al. (1986) concluded that these factors all contribute to QC effectiveness. Given the design, however, it is impossible to determine the direction of causality. For example, contrary to the authors' conclusions, QC effectiveness may cause higher levels of satisfaction and cohesion, rather than being a result of these factors.

In another study concerned with QC success factors, Honeycutt (1989) surveyed 83 QC members at an aircraft manufacturing plant. Results of a multiple regression analysis indicated that member training and perceived management support were significantly related to member-rated QC effectiveness. Honeycutt concluded that, based on these results in combination with past findings, no single success factor seems to emerge in QCs, although member training seems to be more potent than others.

In another survey study, Drago (1988) investigated QC survival rates in 42 organizations. Results of this investigation revealed that participative management practices, union support and job insecurity (measured as layoffs) were all positively related to QC survival. One variable, skill level of members, was negatively related to survival. Those factors that did not affect survival included worker interdependence, minority participation, number of blue collar workers, organization size, and whether the organization was in the private or public sector (Drago, 1988).

Two recent studies were concerned with the differences in QC performance based on whether or not the QC was initiated by management or workers. Results of the first study (Tang, Tollison, & Whiteside, 1987) suggested that self-initiated QCs (i.e., initiated by employees) had more members than management-initiated, but that management-initiated QCs solved more work related problems and solved problems significantly faster. In the second study, Tang, Tollison, and Whiteside (1989) added the variables of upper management attendance and collar color as predictors of QC performance. Results indicated that these two variables interacted with initiation source such that self-initiated QCs with low management attendance had slower problem-solving speed compared to those with higher management attendance. In addition, self-initiated QCs whose members were white collar solved problems more slowly than blue collar counterparts. There was also a main effect for upper management attendance; those QCs with high attendance outperformed those with low attendance (Tang et al., 1989). Taking the results of these studies together, it appears that the source of QC initiation and management involvement are important factors in QC efficacy.

A final study related to QC performance, conducted by Stohl and Jennings (1988), focused on the differences between employees who volunteered for QC participation versus those who did not. Since most QCs in the U.S. are voluntary, these authors reasoned that it is important to determine the characteristics of those who are willing to engage in QC activity, particularly as these are related to QC success. Results of this study revealed that, compared to nonvolunteers, volunteers tended to have lower intrinsic job satisfaction, perceived a less positive communication climate, were younger, had more education, and had shorter organizational tenure. Volunteers also tended to believe that the organization was supportive of innovation and were slightly more committed to the organization than nonvolunteers (although not significantly so).

Stohl and Jennings (1988) interpreted these findings as an indication that QC volunteers were "dissatisfied with key aspects of their jobs, but were not yet alienated from the organization" (p. 247). Further, volunteers believed that they could effect positive changes in their workplace and were willing to try. Such expectations at the onset of a QC can be both good and bad, according to the authors. On the one hand, QC volunteers will be motivated to initiate positive changes. On the other, since QCs are often narrow in scope, they may not have an impact on important issues such as wages or rewards, and offer only limited participation opportunities (Stohl & Jennings, 1988). In fact, frustration resulting from unfulfilled expectations of QCs may be a primary cause of QC failure.

Results presented above provide insight into factors that may contribute to the success of QCs in American industry. Perhaps the most damaging criticism of these studies, however, deals with generalizability of results. Given the complexity of organizational contexts, it is reasonable to expect that organization-specific factors may have an impact on QC efficacy. Intraorganizational comparison of QC success factors is needed to investigate this possibility.

Semiautonomous Work Groups

The use of *semiautonomous work groups* (also called *autonomous work groups, self-regulating work groups,* or *self-managing teams*) represents one approach to organizational structure that grew out of the Sociotechnical systems movement of the 1950s (Davis & Trist, 1979). Briefly, sociotechnical systems interventions seek to optimize the relationship between the social (human) systems of an organization and its technology (Pasmore, Francis, Haldeman, & Shani, 1982). Examples of such interventions include redesigning of jobs or work methods, redesigning of social structures, or modification of technology (Pasmore & Sherwood, 1978; Pasmore et al., 1982). Semiautonomous work groups (SAWGs) are intended to facilitate integration of social and technical systems by allowing groups of employees to manage themselves (Pearce & Ravlin, 1987).

SAWGs have several distinguishing characteristics, including group control of work task assignments, a multiple-skill-based task, a whole identifiable piece of work, control of group maintenance functions, and a relatively permanent lifecycle (Pearce & Ravlin, 1987). Typically, SAWG interventions organize workers into groups that are responsible for an entire task or product. Group members are interdependent, jointly accountable for group functioning, and self-regulating. The arrangement of work is such that cooperative interaction is encouraged, workers have the opportunity to learn all jobs in the group, and groups have the authority, materials, and equipment to perform their jobs (Pearce & Ravlin, 1987). Susman (1975) adds that, to be effective, SAWGs must also offer continuing challenge to group members via nonroutine decision making and task uncertainty.

SAWGs have been employed fairly extensively in Europe, but have only recently received acceptance in the United States. In a recent review of sociotechnical systems theory in North America, Pasmore et al. (1982) found that SAWGs were the most popular form of sociotechnical systems intervention. Of the 134 studies they reviewed, 53% included SAWGs. Overall, proponents of SAWGs maintain that they are an intrinsically motivating form of organization that will lead to enhanced productivity, quality, and motivation, as well as to improved employee attitudes toward their jobs, the organization, and themselves.

The state of research aimed at evaluating the effectiveness of SAWGs in organizations is much like the research concerning quality circles. Specifically, few scientifically rigorous investigations of SAWG effectiveness have been reported (Pearce & Ravlin, 1987; Pasmore et al., 1982). Further, since SAWGs are often only one component of a larger, multifaceted organizational development program, it is difficult to determine which outcomes can be attributed to SAWGs alone.

The following section provides an overview of SAWG effectiveness research conducted in recent years. First, studies will be reviewed that have attempted to assess the impact of SAWGs on organizational outcomes. Following this, studies concerned with input/process factors in SAWG effectiveness will be reviewed.

Impact of SAWGs on Individual and Organizational Outcomes

A study by Trist, Susman, and Brown (1977), conducted in a coal mine, made both longitudinal comparisons (i.e., before and after the introduction of SAWGs into the organization), and cross-sectional comparisons between autonomous and nonautonomous groups on a number of variables. Results indicated that violations of health and safety rules, accidents, and lost time all decreased as a function of SAWG organization. In addition, while productivity decreased in nonautonomous groups due to new safety rules, it was maintained in SAWGs. Also positively affected were perceived autonomy by workers, interdependence of team members, and the belief that supervisors had to make fewer decisions. Interview data suggested further that workers liked the system. Upon union vote, however, workers declined to institutionalize SAWGs, and the program was discontinued. Trist et al. cite several possible reasons for this action: jealousy by other groups in the organization, perceived inequity among workers, and union busting (Trist et al., 1977).

Kemp, Wall, Cleg, and Cordery (1983) also reported some positive changes due to SAWGs in a greenfield site (i.e., a newly formed plant). Compared with controls, perceived intrinsic job characteristics, job satisfaction, work complexity, and involvement in decision making all increased in SAWG groups. No differences were found, however, in motivation, mental health, or trust in management. Wall, Kemp, Jackson, and Clegg (1986), reporting results from the same site, added that turnover was higher in SAWGs and that productivity did not improve. Overall, the results of these two investigations cannot be taken as strong support for the SAWG concept.

Another set of studies that have reported changes in organizations due to introduction of SAWGs have in common the fact that no control or comparison groups were employed, and no statistical analyses of data were performed (e.g., Aquilano, 1977; Archer, 1975; Burden, 1975; Walton, 1977; Poza & Markus, 1980). Interestingly, these studies uniformly reported that positive changes resulted from the introduction of SAWGs in such dependent variables as productivity, absenteeism, turnover, meeting deadlines, customer complaints, cost savings, satisfaction, and job involvement. In at least two cases, however, SAWGs were dropped or phased out after the investigation. Due to a lack of experimental rigor, it is impossible to evaluate fully the significance of these results.

Input/Process Factors in SAWGs

A recent study by Seers (1989) investigated the relationship of *team-member interaction quality* (TMX) with satisfaction measures, cohesiveness, and leader–member exchange quality in SAWGs. Conducted in a small, unionized automotive plant, results of this study indicated that TMX was moderately correlated with all satisfaction measures (i.e., work, supervisor, co-worker, pay, and general) and with leader–member exchange quality. Further, TMX predicted rated performance, and interacted with perceived peer motivation such that the impact of low TMX was compensated for by high peer motivation. Finally, in a follow-up data collection effort, Seers found that "team-oriented" groups (i.e., more autonomous) had higher TMX than more traditionally structured groups.

Seers (1989) concluded from this investigation that the quality of intrateam interactions is important to desired organizational outcomes. Further, these results indicate that autonomously managed teams will experience higher quality team-member interaction than more traditionally structured teams.

In an investigation of leadership behavior in SAWGs, Manz and Sims (1987) recently reported that traditional leader behaviors may be inappropriate in SAWGs. Based on observation and interviews in a small, nonunionized plant, these researchers developed a *self-management leadership questionnaire* (SMLQ) that included items such as encourages self-reinforcement, encourages self-criticism, encourages rehearsal, and communicates to/from management. Analysis revealed that the scale was significantly related to assessments of leader effectiveness by team members. The strongest relationship was between effectiveness ratings and the item "encourages self-observation/self-evaluation." Manz and Sims concluded that effective leadership in SAWGs is different from what is traditionally considered effective leadership. In fact, the difference between them is fundamental; traditional leadership behaviors assume that influence flows from the top-down, while self-managing leadership assumes a bottom-up perspective (Manz & Sims, 1987). This suggests that SAWG effectiveness may depend upon a form of leadership that is not commonly practiced in organizations.

Koch (1979) reported a study involving introduction of group-centered goals and feedback on workers in a sewing factory. Results of this investigation indicated that positive changes were recorded in the experimental group in terms of increased group cohesion, commitment, quality, goal emphasis, and group process. In addition, turnover decreased in the experimental group, but this change could not be attributed solely to the goal setting intervention. Koch also reported that job satisfaction and job challenge declined in both experimental and control groups. While it is difficult to draw conclusions from these data, Koch suggested that group-level feedback may be a useful intervention when transitioning to SAWGs, due to its positive effects on cohesion, goal emphasis, and group process.

Two other studies investigating factors that affect SAWGs involved status of members. First, Susman (1970) found in an oil refinery that high status group members were more successful in obtaining the job of their preference. Susman concluded that formal position differentiation in work groups may result in lower status members remaining underskilled; as a result, work group potential may not be exploited fully. In a second study investigating status, O'Reilly and Roberts (1977) found a positive main effect of group status on performance effectiveness. Other results indicated that group size was negatively related to group connectedness, and that information accuracy and communication openness were significantly related to effectiveness.

A final study of SAWGs to be presented here was conducted by Blumberg (1980) and involves job switching (i.e., job rotation). Blumberg hypothesized that not all employees in a coal mine would be satisfied with job switching.

Results of this multivariable study suggested that several factors were significantly related to a worker's tendency to engage in job switching, including positive association with education, attitude, degree of task hazard, task identity, and feedback; and negative correlations with authoritarianism, job satisfaction, seniority, age, and status. Blumberg concluded that work group designers must recognize the dynamics of job switching, and provide a "path for job switching" for those who desire it (p. 304).

As is obvious at this point, a host of variables have been studied in conjunction with SAWG performance. Many of these support the notion that identifiable input and process factors have an impact on how well SAWGs function. Unfortunately, as with research associated with QCs, results have been largely inconsistent and fragmented. By and large, the lack of scientific rigor characteristic of these studies precludes formation of generalizations regarding SAWG effectiveness or design.

Research and Development Teams

Another form of work group organization popular in industry involves groups of professionals whose mission is to conduct research, design, and planning (Sundstrom & Altman, 1989). Such groups include engineering product groups, technical service groups, product development teams, and planning commissions. These work structures are often permanent components of the organization, although group membership may vary from project to project. A popular form of this latter type of structure is the matrix organization.

Matrix organizations seek to cope with environmental uncertainty or turbulence by superimposing a project structure over a functional structure (Szilagyi & Wallace, 1983). The vertical components of the organization represent typical organizational departments (e.g., marketing, manufacturing, contracting, etc.), while the horizontal components represent projects with their specific needs. When a project is initiated, a team of individuals is brought together from different departments so that an optimal collection of expertise is achieved (Szilagyi & Wallace, 1983). The logic behind such organization stems from the fact that dynamic environments require organizations to make rapid adjustments under conditions of high complexity and information-processing demands. The matrix structure, with work teams at its core, allows the organization to adapt quickly to the particular needs of a project via manipulation of group composition and expertise. The following sections describe research into R&D team communication and effectiveness.

Communication Factors in R&D Teams

The majority of studies investigating R&D team effectiveness conducted in the past are related to communication, particularly communication between R&D

teams and extragroup entities (including other organizational groups and extra-organizational constituents).

In an early study, Rubenstein, Barth, and Douds (1971) investigated factors that contributed to effective communication between 60 R&D groups in public and private laboratories. They found that differences in work-related values did not impede communication between groups, and that groups who perceived themselves to be mutually interdependent tended to have fewer communication problems. In addition, level of technical respect, communication frequency, and preference for participative decision making all contributed positively to communication effectiveness (Rubenstein et al., 1971).

In another early study, Allen and Cohen (1969) investigated information flow in R&D laboratories. These authors concluded that the structure of technical communication within the laboratories was a function of both social relations and formal structure. They also found evidence that "gate keepers" existed in each laboratory who served as a link between the group and external technical information. This finding was later supported by Tushman (1977).

In a series of investigations, Tushman and colleagues studied the relationship between communication patterns, task characteristics and project performance. To begin with, Katz and Tushman (1979) classified 61 R&D teams in an industrial laboratory into four distinct types: basic research, general research, development, and technical service. They hypothesized that, due to varying informational demands among these task types, effective team performance would require different communication patterns. Results indicated that overall communication frequency (both within and outside the organization) was not significantly related to project performance for any task type.

Perhaps more interesting, however, was the finding that significant differences did exist between task types with respect to the kind of communication being considered. For research tasks, frequency of problem-solving communications with external professionals, other organizational divisions, and within the group combined to predict performance. In addition, administrative communication at the corporate level was negatively related to research project performance. Performance for development projects, on the other hand, was significantly related only to the extent of problem-solving communication at the corporate level. Finally, technical service projects appeared to benefit from problem-solving contacts with external professionals but were hindered by administrative communication within the group and within the laboratory (Katz & Tushman, 1979).

This study found further that the nature of the communication linkage between project teams and external groups varied as a function of task types. Specifically, research projects appeared to benefit from widespread, direct contact of all members with external groups, while technical service projects were more successful when a single "boundary spanning" (i.e., gatekeeper) individual mediated communications (p. 159). This finding was replicated by Allen, Lee, and Tushman (1980). In fact, Allen et al. concluded that, when one or only a few research or development team members are responsible for communication, project performance is likely to be impaired. Further support for results regarding gatekeeper functions and effectiveness was found in a study by Tushman and Katz (1980). Briefly, gatekeepers were found to be more important for locally oriented projects (i.e., routine, technical service tasks) than for universally oriented projects (i.e., complex, research tasks).

In two more studies Tushman (1979a,b) added the variable of environmental uncertainty to assess the degree to which it affects optimal communication structures in R&D teams. To summarize the findings of these studies, Tushman reported first that, in high-performing groups, environmental uncertainty was handled differently according to the nature of the project (1979a,b). Second, both studies found that complex research projects increased intrateam communication in response to greater environmental uncertainty, while more routine technical service projects relied on less intrateam communication. In addition, research projects were less hierarchically structured then technical service projects, particularly when considering only high performing teams (Tushman, 1979b). High environmental variability also led to more decentralization in research projects, but to more centralization in technical service projects.

Tushman concluded from this work that increased task complexity appears to demand higher degrees of teamwork in the form of shared decision making, information exchange, support, and feedback, and that this is particularly true when environmental uncertainty is high. Finally, results of these studies suggest that teams who display high degrees of intrateam task interdependence required a decentralized structure for effective performance, while high degrees of organizational interdependence (i.e., between the team and other organizational units) required centralization to be effective (Tushman, 1979a,b).

In a final study regarding information flow in R&D teams, Dewhirst, Arvey, and Brown (1978) hypothesized that task type would moderate the relationship between information accessibility, satisfaction, and performance in 14 R&D teams. Results partially supported this prediction. Access to goal-related information was more strongly related to satisfaction and performance for development groups than for research groups. In addition, access to external information was more important for research groups (in terms of satisfaction and performance), but this relationship failed to reach statistical significance.

Overall, the pattern of results from studies of R&D team communication suggests that optimal organization and management of such groups is highly task dependent. Complex, universally oriented research tasks appear to benefit from decentralized structure and decision making, diffuse responsibility for external communications, and high degrees of intrateam interaction. Less complex, locally oriented technical service type tasks, on the other hand, seem to be best structured more centrally, with the boundary-spanning role limited to one (or a very few) team members.

R&D Team Effectiveness

Several investigations have sought to identify factors that contribute to R&D team effectiveness (other than communication factors). In an early study by Smith (1970a), R&D team effectiveness in a petroleum-engineering laboratory was measured by rated technical contributions and usefulness, number of patents, and number of technical papers produced by each group. Results indicated that a "loose" organizational structure (i.e., participative, decentralized) was characteristic of high scientific performance. When more practical contributions were sought, however, teams benefited from a more formalized organizational structure, provided that the hierarchy allowed for needed consultation contacts (Smith, 1970a). Interestingly, these results are in keeping with Tushman and associates' findings reported above. While Tushman et al. speak of *communication patterns*, Smith calls them *structure;* operationalizations and empirical results suggest, however, that they are referring to a similar construct.

In a more recent study, Keller (1986) included multiple predictors in order to determine their impact on the performance of 32 R&D teams in a major corporation. Performance was measured by rated budget/cost, meeting deadlines, rated value to the company, and rated group performance. Results revealed that group cohesiveness was the only independent variable positively associated with all four criterion measures. This is in keeping with the results of an earlier study by O'Keefe, Kernagham, and Rubenstein (1975), which found that cohesive groups were more responsive to change than noncohesive groups.

Keller (1986) found further that physical distance (negative) job satisfaction (positive) and innovative orientation (positive) were significantly related with at least one criterion variable. However, the type of management influence in the group did not affect performance. Finally, Keller did not replicate a previously found result that project longevity is related to performance in a curvilinear fashion (see Peltz & Andrews, 1966).

A study by Smith (1970b) may help explain why the curvilinear performance/longevity relationship was not upheld by Keller (1986). Using 52 R&D teams, Smith found that, when performance was measured as rated team contributions and general usefulness, the curvilinear relationship was supported. When performance was defined as patents and technical papers, however, a direct relationship between performance and longevity was found. Smith concluded that the longevity/performance relationship is an intricate one; it appears to be affected by group heterogeneity as well as communication patterns.

Katz (1982) found in this regard that older groups communicated significantly less with key information sources than younger groups. In addition, Smith (1971) reported that heterogeneously composed R&D teams perform better than homogeneous ones, particularly if the group is young. Further, while young groups seemed to benefit from the intellectual stimulation derived from heterogeneous problem-solving techniques, they require supportive leadership functioning for effectiveness. Results of these studies, therefore, support the notion that longevity and performance are not related in a simple manner; it appears that other factors mediate this relationship.

Finally, a study by Katz and Allen (1985) investigated the relationship between influence structure and performance in R&D teams. Using 86 project teams in nine organizations with matrix structures, these researchers concluded that team performance is maximized when project (i.e., administrative) managers are concerned with administrative/organizational matters, while functional (i.e., technical) managers have influence over technical aspects of the project.

Overall, the research into R&D teams leads to several important conclusions: (a) communication patterns (both internal and external) are important to R&D team functioning, (b) the type of R&D task being considered moderates the relationship between structure/process and effectiveness, (c) R&D tasks can be distinguished by the degree of complexity and orientation of the project (moving from basic research to technical service tasks), and (d) the relationship between team longevity and effectiveness is a complex one.

SUMMARY AND CONCLUSIONS

The review of work group effectiveness literature presented here leads to a number of conclusions and suggests several recommendations that can enhance the quality of work group effectiveness studies. In terms of conclusions, it is clear that work groups occupy a central role in modern American industry. Evidence for this contention is derived from the sheer volume of work devoted to this topic over the past few decades. A second conclusion is that work groups do, on occasion, achieve desired outcomes (both individual and organizational) in industry. Unfortunately, the state of the literature is such that it is difficult to draw specific conclusions regarding work group design or effectiveness.

This leads to (or is more accurately a function of) the third conclusion, namely, that the inherent complexity of work group functioning in industry and difficulties associated with conducting action research make it particularly challenging to design and execute scientifically rigorous, enlightening studies. Taken together, these conclusions suggest that work groups are important and offer enough potential to warrant creative, innovative theoretical and methodological approaches to the study of their design and effectiveness.

Guidelines for Team Design and Effectiveness

The review presented here suggests that despite a good deal of empirical study, little in the way of specific guidance is available for those interested in understanding team design or effectiveness. One reason for this is that, while many theorists recognize the importance of task demands as a factor in team effectiveness, little effort has been directed in past research toward systematically classifying work teams based on the demands of the task they must accomplish, or on the kinds of outcomes that are expected from team based organization. What is needed is an organizing framework or classification scheme for work teams that would allow researchers and practitioners to draw commonalities among teams, and delineate factors that are most critical to a *particular* team's design and effectiveness. Without such a framework, it is difficult to anticipate the impact of specific team design features or delineate outcome factors that can be reasonably expected to change as a function of the team structure.

Recently, Sundstrom and Altman (1989) presented a classification scheme for work teams as part of a larger ecological framework for studying team effectiveness (Sundstrom et al., 1990). This scheme is based on the nature of the team's boundaries, specifically, the team's level of integration into, and differentiation from, the larger organization. The typology describes four discrete types of work teams that are hypothesized to vary in their work team differentiation, external integration, work cycles, and typical outputs. Further, what constitutes team effectiveness is hypothesized to vary as a function of work team type (Sundstrom et al., 1990). While the Sundstrom and Altman classification scheme is useful in highlighting important work team differences, its focus is on boundaries; it does not consider explicitly other factors in the framework, that is, organizational context (including task demands) and team development. It is limited, therefore, in the degree to which it can provide specific guidance to those interested in team design and measurement.

Proposed Framework for Designing and Studying Teams

Table 13.2 displays a proposed framework for designing and studying teams that is based on two factors: the amount of teamwork needed for task accomplishment, and the nature of expected team outcomes. It is based on several assumptions: (a) that task and situational demands are paramount to team functioning (see Sundstrom et al., 1990), (b) that task demands determine the degree of teamwork needed for task accomplishment (preliminary evidence for this contention was found by Stout, Cannon-Bowers, Salas, & Morgan, 1990), and (c) that the outcomes expected from team-based organization can range from attitudinal factors (e.g., satisfaction, involvement), to task-related factors (e.g., productivity, quality), to organization-level factors (e.g., turnover, absenteeism). Further, it is proposed that teamwork demands and expected outcomes have implications for team design and team measurement. Determining the teamwork needs and expected outcomes for a team can, therefore, provide guidance to those who are interested in the design of teams and team-based tasks, or the measurement of team performance.

Table 13.2.   Framework for Team Design and Study: Design and Effectiveness Issues Affected by Degree of Teamwork Needs and Expected Outcomes

	Design Features	Effectiveness Measures
Teamwork Needs	Training Leadership Team Size Team Composition Member Selection Communication Channels Group Goals Redundancy of Function	Team process measures: Coordination Communication Cohesion Flexibility Compensatory Behavior Mutual Adjustment Individual Measures Aggregate Outcomes
Expected Outcomes	Autonomy Variety Significance Challenge Scope Recognition Outcome Responsibility Resources Procedures Physical Layout Organizational Support Organizatinoal Culture	Attitudes: Satisfaction Involvement Commitment Self-Esteem Motivation Task Related: Productivity Quality Quantity Accuracy Waste Organization-level Turnover Absenteeism Grievances Safety

Turning first to teamwork needs, it has been hypothesized that a number of task/situational factors affect the amount of teamwork required for effective functioning (Boguslaw & Porter, 1962; Oser, McCallum, Salas, & Morgan, 1989; Prince, Cannon-Bowers, Salas, Owens, & Morgan, 1989). *Teamwork* is defined here as consisting of a complex of behaviors including: coordination, mutual adjustment, compensatory behavior, communication, flexibility/ adaptability, and cohesion (McIntyre, Morgan, Salas, & Glickman, 1988). Based on past work, it can be hypothesized that the following task demands contribute to teamwork needs: complexity (i.e., information processing and memory demands), standardization/predictability, interdependence, time compression, criticality, and taskload. The degree of teamwork needs, in turn, has implications for the design and measurement of teams. Table 13.2 displays a preliminary list of design features that are hypothesized to be affected by teamwork needs. For example, high teamwork needs suggest that training interventions be directed at enhancing members' teamwork skills. Selection of team members, team size and team composition are also expected to be different in tasks with high teamwork needs. Systematic research is needed to establish the relationship between each of these design features and the degree of teamwork needs. In addition, it is possible that other design factors are also affected by teamwork needs; research is needed to validate and expand the list shown in Table 13.2.

Teamwork needs also have an impact on the type of effectiveness measures that are appropriate for a particular team (shown in Table 13.2). When teamwork needs are high, process measures designed to assess the quality of teamwork displayed by team members are an important measure of team performance. In military contexts, several studies to date have found that teamwork ratings are associated with mission performance (Oser et al., 1989; Stout et al., 1990). Further, work by Glickman et al. (1987) and Morgan, Glickman, Woodard, Blaiwes, and Salas (1986) provides support for the use of behavioral observation scales as a means to assess team process. Such devices are also important as a way to diagnose team performance and provide team-level feedback. Low teamwork needs may require effectiveness measures that are less process oriented. Again, research designed to identify classes of performance measures appropriate for different levels of teamwork is required.

Turning to expected outcomes, the framework presented here maintains that the type of outcome desired from team-based organization also has implications for team design and measurement. Table 13.2 displays a number of job-related factors that have been shown, for example, to increase employee attitudes (i.e., satisfaction and involvement). These factors include: autonomy, variety, significance, challenge, scope, and recognition (Hackman & Oldham, 1980; Cummings, 1981; Sundstrom et al., 1990). When desired outcomes are product related, then availability of resources, procedures, and physical layout are critical as well. When changes in organizational outcomes are the focus of the effort, organizational-level variables such as organizational support and culture are also likely to be important. This kind of information can be useful to designers because it identifies factors that must be considered in the design cycle that will affect the probability that desired outcomes will be achieved. For example, it may be unreasonable to expect that team tasks designed to enhance productivity will also (automatically) improve attitudes. With respect to effectiveness measures, different expected outcomes dictate what should be measured. Effectiveness measures must be designed, therefore, to assess changes only in those variables that are likely to be affected by team task design.

Overall, the proposed framework presented here represents a preliminary attempt to highlight the importance of two critical factors, teamwork needs, and expected outcomes, in terms of both design considerations and effectiveness measures. It is incomplete at present, since empirical work is needed to specify in detail the manner in which teamwork needs affect optimal team design and measurement. On the expected outcome side, past work provides a fairly good foundation upon which to make design and measurement decisions. In its present form, the value of this framework is to enlighten those interested in studying or designing work teams by highlighting important factors to be considered, and areas that require further study. With development, it has the potential to be a prescriptive tool by providing team designers and researchers with specific design and measurement guidance.

REFERENCES

Allen, T. J., & Cohen, D. I. (1969). Information flow in research and development laboratories. *Administrative Science Quarterly, 14,* 12–25.

Allen, T. J., Lee, D. M. S., & Tushman, M. L. (1980). R&D performance as a function of internal communication, project management, and the nature of the work. *IEEE Transactions on Engineering Management, EM-27,* 2–12.

Archer, J. T. (1975). Achieving joint organizational, technical and personal needs: The case of the sheltered experiment of aluminum casting team. In L. E. Davis & A. B. Cherns (Eds.), *The quality of working life: Cases and commentary.* New York: Free Press.

Aquilano, N. J. (1977). Multiskilled work teams: Productivity benefits. *California Management Review, 29,* 17–22.

Barrick, M. R., & Alexander, R. A. (1987). A review of quality circle efficacy and the existence of the positive-findings bias. *Personnel Psychology, 40,* 579–591.

Berman, S. J., & Hellweg, S. A. (1989). Perceived supervisor communication competence and supervisor satisfaction as a function of quality circle participation. *Journal of Business Communication, 26,* 103–122.

Blumberg, M. (1980). Job switching in autonomous work groups: An exploratory study in a Pennsylvania coal mine. *Academy of Management Journal, 23,* 287–306.

Boguslaw, R., & Porter, E. H. (1962). Team functions and training. In R. M. Gagne (Ed.), *Psychological principles in system development.* New York: Holt, Rinehart and Winston.

Burden, D. W. E. (1975). Participative management as a basis for improved quality of jobs: The case of microwax department, Shell U. K., Ltd. In L. E. Davis & A. B. Cherns (Eds.), *The quality of working life: Case and commentary.* New York: Free Press.

Cummings, T. G. (1981). Designing effective work groups. In P. C. Nystrom & W. Starbuck (Eds.), *Handbook of organizational design* (Vol. 2). London: Oxford University Press.

Davis, L. E., & Trist, E. (1979). Improving the quality of working life: Sociotechnical case studies. In L. E. Davis & J. C. Taylor (Eds.), *Design of jobs.* Santa Monica, CA: Goodyear Publishing Co.

Dewhirst, D., Arvey, R. D., & Brown, E. M. (1978). Satisfaction and performance in research and development tasks as related to information accessibility. *IEEE Transactions on Engineering Management, EM-25,* 58–63.

Drago, R. (1988). Quality circle survival: An exploratory analysis. *Industrial Relations, 27,* 336–351.

Ferris, G. R., & Wagner, J. A., III. (1985). Quality circles in the United States: A conceptual reevaluation. *Journal of Applied Behavioral Science, 21,* 155–167.

Glickman, A. S., Zimmer, S., Montero, R. C., Guerette, P. J., Campbell, W., J., Morgan, B. B., Jr., & Salas, E. (1987). *The evolution of teamwork skills: An empirical assessment with implications for training* (Tech. Rep. No. 87-016). Orlando, FL: Naval Training Systems Center.

Greenbaum, H. H., Kaplan, I. T., & Metlay, W. (1988). Evaluation of problem-solving groups: The case study of quality circle programs. *Group Organizational Studies, 13,* 133–147.

Griffin, R. W. (1988). Consequences of quality circles in an industrial setting: A longitudinal assessment. *Academy of Management Journal, 31,* 338–358.

Guest, R. H. (1986). *Work teams and team building.* New York: Pergamon Press.

Hackman J. R., & Morris, C. G. (1975). Group tasks, group interaction process and group performance effectiveness: A review and proposed integration. In L. Berkowitz (Ed.), *Advances in experimental social psychology* (Vol. 8). New York: Academic Press.

Hackman J. R., & Oldham, G. R. (1980). *Work redesign.* Reading, MA: Addison-Wesley.

Henry, R. F., & Malmstrom, F. V. (1985). A test of the quality circle approach to problem solving. *Proceedings of the Human Factors Society—29th Annual Meeting. 1,* 608–609. Santa Monica, CA: Human Factors Society.

Honeycutt, A. (1989, May). The key to effective quality circles. *Training and Development Journal,* pp. 81–84.

Katz, R. (1982). The effects of group longevity on project communication and performance. *Administrative Science Quarterly, 27,* 81–104.

Katz, R., & Allen, T. J. (1985). Project performance and the locus of influence in the R&D matrix. *Academy of Management Journal, 28,* 67–87.

Katz, R., & Tushman, M. L. (1979). Communication patterns, project performance, and task characteristics: An empirical evaluation and integration in an R&D setting. *Organizational Behavior and Human Performance, 23,* 139–162.

Keller, R. T. (1986). Predictors of the performance of project groups in R&D organizations. *Academy of Management Journal, 29,* 715–726.

Kemp, N. J., Wall, T. D., Clegg, C. W., & Cordery, J. L. (1983). Autonomous work groups in a greenfield site: A comparative study. *Journal of Occupational Psychology, 56,* 271–288.

Kidd, J. S. (1961). A comparison of one-, two-, and three-man work units under various conditions of workload. *Journal of Applied Psychology, 45,* 195–200.

Koch, J. L. (1979). Effects of goal specificity and performance feedback to work groups on peer leadership, performance and attitudes. *Human Relations, 32,* 819–840.

Krigsman, N., & O'Brien, R. M. (1987). Quality circles, feedback, and reinforcement: An experimental comparison and behavioral analysis. *Organizational behavior management and statistical process control, theory change, and behavior analysis.* New York: Hawthorne Press.

Likert, R. (1967). *The human organization.* New York: McGraw-Hill.

Manz, C. C., & Sims, H. P., Jr. (1987). Leading workers to lead themselves: The external leadership of self-managing work teams. *Administrative Science Quarterly, 32,* 106–128.

Marks, M. L., Mirvis, P. H., Hackett, E. J., & Grady, J. F., Jr. (1986). Employee participation in a quality circle program: Impact on quality of work life, productivity, and absenteeism. *Journal of Applied Psychology, 71,* 61–69.

McIntyre, R. M., Morgan, B. B., Jr., Salas, E., & Glickman, A. S. (1988). *Team research in the eighties: Lessons learned.* Unpublished manuscript, Naval Training Systems Center, Orlando, FL.

Mohrman, S. A., & Lawler, E. E. (1984). Quality of work life. In K. M. Rowland & G. R. Ferris (Eds.), *Research in personnel and human resource management* (Vol. 2). Greenwich, CT: JAI Press.

Morgan, B. B., Jr., Glickman, A. S., Woodard, E. A., Blaiwes, A. S., & Salas, E. (1986). *Measurement of team behaviors* (Tech. Rep. No. 86-014). Orlando, FL: Naval Training Systems Center.

Nagamachi, N., Nakai, L. V., Hatamoto, K., & Matsushima, K. (1989). Organizational factors in quality circle activities. *Proceedings of the Human Factors Society— 33rd Annual Meeting. 2,* 841–845. Santa Monica, CA: Human Factors Society.

O'Keefe, R., Kernaghan, J., & Rubenstein, A. (1975). Group cohesiveness: A factor in the adoption of innovations among scientific work groups. *Small Group Behavior, 5,* 282–292.

O'Reilly, C. A., & Roberts, K. H. (1977). Task group structure, communication, and effectiveness in three organizations. *Journal of Applied Psychology, 62,* 674–681.

Oser, R., McCallum, G. A., Salas, E., & Morgan, B. B., Jr. (1989). *Toward a definition of teamwork: An analysis of critical team behaviors* (Tech. Rep. No. TR-89-004). Orlando, FL: Naval Training Systems Center.

Pasmore, W., Francis, C., Haldeman, J., & Shani, A. (1982). Sociotechnical systems: A North American reflection on empirical studies of the seventies. *Human Relations, 35,* 1179–1204.

Pasmore, W., & Sherwood, J. (Eds.). (1978). *Sociotechnical systems: A sourcebook.* San Diego: University Associates.

Pearce, J. A., & Ravlin, E. C. (1987). The design and activation of self-regulating work groups. *Human Relations, 40,* 751–782.

Peltz, D. C., & Andrews, F. M. (1966). *Scientists in Organizations.* New York: John Wiley & Sons.

Poza, E. J., & Markus, M. L. (1980, Winter). Success story: The team approach to work restructuring. *Organizational Dynamics,* pp. 3–25.

Prince, C., Cannon-Bowers, J. A., Salas, E., Owens, J., & Morgan, B. B., Jr. (1989). *Aircrew coordination training: Requirements and challenges.* Unpublished manuscript, Naval Training Systems Center, Orlando, FL.

Rubenstein, A., Barth, R., & Douds, C. (1971). Ways to improve communication between R&D groups. *Research Management, 14,* 49.

Seers, A. (1989). Team-member exchange quality: A new construct for role-making research. *Organizational Behavior and Human Decision Processes, 43,* 118–135.

Shea, G. P., & Guzzo, R. A. (1987). Group effectiveness: What really matters? *Sloan Management Review, 3,* 25–31.

Smith, C. G. (1970a). Consultation and decision processes in a research and development laboratory. *Administrative Science Quarterly, 15,* 203–215.

Smith, C. G. (1970b). Age of R and D groups: A reconsideration. *Human Relations, 23,* 81–96.

Smith, C. G. (1971). Scientific performance and the composition of research teams. *Administrative Science Quarterly, 16,* 486–495.

Steel, R. P., & Shane, G. S. (1986). Evaluation research on quality circles: Technical and analytical implications. *Human Relations, 39,* 449–468.

Steiner, I. D. (1972). *Group process and productivity.* New York: Academic Press.

Stohl, C., & Jennings, K. (1988). Volunteerism and voice in quality circles. *Western Journal of Speech Communications, 52,* 238–251.

Stout, R., Cannon-Bowers, J. A., Salas, E., & Morgan, B. B., Jr. (1990, October). *Does crew coordination behavior impact performance?* Abstract submitted for presentation to the Human Factors Society Meeting.

Sundstrom, E., & Altman, I. (1989). Physical environments and work-group effectiveness. In L. Cummings & B. Staw (Eds.), *Research in organizational behavior* (Vol. 2). Greenwich, CT: JAI Press.

Sundstrom, E., De Meuse, K. P., & Futrell, D. (1990). Work teams: Applications and Effectiveness. *American Psychologist, 45,* 120–133.

Susman, G. I. (1970). The impact of automation on work group autonomy and task specialization. *Human Relations, 23,* 567–577.

Susman, G. I. (1975). Technological prerequisites for delegation of decision making to work groups. In L. E. Davis & A. B. Cherns (Eds.), *The quality of working life: Problems, prospects and the state of the art.* New York: Free Press.

Szilagyi, A. D., Jr., & Wallace, M. J. (1983). *Organizational behavior and performance* (3rd ed.). Glenview, IL: Scott, Foresman.

Tang, L. T., Tollison, P. S., & Whiteside, H. D. (1987). The effect of quality circle initiation on motivation to attend quality circle meetings and on task performance. *Personnel Psychology, 40,* 799–814.

Tang, L. T., Tollison, P. S., & Whiteside, H. D. (1989). Quality circle productivity as related to upper-management attendance, circle initiation, and collar color. *Journal of Management, 15,* 101–113.

Trist, E. L., Susman, G. I., & Brown, G. R. (1977). An experiment in autonomous working in an American underground coal mine. *Human Relations, 30,* 201–236.

Tushman, M. L. (1977). Special boundary roles in the innovation process. *Administrative Science Quarterly, 22,* 587–605.

Tushman, M. L. (1979a). Impacts of perceived environmental variability on patterns of work related communication. *Academy of Management Journal, 22,* 482–500.

Tushman, M. L. (1979b). Work characteristics and subunit communication structure: A contingency analysis. *Administrative Science Quarterly, 24,* 83–98.

Tushman, M. L., & Katz, R. (1980). External communication and project performance: An investigation into the role of gatekeepers. *Management Science, 26,* 1071–1085.

Wall, T. D., Kemp, N. J., Jackson, P. R., & Clegg, C. W. (1986). Outcomes of autonomous workgroups: A long-term field experiment. *Academy of Management Journal, 29,* 280–304.

Walton, R. E. (1977). Work innovations at Topeka: After six years. *Journal of Applied Behavioral Science, 13,* 422–433.

Wayne, S. J., Griffin, R. W., & Bateman, T. S. (1986, March). Improving the effectiveness of quality circles. *Personnel Administrator,* pp. 79–88.

Zahra, S. A. (1984, August). What supervisors think about QCs. *Supervisory Management,* pp. 27–33.

14

Team Skills Training in Nuclear Power Plant Operations

Catherine D. Gaddy
Jerry A. Wachtel

INTRODUCTION

Amid the milling around and mounting low-grade apprehension is an overcast of unreality: this isn't really happening—like the classic recurrent school nightmare in which you show up for a final exam and discover you have been studying the wrong textbook for a whole semester. These are confident people, accustomed to reading and responding to—controlling—this reactor plant. . . . The persistent failure of the . . . operating crew—and of the monitoring personnel in the control room—to recognize and react to these symptoms is one of the abiding mysteries of the first day of the accident.

So the Rogovin Commission reported in its analysis of the accident at Three Mile Island (TMI) in 1979. (Rogovin et al., 1980)

Then, 7 years later, on April 25, 1986, the staff of the Chernobyl Unit 4 nuclear power plant began a test before the plant shut down for its annual maintenance. Twelve hours later, two explosions blew off the 1000-ton concrete cap of the reactor, resulting in the worst accident in the history of commercial power generation. The accident led to the loss of 30 lives, contaminated approximately 400 square miles of land, and increased significantly the risk of cancer deaths over a wide area of Scandinavia and Western Europe (Reason, 1987).

Historically, most disasters of this magnitude are found to be caused by a combination of human and mechanical failures. Chernobyl was different; the accident was due almost entirely to human actions and decisions. At least six violations of procedures occurred during the hour before the explosions, and eight major operational errors and management control breakdowns contributed to the accident (USNRC, 1987). The U.S. Nuclear Regulatory Commission concluded that:

> The plant operators and station management did not demonstrate an adequate understanding of the safety implications of their actions. Their willingness to conduct the test at a very low power level, with abnormal and unauthorized control rod configuration and core conditions, and with safety features bypassed indicates an insufficient understanding of the reactor and its potential behavior. (1987, pp. 5–7)

Several "teams" were responsible for the Chernobyl accident: at least two operating shift crews (the plant evolution that culminated in the accident occurred over a 24-hour period); senior plant management staff, responsible not only for overall control of the test and its integration with plant operations, but also for approval of the test plan despite safety compromises made in order to conduct the test; the power station technical safety group, responsible for reviewing thoroughly the test procedures, conditions, and precautions; and, finally, the team of "electrotechnical rather than nuclear experts" (INSAG, 1986) responsible for developing the test and establishing the test conditions without a thorough understanding of its implications.

These two major nuclear power plant accidents occurred 7 years and 10,000 miles apart. The accidents occurred under very different circumstances, with equipment of radically different designs, controlled by dissimilar work stations. Was there a common thread to these headline-causing events? This chapter will suggest that there is.

Nuclear Technology and Nuclear Power

Nuclear technology is used in numerous applications such as medicine, weapons, propulsion, research, and power generation. The focus of this chapter is on the latter application, nuclear power generation, and more specifically on the human aspects of team performance. Before delving into team performance issues, a brief background is in order to describe the unique characteristics of nuclear power plants that affect team performance.

In December 1942, Enrico Fermi demonstrated that uranium fission could produce energy in a controllable manner. His experiment became the basis for nuclear power technology. As Deutsch (1987) has described, the success of the U.S. Navy program in the mid-1950s under Admiral Hyman Rickover demonstrated the safe and reliable use of nuclear propulsion on board submarines.

While the naval reactors produced much less energy than necessary for a commercial power plant, the basic processes were similar.

A demonstration commercial nuclear power plant, the Shippingport Atomic Power Station, was started in 1953 and was commissioned to operate in 1957. Shippingport demonstrated the safety and feasibility of such plants. In the late 1960s and early 1970s, orders for commercial nuclear power plants were at a peak. Many electric power utility companies added nuclear plants as a resource to supplement their existing power generation facilities.

The processes used in fossil and nuclear plants are similar in a number of ways. In a fossil fuel plant, combustion of coal or oil produces heat that is converted to steam to turn a turbine and generate electricity. In the case of a nuclear plant, the fission of uranium produces the heat; the remainder of the process is essentially the same. A major difference between fossil and uranium fuel plants is the potential hazard of leakage of radioactive materials in the latter case. As a result, significant attention is paid to the quality of materials and construction, and to safety procedures in daily operation. Further, redundancy within safety systems provides "defense in depth."

By the late 1980s, there were just over a hundred nuclear power plants licensed to operate in the United States. These plants provided about one-fifth of our nation's electricity (Deutsch, 1987). More than 250 nuclear power plants are in operation in other countries; in France, for example, more than half of the nation's electricity is generated by nuclear power (Deutsch, 1987).

A nuclear power plant site can be comprised of one or more units. In general, each unit is a separate power-producing plant. However, sites that include multiple units sometimes combine control rooms into one area and share certain systems and personnel between units.

The typical nuclear power plant is large in area and complex in the number of systems and system interactions (see Figure 14.1). The number of plant systems may be well over a hundred, including systems such as containment, feedwater, and radiation monitoring. As in any process control plant, these systems are linked in a process flow or loop. Some systems can be configured for different functions, such as by opening or closing valves in a flow line.

Each system includes some type of display such as meters or digital readouts, to provide feedback to the operators and other personnel throughout the plant; and some type of control mechanism, ranging from a valve that is turned by hand to a graphical computer interface.

The Human Side of the Plant

Given the size and complexity of present-day nuclear power plants, a couple of hundred or more people are needed to run the plant. These people perform functions such as operation, maintenance, engineering, testing, and administra-

Figure 14.1.   A Nuclear Power Plant Site.

tion. For the purpose of this chapter, the focus will be on operation, since the control room crew has received the most attention regarding team performance. Control room crew members have the ultimate responsibility for daily operation, never perform work alone in the control room, and coordinate the immediate response to emergency situations. Other teams in the plant that perform maintenance, engineering, testing, or administrative functions have received less attention to date. A somewhat analogous situation in the commercial aviation field may be the attention paid to cockpit crews in contrast to ground maintenance crews.

The U. S. Nuclear Regulatory Commission (NRC), the federal agency responsible for protecting the public health and safety from the risks of the nonmilitary use of nuclear materials, requires a minimum staffing level for nuclear power plant control room crews (Code of Federal Regulations, 1989). Each plant meets the minimum and then may vary considerably in the size, makeup, and organization of the crew. While there are differences specific to each electric power utility company, and in some cases among plants within a company, crews in general are comprised of: two licensed Senior Reactor Operators, one of whom is the supervisor; and two licensed Reactor Operators, who share the duties of monitoring and controlling the plant. A Shift Technical Advisor who has an engineering background is available as a resource to the crew but is not in direct line within the crew organization.

Each unit has five or six crews, one of which is in the control room at all times. When the plant is operating, a crew is always present. As a result, crews must work shifts around the clock and deal with the stresses of being attentive through the night.

Since the job requires continuous coverage, crews are not always composed of the same people. Vacations and other personal situations require crews to change composition relatively often. As a result, team-building activities often used in other industries for focused project teams that encounter minimal personnel changes may not be as appropriate in the nuclear industry as team skills training. Nuclear power plant control room crews must adapt to working with members of other teams relatively often. While this situation could be viewed as problematic, some variability in crew composition can provide cross-fertilization among crews and minimize the likelihood of complacency that often results from dealing with the same people all the time.

The Control Room Environment

A picture of a typical nuclear power plant control room simulator is shown in Figure 14.2. With minor exceptions, the simulator is similar in physical layout, appearance, and function to the actual control room. The windowless control room has vertical panels and benchboards (on which displays and controls are

Figure 14.2. Typical Nuclear Power Plant Control Room Training Simulator.

mounted), computer equipment, and desks—much like any process control room.

Crew members have specific, step-by-step procedures for dealing with the symptoms of plant problems, such as high pressure or low water level. Most of the time, however, they maintain a vigil over a process that changes relatively infrequently and changes slowly when it does. They also spend a good part of each day testing equipment and completing paperwork. Again, the situation is somewhat analogous to the commercial airline crew experience of a proceduralized routine and long periods of vigilance, with infrequent but "memorable" problems to solve. In contrast, for nuclear control room crews, the level of stimulation is typically lower, the feedback on performance is less apparent and less immediate, and the degree of control over the system is less. However, the responsibility of control room crew members is potentially greater in terms of risk to public health and safety.

To prepare control room crew members for the complex system over which they have responsibility, rigorous training programs have been developed. Crew members undergo technical training in areas of knowledge such as thermodynamics, and for skills such as control manipulation. In the past 5 years, crews have also received increasing exposure to team skills, and other related interpersonal and management types of training. Prior to reviewing these efforts, however, let us take a brief historical look at training in the nuclear power industry.

Historical Background

Most human factors and personnel-related issues to which attention has been paid in the U.S. nuclear power industry stem from lessons learned as a result of the TMI accident. Early efforts related to the area of team training were no exception. One of the first sets of recommendations based on the TMI experience was known as the "lessons learned" report (USNRC, 1979). The report included a recommendation that commercial nuclear power plants conduct "in-plant drills" based on the idea of casualty drills conducted in naval reactor operations. The report writers suggested that each utility review its training program and identify tasks performed by shift operating personnel in response to off-normal or accident situations. Plants were to assure that "sufficient in-plant drills are conducted to enable personnel to maintain proficiency in those tasks" (p. A-5). The drills were to be conducted in simulators, where available, or in plant walkthroughs.

The recommendations made in the "lessons learned" report were later expanded in a document known as the "TMI Action Plan" (USNRC, 1980), and one of the action items required plants to develop and conduct drills. At about this same time, the NRC assembled a human factors staff and began to implement the recommendations of the plan. It soon became clear that the plant drills involved team training. As a result, the NRC expanded its attention beyond the mere conduct of drills. Despite these efforts, the relevant action plan item was not fully addressed to the satisfaction of the NRC, and in 1983, a congressional mandate (United States Congress, 1982) directed that the NRC develop new regulations for operator training and licensing.

NRC staff specialists began a complete review of the licensing process, including the psychometric, behavioral, and administrative aspects of the examination. The exams consisted of written, oral (during plant walkthroughs), and simulator portions. Despite the fact that control rooms were staffed by teams of three or four licensed operators, all aspects of the exam were conducted based strictly on individual performance. Thus, it became clear that some evaluation of how well the crew performed as a team was needed in addition to evaluation of individual operators for their licenses. The NRC handbook for examiners was revised to reflect this concern (USNRC, 1989). The handbook recognized the need to develop exams based upon a systematic approach to training which was coming into wide use in the industry. Exams would, for the first time, include "team dependent behavior" in simulator-based evaluations.

TEAM SKILLS

As was evident from the descriptions of the situations at TMI and Chernobyl, attention to technical and interpersonal skills could benefit the crew in unusual circumstances. After TMI, the NRC sponsored numerous studies of operator training (e.g., Davis, Mazour, & Zaret, 1981) and control room design (USNRC, 1980). In the area of team skills, the experience of other industries was sought during an NRC-sponsored workshop (Davis, Gaddy, & Turney, 1985; Davis, Gaddy, Turney, & Koontz 1986).

For this workshop, organizations known to provide team training or to support team performance research were contacted. Individuals from organizations representing the military, commercial airlines, aerospace, maritime industry, hospitals, and universities were asked to assist in developing team skills guidelines for the nuclear power industry. Participants who attended the workshop represented the following organizations: Air Force Human Resources Laboratory, Naval Training Systems Center, Office of Naval Research, NASA-Ames, United Airlines, Seville Training Systems Company, Duke Power Company, Northern States Power Company, Pennsylvania Power and Light Company, and the NRC.

One of the first topics tackled during the workshop was: what are team skills? The workshop participants had been involved in team training but few had addressed team skills directly. In fact, there was considerable debate among these team-training experts regarding the distinction between a team member's individual skills and team skills. The conclusion was that team skills come into play any time a team member communicates with another team member. A member of the crew may have superior private technical knowledge. However, if he or she cannot communicate this understanding publicly, team performance may suffer. In other words, a breakdown in team skills can undermine the best technical skills.

Generic Team Skills

With respect to specific team skills, workshop participants from the diverse organizations discussed certain skills that were beneficial to team members regardless of the work setting. The term *generic team skills* was used to distinguish team skills that have broad applicability from *operational team skills,* which are more mission specific. The generic team skills agreed upon by workshop participants were: communications, feedback, effective influence, conflict resolution, and leadership. Certainly a much longer list of team skills could be compiled based on the literature, but these five skills received consensus support from participants as being fundamental to team performance, and as evocative of specific behavioral examples. Skills labeled "cooperation" or "coordination" in the literature required further explanation to be useful.

The first of the generic team skills, communications, has been described as a fundamental team skill by most every researcher of the subject (e.g., Dyer, 1984; Turney & Cohen, 1981). The basics of effective message-sending and -receiving skills are also documented widely (e.g., Fisher, 1981; Haney, 1979; Randolph, 1985). The challenge in the team skills context is identifying the absence of needed communication, the presence of unnecessary and distracting messages, and the appropriateness of message content. In the scope of some job/task analyses of crew performance, the content of verbatim transcripts of crew communications has been analyzed. For example, the information on cockpit voice recorders has been scrutinized following aviation accidents. The challenge to team skills improvement in an operational context is to sample communications in some representative way and provide guidelines for crews in daily operation.

A related but distinct skill discussed by participants was feedback. This team skill was described separately from communication per se, to stress the importance of two-way communication. The feedback described by workshop participants pertained to both technical performance feedback—about how the plant process or operators were doing, and personal feedback—about how crew members were relating to one another.

The third generic team skill was effective influence. Effective influence refers to skills used by team members to query the course of action, and to persuade other crew members to consider alternatives. The two components of effective influence are inquiry (or questioning) and advocacy (or assertiveness). Effective influence has received considerable attention over the past 15 years in assertiveness training and counseling programs (e.g., Alberti & Emmons, 1982).

Conflict resolution was identified as a fourth generic team skill. Techniques for conflict resolution have been described by numerous authors (e.g., Blake & Mouton, 1978; Filley, 1975). With these techniques, team members are encouraged to find solutions to technical and interpersonal areas of disagreement that are at least supported, if not accepted, by all the crew members.

The last generic team skill was leadership. The unique connotation of the concept of leadership discussed by workshop participants was that it was a useful skill for all crew members, not just the team supervisor. Leadership functions can be filled by any crew member, even though the supervisor maintains ultimate authority.

Operational Team Skills

In addition to the generic team skills, workshop participants described operational team skills that were job specific. This second tier of team skills was developed to provide descriptions of team skills that could be linked directly to job/task analyses and performance evaluation criteria. For example, deciding whether a crew communicated effectively might require too general an assessment. However, evaluating how well a crew kept its members informed of plant

Figure 14.3.   Examples of Operational Team Skills.

Information exchange
Information evaluation
Task assignment
Performance direction
Performance feedback
Coordination in sequencing of tasks
Strategy development
Problem solving and decision making

status throughout an operational scenario would be easier to critique. Examples of operational team skills are provided in Figure 14.3.

At the operational team skills level of description, the development of team skills performance objectives and criteria based on job/task analysis is relatively straightforward. This process is described in the next section as applied in the nuclear power plant environment.

TEAM SKILLS TRAINING

After discussion of team skills, workshop participants turned their attention to the process of team skills training, using the instructional systems development approach as the foundation.

As in the development of any type of training, the *job/task analysis* (JTA) can be reviewed to identify requirements for team skills. A straightforward search of a JTA database for relevant task action verbs such as *inform, direct,* and *decide* will identify many tasks that require team skills. However, due to the dynamic nature of crew interactions, a table-top review of the JTA by *subject matter experts* (SMEs) is especially important. SMEs can be asked to identify those tasks or scenarios that potentially have critical, complex, or frequent crew interactions. Communications among nuclear power plant control room crew members are not structured, unlike the lexicon for air traffic control or interior communications on a submarine. As a result, the format or content of expected communications cannot be predicted as specifically. In addition, the complexity of system interactions and the multiplicity of possible paths based on operator actions make rigid evaluation criteria impractical. Examples of team skills objectives and evaluation criteria are provided in Figure 14.4.

Figure 14.4.   Examples of Team Skills Objectives and Evaluation Criteria.

Typical team skills objective: Determine that the level decrease is due to a misaligned residual heat removal configuration resulting from an instrumentation and control surveillance test.

    Associated evaluation criteria: Crew members communicate that they realize the decrease in vessel level began when the surveillance test was started at the remote shutdown panel.

Typical team skills objective: Recognize that the reactor has scrammed.

    Associated evaluation criteria: Based on one or more of the annunciator alarms and other displays, crew members communicate among themselves and to management that the reactor has scrammed.

Basic Team Skills Training

After objectives and criteria for team performance have been developed, training in generic team skills can be planned. Basic skills training in mathematics, physics, chemistry, and electricity is provided before task-specific technical training. In the case of team skills, crew members may bring an even greater variability in their backgrounds in basic team skills. For example, high school curriculum prepares most graduates for the mathematics required to begin technical training. However, fewer novice crew members will have had a course in communications or interpersonal relations. As a result, the generic team skills need to be covered thoroughly.

While the generic team skills training can be generalized from other organizations, the inclusion of plant-specific examples, case studies, and exercises can enhance the acceptance of training by crew members. They can readily see the applicability to their future job positions.

Some training programs in the past have presented only generic-type training and have not included training to transfer these skills to the operational context. As researchers have pointed out for many years (e.g., Campbell & Dunnette, 1968), training that is limited in this way has failed to demonstrate actual performance changes in organizations. Thus, the team task training described in the next section is particularly important.

Generic team skills have often been addressed as part of supervisory or management training programs provided by most electric power utility companies. However, these programs often lacked the transfer of training back into the operational environment. Further, this training was usually not offered to non-supervisory members of the crew.

Team Task Training

The next phase of team skills training for control room crews provides task-specific team training in an operational context. For many years, some utility companies have provided training for nuclear power plant control room crews using high-fidelity simulators of the control room (as pictured in Figure 14.2). The simulators allow crews to practice responding to events that are too dangerous to practice in the actual control room. Until recently, however, due to the limited availability of simulators and to the task-oriented approach of most trainers, little formal or systematic attention was paid to team skills per se. In the aftermath of TMI, the NRC has required all nuclear utilities to acquire simulators and to certify their fidelity to the plant. Thus, access to these training tools is becoming easier. In addition, attention to people skills has increased, as attested to by the numerous courses now available for the instructors themselves in various types of instructional and interpersonal skills. Now, instead of spending every possible moment during simulator training with crew members responding to a simulated event, crews and trainers are spending more time in debriefings for technical and team skills. Also, with the introduction of a systematic approach to training in the industry after TMI, more time and other resources are now allocated to prepare for team training.

Although some practice of team skills was implicitly part of simulator team training a decade ago, emphasis on team skills may well improve overall crew performance. In the aviation industry, Foushee (1984) described studies in which teams that exhibited less communication, information exchange, and coordination tended to commit more errors. Studies of this type are currently underway in the nuclear power industry (as described later in this chapter). Experience from other industries has shown the potential for benefit from team skills training.

Considerations in team task training are described in the remainder of this section. In preparation for the training, tasks must be identified and scenarios created. Then, some of the logistics in conducting team task training are discussed.

Selection of tasks. As mentioned earlier in discussion of the development of objectives for team performance, tasks can be identified that have relatively greater requirements for crew interactions than others. Characteristics of crew interactions that may challenge team skills include: criticality, complexity, and frequency.

Interaction criticality refers to the extent to which interactions affect task performance. The team skills literature has included the distinction between *established* and *emergent* tasks (Boguslaw & Porter, 1962; Wagner, Hibbits, Rosenblatt, & Schulz, 1977). Established tasks involve predictable sequences that can be specified in advance. Since these tasks are straightforward, little variation would be expected based on team member interactions. In contrast, emergent tasks involve unpredictable events that cannot be specified fully in advance. Thus, team skills training might best focus on emergent tasks.

Interaction complexity refers to the amount of group problem solving and decision making that arises during task performance. Training for complex tasks will be more challenging than for structured or rote tasks.

Interaction frequency refers to the number of communications required among crew members. For cases in which a high frequency of communications was necessary for task performance, Briggs and Naylor (1965) found that the ability to effectively handle frequent communications was a key factor in successful team performance. In addition, as the number of crew members in the control room increases, as would happen in most emergency situations, the frequency of communications is likely to increase. With this increase comes the attendant increase in the probability for communication errors to occur. Thus, tasks that require frequent communications may also be good candidates for team task training.

Scenario development. During simulator training, nuclear power plant crews rarely perform just one task in isolation. More often, numerous tasks are combined to develop a scenario that takes the simulated plant from one condition, such as an abnormal situation, to another, such as a normal condition. For the purposes of team skills training, points during a scenario that are likely to involve critical, complex, or frequent communications can be flagged in advance so instructors can be prepared to observe them. Due to the dynamic nature of the scenarios, many other interactions will occur. Some of these will be necessary for the task at hand, some will clearly not be necessary, and still others will be of questionable value to task performance. For this reason, instructors have a demanding workload consisting of observing interactions and noting representative examples of successes and potential problems. Preparations for the scenarios are essential to work out any technical bugs and acquaint the instructors with the scenarios.

Conduct of team training. Two considerations in conducting team training are: how often should it be conducted, and who should participate? With respect to the frequency of team skills training, long-term retention of some technical skills has been studied (Dyer, 1984), but in most cases the length of time between refresher-training sessions has been decided without the support of data. The nuclear plants provide approximately 1 week of training every 6 weeks. Within this framework, team skills training is incorporated differently at each plant. An annual requalification examination is required by the NRC. Team skills are a component of this exam.

With respect to who should participate, inclusion of the entire team is recommended in the literature (Dyer, 1984). However, defining the entire team in a nuclear power plant is not straightforward. The control room crew is assisted by numerous other personnel during emergency situations. To include all these other personnel is complicated. Plants do conduct emergency drills on a periodic basis, but these are extremely labor intensive to do for regular training.

A compromise situation has been tried at some sites. The auxiliary plant operators who interface frequently with the control room crew are included in simulator training. However, since the tasks of these auxiliary operators are not usually simulated, the training is somewhat limited for them. Further, since the NRC examines only licensed operators, and since training is generally oriented toward licensure, the inclusion of nonlicensed personnel in training may not be straightforward.

Team Training Evaluation

Evaluation of team skills training can be addressed at two levels: for the crew members, and for the training program.

Evaluation of team skills of crew members. In the nuclear power industry, team skills are now evaluated in a similar format as technical skills. Objectives and criteria, such as were presented earlier in Figure 14.4, are used to structure the evaluation process. After a scenario is conducted on the simulator, crew members and instructors have a debriefing session.

During the NRC-sponsored workshop described previously, participants stressed the importance of self-critique by crew members. This crew-centered approach to debriefing has a number of advantages. Once crews are used to taking the lead in debriefing, they are usually more self-critical than instructors would have been for the same scenario. While crew members themselves do not see everything that happens during a scenario, they certainly have first-hand knowledge. Finally, crew members may understandably be less defensive about peer critiques than comments from the sidelines. This approach in no way lessens the importance of the potentially more objective instructor. However, it does allow crew members to practice feedback skills and critique themselves first.

The use of videotape playback of scenarios has been tried by increasing numbers of plants as the equipment available on the market has improved. However, the audio and visual challenges of taping a large area in which multiple people are responding is not trivial. The videotape can facilitate debriefing sessions by permitting playback of selected segments of the scenario.

Evaluation of training program. Standard approaches to training program evaluation can be applied to team skills training assessment. Internal approaches such as pre- and posttests of trainees, and external approaches such as follow-up supervisors' ratings of team performance, will be useful.

ONGOING RESEARCH

As part of team skills evaluation, each plant constructed rating scales or check-lists for use in assessing crews during simulator training. The NRC also developed rating forms for use during requalification examinations. However, these scales were general in nature; crews could fail their exam due to team skills problems but not know specifically what they had done wrong or what to do differently in the future. In addition, the relative importance of team skills in crew performance was not known. As a result, evaluators did not know how much emphasis to place on team versus technical skills. To remedy this situation, the NRC is sponsoring research in team skills evaluation.

The primary objectives of the NRC-sponsored research program are to: (a) develop reliable, valid measures of team skills, and (b) explore the relationship between team skills and overall safe crew performance. A first step in the program was to collect examples of team skills evaluation forms. These examples were used to develop rating scale dimensions and supporting descriptions of team skills behaviors.

Method

Rating scales were reviewed on a table-top basis with operations and measurement experts. The scales were then used to rate crews. Crews at three nuclear power plant simulator facilities have been rated using the scales for research purposes. A total of 18 crews have been observed responding to multiple scenarios.

Training materials were developed for presentation to crew members and other raters. This training introduced raters to three types of rating scales. The first type consisted of behaviorally anchored, seven-point scales for the team skills: two-way communication of objectives and plant status, resource management, inquiry, advocacy, conflict resolution and decision making, stress management, team spirit, and overall team skills and performance. The second type included frequency ratings for behaviors representative of the seven team skills. As an example, for the team skill of resource management, one of the behaviors was "step in to assist others who are overloaded with work." Raters used a seven-point frequency rating scale that ranged from "always" to "never," and included a "not observed" option. The third type consisted of technical crew performance ratings currently in use by the NRC. These three-point behaviorally anchored rating scales were organized into dimensions such as "understanding/interpretation of annunciator/alarm signals," and "diagnosis of events/conditions based on signals/readings." During the training session to introduce these three types of scales, raters were also cautioned about rating biases such as halo effect and severity/leniency.

Crew members were asked to provide self-ratings, and observers, such as instructors, were asked to rate crews after each simulated scenario. Additional information such as parameter recordings and other instructor ratings were collected for use in characterizing crew technical performance.

Ratings are being analyzed for interrater reliability and concurrent validity. As the industry moves toward more detailed, quantitative evaluation of crew performance, the availability of more precise measures will improve attempts to identify the role of team skills in overall crew performance.

FUTURE RESEARCH

The ongoing team skills research sponsored by the NRC is part of a larger program to address issues of team performance. The NRC recognized the need for a stronger empirical base to support regulations for team skills evaluation standards; linkages between team skills standards and the training programs currently in place at nuclear power plants; training of license examiners; and others who evaluate plant performance in the development, conduct and analysis of team performance evaluations. Reviewers outside the industry have taken notice as well. The National Research Council was asked to review human factors research needs for the safe operation of nuclear power plants. The Council's report (Moray & Huey, 1988, p. 62) stated:

> team training is an issue that has great potential for safety improvements in nuclear power plant operations. The key is to develop a research program that deals with the types of skills required in the nuclear power plant context and that feeds into the systems approach to training that has been widely adopted by industry.

In response to these identified needs, the NRC Office of Nuclear Regulatory Research has identified a plan for research in the area of team skills and team skills training. The focus of near-term research is on the development and evaluation of indicators of control room team performance during emergency operating conditions (Stello, 1989). The results of this research will be coordinated with other NRC programs such as the operator examination process, severe accident planning, and research into plant organization and management. In addition, the importance of team skills for teams outside the control room, and outside the plant are also being considered. Team performance issues in related areas regulated by the NRC such as transportation of nuclear materials, operation of hazardous waste sites, and the practice of nuclear medicine have begun to receive attention.

Despite the growing efforts to apply tools and techniques of psychology to issues of human performance in complex technological environments such as nuclear power plants, human performance continues to be implicated in most of the significant plant problems each year in nuclear power facilities (Bishop & LaRhette, 1988). Only within the last 10 years has the nuclear industry recognized the importance of human factors to safe operation of nuclear power plants (a few reports highlighted potential problems before TMI, but they received relatively limited attention, e.g., Seminara, Gonzalez, & Parsons, 1977). The vital role that teams play in nuclear power plants has received attention even more recently. While a start has been made, much remains to be done. The nuclear power industry, and indeed the world, cannot afford another TMI or Chernobyl to bring the point home.

REFERENCES

Alberti, R. E., & Emmons, M. L. (1982). *Your perfect right.* San Luis Obispo, CA: IMPACT.

Bishop, J., & LaRhette, R. (1988). Managing human performance—INPO's Human Performance Evaluation System. In E. W. Hagen (Ed.), *Conference Record for 1988 IEEE Fourth Conference on Human Factors and Power Plants (88CH2576-7).* New York: Institute of Electrical and Electronics Engineers.

Blake, R. R., & Mouton, V. S. (1978). *The new managerial grid.* Houston, TX: Gulf.

Boguslaw, R., & Porter, E. H. (1962). Team functions and training. In R. M. Gagne (Ed.), *Psychological principles in system development.* New York: Holt, Rinehart & Winston.

Briggs, G. E., & Naylor, J. C. (1965). Team versus individual training, training task fidelity, and task organization effects on performance by 3-man teams. *Journal of Applied Psychology, 49,* 387–392.

Campbell, J. P., & Dunnette, M. D. (1968). Effectiveness of T-group experiences in managerial training and development. *Psychological Bulletin, 70,* 73–85.

Code of Federal Regulations, Part 10, Section 50.54(m). (1989).

Davis, L. T., Gaddy, C. D., & Turney, J. R. (1985). *An approach to team skills training of nuclear power plant crews (NUREG/CR-4258).* Washington, DC: U.S. Nuclear Regulatory Commission.

Davis, L. T., Gaddy, C. D., Turney, J. R., & Koontz, J. L. (1986). Team skills training. *Performance & Instruction, 25*(8), 12–17.

Davis, L. T., Mazour, T. J., & Zaret, R. (1981). *Analysis, conclusions, and recommendations concerning operator licensing* (NUREG/CR-1750). Washington, DC: U.S. Nuclear Regulatory Commission.

Deutsch, R. W. (1987). *Nuclear power: A rational approach.* Columbia, MD:GP Courseware.

Dyer, J. L. (1984). Team research and team training: A state-of-the-art review. *Human Factors Review,* pp. 285–323.

Filley, A. C. (1975). *Interpersonal conflict resolution.* Glenview, IL: Scott, Foresman & Company.

Fisher, D. (1981). *Communication in organization.* St. Paul, MN: West Publishing.

Foushee, H. C. (1984). Dyads and triads at 35,000 feet: Factors affecting group process and air crew performance. *American Psychologist, 39,* 885–893.

Haney, W. V. (1979). *Communicational and interpersonal relations.* Homewood, IL: Richard D. Irwin.

INSAG (International Nuclear Safety Advisory Group). (1986). *Summary report on the Post-Accident Review Meeting on the Chernobyl Accident.* Vienna, Austria: International Atomic Energy Agency.

Moray, N. P., & Huey, B. M. (Eds.). (1988). *Human factors and nuclear safety.* Washington, DC: National Academy Press.

Randolph, W. A. (1985). *Understanding and managing organizational behavior.* Homewood, IL: Richard D. Irwin.

Reason, J. (1987). The Chernobyl errors. *Bulletin of the British Psychological Society, 40,* 201–206.

Rogovin, M., Frampton, G. T., & the Nuclear Regulatory Commission (NRC) Special Inquiry Group. (1980). *Three Mile Island: A report to the Commission and the public* (NUREG/CR-1250, Vol. 1). Washington, DC: U.S. Nuclear Regulatory Commission.

Seminara, J. L., Gonzalez, W. R., & Parsons, S. O. (1977). *Human factors review of nuclear power plant control room design* (EPRI NP-309). Palo Alto, CA: Electric Power Research Institute.

Stello, V., Jr. (1989). *NRC's human factors programs and initiatives* (SECY-89-183). Washington, DC: U.S. Nuclear Regulatory Commission.

Turney, J. R., & Cohen, S. L. (1981). *Defining the nature of team skills in Navy team training and performance* (Contract No. N0014-80-C-0811). Alexandria, VA: U.S. Army Research Institute.

United States Congress. (1982). *Section 306 of the Nuclear Waste Policy Act of 1982 (Public Law 97-425).*

USNRC (U.S. Nuclear Regulatory Commission). (1979). *TMI-2 Lessons Learned Task Force–Final report* (NUREG-0585). Washington, DC: U.S. Nuclear Regulatory Commission.

USNRC. (1980). *NRC action plan developed as a result of the TMI-2 Accident* (NUREG-0660). Washington, DC: U.S. Nuclear Regulatory Commission.

USNRC. (1987). *Report on the accident at the Chernobyl Nuclear Power Station* (NUREG-1250). Washington, DC: U.S. Nuclear Regulatory Commission.

USNRC. (1989). *Operator licensing examiner standards* (NUREG-1021). Washington, DC: U.S. Nuclear Regulatory Commission.

Wagner, H., Hibbits, N., Rosenblatt, R. D., & Schulz, R. (1977). *Team training and evaluation strategies: State-of-the-art* (Tech. Rep. HumRRO TR-77-1). Alexandria, VA: Human Resources Research Organization.

Author Index

Subject Index